PRIVA

RAILW

CW00537298

John Glover

IAN ALLAN

Publishing

First published 1998

ISBN 0 7110 2571 1

© Ian Allan Publishing Ltd 1998

Published by Ian Allan Publishing

an imprint of Ian Allan Publishing Ltd, Terminal
House, Station Approach, Shepperton, Surrey
TW17 8AS.
Printed by Ian Allan Printing Ltd, Riverdene,
Molesey Road, Hersham, Surrey KT12 4RG.

Code: 9806/C2

Picture Credits
All photographs have been taken by the author
unless otherwise credited.

Front cover:
EWS-liveried No 73131 heads the privately-owned
Venice-Simplon-Orient Express set during 1997.
Brian Morrison

Back cover:
Virgin Trains (Cross-Country)-liveried HST power car
No 43063, July 1997. *Hugh Ballantyne*

Title page:
EWS No 60086 *Schiehallion* hurries north through
Wigan North Western on 22 November 1997 with
an Enterprise service.

Contents

Introduction

The purpose of this book is to describe the principal changes to the organisation of Britain's railways under the Railways Act 1993.

This was not a minor event, since the Act has spelt the end of the integrated railway system owned and operated by a single body, which was established upon nationalisation on 1 January 1948. Yet, the years since World War 2 can hardly be said to have been an unqualified success for British Railways. Quite why this should have been so is open to question, but a fully successful remedy has so far eluded a succession of governments, of both political complexions. It will be several years before the results of the Conservative British Government's initiative become fully apparent, even if future circumstances do not force adjustments to the chosen course.

First, some of the key events of the last few years and their dates.

The book starts by considering the background to the changes, which began in earnest with the publication of the Government's White Paper 'New Opportunities for the Railways' on 14 July 1992. One immediate result was that the House of Commons Transport Committee set up an inquiry into 'The Future of the Railways...'; its first report was published on 13 January 1993 and a second, much fuller, report on 20 April 1993. The Railways Bill itself was published on 22 January 1993, and progressed through Parliament in the usual manner.

With limited changes, the Railways Bill became law on 5 November 1993. After a period to allow for the necessary restructuring of the railway, the main provisions came into force on 1 April 1994. Briefly, the most far-reaching changes were perhaps:

- the separation of operations from the infrastructure on which the services run, with the infrastructure passing to the ownership of the newly set up company, Railtrack;
- the creation of the post of Director of Rail Franchising, whose duties include the securing of railway passenger services by a series of franchise agreements with private operators;
- the parallel creation of a Rail Regulator, whose duties include the licensing of operations, the approval of operator access agree-

Above:
The diesel multiple-unit was an attempt to cut costs and at the same time provide a more attractive passenger environment. Over 4,000 vehicles were bought by British Railways in the late 1950s and early 1960s. Wickham's of Ware, Herts, was not perhaps the most successful of purveyors; this is a contemporary advertisement by the company.
Author's collection

ments with Railtrack and the enforcement of competition law;
- the setting up of three rolling stock companies to own the locomotives and rolling stock, which are then leased to the passenger operating companies; and
- the restructuring of the freight businesses with a view to their subsequent sale.

The Railways Act contains 154 sections and 14 schedules, spread over 244 pages. (By comparison the Transport Act 1947, which nationalised virtually the whole of the inland transport industry in Britain, confined itself to 170 rather smaller pages.) There is, of course, much more to the Railways Act, and various aspects are discussed in successive sections. Neither is it only the Railways Act to be considered, since European legislation, after remaining relatively dormant in the transport sector for several years, is now assuming a more prominent role.

This is a story of which only the early chapters can as yet be written. It is hoped that the reader will find it of value in getting to grips with what is happening to the railway as it approaches the millennium.

Finally, whatever misgivings we might have, let us cheer ourselves with s4(1)(b) of the Act. This gives the Regulator the duty 'to promote the use of the railway network in Great Britain for the carriage of passengers and goods, and the development of that railway network, to the greatest extent that he considers economically possible'. And who could argue with that?

So they were described by the historian G. M. Trevelyan, half a century ago. Who would thus describe the railways now? This section looks briefly at their formative years to see what lessons might be drawn.

Before Railways

The first major transport infrastructure construction in inland Britain was carried out by the Romans. Many of their road alignments, albeit subsequently improved beyond recognition, remain in use today. But the resources which can be harnessed by invading armies who need to move troops and supplies are not available to the general population. With the Roman withdrawal in AD410, both the need for the roads and the ability to maintain them disappeared; it was well over a thousand years before any serious attention was given to them again.

The Industrial Revolution of the late 18th century marked a decisive change. Factories were built for textile manufacture and iron making, producing industrial towns. They depended first on water power, then on coal power—and hence the establishment of the coal mining industry.

In transport, the whole lived off a combination of inadequate and poorly maintained roads, navigable rivers which were later supplemented by canals, and coastwise shipping. 'Plateways' for metal-wheeled vehicles, albeit horse-drawn, made a slow appearance. It was the coupling of this embryonic technology with the possibilities afforded by the steam engine which allowed the 'Railway Age' to take off.

Above left:
Was there a better solution for local services? This is the experimental railbus of Class 140, seen here undergoing passenger trials on 30 July 1981 at The Lakes on the 16.11 Birmingham Moor Street to Stratford-upon-Avon. The eventual result was the 'Pacer' railbuses, using bus bodies.

Left:
Push-pull operation on medium (if not high) speed service was a feature of the Edinburgh-Glasgow Queen Street operation from 1979. A Brake Second Open converted to DBSO format arrives at Queen Street.

The Railway Arrives

The Stockton & Darlington Railway opened in 1825 to transport coal from the Durham coalfield to the River Tees. It did exceedingly well, to the extent that congestion was rife. The authorising Act provided that any person could, by paying the charges, put his own horse and carriage on the railway, and a number of competing services were running simultaneously.

In this, the conditions and pricing of access were not dissimilar to those applying to roads and canals. Parliament of the day had supposed that once free access to the line had been secured for carriers, and the tolls payable by those carriers to the railway company were fixed, free competition would secure the best and cheapest service in the interest of the public[1]. Such conditions were not to be seen again on a railway in Britain for 170 years.

In concept, however, the Stockton & Darlington was completely overshadowed by the Liverpool & Manchester Railway of 1830. Steam power in the form of Stephenson's *Rocket* unquestionably triumphed, and the railway itself broke decisively with the canal and turnpike business practices. Thus, the Liverpool & Manchester:
- both owned and operated the railway itself;
- forbade its use by outside parties on payment of a toll;
- employed a regular staff, without subcontracting any operations; and
- lifted the scale of investment to a new order of magnitude.

There was a clear emphasis on passenger traffic right from the start, and it carried on average well over 1,000 passengers a day in its first three years of operation. For the 30 miles between the two important commercial cities, trains averaged 20mph. It was a huge improvement on the only passenger alternative, the horse.

Interestingly, Parliamentary Papers of 1839 suggested that even if on-line competition were practicable, it was not desirable, since:

'...the safety of the public also requires that upon each railway there should be one system of management... On this account it is necessary that the company should possess complete control... although they should therefore acquire an entire monopoly. (Thus) it becomes most important that (the railways themselves) should be so controlled as to secure the public as far as possible from any abuse that might arise'.[2]

Shortly afterwards, the Government set up the Railway Department in the Board of Trade, under the Railway Regulation Act of 1840. This was the origin of today's Railway Inspectorate.

With the Liverpool & Manchester showing the way, the embryonic railway industry moved into a major role. Its route between two of the country's major cities and in a major industrial area was undoubtedly well chosen, while the consistent 9.5% dividend paid by the L&M to its shareholders was generally admired. The highly competitive technical attributes of railways made system expansion prolific, since the possession of a railway station was a clear indication that the locality had 'arrived'.

Thus, the railways grew, fuelling industrial expansion and urban growth in countries around the world. In Britain though, there was nothing which could even remotely be called centralised planning in railway provision. Development of the network was left entirely to market forces. An Act of Parliament had to be obtained on each occasion, and no little energy was expended in trying to adjudicate between the competing commercial objectives of opposing promoters. But the railways as built, largely in the middle years of the 19th century, were wholly private undertakings.

Evolution

The expansionist years were not without their problems. In a settled land, the interests of landowners had to be considered as well as those of the industrialists who were more likely to provide the traffic. It is widely accepted now that many landowners were over-compensated in relation to the earning potential of the lines, and that much construction was over-optimistic in relation to the potential benefits. Here, one might interpolate, there are distinct parallels in today's climate with the economic benefits of the Channel Tunnel rail link and how generously local property owners should be compensated.

Pre-1923 British railway companies had extensive trading arrangements with each other for good commercial reasons. These included:

- Jointly owned railways (eg the Great Northern and Great Eastern Joint Line between March and Doncaster, or the Cheshire Lines Committee).

- Stations with multiple operators (eg Carlisle with the London & North Western, the Maryport & Carlisle, the North Eastern, the Midland, the North British and the Glasgow & South Western).

- Running powers over each other's tracks (eg the North British over 40 miles of the Caledonian to gain access to Aberdeen).

None of these historical arrangements was necessarily ideal, but they were made to work in an era when railways were indeed acknowledged to be effective monopolies. There is also a modern example: Eurotunnel accords broadly with the principle of running powers exercisable by other companies (as well as the owner) on payment of a fee. There are, one might note, several different means of organising railway undertakings.

While the railways of Britain were as a whole profitable, this was at the expense of what became excessive cross-subsidisation. Although this could be tolerated under near monopoly conditions, it was to be a major drawback when real competition later became apparent.

New markets also emerged. City growth led to the separation of homes and employment, and this in turn led to the establishment of the suburban railway. Some railway companies encouraged suburban growth; others considered the traffic as having more of a nuisance value. However, the railways, and later trams and then buses, had a considerable effect on the shape and extent of cities before planning legislation in much more recent times became effective.

Within cities the problem was, if anything, worse. The decision not to allow the main line railways into the centre of London (with a few very limited exceptions) made movement within the capital exceedingly difficult. Salvation came with the development of the Underground railway from 1863.

After World War 1, the Government decided that the fragmented state of the main line railways with their plethora of companies would be more economically combined into four major operators. The 'Grouping' into the 'Big Four' companies took effect from 1923. The principal idea was that inter-company rivalry would be reduced, together with the cost and inefficiency of the duplication of facilities. But the General Strike and the economic depression of the interwar years were to make the new companies' task an uphill struggle.

A welcome development was the streamline era of the 1930s. Competition took the form of emulation, with the development of high quality express passenger trains on the principal routes. It was the era of the 'Coronation' (LNER) and 'Coronation Scot' (LMS). Steam remained the source of power for railway operations generally, which allowed the locomotive engineers to demonstrate their prowess. Diesel traction was still confined to a handful of shunting locomotives. Electricity had received rather greater exploitation, but mainly for suburban links.

Suburban expansion in the London area was extensive in the interwar years. London Underground extensions, such as the Piccadilly Line to Cockfosters, were financed by cheap loans. On the Southern Railway, a new line was constructed to Chessington South.

For freight traffic, the railway was still a major carrier. The following is gleaned from a contemporary description of the rebuilt Surbiton in 1936:

'Of particular note is the extent to which provision for freight traffic is made. On the south side of the main line are four sidings with a coal wagon capacity of 97, and three sidings for merchandise, capacity 50 wagons. There is also a goods shed. Alongside is a Carter Paterson & Co (carriers) depot. On the north side are sidings for 62 wagons and 14 coaches, also a cattle dock and a milk dock. In the station itself are two parcels offices.'

By this date, commercial road transport was becoming an unwanted but prolific competitor, which unlike the railways had no restrictions on its charging policies. It seems incredible nowadays that railway freight rates had both to be determined in advance and applied impartially to all comers. No wonder there was scope for undercutting them. In 1938, the railways launched a demand for a 'Square Deal' to even up the terms of business. No progress was made before minds turned to greater things and the onset of World War 2.

War and its Aftermath

World War 2 put an enormous strain on the railways, from civilian evacuation, through the need to help the war effort in offence and defence, to troop transport and the movement of food supplies. Most debilitating in the longer term was the enforced inadequacy of maintenance, the lack of new construction and the effects of enemy damage. The railway is a long-term organisation, and it is just not possible to compensate for such shortcomings quickly.

Nationalisation in 1948 was the response of the postwar Labour Government era, with the newly created British Railways placed under the aegis of the British Transport Commission. However, materials were short, as was the political will to give priority to righting the (by then) extensive shortcomings of the railway system. Road transport was less inhibited. Its expansion was boosted by the sale of surplus vehicles from the armed services and the end of petrol rationing. The bus industry peaked in 1952/3, and has declined steadily ever since.

The railway Modernisation Plan appeared in 1955, with a clear (if perhaps misguided) aim to restore prewar standards and to make up for the missed years. The world had moved on. Large scale electrification and dieselisation were to replace the steam locomotive, and investment in virtually everything was promised.

Sadly, progress was relatively slow, while the financial results were exceedingly doubtful. They attracted withering comment. In 1960, the Permanent Secretary at the Ministry of Transport said that it was difficult to understand 'how the whole of the modernisation scheme could possibly have the economic results forecast by the BTC in their last reappraisal'. In that same year, Swindon Works turned out the last steam locomotive, *Evening Star*.

What was lacking for the railways, then as now, was any real analysis of what they were there to do. The unpublished Stedeford Committee was set up, numbering amongst its member a certain Dr Richard Beeching. Appointed Chairman of the newly formed British Railways Board, his masterwork was the report 'The Reshaping of British Railways' published in 1963. At the launching press conference he quoted Macbeth: 'If it were done, when 'tis done, then 'twere well it were done quickly.' What he did *not* say is that Macbeth himself was referring to the coming assassination of King Duncan.

Much of the Beeching plan was concerned with ridding the railways of their economically hopeless elements. Politically, it caused a monumental furore. Basically, the plan dismissed local rural passenger services and stopping services on main lines, and criticised the excessive size of the freight and passenger rolling stock fleets. More positively, it looked forward to the quickest possible replacement of steam traction, and new markets for freight using modern containers on the new 'Freightliner' services. A later plan included proposals for the development of the major railway trunk routes and, by inference, the slimming down of the less major ones. Of particular import in 1966/7 was the completion of the electrification of the Euston-Birmingham-Manchester/

Liverpool main line, though this was after Dr Beeching had departed.

Barbara Castle's Transport Act 1968, the same year as steam traction finally ceased, predictably had a different emphasis. The needs of the (eventually seven) major conurbations outside London were to be met by giving each of them their own Passenger Transport Executives, whose tasks included integrating bus and rail services in their areas and funding them as required. Outside those areas, specific Government grants were to be paid for socially necessary services, on a stabilised network.

This brought stability, albeit at a price. The modern railway developed in the 1970s, while service quality and provision generally surpassed anything that had been achieved previously. On the main lines it saw the introduction of the InterCity 125. Investment proceeded, albeit not as fast as many would have wished.

In 1979, the modern railway was still seen to be performing commercially less well than it might, especially in the face of the Conservative Government's wishes to contain its financial contributions. One outcome was the sector-led railway.

The Present Scene

Times change, but the railway system remains much in the form in which it was constructed. Railways are essentially long lasting; while technology advances and equipment is renewed, the physical railway itself remains more or less unchanged other than in a reduction in system mileage. The inevitable mistakes which are the lot of the pioneer are also with us. Of these, the most conspicuous is the result of the perhaps apocryphal story that George Stephenson used the biggest vehicle he could conceive to determine the loading gauge, to which virtually the entire system was built. This was a horse with a fully laden hay cart.

Today's railway faces a very different scene from that during most of its history. Railways have many strengths; for instance, they:
- offer high speeds and/or high carrying capacity, with safety;
- are responsible for the movement of four-fifths of central London commuters, or about 800,000 people in each direction every day;
- have a modest land take in relation to line capacity; and
- can, if electrified, use coal, oil, nuclear or hydro-electric as indirect power sources.

But there are limitations also, and the business in which they do not excel is the economic movement of small volumes, whether they be freight or passenger. The exclusively provided railway infrastructure of track and signalling is costly, whether in terms of initial provision, its maintenance or its renewal. Rail is essentially a mass mover; preferably, though not essentially, over longer distances.

Also, railways cannot offer door-to-door transit for freight without transhipment, other than where industrial premises are directly connected by private siding. Passengers also have to get to and from stations; railways can never offer the door-to-door convenience of the private car.

Meanwhile, how has the railway been getting on in the postwar years?[3]

Thus while the railway infrastructure, measured in terms of route km, has almost halved, passenger traffic has declined much less significantly. Freight, though, has fallen dramatically. The railway has thus failed to maintain its carryings. This would be serious in a stable market, but the reality is that the market itself has expanded enormously. From being a prime market provider of both passenger and freight traffic in 1951, National Railways now account for a melancholy 4% of the British passenger market and 6% of the freight. (The passenger figures exclude London Underground and other urban rail systems.)

There have, however, been many positive developments. From 1988, the non-commercial passenger railway was defined by Government as excluding InterCity. The development of the InterCity shuttle concept was but one part of the response.

The efforts of Regional Railways deserve recognition. The introduction of Regional Express services linking (for instance) Liverpool with Ely on an hourly basis, with trains diverging thence to Stansted Airport and Norwich alternately, was a major and welcome innovation. The service

Table 1: National Railways traffic and infrastructure since 1951					
Passenger km	1951	33,500 million	1996/7	32,200 million	change – 10%
Freight net tonne km	1951	37,229 million	1995/6	13,300 million	change – 64%
Route km open	1951	31,152 million	1996/7	16,666 million	change – 47%

beyond Cambridge to Stansted proved, however, to be before its time.

In the seven PTE areas, the Passenger Transport Authorities defined service provision requirements with some considerable precision, and accepted a collective annual bill of £115 million in return.

However, other Regional services were operated formally merely 'to provide a public service comparable generally with that provided on 1 April 1988'. In practice, there was little difference between that and the previous Direction, dating from 1975. The same Direction applied to Network SouthEast, and it was Government who issued the Directive.

Times change, and the Regional Railways commitment to working in conjunction with local authorities to explore and then to maximise the benefits which rail could bring to their areas, especially in towns with 250,000 plus population, was a very positive move. This was a considerable advance over the 'do as you have always done' approach embodied in the PSO concept. On the other hand, where there is effectively no accountability, there is always extreme local reluctance to accept any lesser service levels, and politicians have always had the 1988 Direction to fall back on.

None of this is to decry the achievements of other sectors, though the change in what was once referred to almost disparagingly as 'Other Provincial Services' is remarkable. Yet, Regional Railways still only covered a small proportion of its costs through passenger revenues. Tight financial control is essential in the management of a

service business; management must know what it is trying to do.

Something, as they say, had to be done. But what? We cannot, and must not try to, rebuild the past. The railway needs to move with the times, particularly in capitalising on the areas in which it can excel. At the same time it might be well advised to minimise its efforts on, and exposure to, the peripheral activities. Apart perhaps from London suburban services, it is nowadays far from a monopoly provider. Can the areas in which it is presently successful be extended? Can the railway be successful in other areas too? What form of organisation and legal background is necessary to achieve change and develop the railway's role?

The Conservative Government's answer was the White Paper of 1992, followed by the Railways Act 1993.

1   *Government and the Railways in Nineteenth Century Britain*, Routledge & Kegan Paul, H. W. Parris, 1965.
2   Parliamentary papers 1839, x, 132-3, quoted in Parris op cit.
3   Sources: British Transport Commission Financial and Statistical Accounts, 1951, and Transport Statistics Great Britain, 1997.

The initial commitment of the Conservative Government towards change was announced by HM The Queen at the State Opening of Parliament on 6 May 1992:

> 'My Government are committed to increasing the role of the railways in meeting the country's transport needs. Legislation will be introduced to enable the private sector to operate rail services.'

First, the White Paper which preceded the Railways Bill, in which the Government's intentions were set out, subtitled 'The Privatisation of British Rail'[1], was published on 14 July. On objectives it was less than expansive, referring only to a wish 'to improve the quality of rail services'. The rest was method.

The White Paper

After an initial foray into the then British Rail of the 'not bad, but could do better' variety, the Government outlined what it saw as the six essential issues. These were:
- Safety—Standards must be maintained and bettered.
- Quality of service—All customers must be offered a higher standard of service.
- Essential passenger services—Continuing subsidy will be available to provide social and other benefits.
- Network benefits—The benefits of a single network for passengers include a national timetable and through ticketing.
- Employee opportunities—Enabled to transfer to the new companies and take a stake in private sector replacements.
- Environmental benefits—To continue to be developed.

Only six weeks earlier, the British Railways Board had completed its (re-)Organising for Quality initiative, which had been some years in the making. This created a number of freestanding businesses, with both infrastructure and rolling stock assets as well as staff divided between them, leaving the Railways Board responsible for finance and to set policies and standards for the running of the railways as a whole. It was also there to settle disputes. Trading arrangements

were set up to cover asset usage by other railway businesses. This was the end of the former regional railway organisations.

The operating businesses, managed through a total of 27 profit centres, were:
- InterCity
- Network SouthEast
- Regional Railways
- Trainload Freight
- Railfreight Distribution
- European Passenger Services
- Parcels

All this work came to naught; as one insider said: 'This was the best reorganisation we never had.' The preferred Government option was to dismantle the vertical integration of the railway where individual management teams were responsible for everything from infrastructure to operations—in short, all that they needed to provide the complete service to the customer. The Government decided to create a track authority (Railtrack), which would be separated from the companies who were to operate the trains. The purpose of the latter was merely to run the passenger services until they were all franchised to the private sector. By then, Railfreight and Parcels would both have been privatised. 'This structure,' said the White Paper, 'offers the greatest prospect for private sector involvement in operations...' However, it was made clear that the Bill would also provide for the eventual privatisation of Railtrack itself.

The Transport Committee

The House of Commons Select Committee on Transport, chaired by the late Robert Adley MP, reported in great detail in April 1993. This was not the committee set up to debate the Bill. Its report ran to 172 pages, with the appendices and minutes of proceedings accounting for a further 1,121 sides.

The report was critical of the Bill, and Adley was widely reported for his remark likening the effects of the then Bill to 'a poll tax on wheels'. A much abridged summary of the principal conclusions appears below:
- The Government is right to search for ways of improving rail services for passengers and freight customers.

- The test of any proposals must be their practicability, coupled with their ability to produce a sustained increase in investment.
- Investment is a basic prerequisite for success.
- The White Paper should have been preceded by a Green Paper discussing the role of railways, encompassed within an overall transport policy.
- Both for railway operating reasons and because of the implications for the viability of franchises, the scope for open access passenger services is very limited.
- Success in the franchising of passenger services needs:
  - a greater degree of vertical integration
  - greater incentives to Railtrack's efficiency
  - gearing the form and length of franchises to investment requirements
  - franchise areas chosen to preserve the coherence of the network
  - strict service standards and controls over fares to protect passengers against misuse of monopoly power
  - arrangements for continuing services in the event of an operator's default.
- The benefits to passengers of a national network must be preserved.
- The Government should commit itself to a system for co-ordinating coherent transport improvements across the country.
- An outline safety case should form an integral part of the formal franchise bidding process.
- A greater degree of simplicity could be achieved if Railtrack and the Franchising Authority were merged to form a single Rail Authority, though there would still be a need for an independent Regulator.
- In terms of international railway experience, the Government's proposals are novel and untested. The risk that something could go badly wrong is therefore higher than would otherwise be the case. This does not mean that the system cannot work, but considerable care and resources will be needed to ensure that it does work.
- Rail users will be the final judge on whether the legislation succeeds in maintaining the railways' social and economic obligations whilst creating opportunities for private profit.

Those were the conclusions of five years ago; much has since happened. Of the various concerns expressed, the concentration on the importance of investment and relating this to the lengths of the passenger franchises is perhaps one of today's more difficult areas. Also, the creation of a Strategic Rail Authority is now on the cards.

The Railways Act

Meanwhile, the Bill continued its passage through Parliament, to become law as the Railways Act 1993 in November of that year. It is a huge document, in three parts:

Part I deals with the provision of railway services
Part II concerns itself with the reorganisation of the railways
Part III is the usual miscellaneous, general and supplemental provisions.

What does the Act actually set out to do? The following is an interpretation of the various sections, starting with Part I. Section numbers appear in brackets throughout, for reference purposes. Many of the bodies mentioned here briefly, such as the Franchising Director and the Regulator, we shall meet again in later chapters.

Introductory

The Act provides for the appointment and functions of a Rail Regulator and a Director of Passenger Rail Franchising (s1), and the setting up of new rail users' consultative committees (RUCCs) for the railways (s2) and the Central Rail Users' Consultative Committee (s3).

Duties of the Secretary of State and the Regulator

The duties of both are to be exercised 'in the manner which he considers best calculated:

(a) to protect the interest of users of rail services;

(b) to promote the use of the railway network in Great Britain for the carriage of passengers and goods, and the development of that railway network, to the greatest extent that he considers economically practicable;

(c) to promote efficiency and economy on the part of persons providing railway services;

(d) to promote competition in the provision of railway services;

(e) to promote measures designed to facilitate the making by passengers of journeys which involve use of the services of more than one passenger service operator;

(f) to impose on the operators of railway services the minimum restrictions which are consistent with the performance of his functions under Part I;

(g) to enable persons providing railway services to plan the future of their businesses with a reasonable degree of assurance'.

Further duties refer to protecting the interests of users and also the price and quality of service offered by facility owners to operators. They also need to take into account the need for operational safety and environmental effects.

The Regulator was obliged to take into account the guidance of the Secretary of State, but only until the end of 1996. In contrast, his need 'to have regard to the financial position of the Franchising Director' is perpetual (s4).

Duties of the Franchising Director

The Franchising Director has to carry out his task in a way calculated to fulfil the Secretary of State's objectives and instructions, in the provision of passenger services. He also needs to ensure that any payments made will achieve those objectives economically and efficiently (s5).

The outpayments by the Franchising Director are made as a result of his entering into franchise agreements with passenger train operators. The franchise operator has the obligation to provide the services specified for the period of the franchise agreement.

Licensing of Operators of Railway Assets

The Act establishes a licensing regime for the ownership and use of railway assets to provide passenger and goods services, and specifies how such licences may be modified. All operators of such assets must either hold a licence or be exempted. The Regulator may modify licences by agreement, or by making a reference to the Monopolies and Mergers Commission (s6-s16).

Access Arrangements

The Act provides that a railway facility owner shall, if so directed by the Regulator, enter into an access agreement with a train operator which allows the operator to use the owner's facilities on terms approved by the Regulator. The legislation on the highly complex question of access is spread

Right:
London commuters on National Railways come predominantly from south of the river or the east. On 6 September 1993, South West Trains' customers descend into the subway at Waterloo, to continue their journey by the Waterloo & City, the Bakerloo or the Northern or, in future, the Jubilee.

across 12 pages of the Act (s17-s22).

Franchising of Passenger Services

The Franchising Director is placed under a duty to designate passenger services as eligible for provision under a franchise agreement (s23).

There are limited exceptions to franchising in that railways as may be specified by the Secretary of State may be exempted (by the use of a Statutory Instrument). London Underground is the principal example and Heathrow Express is another, but others such as Tyne and Wear Metro and preserved railways would also otherwise be included. However, this section does not prevent subsequent governments from changing direction, such as exempting certain former BR services from franchising (s24).

Public sector bodies may not be franchisees, apart from the British Railways Board under very restrictive circumstances (s25). Franchisees must be financially sound, competent and 'otherwise a suitable person' (s26).

Franchise assets will be transferred to the successful franchise bidder and returned at the end of the franchise period (s27). The franchise itself may include specification on fares to be charged and a mandatory requirement to participate in approved discount fares schemes. The Act specifies such schemes as those for the young, the elderly or the disabled (s28). Other railcards are not protected.

The next section sets out the other terms and conditions of a franchise agreement, including the obligations of the franchisee to pay the Franchising Director or, alternatively, to be paid by him. The agreement must also contain the franchise term and its possibility of extension, rights

of acquisition of property, and liabilities (s29). Provision is also made for the means of continuing a service once a franchise has come to an end and no further franchise agreement has been reached (s30). Franchise assets are not leases (s31).

Passenger Transport Authorities and Executives

The respective roles of the PTAs and the PTEs in connection with the franchising of passenger train services in their areas are also defined. Among them, the PTE has the power to specialise the services to be operated, the service quality required and fares levels to be charged where it has an s20 agreement under the 1968 Act. (s32-s36).

Closures

The Act establishes new railway closure procedures to replace those which applied previously to the British Railways Board. These have to take account of the now separate issues concerning the operation of services and the provision of the infrastructure, including depot facilities. The Franchising Director initiates the notifications of a proposed closure and the Regulator decides on its merits, attaching conditions such as replacement bus service provision as he thinks fit. The Secretary of State, however, only becomes involved if there is an appeal against the Regulator's decision. Lesser procedures are invoked where experimental new railway services are involved (defined as those which have been running for less than five years) or the closure is classified as minor. Minor closures do not involve service withdrawal from any passenger station and trains can run via an alternative route (s37-s50).

Supplementary Powers of the Franchising Director

The legislation also provides for means by which the Franchising Director can ensure that services continue by subcontracting, for instance after a franchise comes to an end and there is no successor (s51), while he can also make agreements with the British Railways Board (s52). He may also form companies to undertake his own franchising or other duties—in a sense, to privatise himself! (s53).

This section offers an interesting freedom to the Franchising Director in the way in which he exercises his franchising functions 'for the purpose of encouraging railway investment' (s54).

This might be used to help address the problem of costly railway assets with long lives, such as new rolling stock, being unattractive propositions to a franchisee with a seven-year contract.

Enforcement and Winding Up

The next sections allow the Regulator and the Franchising Director to ensure compliance with the regulatory regime established by the Act and make provision in respect of railway administration orders, winding up and insolvency (s55-s65).

Consumer Protection

Consumer protection and the relationship of the Regulator with other established bodies are clarified. The Regulator is given some of the functions of the Director General of Fair Trading under the Fair Trading Act 1973 and Competition Act 1980 (s66-s67).

Other Functions

Other functions of the Regulator and the Franchising Director include the maintenance of registers, the collection of information and the publication of reports (s68-s75).

Consultative Committees

The duties of the consultative committees are specified. These refer to the provision of railway passenger services or station services (s76-s79).

Information and Interpretation

The Franchising Director can require information from licence holders or the Board and its subsidiaries, with penalties for non-compliance (s80).

Sections dealing with interpretation (s81-s83) include the definition of a railway as that of the Transport and Works Act 1992 s67(1), which is:

'A system of transport employing parallel rails which:
(a) provide support and guidance for vehicles carried on flanged wheels, and
(b) form a track which either is of a gauge of at least 350mm or crosses a carriageway (whether or not on the same level), but does not include a tramway.'

So, now we know. It will be noted that this definition includes the Romney, Hythe & Dymchurch Railway on all three counts. The 15in gauge of the RH&DR equates to approximately 380mm.

Sometimes, the 1993 Act specifies that 'railway' shall have a wider meaning. This

Above:
A 20-year agreement was signed by BR with road haulier Tartan Arrow in October 1965, which provided for a nightly chartered train between Kentish Town and Bridgeton, Glasgow. Trains were painted in the company's red and white livery, as with this Covered Carriage Truck (CCT). Private operations were never quite extinct. Lawrie Williams

includes tramways, which are distinguished in the T&W Act 1992 by being 'laid mainly or wholly along a street or in any other place to which the public has access (including a place to which the public has access only on making a payment)'. They are also wholly or mainly for passenger traffic. In this wider context, 'railway' also includes other guided transport, other than trolleybuses or similar.

Other useful definitions include, for instance, 'light maintenance'. This means:

• the refuelling, or the cleaning of the exterior, of locomotives and other rolling stock; or
• the carrying out to locomotives or other rolling stock of maintenance work (including the detection and rectification of any faults) of a kind which is normally carried out at regular intervals of 12 months or less to prepare the locomotives or other rolling stock for service.

Another is 'information', which includes 'estimates', but not perhaps as in estimated time of arrival. There is also a definition of goods; Acts of Parliament eschew the use of Americanisms such as freight. 'Goods' includes mail, parcels, animals, plants and any other creature, substance or thing capable of being transported, but does not include passengers.

Part II of the Act (s84-s116) is concerned with the British Railways Board. The Act conferred new powers on the Board with respect to the formation of subsidiary companies and the transfer by scheme of property, rights and liabilities in connection with franchising or in preparation for disposal to the private sector.

The Act also conferred powers on the Secretary of State in connection with transfer schemes, including powers to give directions to the Board and to require information from it. The Secretary of State was also given the power to transfer to either himself or the Franchising Director the Board's function of making transfer schemes. The Act also made financial provision relating to the Board as well as successor companies to the Board's undertakings.

Perhaps the most notable Section in Part II of the Railways Act is s113(1) which states: 'It shall be the principal objective of the Secretary of State...to secure as soon as, in his opinion, is reasonably practicable the result that the function of providing railway services in Great Britain is performed by private operators.' This does, however, refer only to Part II. In performing this task, s113 goes on to require the Secretary of State 'to have regard to the desirability of:

(a) encouraging competition between those who provide railway services;

(b) maintaining efficiency, economy and safety of operation in the provision of railway services in Great Britain;

(c) providing opportunities for persons employed in railway undertakings...an interest in the ownership of the undertakings in which they are employed; and

(d) securing that the disposal takes place on the most favourable terms that can reasonably be obtained...'

Readers will note that this requirement extends equally to the present Government, to whom repeal is the only remedy should they not wish to continue this policy.

Part III is rightly referred to as Miscellaneous Provisions.

Safety, Emergencies, Security, etc

The Act makes provision with respect to the safety of the railways, which includes control of the railways in times of hostilities or great national emergency. The latter even warrants a statutory definition: 'Any natural disaster or other emergency which, in the opinion of the Secretary of State, is or may be likely to give rise to such disruption of the means of transport that the population, or a substantial part of the population, of Great Britain is or may be likely to be deprived of essential goods or services.' Effectively, the Government retains the right to give directions to all those involved in service provision in such circumstances (s117-s121).

Statutory Authority

If you are involved in running a railway, it is important that you are not open to a charge of causing a nuisance; this section confers the status of statutory authority on operators and others (s122).

Miscellaneous

In a similar vein, the legal status of common carrier by railway, which obliges operators to refuse neither passengers nor consignments of goods is specifically removed, as it has been since the 1962 Act (s123), while the Post Office can no longer compel railways to carry mailbags (s124).

The disposal of historical records or artefacts from the public sector is to be overseen by a new committee (s125); this provision failed to take into account that most of the railway was about to enter the private sector.

Consequential changes in the powers and duties of the BRB (s126-s128) are followed by the power to make byelaws being extended to new operators. These may be for matters as diverse as ticketing, smoking and obstruction of the railway (s129), followed by three pages of detail on the regulation of penalty fares by the Secretary of State (s130).

The Restrictive Trade Practices Act 1976 could make co-operation between operators over such matters as varied as track access, ticketing or rolling stock maintenance extremely difficult. Such agreements may be exempted under this section to ensure that network benefits are achieved and to avoid nonsenses similar to those which have occurred in the bus industry (s131).

The next sections make provision in respect of the BT Police (s132-s133), pensions (s134) and staff travel (s135).

Financial Provisions

The Regulations of the European Economic Community 1191/69 and 1893/91 for the payment of subsidy in respect of passenger rail services (the Public Service Obligation grant) themselves remain unchanged. The Railways Act designates competent authorities who may impose such obligations as the Secretary of State, the Franchising Director and, on a more limited basis, the PTEs and local authorities (s136).

The Act also makes provision for track access charges for freight operators to be paid for, in part or in total, by the Secretary of State, 'for the purpose of securing the provision of adequate services for the carriage of goods by railway'. There must be benefits of a social or environmental nature (s137).

Capital grants made under Section 56 of the 1968 Act have had an uncertain status if they were intended for use for access to airports or harbours. This new section confirms that they may be thus used (s138).

The authority for freight facilities grants of the 1974 Act is re-enacted and made more general by applying a simpler public interest criterion (s139), while similar grants are available for freight by inland waterway (s140).

Financial assistance for the Board's management or staff buy-outs is available (s141) as it is for administrative expenses deriving from the Act (s142).

Supplemental

The remaining sections are also administrative in nature (s143-154).

There are also 14 schedules, which include amendments to existing Acts of Parliament and repeals.

It is fully realised that the foregoing is somewhat indigestible, but it does represent a concise *résumé* of the Act's overall contents. It concentrates on some of the principal sections of the Act, though their individual importance is perhaps better judged with the benefit of hindsight.

Some aspects are conspicuous by their absence—for instance, there is no mention anywhere of Railtrack. Acts of Parliament provide powers and may also prescribe method and introduce prohibitions. They may repeal earlier legislation. But they cannot undertake the job itself.

How this is being achieved is the subject of the next chapter.

1 'New Opportunities for the Railways', Cmd 2012, HMSO, £5.40

Compared with the unitary British Rail, the new railway organisation is complex and has a number of players. The principal components are as follows:

- Railtrack PLC, the infrastructure owner.
- The Franchising Director, who lets passenger franchises and may provide Government support.
- The Rail Regulator, who ensures fair play.
- The Passenger Train Operating Companies (TOCs) and freight companies.
- The Rolling Stock Companies (ROSCOs) who own and lease out rolling stock.

These organisations are shown in the diagram, and all will be discussed. Railways are substantial businesses; in terms of cash flows, the following are the principal movements.

The originator is the Treasury, which dispenses moneys via both the Franchising Director and the PTEs to most of the Train Operating Companies. The TOCs then have to pay their rolling stock leases to the ROSCOs, plus their track access charges to Railtrack, as well as incurring the costs of running their businesses. They also collect the fares revenue.

Below:
New stations may be built to a basic standard, such as this one at Sinfin North, south of Derby. It was opened on 4 October 1976, and there is no public access; usage was thus confined to those at the adjacent factories. According to the timetable, there is now one train a day at 07.02, Mondays to Fridays only, to Derby.

Freight companies also have to pay Railtrack access charges, but they own most of their rolling stock outright. They too collect revenue from their customers. Railtrack uses the proceeds of the access charges for operational control of the network. It also has to maintain and renew the network, these tasks being carried out mostly by contractors.

Railtrack: The Heart of the Railway

Railtrack is the organisation which owns the freehold and manages the track and other railway infrastructure. It is a commercial enterprise, earning a return from its assets. Railtrack is responsible for timetabling, train planning, signalling and control of the system, infrastructure maintenance and investment. It also co-ordinates the national passenger timetable.

The Government gave four main reasons for creating Railtrack:

- to provide a national infrastructure company which will give track access to every train operator on a fair basis;
- to secure appropriate levels of investment in rail infrastructure on a national strategic basis;
- to ensure that safety standards and procedures are co-ordinated in a clear and systematic way; and
- to ensure that timetabling is co-ordinated efficiently across the whole network.

Initially a Government-owned company, Railtrack was floated on the London Stock Exchange in

May 1996. For this to be possible, it was first necessary to take four steps:

- Railtrack had to be vested as an independent, Government-owned company.
- There had to be a performance framework.
- An industry contractual framework had to be in place.
- Railtrack had to demonstrate a record of trading and performance achievement.

Railtrack has an important role in the restructured industry. The company's objective is to provide the safe, efficiently run network which is critical to the overall success of the railway.

The goals which Railtrack has set itself are:

- to provide our customers with safe, efficient, cost-effective services with targeted improvements in every activity;
- to develop a fair contracting relationship with our suppliers that builds in performance incentives;
- to offer our employees a fulfilling and challenging career in which all share equal opportunities; and
- to grow our business and increase the value to our shareholder.

'If it doesn't move, it belongs to Railtrack' is still a useful short description of the company's range of assets. The most obvious asset is the 31,849km of track. By permissible line speeds, this divides up as follows:

<20 mph	2,345km	7%
25–35mph	2,174km	7%
40–75mph	17,973km	56%
80–105mph	7,289km	23%
110-125mph	2,068km	6%

In terms of length of route, this is around 16,000 route km. Other assets are:

- 750 tunnels
- 40,000 bridges and viaducts
- 9,000 level crossings
- 2,500 stations
- 90 light maintenance depots
- connections to over 1,000 freight terminals
- 37,500 other property units. These include non-operational stations, retail outlets on stations such as W. H. Smith, offices (eg those of catering companies) and the businesses occupying railway arches comprising anything from a laser gun shooting range to pine bed manufacturers.
- 1,200 signalboxes, but decreasing in numbers.

Expenditure on keeping these assets in shape will cost £16 billion over a decade, or a rate of £4

Above:
The repeater signal is commonly placed in locations where the guard cannot see the starting signal because of line curvature, or obstructions such as a station canopy. This example is at Wigan North Western.

million per day. Proportionately, just over half (or 52%) will be spent on infrastructure, 36% on maintenance and 12% on major projects.

Of interest is the life of assets, as used for depreciation purposes. Track and other route structures are estimated to last 100 years, and stations or depots for 50. Third rail electrification equipment is also judged to last 50 years, but the new-fangled overhead line equipment for 40 years. Similarly, with signalling, mechanical systems have a 50-year life, which reduces to 35 years for powerboxes (PSBs) and a mere 15 years for Integrated Electronic Control Centres (IECCs).

Railtrack's annual revenue in 1996/7 was nearly £2.5 billion. The vast majority of this—£2,119 million or 87%—was derived from selling track access to passenger franchise operators. Of the remainder, £159 million or 6% was from freight, £120 million or 5% from property rental and £39 million (2%) from open access passenger (as opposed to franchised) operators. These latter include all special trains and excursion workings, but mostly the operations of Eurostar (UK) Ltd.

It may be said that track access charges, which

form a large part of Railtrack's income and TOC's expenditure, are not a simple calculation. The structure of how charges were to be formulated was initially defined as follows, with proportions represented by each for a typical franchisee shown in brackets:

Track Access Variable Component (25%)

User-related charges refer to the costs incurred by an operator which vary with the volume of that operator's traffic, with the nature of the equipment used and, to some extent, with the timing of the trains concerned. This is further subdivided into track usage charges for wear and tear, and charges for electric traction current as might be applicable.

Peak charges are incurred where the railway is congested to the extent that there is an overall shortage of paths. A path allocated to an operator in the timetable is therefore charged to him, since it is not available to others. The charge is thus maintained, even if the path is not used.

Track Access Fixed Component (65%)

Directly attributable fixed costs (30%). These long-run avoidable costs are specific to the services being provided by the franchisee, but do not vary with short-term changes in usage. Essentially, these are the parts of the railway infrastructure which would not be needed if the franchisee's services were not being operated. An example might be the bay platforms and the associated track and signalling used by local passenger services at a larger station.

A complication arises if other franchisees share the use of that facility. If there are no others, then the whole of the costs could be saved, at least in the longer term. Where there are other operators,

the avoidable elements are much less or even nil. Costs which are not attributable have to be treated as common costs.

Common Costs (35%)

There are three categories of costs as follows which cannot be allocated specifically to one operator and which would therefore not be avoidable if that operator ceased to provide services:

(a) Those costs which can be allocated to specific sections of track but not to individual operators. Unless there is only one operator, these costs, such as the maintenance of a particular viaduct or tunnel, have to be divided between the operators using that section.

(b) Those costs which can be allocated geographically. These are costs which are specific to an area but not to particular sections of track, such as those of a large power signalling centre.

(c) Network costs, comprising essential overheads like administration and payroll costs, which can only be spread overall.

Station Rents (10%)

The vast majority of Railtrack's stations are leased to and managed by the passenger train operator who is the sole or perhaps main user of the station; this will be normally by a lease which is granted for the same period as the duration of the service franchise.

Fourteen stations have been identified as being suitable for greater commercial trading and longer-term property development. Initially, these stations are operated by Railtrack themselves.

Independently managed stations

Charing Cross	Euston
King's Cross	Liverpool Street
London Bridge	Paddington
Victoria	Waterloo
Birmingham New Street	Edinburgh Waverley
Gatwick Airport	Glasgow Central
Leeds	Manchester Piccadilly

Left:
Cambridge is notorious for its very long single through platform which can contain two trains simultaneously along its length. Subject to necessary signalling constraints, these can run independently of each other via the central crossover, seen here in part. The solidity of construction of this much used piece of permanent way is evident and one suspects also that maintenance is expensive.

Above:
The south end of Carlisle station and the protecting signals are seen here on 11 November 1997.

Income from retail activity at stations is about £34 million per annum in total, of which this select list generates around £20 million. And what will this new approach mean? The following describes the Nagoya station development in Japan:

'The station will have a deluxe hotel, offices, a department store and shops, in a high-rise block both above and below ground level with an emphasis on the convenience, comfort and elegance that will characterise the sophisticated life-styles of the 21st century.'[1]

It doesn't sound like any of the stations named opposite, does it? But, if the town centre moves away from the station, one remedy might be to develop the station in its own right to redress the balance. And, if the treatment described sounds slightly staid, why not a high quality entertainment centre or theme park? We shall see.

Back to more mundane matters. The charging structure by Railtrack outlined above was intended to give sufficient detail on how costs would be incurred by operating companies to help shape Railtrack's investment decisions. Track charges would reflect the quality of the track and other facilities provided during the period of the access contract. New investment costs by Railtrack would be recovered by variations to access charges as might be agreed between the parties concerned. These might, for instance, include the Franchising Director were he to specify service patterns which required infrastructure changes.

Fair enough, but what happens if the operating companies all disagree with each other as to what is needed and in what timescale? Who decides what is necessary and what is optional? How is technical compatibility between trains and infrastructure to be guaranteed? This extends to highly costly areas such as Automatic Train Protection (ATP) systems and the priority which may be attached to them.

Let us remind ourselves of a crucial railway characteristic. The need to have a specialised infrastructure and to meet its provision costs mean in turn that it has to be well used. Heavy usage will help to spread Railtrack's costs sufficiently to keep unit charges down to an acceptable level for the operating businesses. The railway is volume hungry; the more traffic, the better. Line capacity is the most valuable resource, but its exploitation has to match the franchisee's (and any other user's) ability and willingness to pay.

Conversely, rail is at its least competitive where demand is low. After all, the track has still to be maintained and paid for. The Franchising Director needs to achieve value for money; this means maximising the benefits from paying support.

This is not to suggest that such railways are necessarily under threat. Service provision needs to develop to match changing social requirements, while economy of both operation and maintenance must be pursued.

The issue of how the cost of future rail infrastructure investment should be recovered through charges, important though it might be for small schemes, is of critical importance to Railtrack with really major investments such as those

19

represented by the West Coast main line modernisation or Thameslink 2000 (both are examined later). These schemes have yet to be finalised, but it is for this reason that possible charging structures have been discussed here in some detail. Any scheme used should reflect the reality of the operating railway, be reasonably free of distorting effects over time and fair in its overall attribution of costs. But it also needs to be administratively practicable and allow Railtrack's operator customers to predict their future access commitments with some certainty.

However, access charges have also to be approved by the Rail Regulator, and the present situation will be found in that section.

So much for charges. On Railtrack's expenditure side, and apart from the 11,375 staff of Railtrack, most of whom are signalmen, there are the bought-in services of what was formerly British Rail Infrastructure Services (BRIS), who presently undertake most of this work.

BRIS was divided and sold during 1996 as seven infrastructure maintenance companies (IMCs), six track renewal companies (TRCs) whose work area is self-explanatory, and seven design offices. The main areas of work covered by the IMCs are:

- track maintenance and inspection, covering up to two-thirds of IMC work;
- maintenance and inspection of signalling and pointwork;
- maintenance and inspection of power supplies and control equipment; and
- project work, especially for Railtrack's Major Projects Division.

Other work includes structure examination, maintenance and renewal, lineside work such as clearing vegetation and mending fences, dealing with adverse weather and the results of accidents, and safety management.

The railway of the future will see further changes. Track quality upgrading to meet greater tonnages and higher speeds on principal lines will make them more fit for their purpose, while simpler and cheaper methods of provision will have to be found for secondary routes. New track installation will have to be accompanied by less total track occupation, with the use of more technically advanced handling equipment, while maintenance programmes will need to result in less frequent attention. There will need to be a detailed measurement of track condition and performance, with sophisticated programmes for giving it the necessary attention for maintenance and renewal.

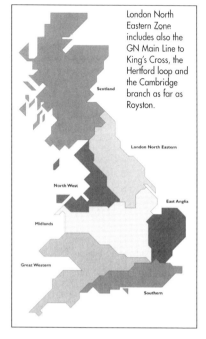

London North Eastern Zone includes also the GN Main Line to King's Cross, the Hertford loop and the Cambridge branch as far as Royston.

The TRC and IMC contracts with Railtrack are worth more than £1 billion a year. As existing maintenance contracts expire, new contracts are being let by competitive tender.

Railtrack's own organisation was divided into 10 geographically based zones, which have sinc been reduced to seven. The zones are the main interface between Railtrack's customers and suppliers, and with local authorities, local industries, user groups and others. They thus have a critical role in the long-term development of the network for increased use by both passenger and freight services. The zones, with their headquarters locations, are listed below. A major project has also been identified and described for each zone, and other projects listed. These are derived from the Network Management Statement, subtitled 'Investing in Britain's Railway'.

Scotland (Glasgow)

Physically, this is the largest zone, on whose tracks run InterCity, rural and suburban passenger operations, and freight. Scotland has 11 train operating companies operating within the zone and has the largest suburban rail network outside

London. These latter are run by ScotRail on behalf of the Strathclyde Passenger Transport Executive. A flagship service is the frequent Edinburgh-Glasgow Queen Street shuttle, for which ScotRail's plans envisage a 15min frequency in future. Beyond Inverness, the debate on how best to secure the far north services rumbles on.

A long-term maintenance strategy has been developed for the Forth Bridge. A key feature is to increase significantly the volume of repairs and painting work to bring the bridge to a condition allowing a steady state maintenance regime. Enhancement to the carrying capacity and line speed may also be realised. Cost £40 million, completion 2000/1.

A similar strategy is being developed for the Tay Bridge. Other schemes at Edinburgh Waverley (£40 million) and Glasgow Central stations (£25 million).

London North East (York)

What might be termed the home territory runs south from Berwick-upon-Tweed to Newark and North Nottinghamshire, and thence via the East Coast main line to King's Cross. This latter includes the Hertford loop. Major conurbations include the Passenger Transport Executive areas of Tyne and Wear, West Yorkshire and South Yorkshire, while the route of the Midland line from Chesterfield to Leeds approximates to the western boundary.

Leeds area infrastructure: extensive renewals of signalling and trackwork in the station area, with options to enhance the infrastructure and meet potential demand increases being investigated. Cost over £25 million, over the next 10 years.

North West (Manchester)

The North West zone is bounded by Holyhead, Wrexham, Crewe and the Settle & Carlisle. This encompasses a population of around seven million and includes the Greater Manchester and Merseyside Passenger Transport Executive areas. A full range of services is operated over North West zone's tracks, including deep rural areas such as the Cumbrian Coast and the line to Blaenau Ffestiniog. Recent investment includes the IECC installation on Merseyside, while the modernisation of the WCML is likely to be a forthcoming task.

Manchester South Resignalling and Remodelling: modernisation and remodelling of the infrastructure and track layout on the southern approaches to Manchester, including centralisation of control, to provide improved performance, operational flexibility and increased capacity. Cost £40 million, completion 2001/2.

A similar scheme is under way for Manchester Victoria area resignalling (£35 million).

Below:
Birmingham International, with its five platforms, opened on 26 January 1976 at a contemporary cost of £6 million. It has a dual purpose as the station for the National Exhibition Centre on the north side of the line, and for Birmingham airport on the south. This view was taken on 22 October 1997, looking west towards Birmingham.

Midlands (Birmingham)

The Midlands zone links Skegness, via Matlock, to Pwllheli and south to the London termini of Euston, St Pancras and Marylebone. This includes the West Midlands Passenger Transport Executive area. Together with North West, Railtrack's Midlands zone encompasses key parts of the national railway system, with the former London & North Western Railway main line as its core. But it also includes rural outposts such as the Leamington Spa-Stratford-upon-Avon branch, castigated by the 1983 Serpell Committee as having a (1981) revenue of a mere £76k, while direct costs alone amounted to £425k.

Trent Resignalling: renewal and centralisation of East Midlands signalling and control, including Nottingham East resignalling, track rationalisation, junction remodelling and Nottingham station remodelling. Cost £30 million, substantial completion by 2003.

Other similar schemes for Derby and Saltley (£35 million each); also remodelling at Euston and at Proof House Junction, Birmingham.

Great Western (Swindon)

With the exception of the once proud main line to Snow Hill and Birkenhead, this zone takes in nearly the whole of the former Great Western territory, plus all railways west of Exeter. Bristol and South Wales are the key industrial areas, while deep rural lines still abound, notably in Cornwall. The Great Western main line and its future electrification or otherwise will be a challenge for the zone, as will the developmental opportunities of Heathrow airport rail links.

Great Western Routes Transmission Based Signalling: strategy to extend the life of existing installations until TBS can be introduced to provide additional facilities, improved performance and reduced maintenance costs. Cost of

Below:
Level crossings are an unwelcome feature of eastern England in particular, both to road users and to railway managers. This automatic half-barrier crossing is outside Ely and was pictured on 8 November 1997.

Right:
Another feature found at Ely and elsewhere on Great Eastern metals at Manningtree is the level crossing for high vehicles and a (very) low under-bridge. A Class 158 enters Ely station from the north on 8 November 1997, while HGVs queue on the right for the use of the crossing.

Phase 1, Slough to Bristol and Oxford: £125 million, completion 2005/6. Cost of Phase 2, Gloucester to Bristol and Bristol to Swansea: £150 million, completion 2007/8.

Other schemes include work at Paddington station (£25 million).

East Anglia (Liverpool Street)

This zone comprises the lines of the former Great Eastern Railway and those of the Tilbury company. Both have heavy suburban traffics, while the GE also has InterCity and rural services. But Railtrack East Anglia also includes the North London line, right through to its Richmond terminus. The North London is a multi-purpose railway, carrying north of London Eurostars, as well as substantial freight from Thames-side and Felixstowe and an intensive local passenger service. What extra constraints will there be on the availability of train paths when the Channel Tunnel Rail Link starts to operate?

West Anglia Route Modernisation: renewal of signalling equipment at the south end of the West

Anglia network. Present assessment of control strategy, future capacity requirements and timetabling, and the potential for improved track layouts and increased line speeds. Cost £65 million, substantial completion 2001/2.

Southern (Waterloo)

The area is very similar to that of the former Southern Region of British Rail. Waterloo station is London's busiest, with 220,000 passengers daily, while the zone as a whole has the busiest network in the country. All major lines are electrified on the third rail system. The predominantly commuter traffic has also to cope with Eurostars and Channel Tunnel freight traffic, and Gatwick Express. The forthcoming Channel Tunnel Rail Link will require a substantial rethink of infrastructure requirements in conjunction with OPRAF and the TOCs.

Waterloo station: Extensive works to floors, platforms, trainshed roof and structural elements of the building. Integration into commercial opportunities. Cost £40 million, timescale not yet set.

Other works include resignalling Woking-Surbiton, Basingstoke, Dartford, Dorset coast and Feltham areas at costs varying between £30 million and £70 million.

Although Railtrack might be funding most schemes itself, local authorities also have an interest in rail investment. A guide to development partnerships was published jointly by Railtrack and the Association of Transport Co-ordinating Officers in 1997.

Local authority interest began with station car parks and other improvements, then moved on to new stations from the 1980s and even new lines. There were some local authority-owned DMUs, while resignalling Pontypridd-Taffs Well in the Cardiff Valleys was local authority-inspired.

Keeping railways open and busier is a contribution to the environment in its widest sense. It might also:

- help people to use cars less
- ease integration between modes through interchange
- move more freight onto rail, a major hope for the future
- make better use of rail corridors
- affect land use and development through partnership.

There are three major issues for local authorities when dealing with the railway industry:

- The costs of projects tend to be high; they *must* be comparable with other modes
- The justification for spending public money is in capturing benefits which would not otherwise be considered
- There is a need to understand what schemes are already planned.

Relationships must be built for the future, to encourage people to use the railway. Meanwhile,

Railtrack want to work in partnership to benefit local communities, and will look for ways to make it happen.

Additional Railtrack headquarters directorates set standards and policy guidelines for the company. These include the Safety and Standards Directorate. Railtrack's Safety Plan provides strategic direction and sets objectives in terms of minimising accident rates. Other Directorates are Commercial, Engineering and Production, Finance, Government and Public Affairs, Human Resources, Legal/Secretariat, and Railtrack Property.

West Coast Main Line

Of all the investment possibilities in the existing railway infrastructure, the West Coast main line modernisation programme is perhaps the most glamorous. However important they may be, overcoming the problems of the rising water table on Merseyrail's underground line or investment in IECC resignalling come into the necessary but politically unexciting category. Total rebuilding of the WCML is another matter.

A full 30 years have now passed since main line electric trains began running accelerated schedules from Euston on 18 April 1966. By today's European standards, the schedules were pedestrian, but they were exciting enough then. 'For the first time in history, start-to-stop times at over 80mph appear in a British timetable. The 08.03 Liverpool Pullman will run the 163.05 miles from Watford to Runcorn in 122min at 80.2mph, and four trains from Stafford to Bletchley, 86.9 miles in 65min, also at 80.2mph' enthused *Modern*

Railways, noting that there would now be trains every 2hr between Manchester and London, with extras in the morning and evening. Today, Virgin Railways' Merseyside Pullman takes 129min for the same journey with four intermediate stops, while Milton Keynes Central has long replaced Bletchley for InterCity purposes.

But, apart from extending electrification to Glasgow, not a lot has happened since. As Railtrack put it: 'Much of the infrastructure is now reaching the end of its life. It is becoming increasingly unreliable and the costs of keeping it going on a "patch and mend" basis are escalating.' Yet, the WCML is designated as a priority Trans European Network (TEN) project as part of the European high speed rail network. This reflects its strategic importance. It links the major conurbations of northwest England and Scotland to the Midlands, London and continental Europe via the Channel Tunnel. It also provides links to Ireland via Holyhead. TEN status provides access to potential funding support from the European Union.

The result was a study, in which the main aspirations of users were:

- reliability
- faster journey times
- increased line capacity
- increased options for freight, including a larger loading gauge.

The study team examined four business approaches to investment:

- the bedrock case, using the minimum patch and mend approach
- the recovery case, using conventional technology to achieve a state of good repair

At South Tottenham station, electrification connects the single line from Seven Sisters via the junction on the right in the medium distance, with Tottenham South Junction and Stratford. The effect on the nearby platform edge of the use of single leads, and the coach overhang which results, is noticeable. What effect will the provisions of the Disability Discrimination Act and others have upon the vehicle to platform gaps which result?

- the cost driven case, with major investment with the aim of cost reduction
- the market driven case, with major investment designed to exploit market opportunities.

The task was to produce a single viable option, but this became a tiered solution consisting of a major renewal programme and two subsequent upgrades. The core investment is the part of the programme designed to significantly improve safety, reliability and journey times, and to reduce costs. The upgrade options were designed to permit significant journey time reductions for both passenger and freight.

All received approval in October 1997. The schemes are as follows:

Core Investment Programme

Its purpose is to restore WCML infrastructure quality in terms of modern equivalent asset values, albeit that the definition of what this means in practice is not as easy as it might seem. This is costed at £1.35 billion and includes:

- modernisation of track and improvement of traction power supplies to meet system performance standards. This involves the removal of permanent speed restrictions, for instance.
- Installation of Train Control System transmission-based signalling, the cost of which alone accounts for £500 million of the total. This replaces lineside signalling.
- Automatic Train Protection as an inherent capability of the train control system.
- The development of a single integrated control centre for the whole WCML.
- An implementation programme involving minimum disruption to train services.

Passenger Upgrade 1

This is the first upgrade, and was negotiated by OPRAF with Railtrack as part of the franchise agreement with InterCity West Coast. This £150 million scheme upgrades track and power supplies

to allow passenger operation by tilting trains at 200km/h. This stage and the core investment programme (excluding the resignalling) are to be achieved by 2002.

Passenger Upgrade 2

This is a further £600 million upgrade. It prepares the infrastructure for 225km/h tilting train passenger operation, for which the new signalling will be required. The track also needs further work to raise ride quality, allow for increased structure gauge clearances in both width and height, new power supplies and new overhead line equipment (ohle). Speeds on the slow lines will also be raised to 160km/h for freight services. Included in the above cost, freight will also benefit from £127 million worth of other infrastructure work such as quadrupling over the Tamworth-Lichfield-Rugeley section and reinstatement of the Nuneaton flyover. All work is for completion in 2005.

The WCML will become, effectively, two separate railways side by side. Crossovers between the 225km/h fast lines and the 160km/h slow lines will mostly be removed, and while facilities will be provided for passenger trains on the slow lines to overtake freight, use by either of these traffics of the fast lines will be a rarity. This will be the situation north from Euston to Rugby, and for much of the distance thence to Crewe.

The core programme meets many of the key aspirations, but the enhancements go further and bring attractive opportunities to operators and users. The study demonstrated that benefits in terms of journey time reductions could be achieved, but that this required the co-operation of others, including decisions on the types of rolling stock used.

To justify such an investment, Railtrack needs to be confident that it would produce benefits in terms of long-term maintenance costs as well as passenger benefits such as greater reliability and journey time savings. As part of the cost/benefit analysis, a socio-economic and environmental impact study was undertaken to examine in more detail the effects and likely benefits of the core programme and enhanced options on UK regions.

As to who benefits, these include the obvious ones of passenger and freight operators, but also those such as OPRAF, ORR, PTEs, the RUCCs, HSE, plus manufacturers and the infrastructure service providers. The study showed:
- Virgin Railways will be able to provide faster, more comfortable, more reliable and more frequent services. The aim is to double the

number of passenger journeys by the time the franchise ends in 2012. Virgin will also have greater flexibility in traffic management through improved train command and control systems.

- For Silverlink and other North London services out of Euston, the remodelling of the station approaches together with the possibilities of double-decker commuter trains will increase reliability, improve services and increase demand while reducing costs.
- For services in the West Midlands, train control improvements will aid increased frequency of services in the Wolverhampton-Coventry corridor.
- Longer freight trains and (perhaps) piggyback will offer greater opportunities to freight operators.
- All trains will be afforded the improved safety benefit of the new train control system.

Without much service disruption during construction, passengers and business users will enjoy:

- a radically improved and more reliable service on the WCML;
- the ability to reach destinations punctually, faster and more often; and
- a competitive alternative to other modes of transport.

The new signalling technology means that existing systems can still be used while the new transmission-based system is being installed, avoiding extensive service disruption during rebuilding.

Overall, the study concluded that there were considerable benefits. Railtrack has negotiated a new West Coast track access agreement, which came into effect from spring 1998. In all, 80% of the charge is fixed and the other 20% is indexed

Above:
The neat Wembley Stadium station area, looking south on 12 November 1997, shows the space which could once again be made available for additional tracks, should they ever be required here. Sadly, capacity problems are rarely so easily solved in real life; legal powers, acquisition, demolition, compensation, construction and access charges are the languages which usually count.

Below right:
Automatic crossings are activated by wheel flanges depressing a treadle, as seen here.

to the level of ridership as expressed by revenues, and of customer satisfaction. If operation is faultless and Virgin Railways meets its own income targets, Railtrack receives the fixed charge, its share of the 20% variable and another 20% from the revenue sharing. Potentially, Railtrack could earn 120% of the standard amount. But shortcomings in any of the identified areas will reduce Railtrack's revenue, maybe substantially. It is hoped that the net effect will be an incentive for operator and Railtrack alike to minimise the disruption felt by the customers.

In prospect is the running of 11 trains per hour per direction on the fast lines in 2005, though the maximum capacity depends also on the mix of train speeds and stopping patterns. Theoretical headways of 90sec (40tph) are in prospect for 225km/h operation, though 15tph is expected to be the practical limit.

However, a standard hour for Virgin Railways in 2005 is likely to consist of:
- four trains to Birmingham, of which one extends to Wolverhampton

- three trains to Manchester
- one train to Liverpool
- two trains to Preston, of which one will be extended, alternately, to Edinburgh or Glasgow
- one train to Chester (IC125).

Virgin's claimed timings achievable at 225km/h in 2005 are less than 1hr 15min to Birmingham, 1hr 45min to Manchester, 1hr 55min to Liverpool, and 3hr 50min to Glasgow. Broadly, this is around one-third less time than the 1997/8 timetable, albeit with fewer stops. It should be said, though, that upgrading work will not take place north of Weaver Junction where services to Warrington and all destinations to Scotland diverge.

The WCML passenger may thus look forward to much higher frequencies and considerably faster services. The result, it is hoped, will be a huge surge in traffic. If it isn't, then the long distance railway can have little future in Britain.

London Projects

Other major projects concern London, where a Director, London Projects has been appointed for Railtrack. A principal development is Thameslink 2000, which is an integration of rail infrastructure north and south of the Thames, with the key benefit of adding enough capacity to allow 24x12-car trains per hour to operate.

The two service groups north of the Thames are the Midland line and its Thameslink services from Bedford, which presently use the route via Blackfriars, and the outer suburban Great Northern services to Peterborough and King's Lynn. Inner suburban GN services will continue to run to Moorgate.

South of the river, the intended destinations are Guildford, Horsham, Littlehampton, Brighton, Eastbourne, Ashford and Dartford, while the Wimbledon-Sutton loop will continue to be Thameslink served.

Costed at £580 million, this scheme requires less than a mile of new track. The main physical work in T2000, for which a Transport & Works Act Order application was made in November 1997, includes:

- Grade separation in the Bermondsey area to minimise interactions between service groups.
- Extra platform and two new tracks at London Bridge.
- Additional track from London Bridge to Borough Market (which involves demolishing two pubs).
- New Blackfriars station with entrances both north and south of the Thames.
- Closure of the 'Widened Lines' Farringdon to Moorgate section, since the extension of Farringdon's platforms to 12-cars can only be achieved at the eastern end.
- The severely congested King's Cross Thameslink station will be closed and replaced by a new station below St Pancras with entrance on Midland Road.
- Connection made to the Great Northern, for which powers are available in the CTRL Act.
- Power supplies upgraded.
- Resignalling needed in central area.

This is Railtrack's first big enhancement project and it is essential to get the structure of the funding methodology for calculating track access charges right for the future.

Other major projects include the £2 billion east-west CrossRail scheme to provide services between Shenfield and Reading/Aylesbury, in whatever form it might take eventually. This links lines east and west of London via a new underground tunnel with stations at Liverpool Street, Farringdon, Tottenham Court Road, Bond Street and Paddington. In 1998 it is still being described as 'a vital part of a rail strategy for London' and its route through central London enjoys planning safeguards. A five-year construction period is anticipated, and funding is expected to be arranged through a partnership between the Government and the private sector. Also under consideration are rail links from Heathrow Airport both to the north and the south of the airport, with or without Terminal 5.

Potential conflict areas exist between such projects, be they for business reasons, capacity constraints, geographical incompatibilities or diverse technical standards. What traffic volumes do we really envisage as attainable in the future, and what is the real ability of a given railway infrastructure to handle much higher and more diverse traffic levels?

But schemes also need funding, and thus a promoter, if progress is to be made. The funding may be private, public or some combination, reflecting perhaps where the various benefits of the schemes are expected to lie. They also require one or more train operators.

Network Management Statement

The Network Management Statement is an annual document setting out how Railtrack intends to manage and develop the railway, and many of the major projects have already been discussed. The NMS sets out the various categories, and programmed expenditure over the succeeding six years (at 1995/6 prices):

renewals	£3.5 billion
property maintenance backlog	£0.7 billion
day-to-day maintenance	£4.0 billion
network development	£0.9 billion
Total	£9.1 billion

Over the period under review, this amounts to a commendable £4 million per day.

The 1997/8 NMS business plan includes actual and current expenditure in the previous and present years, plans for the years 1998/9 to 2007/8 and outline plans beyond that.

There are three levels of geographical disaggregation:
- a national picture for the period to 2008
- division into seven zones up to the year 2001
- each zones divided into routes (33 in all and taking into account both passenger and freight) to 2001.

The NMS contents include:
- network demand and capacity analysis
- network maintenance and renewal plans, which account for the bulk of expenditure
- network development plans—the interesting bit!
- methods of finance, made up of Railtrack's own resources and those of others such as local and central government.

There is a forecast of future demand, both passenger and freight. For passenger this extends into time periods beyond the existing franchises, but recognises and includes the requirements of existing TOCs. Railtrack makes its money from selling train paths, and a key requirement is that there should be adequate network capacity. Between 12 and 15 significant bottlenecks have been identified.

What might Railtrack's various customers want? Those that have been identified include, for passenger traffic: attention to station access, interchange facilities between rail and road, information provision and service reliability; for freight: intermodal access to rail, loading gauge enhancement work and international traffic; for all train operators: facilities which help them to reduce their operating costs, and to increase line capacity by eliminating bottlenecks where these are a constraint on service provision.

The NMS includes a physical description of works, the projected timescales and target dates for completion. Growth, in passenger or freight traffics, has to be accommodated. The decision-making process covers safety, customer and community requirements, impact of new technology, and capacity levels.

The NMS sets out project justification, seeking to answer two questions:
- Why do it?
- Who gets what out of it?

Output measures cover network capability (matters such as trains per hour) and quality (such as maximum speed/axle loads). They also cover journey times and the provision of disabled facilities. Targets are set for some measures.

It should perhaps be recorded here that Railtrack does not own quite all the rail infrastructure on which National Railways operate. Track on the approaches to and within Heathrow Airport is owned by BAA. St Pancras station is owned by London & Continental, who were expected to construct and own the Channel Tunnel Rail Link. That of the Channel Tunnel itself is owned by Eurotunnel, while private sidings and terminals retain their traditional status.

Railtrack needs to take a long-term view to produce a railway which is fit for purpose in the 21st century. Finally, a view from the Regulator:

> 'Railtrack has a central position in the railway industry. Thus not only is the future success of the railway in Great Britain dependent on Railtrack, but the success of Railtrack is dependent on those who provide services to Railtrack and on those who as train operators or funding bodies purchase services from Railtrack.'

Regulatory controls on Railtrack are discussed further in Chapter 6.

1 Annual Report and Accounts, Central Japan Railway Co, 1992.

O P R A F

Office of Passenger Rail Franchising

This section considers the work of the Office of Passenger Rail Franchising (OPRAF). The Franchising Director is appointed by the Secretary of State. He is a statutory officer for franchising the railway but also an accounting officer who has to show value for money for the funds he expends.

Franchise Sales

The result of the sale programme was the franchising of 25 companies between February 1996 and April 1997. The initial public expenditure of £2,102 million in 1996/7 is to fall to £926 million by 2002/3. Major committed investment as a condition includes £1.5-£2.0 million in rolling stock and £600 million in Thameslink 2000. The WCML upgrade includes £150 million of public money as well as that committed by Railtrack.

The Train Operating Companies were all franchised individually, but several of the purchasers were awarded more than one company. Against each entry is shown the location of the head office and the date on which the franchise was awarded.

National Express Group

Top of the list with no less than five franchises, the company has wide public transport interests ranging from coaches to airports, and now rail. As may be seen, the group's franchises have a wide geographical spread and cover examples of all types of services as defined previously by the British Railways Board. The companies are:

- Central Trains Ltd
  Birmingham   17 February 1997
- Gatwick Express Ltd
  London   3 April 1996
- Midland Main Line Ltd
  Derby   22 April 1996
- ScotRail Railways Ltd
  Glasgow   24 February 1997
- Silverlink Train Services Ltd
  Watford   7 February 1997

National Express also has a 17% shareholding in London & Continental Railways Ltd, the company formed to own Eurostar (UK) Ltd and to construct the Channel Tunnel Rail Link.

Prism Rail PLC

The four companies in this franchise are mostly suburban in nature, but Wales & West serves large rural areas.

- Cardiff Railway Co Ltd
  Cardiff   17 September 1996
- LTS Rail Ltd
  Southend   9 May 1996
- Wales & West Passenger Trains Ltd
  Cardiff   17 September 1996
- West Anglia Great Northern Railway
  London   6 December 1996

First Group plc

First Group was awarded the Great Eastern Railway initially, but subsequently acquired Great Western Holdings Ltd in which it had a minority stake. First Group thus now have three rather different operations.

- Great Eastern Railway
  London   4 December 1996
- Great Western Trains Co Ltd
  Swindon   20 December 1995
- North Western Trains
  Manchester   5 February 1997

Virgin Rail Group Ltd

These two former InterCity companies are now managed as one group, albeit that they remain two franchises. Substantial upgrading is required in both cases.

- Virgin Trains (Cross Country)
  Birmingham   28 November 1996
- Virgin Trains (West Coast)
  Birmingham   19 February 1997

Virgin Rail also has a 17% shareholding in London & Continental Railways Ltd.

Compagnie General d'Entreprises Automobiles (CGEA)

This French group has extensive interests in passenger transport and utility operations. The two Connex companies form a large part of the former BR Southern Region operations.

- Connex South Central Ltd
  Croydon   12 April 1996
- Connex South Eastern Ltd
  London   21 August 1996

Stagecoach Holdings plc

Stagecoach has substantial UK and overseas bus interests. Also wholly owns the Porterbrook ROSCO, acquired on 28 August 1996. The rail franchises represent the rest of the old Southern Region!

- Island Line Ltd
  Ryde IoW   13 October 1996
- South West Trains Ltd
  London   19 December 1995

MTL Trust Holdings Ltd

Parts of RRNE operations are wholly urban, as is the Merseyrail company, but large rural areas are also served. The MTL group has bus industry connections.

- Merseyrail Electrics Ltd
  Liverpool   20 December 1996
- Regional Railways North East Ltd
  York   10 February 1997

Other Owners

- Anglia Railways, owned by GB Railways Group plc.
  London   6 December 1996
- Chiltern Railways, owned by M40 Trains Ltd, a management buy-out backed by 3i and John Laing plc.
  Aylesbury   25 June 1996

- Great North Eastern Railway Ltd, owned by Sea Containers Ltd.
  York   29 March 1996
- Thames Trains, owned by Victory Railway Holdings Ltd. Victory Railways is owned by the Go-Ahead Group plc (65%), principally bus interests, and a management buy-out (35%), but subsequently became wholly owned by the Go-Ahead Group.
  Reading   19 September 1996
- Thameslink Rail Ltd, owned by GOVIA, a joint venture between the Go-Ahead Group plc (65%) and Via GTI (35%), a French public transport operator.
  London   11 February 1997

Each Train Operating Company is discussed in detail in Chapter 7; here we are concerned only with the results by owning companies. For the most recent period available, these appear as set out in the table below. They are rated in diminishing order of cumulative revenues, including Government grant to the franchisee.

Such results should be taken as no more than the starting point; the annual Government support will have reduced by half that shown to £926 million by 2002/3, while several TOCs have claimed worthwhile traffic and revenue growth. It does, however, illustrate the imbalance between commercial revenues and support profiles from which the exercise has started, and also the differing sizes of the 12 owning groups. Effectively, three-quarters of total fares revenue is in the hands of half-a-dozen groups. The same is true of the total revenue when the support payments are included, although in this latter list MTL replaces Stagecoach.

Owning company profiles

Table 5.1

Group	Fares revenue 1995/6 £m	Support Year 1 £m	Total income £m	Cumulative franchise revenue £m	%
National Express	310	528	838	838	20
First Group	395	267	662	1,500	35
Connex Rail	390	211	601	2,101	49
Virgin Rail	327	190	517	2,618	61
Prism Rail	225	173	398	3,016	70
MTL Trust Holdings	87	305	392	3,408	79
Stagecoach	281	57	338	3,746	87
Sea Containers	206	65	271	4,017	94
Victory Railways	47	33	80	4,097	96
GOVIA	76	3	79	4,176	97
GB Railways	38	36	74	4,250	99
M40 Trains	22	17	39	4,289	100
National Railways	2,404	1,885	4,289		

Principles

The basic principles of franchising were identified in 1859 by Chadwick, who argued in favour of competition *for* the market as opposed to competition *in* it. In other words, you make a bid against others to run the business for a fixed term. If successful, you have exclusive but temporary monopoly rights, so that you can operate the designated services profitably. In his view, this was preferable to a general free-for-all, as applies today in the bus industry outside Greater London.

The Conservative Government set out its stall on rail franchising during the passage of the Railways Bill. The following was contained in the Department of Transport's Consultation Document 'The Franchising of Rail Passenger Services', issued in October 1992:

- 'Central to the [Government's] proposals for passenger services is the intention to franchise their operation... The Government wants franchising to be responsive to the market.' (Introduction, paras i and ii)
- 'The aim will be to preserve as much flexi-

Left:
The Porterbrook Leasing Company-owned No 47810 carries the company's livery although it is leased to Virgin Cross Country. It is seen here at Birmingham New Street on 11 October 1997 alongside the symbol of the Black Country Development Corporation.

bility as possible in...the duration and geographical extent of franchises, and the functions to be carried out by franchisees.' There is a 'need to enhance competition...' (para 3.1)

- The rights of a franchisee are 'to provide an identified group of services, be guaranteed the necessary track access to do so, receive passenger revenue and any other income his services generate, and, where necessary, receive subsidy'. (para 4.1)
- The obligations of a franchisee are 'to provide at least the minimum level of service specified in his contract, and to meet at least the minimum standard specified therein, for the duration of the contract'. (para 4.1)

These objectives have since been set out in formal instructions to the Franchising Director from the Secretary of State. They have been updated as matters progressed, but also following the change in Government on 1 May 1997. Extracts from the present version dated 6 November 1997 may be found in Appendix 2. This contains a distinct move away from how to set about franchising, which is now complete. Emphasis is now on managing the franchised railway and protecting passenger interests, together with progressing investment issues.

The first of the principal objectives for the Franchising Director is to increase the number of passengers travelling by rail.

Responsibilities

In its early days, OPRAF's main responsibility was to develop an attractive and saleable business opportunity, and also to sell the 25 passenger franchises. Although this was the remit, franchising is little to do with selling anything. A more explanatory way of looking at it is to think of the duties as:

'To receive competitive bids for a level of public funding to run a rail service for a period of time, the service levels themselves being specified to a greater or lesser extent.'

In letting the franchises, the Franchising Director has tried:

- to secure an overall improvement in the quality of passenger and station services;
- to obtain value for money for the taxpayer by encouraging efficiency and economy;
- to offer the prospect of success and profit for the franchisees; and
- to promote passenger usage and the long-term cost-effective development of the network.

There is a fundamental problem in balancing the aspects of service quality for the user, the constraints on taxpayer funding, and ensuring that the franchisee is not denied a successful business outcome. These tensions need to be present, but their resolution is a major challenge.

The development of the network can be influenced by the content and terms of the contracts (mostly seven years). To what extent is this itself a problem when considering the long term? It is important that the railway and the services it offers do not become fixed. Both have to change with the times, and the framework must enable this to happen.

A quality railway is a laudable objective, but what is meant by the concept and how long will it take to implement? A suggested definition is:

- driven by the market, rather than bureaucracy;
- responsive to customer needs;
- seeking out and developing new opportunities;
- attracting capital from outside; and
- an industry where real improvements can happen.

There is a need to focus on commercial incentives.

Meanwhile, OPRAF has tried to improve quality in a more basic sense, by retaining those network benefits which stem from a co-ordinated system, giving the maximum autonomy to management, and controlling levels of risk.

Again, a political objective was to transfer risk from the public sector to the private sector. Initially, anyway, the competition was *for* the franchise, rather than head-to-head competition between operators on the railway itself. This is one of the reasons that a definition of quality targets is so important.

Franchise Award

The franchise process first required the creation of the 25 Train Operating Companies, each with its licence to operate and a safety case to demonstrate that it could manage operations safely and meet required safety standards. The subsequent stages were as follows:

- pre-qualification to bid
- issue of invitation to tender
- due diligence investigations
- bid made
- negotiation
- completion, including the formal acquisition of the TOC by the franchisee and final approval by the Rail Regulator.

The transfer of the TOCs took place with the necessary contracts in place relating to track, stations, depots, rolling stock and inter-operator agreements. Some of the bidders clearly needed more time to come to terms with the magnitude of what they were proposing to undertake, and betrayed a distinct lack of understanding of the rail industry.

Bid assessment was based on the following criteria:

- value for public money
- financial stability of the franchisee
- risk transfer
- management competence
- employee involvement.

However, for the management of the franchise itself, this was essentially the beginning of a long-term relationship. The award to a bidder is only the start of a continuing arrangement, in contrast to the earlier utility privatisations.

Agreements

What does a franchise agreement offer? It gives the franchisee the right to run passenger services for a specified number of years, in return for an agreed level of public subsidy or payment to public funds. It also confers ownership of the Train Operating Company running the franchise.

When it comes to bidding the next time round,

this will be based on the deals which the potential franchisee can do, rather than having it all set up for them as with the initial round completed on 31 March 1997.

The characteristics of a railway franchise are:
- few fixed assets of any substance;
- low initial capital requirements;
- the need to deposit performance bonds, to ensure that the franchisees do not lose interest in what they are doing;
- operational flexibility within the Passenger Service Requirement (qv); and
- a contractual entitlement to subsidy to offset fixed costs, though in most franchises this diminishes over the term of the contract and in some cases becomes a reimbursement to the Government.

Put another way, the subsidy/reimbursement element is the way in which Government has chosen to support the railway businesses, according to what the businesses themselves have estimated as necessary. It also immunises the franchisee (and thus the railway itself) from the variability of public funding. The Treasury influence, in particular, is reduced.

The agreement between the franchisee and OPRAF has to get the balance right, whether between obligations and business freedom, or between risk and reward.

PSR

The Passenger Service Requirement (PSR) is the central element of the franchise agreement. It specifies the level of service which the franchisee *must* provide, on a route-by-route basis. Although he is free to provide more, he cannot provide less. The scheme is designed to prevent bidders from 'cherry picking'. Extracts from a specimen PSR are included as Appendix 3.

There are three types of passenger railway: essentially these are the InterCity, commuter and regional types, based on previous definitions. Some, such as Anglia, cover more than one service type in different parts of their operations. The question which has to be asked is: What is OPRAF purchasing with the taxpayer's money?

With InterCity services, previously provided more or less commercially by the British Railways Board, some attention needs to be given to frequencies. For commuter (and particularly London commuter) services, the peak demand has to be satisfied in terms of both frequencies and volumes, but this gives the opportunity for off-peak services to be demand driven. For regional

services, the service provision has to be justified and tightly specified; overall, this is the least financially satisfactory part of railway operations.

The specification to safeguard passenger needs takes the following structure. The whole is remarkably complex and needs to include:
- frequency
- times of first and last trains
- weekend services
- stations served
- journey time
- provision of through services
- preservation of key connections
- capacity standards, where applicable.

The key benefits for passengers are a new level of safeguards, under which for the first time the operator has clear obligations on a route-by-route basis, with every route and every station protected. The incident over the attempted withdrawal by stealth of the Fort William sleeper demonstrated that such issues cannot be fudged.

There is a long lead time when timetables are to be changed; this needs stringent controls in the PSR, including consultation. The benefits for franchisees are that their obligations are clear from the outset and that they have flexibility in how to respond to passenger needs.

Fares

Fares regulation is aimed at the control of monopoly power in areas in which it is thought to exist. The formula which has emerged where fares are to be regulated is Retail Price Index +0% for the three years to 31 December 1998, followed by RPI -1% for the following four years until the end of 2001. It is the overall fares basket which is limited, rather than individual fares, which may rise by up to 2%. What happens after 2001 remains unclear.

This betrays an interesting political perspective rather than a railway one, in that ministers in the last government had previously been looking for real fares increases. The present formula, which relates to the seven-year franchise period enjoyed by most (but not all) train companies, could conceivably even lead to fares decreases with very low inflation. This would play havoc with season ticket revenue; the London Tilbury & Southend is one business where huge amounts of money for annual season tickets are taken during December to avoid the January fares increases.

For commuter journeys, the pricing formula applies to standard singles and returns, and also season tickets, for journeys to work in and around the London area, Edinburgh and Cardiff. Some fares may rise by up to 2% above inflation but, if so, compensating changes below the regulated level must be made to other fares. In the Passenger Transport Executive areas, the PTEs themselves regulate fares.

Elsewhere, Saver tickets are price regulated and, where there are no Savers, the unrestricted standard returns. Such tickets must:

• be valid for at least one month;
• be valid on any day of the week; and
• be valid at any time of the day, except that they need not be valid before 10.30 (Mondays to Fridays) or for journeys leaving Greater London and other major stations near London between 15.00 and 19.00 (Mondays to Fridays).

The key point is that less onerous conditions may be applied by operators; what they cannot do is to be more restrictive. For instance, there is no *requirement* to restrict the use of the return portion of a Saver journey, only that operators may do so if they wish.

OPRAF has sought to safeguard the essential features of the Saver ticket while leaving the operator some flexibility in the application of these restrictions. The SuperSaver, it will be noted, is not controlled. Some companies have withdrawn it for their own domestic operations, replacing it, for instance, with day returns.

Another element is the quality of service performance. As the present Passenger Charter statistics show, results are patchy. Since January 1997, in London, operators who failed to meet performance standards set by OPRAF have had their fares held down by up to 2% below the regulated level. If, on the other hand, they improve their performance, fares may be raised by up to 2% above the regulated level. Later, similar arrangements may be applied in Edinburgh and Cardiff.

Other areas covered by the franchise agreements include payments between the Franchising Director and the franchisee, the term of the franchise, and the incentive regime. There is also a requirement to participate in what is styled 'Network Benefits', matters such as through ticketing and the national rail enquiry service.

There are financial and corporate safeguards. These last are designed to ensure that the Franchising Director is not left high and dry in the case of a franchisee's failure. They include the franchisee's provision of share capital and a performance bond. Specified operational and financial data must also be supplied to enable

performance to be monitored and audited.

The above are common to all franchises. Franchise Plans are the additional commitments which were made by would-be franchisees in preparing their bids; these are discussed in Chapter 7 under each Train Operating Company.

Monitoring

OPRAF has to ensure that the public money committed continues to be justified and that the TOCs are fulfilling their side of the franchising agreements. Fundamentally, the objective is to ensure compliance.

This alone, though, is not enough. OPRAF is looking also to encourage improvements in the quality of services, to safeguard the continuity of service provision, to treat all service providers consistently and ensure continued confidence, and to develop the market for franchises.

To achieve this, OPRAF needs to manage the contracts, but *not* the railway. The latter is the job of the franchisees, who have the freedom to pursue commercial objectives. It is OPRAF's aim to drive further performance improvements with the incentives programme. There must always be clear boundaries of responsibility between OPRAF and the franchisee, and there must be flexibility.

Operator Obligations

Operator obligations may derive from those placed upon all franchisees, commitments made by individual companies, or industry obligations such as Association of Train Operating Company (ATOC) schemes and licences.

All franchisees have to operate the base level service (PSR), give notice when and where the timetable will change, undertake customer satisfaction market research and maintain station standards of shelter, lighting, etc. They are subject to capacity and fares regulation, and must provide a passenger charter. They will also have obligations which are designed to enable the smooth transfer of the franchise to another party.

Additional commitments may refer, variously, to existing train mileage being maintained, new services and recasts, as on Chiltern, Midland Main Line, North Western Trains and Virgin CrossCountry, investment in stations and passenger security, and intermodal initiatives in terms of car parking, taxi links and bus integration. Many have been active in this last field.

OPRAF has to ensure that the commitments are delivered.

Above:
Eurostar services run from Waterloo International, seen here at platform level before it was opened.

Tools of the Trade

The largely fixed costs of a franchisee are in themselves an incentive to increase passenger volumes, as are the decreasing subsidy profiles. The commercial incentive regime includes punctuality (Performance Incentive Payments [PIP]), short formations (SFIP) and timetable change (TCIP).

There is also the customer satisfaction benchmark of SQUIRE (service quality incentive). This also applies in the Greater Manchester and West Yorkshire PTE areas, where the operators take the revenue risk.

Alternatively, TIRE (ticketless travel) is in place in the other five PTE areas, where the PTE takes the revenue risk and not the franchisee. Here, there must be an incentive on the operator to collect fares, or he might not bother!

Regular reports are made by the franchisee to OPRAF. OPRAF also has checks on timetables through the PSR compliance system, fares increase regulation monitoring (FIRM) and train running analysis (TRACS). This latter determines the eligibility for incentive payments by OPRAF and gives advance notice of problems.

The incentive regime penalises the operator for non-provision of service in the case of engineering works whether foreseen or not, but the operator may also have a claim against Railtrack. The enforcement regime consists of the three stages of Call-In, Breach and Default, the last of which recognises that performance is exceptionally poor or there has been serious failure. The Franchising Director has an option to terminate the contract in these circumstances.

However, while breach and default can be pursued in the courts if absolutely necessary, OPRAF's preferred commercial approach is to prevent events which give rise to such costly and time-consuming actions from happening in the first place. This is much more productive than pursuing compensation issues to the bitter end.

The Act requires the Franchising Director to ensure continuity of service to the public, whatever the reason for a franchise coming to an end. Reasons for failure may be premature termination or a failure to relet a franchise at the end of its term. Termination affects the legitimate interests of the ORR, Railtrack and ROSCOs, which must be taken into account. The successor operator may be a Franchising Director company (shell companies have been set up) or another franchise operator. There may be primary or specific assets for transfer, key contractual obligations, handover arrangements and specified personnel.

Results So Far

New and refurbished rolling stock is being provided, either contractually or conditionally, by a number of companies.

There are signs of new services, such as Connex South Central's Gatwick-Rugby and SWT's Portsmouth-Reading operations. Gatwick Express now runs throughout the night. Ticketing initiatives by GNER, Midland Main Line and others offer group travel rates, while passengers between London and Birmingham have a number of operator and ticketing choices.

Not all operations are running smoothly. In 1996/7 there were eight call-ins: six due to cancellations and two to short formations. Breaches were due to Chiltern (late ordering rolling stock), Midland Main Line (peak capacity) and South West Trains (franchise plan delivery).

On reliability, 15 route groups were better, 14 the same and 31 worse (second quarter 1997/8 compared with same period previous year). On punctuality, 16 were better, one the same and 43 worse. This suggests 'some falling back' in performance, with incentive payments only 80% of those in 1996. Punctuality and reliability are the essence of the customer charter objectives.

Passenger volumes were up 7.5% in 1996/7, and growth is continuing.

Conclusions

The future is promising but uncertain. Transport providers are always vulnerable to changes in the fortunes of the national economy, and resultant changes in TOC revenues may be very different in the London area from those in Cardiff or those in Glasgow. Secondly, what regulatory changes will be made, both in access charging and the moderation (or otherwise) of competition?

There remains the slightly uncomfortable interface between the Franchising Director and the Rail Regulator, particularly in retailing and ticketing. OPRAF is interested in the service experienced by the passenger, while ORR regulates infrastructure and the information provider. It may be noted that, unlike ORR, OPRAF has no freight responsibilities. Further away perhaps, there is the promise of an integrated transport policy and a Strategic Rail Authority.

Franchising management is a commercial process which needs:
- a sound contractual framework
- good quality operators
- keen commercial terms, including incentives
- effective relationships

- ongoing benefits for passengers
- value for money for taxpayers.

It would not be unreasonable to expect 'value for money for taxpayers' to rank highly in future tendering exercises. What is the justification for spending large sums of public funds? The work of the Association of Transport Co-ordinating Officers (ATCO), whose members' responsibilities include securing non-commercial bus services for local authorities and PTEs throughout Britain, is illuminating:

> 'Any evaluation of the social value obtained by the community...should take all costs and benefits, both internal and external, into account before reaching a conclusion. The external factors are particularly relevant in urban areas, where significant benefits may be experienced by non-users through relief of traffic congestion.'

There are five main groups of financial criteria, which may be used singly or in combination with each other:
- volume of travel (measured by passenger journeys or passenger km)
- journey purposes (work, education, shopping, leisure, etc)
- category of beneficiary (adult, pensioner, child, student, etc)
- type of area served (urban, suburban, rural)
- availability of alternatives (geographical, by time, etc).

ATCO argued that it is the combination of these factors, weighted to reflect their relative priorities, which determines the social benefits which may be derived. It also argued that such matters should be looked at first, before applying financial criteria. The unit costs of provision add another dimension, as indeed does the political input.[1]

Nobody, least of all ATCO, would suggest that this is the last word in such matters. It concentrates also on local rather than longer distance services. The approach does, however, indicate some of the areas for consideration. Their resolution will become more pressing as services come up for retendering as part of the second franchise round.

However, it remains relatively early days of the franchised railway. As a process, franchising is not without its detractors. There has been a long-standing antipathy to it in the old Department of Transport. In March 1985, its Economics Directorate published a document 'Problems With Franchising'. The context was the Government's

then proposal for the deregulation of bus services. Many thought that bus services should instead be franchised out by the local authorities. The DoT paper concluded:

- Franchises afford a measure of protection to the incumbent, since the natural pressures are to accommodate operators' difficulties in order to maintain service and minimise public dispute. This might, for instance, lead to allowing cost pressures to result in price rises.
- The franchise needs to be sufficiently long to encourage investment and secure a return, but the longer the period, the greater the chance that monopolistic practices would develop.
- Franchises involve contracts between a public authority and a supplier, and require a performance specification. This can never reflect fully the detail of consumers' wishes. The specification must be imperfect, since the future is uncertain.
- The actual award criterion of the franchise will be to a degree artificial or obscure. It is impossible to reduce competitive bids to a single criterion.
- Franchisees may use any imprecision in the specification to their advantage. Only gross infringements can result in termination, since litigation and the exercise of penalty clauses are not costless.
- Performance needs to be monitored, a substantial and bureaucratic and regulatory task.
- Changes in circumstances lead to pressures for renegotiation and extension of the franchise, away from the pressures of the market. The incumbent has an advantage over others when rebidding, and the record shows that franchises do not frequently change hands.

Above:
Most Great North Eastern Railway operations are based on the Class 91 plus Mk 4 coaches and a Driving Van Trailer. With a DVT leading, the 06.00 from Newcastle arrives at King's Cross on 8 November 1997.

Technically, local bus services are only partially akin to rail passenger services. Thus the capital requirements are of an entirely different magnitude, while the scale of rail operations is generally much larger. Rail services have to operate as part of a system, since the infrastructure of track and signalling is, at any one time, of finite capacity. As a business, the railway is characterised as having costly assets, which have an extremely long life.

The franchised passenger railway is, however, a reality. How successfully these issues have been addressed is perhaps still to be determined, but there are certainly signs that the seven-year franchise holders are dangling carrots to secure extensions. For instance:

'Stagecoach has offered to spend more than £400 million on new carriages for its South West Trains network if John O'Brien, the Franchising Director, agrees to extend its franchise for a further seven years. Brian Souter has told Mr O'Brien that Stagecoach will make the London Waterloo commuter line the most modern rail franchise in Britain, if it is given the chance to keep running it until 2010. The offer will stand until the franchise is retendered.'[2]

1 ATCO Performance Criteria Working Party Report, November 1989.
2 *The Times*, 3 December 1997.

The Rail Regulator

To ensure that 'fair play' is achieved, a Regulatory Authority has been set up. First, who are the users of rail services? For the Rail Regulator, there are two distinct groups:

- The passengers of the train operating companies and the consignors using rail freight services; and
- Operators of passenger/freight/open access services, as users of Railtrack.

The Rail Regulator has three main roles:
- overseeing the arrangements for track access and charging over the whole network;
- promoting competition and preventing abuse of monopoly power and anti-competitive practices; and
- promoting the interests of consumers and ensuring that network benefits are maintained.

This is where the rail version of the nearest equivalent to the traditional Traffic Commissioner role in the bus industry is based. The Regulator sets out the rules and enforces them; he is also the arbiter. Attention is drawn to the scope for monopoly abuse in the railway; this is seen as being mostly in the London commuter network, and in the activities of Railtrack.

A further activity is the issuing of licences to railway operators. In general, all companies operating railway assets (a network, a station, a light maintenance depot or a train) need to be licensed. Licence exemptions will be granted to the operators of preserved railways and most others outside the National Railways umbrella. Licence holders are required to establish a policy to protect the environment from the effects of their activities. This includes compliance with environmental legislation, and using technological developments to upgrade their environmental performance.

Operators have to undergo a safety validation process overseen by the Health and Safety Executive before a licence is granted. The Regulator is responsible for enforcing licence conditions concerning such matters as policing, the environment, insurance requirements and through ticketing.

On closures, the Regulator will make the decision on whether a closure should be allowed to occur, subject to reference of the matter by an aggrieved person to the Secretary of State. In exercising his functions with respect to closures, the Regulator will take evidence from the consultative committees, which it is also his duty to establish and maintain. The Regulator is able to attach conditions to any closures and enforce compliance with those conditions.

The Regulator has set out his stall on a number of issues. For the passenger railway (those

Below:
Another innovation at Marylebone is the automatic ticket barriers; at least three other London area TOCs are in the process of undertaking similar installations.

pertaining mostly to freight are discussed in Chapter 8), the principal ORR Policy Statements are as follows. These followed a series of consultation documents:

- Criteria for the Approval of Passenger Track Access Agreements (September 1994)
- Railtrack's Track Access Charges for Franchised Passenger Services: Developing the Structure of Charges (November 1994)
- Competition for Railway Passenger Services (December 1994)
- Railtrack's Track Access Charges for Franchised Passenger Services: The Future Level of Charges (January 1995)
- Ticket Retailing (April 1995)
- Investment in the Enhancement of the Rail Network (March 1996)
- Charter Train Services (April 1996)
- Penalty Fares (August 1996)
- Railtrack's Network Management Statement (September 1996)
- The Regulatory Objectives for Railtrack (January 1997)
- Accurate and Impartial Retailing (January 1997)
- Railtrack's Investment Programme: Increasing Public Accountability (July 1997)
- New Service Opportunities for Passengers (for consultation, September 1997)
- The Timetabling of Railtrack's Network (for consultation, October 1997).
- The Periodic Review of Railtrack's Access Charges (for consultation, 12/97)
- Railway Group Standards Code (for consultation, 1/98)
- Rolling Stock Companies (for consultation, 1/98)

Each document is discussed in turn.

Criteria for the Approval of Passenger Track Access Agreements

As a general requirement, the Regulator will normally require to be satisfied that proposed access agreements are not framed in such a way that may unduly limit competition in service provision, create undue discrimination between users or represent abuse of a monopoly position.

A track access agreement is a bilateral agreement between Railtrack and a train operator. Areas of particular concern for the Regulator are likely to be as follows:

Timetable Rights

These will need to be clearly defined and complete. They also need to be flexible enough to make changes, but not to constrain Railtrack in granting access rights to others. Normally, the Regulator will expect the amount of track capacity taken up to be defined in terms such as the following:

- rights to run a number of trains in a given period, which might be a whole day or parts of the day such as the peak periods;
- a right to run a train within a given broad time period (eg to run a train from Manchester to Bournemouth between 08.30 and 09.00);
- a right to run trains according to a specified interval pattern; or
- 'hardwired' rights to a specific time slot (eg the 'Flying Scotsman' must leave King's Cross at 10.00). This is expected by the Regulator to be by exception only.

Operators and Railtrack may also enter into other contractual rights, such as times of first and last trains, connectional requirements, stopping patterns, through train requirements and use of rolling stock and train crew.

Specific matters of concern to the Regulator are likely to be:

- whether the proposed rights contain any in-built provisions which unduly reduce the capacity available on the network;
- the impact on the capacity available for other operators of any rights to service expansion; and
- the cumulative effects of restrictions on Railtrack's ability to flex an operator's timetable bid on the access rights which Railtrack can then agree with other operators.

Output Standards

Operators will want to specify infrastructure standards to make sure that their business requirements such as ride quality and journey times are maintained, and that the access charges which they pay to Railtrack for the route will result in its being renewed as required.

Performance Incentives

Service performance can be adversely affected by infrastructure problems. In turn, these can result in reduced fares revenue and lower franchise payments. The Regulator will welcome arrangements which shift such income risk to Railtrack, provided they are workable! The Regulator may also require Railtrack to outline policy and procedures in respect of train service regulation. However, the net effect must work in the interests of rail users.

Charging Arrangements and Moderation of Competition

Any exclusivity agreement will need to have alternative means of providing incentives contained in the franchise agreement.

Engineering Strategy

The Regulator suggests that Railtrack and the operators may wish to negotiate procedures which compensate the operators for excessive line closures caused by engineering works and to reduce their payments if agreed renewals are not carried out.

Arrangements for Operational Disruption and Contingency Plans

Such plans need to exist, but the Regulator does not intend to review them in detail.

The Regulator holds the crucial key, in approving access agreements. This duty will need to be exercised with great care.

Railtrack's Track Access Charges for Franchised Passenger Services: Developing the Structure of Charges

So, how are those access charges to be structured? The basis of the original unregulated track charges introduced in 1994 comprised:

- Track usage: These charges, 6% of the total, reflected the short-run 'wear and tear' effects on maintenance and renewal costs of running trains of different types for different distances.
- Traction current: This was the mechanism to recover the cost of electric current, varying geographically and by period of time, reflecting distance covered and type of vehicle. These accounted for 3% of charge totals.
- Fixed charge: This accounted for the remaining 91% and was payable irrespective of the number and types of train run, or passenger revenue.

From his consultations, the Regulator agreed that there was a need for operators to be able to determine how their actions affected the charges which would be levied, that some mechanism was needed to enable operators to make access cost savings if revenue fell and they wished to reduce services, while the whole structure needed to reflect greater variability in charging.

The Regulator's response was to require greater transparency through the disaggregation of Railtrack's charges and that operators should be able to seek from Railtrack an assessment of the effect of changes in both short- and long-term variable costs as a result of different access requirements. Any financial benefits which resulted, whether they concerned the reduction of costs incurred by Railtrack or the freeing up of more track capacity which another operator was prepared to purchase, should be shared between the original operator and Railtrack.

Competition for Railway Passenger Services

The main purpose is to try and reconcile the benefits to consumers which would result from open competition and the uncertainty among potential bidders for franchises that such competition would engender.

The Rail Regulator advanced two reasons for his concluding that it is necessary for competition between passenger train operators to be substantially restricted during the initial period. First, he recognised that the franchising process itself will produce increased competition because of geographical overlap, even without allowing for entry by so-called 'open access' operators. Second, the Rail Regulator noted that the railway industry is at an early stage in a period of fundamental restructuring and that unrestricted or uncontrolled competition would expose all parties to undue risks. These might negate the benefits of privatisation.

Consequently, no significant competitive new entry will be allowed before 31 March 1999 and substantial restrictions will remain for at least a further three years after that date. The restrictions will be reviewed in 2001, as will the level and structure of Railtrack's track access charges for franchised passenger services. The ORR has not determined the form which the competitive regime will take. However, the review will continue to reflect the policy framework and it is likely that changes after 2002 will be incremental.

The Rail Regulator decided that it would not

Above:
Piping to carry cables beneath the running lines to avoid damage is distinguished (usually) by bright orange colouring. Sheathing also prevents electrical contact should the insulation be damaged.

be appropriate to moderate competition by modifications to the current charging regime and therefore considered two broad options for implementing policy. One was on a case-by-case approach; the other was to use some kind of formula. The ORR decided to publish a framework, which would be used to establish the level of competitive new entry that would be allowed in each franchise area. Nevertheless, this would not preclude the investigation of individual cases.

The following detailed principles for moderating competition are to be adopted:

- Train operators should expect to face either early exposure to possible competition (as a result of the franchising process) or the firm prospect of increased exposure to competition during the term of their initial regulated access agreements.
- The potential financial impact of competition on franchisees should be limited and sufficiently predictable that franchises are capable of being sold at a price the Franchising Director can afford.
- Franchisees should have the opportunity for commercial expansion as well as protection from excessive competitive risk.
- Entry of non-competing services should not be constrained.
- Within the controlled framework for the introduction of competition, the location of competitive entry should be market led rather than centrally determined.
- The new owners of the passenger railway industry should have some say over where they feel that protection from competition is needed, and decisions should, if possible, be taken in the light of actual experience of private sector behaviour.

Essentially, in the early years, involvement in operating passenger train services will be limited by the franchising process. Open access will be the exception, rather than the rule.

Briefly, the proposed mechanism consists of two stages. The first starts at the point at which the last of the BR TOCs has its long-term track access agreement approved and will expire on 31 March 1999, while the second stage will start at that point and expire on 31 March 2002. The protection is based on assessing the market in terms of point-to-point flows, reflecting the origin and destination stations of passengers carried by the operator.

In the first stage, operators will be able to nominate a list of point-to-point flows, subject to limited constraints, on which new entry for scheduled passenger services will not be permitted without the operator's agreement. In advance of the second stage, operators will be able to nominate a revised list to be used as the basis for restrictions on nominated flows up to a threshold limit, which will be 20% of those flows by revenue. New entry will be unrestricted on any flows not so nominated. Finally, it should be noted that restrictions are subject to the access rights agreed between Railtrack and neighbouring operators which may well permit a level of inter-operator competition.

The topic was raised again in 1997.

Railtrack's Access Charges for Franchised Passenger Services: The Future Level of Charges

The Regulator considered that Railtrack had scope to reduce its own costs by 3% a year and that the company could secure significant reductions in real terms in infrastructure maintenance costs. He also thought that access charges should cover depreciation on a current cost basis and that this should be enough to renew those assets, continue the operation of the national network and the national timetable of services. To ensure that the network *is* maintained and renewed, the Regulator would monitor Railtrack's expenditure and performance at the national level.

Overall, and after allowing for inflation as measured by the RPI, the Regulator decided that Railtrack's charges should be reduced in 1995/6 for franchised passenger services by 8% and that they should fall by 2% per annum in real terms from 1996/7 onwards. On property assets, the Regulator decided that variations in net income from property from the levels in Railtrack's projections should be shared between the company and train operators.

Access charges will be further reviewed in 2000, with the conclusions implemented from 1 April 2001.

Ticket Retailing

In his consultation document, the Regulator said that he would be guided by the following issues:

- consumers should continue to enjoy widespread and easy access to through tickets;
- the new arrangements should assist in promoting the use of the network;
- within a framework which protects existing consumer benefits, operators should have scope to innovate and take advantage of the opportunities of new technology and new ways of selling;
- as a consequence of offering a greater range of choice to consumers, retailing is likely to become a more complex activity. The costs which operators may have to meet in order to satisfy the Regulator's requirements should be proportionate to the resulting benefits which consumers will enjoy; and
- to enable monitoring of compliance against the licence obligation, clear standards for levels of service will need to be established. So far as possible, these standards should be based on objective criteria.

In the light of the responses he received (and this included a debate in the House of Commons), the Regulator concluded that on the issue of ticketing, 'public opinion and public interest are at one'. BR's current arrangements (as at April 1995) for retailing tickets generally met customer requirements, and that to maintain them would not impose significant costs on operators for the immediate future. The approach of the Regulator would be that of incremental change, based on a clear definition of the service provided. This would cover:

- the product range of tickets sold at each outlet (based presently on APTIS and SPORTIS machines etc);
- the opening hours of ticket offices;
- more complex transactions, such as seat reservations;
- commission arrangements for selling tickets of other operators;
- how change might be progressed in the future, while avoiding undesirable side effects.

The arrangements would be reviewed in 1997.

Investment in the Enhancement of the Rail Network

This document concentrates on new investment in excess of the £3.5 billion required over six years for the replacement and renewal of existing assets. It depends, critically, on an effective partnership between Railtrack, train operators and funding bodies such as the Franchising Director, the PTEs and local authorities. In particular, a shared

understanding of investment priorities and plans needs to be reached; Railtrack's annual Network Management Statement is seen by the Regulator as a means by which this can be developed.

The Regulator's general presumption is likely to be that ownership or operation of a railway facility should not be used to create a monopoly position for one or more train operators, and that capacity should be shared by all those able and willing to use it, based on the public interest criteria in s4 of the Act. Furthermore, capacity sharing must be on a fair financial basis, although vertical integration with the infrastructure owner having an interest in, or full ownership of, the operation of trains is not ruled out. However, the accounts of the infrastructure and operating arms would need to be fully separated as required in principle by European Council Directives 91/440 and 95/19.

Railtrack is seen by the Regulator as having a vital role but, by having a monopoly position, train operators and their customers are dependent on the company. He therefore expects Railtrack to be proactive in the development of investment proposals, if they receive an appropriate return through access charges. These charges should be designed at least to cover avoidable costs, including that of capital. Generally, facility owners should receive a share of the benefits from investment, depending on the relative risks being taken by the parties involved and the source and level of the overall benefit. Exposure to revenue risks is particularly important here.

However, the charge structure might be designed to benefit Railtrack through higher returns if the company executes the project more quickly and more cheaply than originally expected.

New stations have been one of the most significant enhancement projects in recent years; in the seven metropolitan areas alone, 54 new stations funded by PTE capital grants have opened since 1988. Other schemes include line openings, electrification, resignalling and station refurbishment, with PTE infrastructure spend totalling £269 million over the period.

Finally, the Regulator points out that though licence and contractual provisions can offer a framework to help reach a shared understanding of investment plans, they are in themselves 'no substitute for effective co-operation between industry parties'.

Charter Train Services

The charter market is very small but, according to the Regulator, it represents 'one of the few areas at present where third parties are seeking access to the network and promoting services'. There is thus some considerable determination on the Regulator's part to get the issue of costing and pricing right.

The consultation document painted a picture of inexperience and uncertainty by TOCs, rather than deliberately trying to cause difficulties in the market. The Board was asked to produce a code of practice for its subsidiaries to set out how charges will be calculated and applied, as also was RES.

The Regulator's criteria were set out, which he is to apply when considering access charges in contracts. However, the whole issue of charter services is to be kept under review and, if difficulties persist, the Regulator will seek further changes.

Penalty Fares

Ticket sales income is worth around £2 billion a year to the railways; even a small percentage shortfall due to ticket fraud is therefore a sizeable sum in its own right. Penalty fares, in which a charge of twice the single fare may be made (minimum £10), are one way of combating the problem. However, as the Regulator has pointed out, Parliament was particularly concerned, when the original legislation was debated, that the innocent passenger should be given every protection from being improperly charged a fine, which is what a penalty fare amounts to. The Regulator is determined that high standards of passenger protection against being wrongly charged should be maintained.

Consequently, he has ruled that schemes should comply with the following:

- Passengers must be fully informed before entering a penalty fares area or boarding a train subject to penalty fares, about what represents a valid ticket or permit to travel, and what liability will be incurred by passengers who do not have one. As the purpose of penalty fares is to encourage passengers to buy tickets at stations, back-up facilities should be provided for use when the ticket office is closed.
- For the liability to take effect, there must be a high degree of assurance of the passenger's ability to first purchase a valid ticket or permit to travel. Scheme integrity must be

maintained; conductors on trains selling tickets in penalty fare areas are a contradiction in terms.

- Passengers must not be penalised if there was no adequate opportunity to purchase a valid ticket or permit to travel beforehand. This is a particular problem where a journey requires a change of train and maybe also a change of operator, if no through tickets are available. Further problems arise if London Underground is involved and different penalty fares rules apply.

The Regulator also ruled that a strengthened appeals procedure was needed, which he would require to approve.

Railtrack's Network Management Statement

The publication of an annual Network Management Statement is a requirement of Railtrack's Network Licence. The content must include future capacity requirements and details of investment schemes. It must also set out how they are to be financed.

The Regulator expects the Network Management Statement to:

Below:
The Networker Classic is a rebodying by Adtranz of Mk 1 vehicles, with a 3+2 layout and sliding doors. They are intended for use as affordable peak use service supplementation. A four-car Class 424/0 unit with this seating layout would seat 310 (standard class only). This DTOS has 77 seats in a length of 20.66m. Within an overall width of 2.80m, five seats and a centre gangway are achieved; in a bus (maximum legal width in UK 2.50m), four seats and a gangway are regarded as the limit. Does this say something about the relative dimensions of bus and rail passengers?

- help him, and all others concerned, to monitor how effectively Railtrack is planning for and actually carrying out maintenance, renewal and enhancement of the network;
- develop a shared understanding of the plans Railtrack has for the management and development of the network and the criteria adopted.

The Regulatory Objectives for Railtrack

Against a background in which he described Railtrack's record of asset renewal as 'disappointing', the Regulator set out four key principles:

- Railtrack should, in a timely fashion, renew the railway infrastructure in the appropriate modern equivalent form;
- Railtrack should take a proactive and positive approach to the development of the railway network in a way which reflects the needs of its customers and rail users;
- Railtrack should make good the current shortfall in expenditure in an efficient and effective way; and
- Railtrack's plans and investment approval processes should ensure delivery of these objectives.

Accurate and Impartial Retailing

The promised 1997 review was preceded by a consultation document in which the Rail Regulator set out the importance 'for information to be accurate and responsive to what passengers want or need to know'. The principal objectives were:

- to establish more clearly the needs of passengers;
- to seek views on how the impartial retailing obligation translates into front line service delivery; and
- to stimulate debate on the practical issues and the financial implications.

The first conclusion from the consultation was that retailing responsibilities should be left with the professional railway operators who have an interest in the business. One third of all passenger revenue comes from sales made by other TOCs, so the interdependence is to a large extent mutual.

The objective of impartial retailing is defined as: 'Providing accurate information and advice on journey and ticket options—irrespective of which company provides the service—to allow passengers to make an informed choice; and providing the means to purchase the product which best meets their needs.'

Other points from the Regulator's policy statement are:

- The Regulator does not wish to prevent retailers from making straightforward sales with the minimum of fuss. However, where a passenger's needs warrant it, the question asked by retailing staff should be widened to include fare and journey options, on-board facilities, service frequency, and preferred origin and destination stations.
- Except where it is clear that passengers have already made a choice of services or are travelling immediately, retailers must provide information about competing services, including from or to another station in the same town.
- It is the responsibility of operators to invest in more support and training for their retail staff, and in modern information systems, and to examine their fares to ensure they offer choice without creating confusion.

How well does it work? The writer was impressed to be offered the opportunity of a cheaper fare from London to Bath Spa recently, if he wished to travel from Waterloo. This was an advance purchase. The retail outlet concerned? Paddington.

The Regulator has been less happy with the overall results. A survey of ticket offices and telephone enquiry bureaux (TEB) showed that, overall, 10% of enquirers were misinformed. The proportion was much higher where APEX tickets or Sunday engineering work was involved. The result is likely to be the setting of quality standards, enforceable through operator licences.

This followed a series of fines on TOCs for the lack of performance of TEBs in answering calls.

Railtrack's Investment Programme: Increasing Public Accountability

Railtrack came in for further attention in mid-1997, when the Regulator proposed formally to modify Railtrack's Network Licence. There were three key changes:

- It established a new General Duty on Railtrack in respect of the maintenance, renewal and development of the rail network and a series of further detailed and enforceable obligations in support of this duty.
- It gave the Regulator powers of investigation and enforcement if Railtrack fails to deliver without good reason.
- It explicitly established obligations on Railtrack both to consult with train operators and funding organisations and to meet their reasonable expectations to the greatest extent reasonably practicable.

In the Regulator's words: 'I have attached primary importance to establishing strong, measurable and enforceable obligations on Railtrack in respect of its investment and stewardship obligations.' The modifications were mutually agreed between ORR and Railtrack, and were confirmed as required by consultees in September 1997.

New Service Opportunities for Passengers

Should operators be able to offer new services to passengers outside their present areas? The regulatory regime gives a large measure of territorial exclusivity to each of the franchised operators. The issue is simple but very important, said the Regulator, for passengers in particular. Should the degree of operator protection from competition be reduced in the period 1999 to 2002, or should it be retained?

There are four main principles which form the base of the current framework for the promotion of rail for the benefit of passengers:

- A duty on the Government, through the Franchising Director, to specify the minimum services which the Government requires to be operated (the Passenger Service Requirement) and to acquire them for the best value for money.
- A duty on Railtrack, as the sole owner of the infrastructure, to provide infrastructure access to all passenger train operators without discrimination, and on public interest criteria established by the Regulator.
- A duty on all licensed train operators to be parties to a set of multilateral arrangements to ensure network benefits for passengers.
- A right of passenger train operators to decide whether to engage in commercial activities which in their best judgement meet passenger demand and thus advance their business prospects during the period of their franchise.

The Regulator requested comment on four main questions:

- What are the features of the railway industry that need to be taken into account to decide whether relaxation of constraints on competition will achieve overall benefits to passengers and taxpayers, and will promote the use of the rail network?
- What are the main opportunities for new services and other passenger benefits that might follow from an extension of competition along the lines envisaged beyond 2002?
- To what extent should private sector operators take the initiative in identifying opportunities for new entry?
- What are the main potential detriments in terms of disadvantages to passengers and effects on existing franchisees? What further controls, if any, need to be built into the regulatory framework to prevent such detriments?

The whole is a highly complex area, and the foregoing can do no more than give an indication of the issues at stake. One franchisee's protection is another's obstacle to expansion. If a franchisee is running no more than the minimum service required by the PSR, there is little that can be done. Nobody can come in and try to do a better job. Having said that, competition carries with it very considerable risks, for operator and service user alike.

As Mr Swift put it in his introduction to the consultation: 'The overriding consideration is: which system is going to produce a better service for passengers generally?'

The Timetabling of Railtrack's Network

The timetable is the basis on which the whole of the railway operates. There is a correspondingly high premium on getting it right. Can we do better, with the public interest aspect particularly in mind?

Under the present arrangements, Railtrack sets out the initial limitations, including planned engineering works. There is then a bidding process. Each operator bids for train paths (which have to reflect their access rights) and Railtrack allocates capacity on the basis of public interest decision criteria. There is an appeal process to settle (or at least adjudicate on) disputes, and the end result is the production and subsequent publication of the timetable by Railtrack.

This twice yearly process results in the Summer (May) and Winter (September) timetables. Spare capacity during the currency of a timetable is allocated through a separate 'spot bidding' process.

The process is to be reviewed; one particular weakness appears to be the length of time taken from a service proposal progressing from being a feasible idea to actually operating on the ground. Franchisees, with a diminishing timescale in which to make service changes which they consider will bring them worthwhile revenue gains, have a special interest in a speedy process. If only a couple of years are left in which to make revenue gains, one conclusion might be that it just isn't worth the effort.

It should be noted that what might be thought of as recent competitive incursions into the territories of others, such as Connex South Central's service to Rugby, were already under consideration at the time franchises were let. They thus enjoy the equivalent of 'grandfather rights'.

Railtrack's Access Charges

How the access charges are working in practice is to be assessed in a full and comprehensive reappraisal. Railtrack's security of income is based on access charges which are contained in the bilateral agreements between it and individual train operators. These charges fall by 2% per annum in real terms until 2001. Mr Swift is looking for changes which will promote investment, growth and operating performance improvements, which both rail users and those who fund the railway are entitled to expect from Railtrack.

Specifically, the Regulator is looking for views on:

- the nature of the control on Railtrack's charges;
- incentives to use and develop the network;
- capability, quality and performance of the network;
- efficiency review of Railtrack's capital and operating expenditure;
- setting the price control; and
- the timetable of the work needed to come to a conclusion by July 2000.

Railway Group Standards Code

Railway Group Standards are the key technical standards and operating procedures for the railway. Compliance with them is a requirement of the Railway Safety Cases held by train operators, station operators and Railtrack. This is also a licence requirement of these organisations and that of depot operators.

The primary purpose of the Railway Group Standards Code is to ensure the safe operation of Railtrack's network and of trains and other railway assets used on it, having regard to the need:

- to promote the use and development of Railtrack's network;
- to promote efficiency and economy by Railtrack and other providers;
- to promote competition in service provision;
- to impose on Railtrack and others the minimum restrictions consistent with purpose; and
- to enable Railtrack and others to plan the future of their businesses with a reasonable degree of assurance.

The code authorises the existing safety standards on the railway and sets out the arrangements under which they can be changed. While the safety objectives may be constant, there will always be an element of choice in the best means of achieving them.

The present proposals are those of Railtrack's independent Safety and Standards Directorate. They are made under the terms of Railtrack's Network Licence, and the Regulator seeks rail industry views.

Rolling Stock Companies

At the behest of the Deputy Prime Minister, the Regulator is conducting an inquiry into the operation and possible regulation of the rolling stock companies. The terms of reference include the assessment of the scope for ROSCOs to abuse their position by setting excessive leasing charges, failing to invest in new or refurbished rolling stock, or failing to improve service performance. Among the possible remedies which might be considered is bringing the ROSCOs under the control of the Rail Regulator.

This is not a consideration of the terms under which the companies were sold initially, which is the subject of a separate inquiry by the National Audit Office.

Consumer Representation

The Rail Users' Consultative Committees (RUCCs), and indeed the umbrella body, the Central RUCC, are another interest of the Rail Regulator. These consumer bodies are channels through which comment, suggestions and complaints from users of the services can be investigated and, where possible, remedial action initiated or appropriate recompense offered. In this capacity they have an appellate role, helping to resolve grievances in cases where an initial direct approach to the operator has failed to secure the desired result.

Where satisfactory resolution cannot be achieved, the RUCC may refer the matter to the Regulator for his action. This applies also if the RUCC believes that any licence condition is being contravened.

The RUCCs provide a forum for public debate on matters which impinge directly upon users. Such matters include timetables, vehicle design, fares structures, ticketing systems, passenger security, waiting facilities, information provision, route patterns and interchange arrangements. Also, they are the agencies through which the quality of service can be monitored and reported.

Conclusions

It is not the purpose of the Regulator to substitute his views for those of the competitive operator. However, he has to watch out for monopolistic practices. It was as long ago as January 1994 that the Office of Fair Trading produced a paper 'Railways: Guidance on Mergers'.

The Regulator must look to the needs of the users first. London customers are largely captive, while some of the former InterCity routes have substantial proportions of the total travel market. There are better deals under the new legislation than the old. But, as Mr Swift, the Rail Regulator, told the House of Commons Transport Committee, if there are no benefits for consumers, the legislation was not worthwhile.

He has since spelt out what he would like on the passenger railway:[1]

'I want to see a railway which develops and thrives, which competes for excellence and attracts more passengers onto the network. I want train operators to achieve commercial success through policies and practices which allow passengers to use the national network easily, flexibly and with confidence...My aim is to regulate an industry which grows, which delivers improved performance and which offers even better value for money.'

The regulatory messages are 'commitment', 'improvement' and 'enforcement'.

1 Regulatory Objectives for Train and Station Operators. ORR, June 1997.

The railway as it was organised under British Rail ceased to exist on 31 March 1994. Latterly, there were three passenger businesses, each divided into a number of constituent parts, as shown below. This was the vertically integrated railway, with the businesses owning the infrastructure which they needed to run the services. Costs were divided where there was mixed use of infrastructure. The statistics relate to the 1993/4 year[1].

InterCity

Gross revenue: £896.8 million; operating profit: £97.9 million; investment (including track renewals): £114.3 million; stations 69. There were five profit centres:

- West Coast Main Line
- East Coast Main Line
- Great Western
- Midland Cross Country
- Anglia & Gatwick Express

Network SouthEast

Gross revenue: £1,114.6 million; operating profit: £71.4 million; Public Service Obligation capital grant (no revenue grant): £371.9 million; investment (including track renewals): £432.4 million; stations: 943. There were nine profit centres:

- London Tilbury & Southend
- Great Eastern
- West Anglia Great Northern
- Thameslink
- Network North
- Thames & Chiltern
- South Western
- South Central
- South Eastern

Regional Railways

Gross revenue (including revenue grant): £817.3 million, operating profit after revenue grant: £15.9 million, PSO revenue grant: £353.0 million, PSO capital grant: £84.0 million, investment (including track renewals): £172.3 million, PTE support: £105.4 million, stations: 1,481. There were five profit centres:

- Regional Railways Central
- Regional Railways South Wales and West
- Regional Railways North West
- Regional Railways North East
- ScotRail

Thus the passenger revenues divided, roundly, into InterCity 32%, Network SouthEast 39% and Regional Railways 29%. This considerably over-states the commercial position of Regional Railways, since it includes the PSO and PTE grants payable.

From 1 April 1994, the passenger railway was instead divided into 25 train operating units (TOUs). These were to become, after vesting, subsidiary BR train operation companies (TOCs). Each operated under its own licence granted by the Rail Regulator, its own Railway Safety Case (approved by the Health & Safety Executive) and a track access agreement with Railtrack (approved by the Regulator). A wide range of station and depot access agreements (also approved by the Regulator), property leases and other contracts such as for rolling stock leases were also required by each train operating business.

While today's privately owned operating companies mostly reflect their origins as being part of their former parents, some additional groupings were created. Thus, InterCity's Midland Main Line was separated from Cross Country. Wales & West and the Cardiff Valleys services were created from Regional Railways SW&W, and from Regional Railways North West we now have Merseyrail Electrics as a separate organisation. In the London area, NSE's Thames & Chiltern was subdivided into the Paddington group (Thames Trains) and the Marylebone group (Chiltern Railways). While Regional Railways Central continues as Central Trains, it no longer provides most of the local services in East Anglia. These have been transferred to the former Anglia part of InterCity, itself separated from Gatwick Express. Another substantial change is in sleeper services, those to and from Scotland now being the responsibility of ScotRail.

However, the concept of geographically defined areas of operation is less relevant than it was previously. Since the infrastructure became the responsibility of Railtrack, the emphasis of the TOCs is on the services which they provide as businesses. The payments which they make, either to Railtrack in the form of access charges, or to rolling stock leasing companies (ROSCOs), are merely business outgoings—though this is not to suggest that they represent a minor part of their overall business expenditure. Somewhere in the order of two-thirds of their total costs appears to be the right order of magnitude, although it will vary greatly. In theory, the situation is little different from that applying to (say) the bus industry, where bus companies run vehicles (which they may lease, rather than own outright) on public roads provided and maintained by local highway authorities and the Highways Agency.

Although still subject to the terms of their agreements with the Franchising Director, the TOCs now have a more direct responsibility for the specification and marketing of their services. The concept of the public service obligation no longer applies. If the Franchising Director does not consider a service suitable for inclusion in a TOC's passenger service requirement (PSR), and the TOC does not think it can run the service profitably, the operator is more or less free to discontinue it. This freedom is subject to statutory closure procedures, if relevant, while capacity requirements as may be set out in the franchise agreement must be satisfied.

To summarise the new organisational arrangements, the diagram overleaf sets out the range of contracts and relationships as seen from the viewpoint of a Train Operating Company.

Let us now look at the overall passenger railway business itself and its characteristics. Firstly, on average journey length, distances are relatively short. Over the whole BR network, this was 25.4 miles in 1994/5. However, when ordinary fares are separated from journeys made on season tickets, the average journey length associated with ordinary fares was 34.2 miles. This compared with seasons at 15.2 miles. This is much more than on London Underground, where the average journey length is 5.0 miles.

Secondly, season tickets must not be considered as a marginal element, since in 1994/5 they accounted for 47% or very nearly half of all passenger journeys made on BR. Travel on ordinary fares (including all discounted fares) made

up the remaining 53%. The revenues associated with ordinary tickets do, of course, reflect the longer average distances and are much higher than with seasons.

The third point is that it would be fair to suggest that the railway as a whole encompasses a huge range of businesses. For instance, the Midland Main Line and Cardiff Valleys have little in common, be it in traffic volumes, service types, revenues or scale of operations. The customers also have different wants and expectations. Generalisations are correspondingly dangerous!

However, on the basis of the foregoing, it is at least plausible to suggest that most passenger journeys are likely to be internal to one particular company's operation. Further, it is probable that relatively few journeys are made which involve the services of more than one operating company—unless that second company is London Underground. For the present purpose, London Underground involvement is not relevant, but it does perhaps indicate a way in which the London situation differs from that of the country as a whole, due to the sheer size of the capital and its surrounding residential areas.

In a 1970 exercise, the origins of East Coast main line passengers departing from King's Cross were identified. This was in the days when ticketing and revenue analysis were relatively primitive. To general managerial surprise, something like 40% of passenger journeys were found to originate somewhere on the (then) Southern Region. Today, many of those passengers might well be period Travelcard holders, but cross-London travel is perhaps likely to be the most common use of more than one Train Operating Company's services.

Nevertheless, the situation everywhere does become more complicated, especially for the return parts of journeys, when more than one train operator provides services over a route. This directly affects ticket pricing and revenue distribution between operators.

Turning to the TOCs themselves, these are each considered in turn. Some statistical data is provided, in most cases from OPRAF sources. For consistency, the initial support figures quoted are in all cases those for 1997/8, which was the first year in which all companies were franchised throughout. The 1996/7 figures include what might best be termed transitional costs.

The adoption of odd months in the lengths of later franchises to be awarded is intended to match their ends with those of full financial years.

All service descriptions refer to the winter 1997/8 timetable, except where specifically stated.

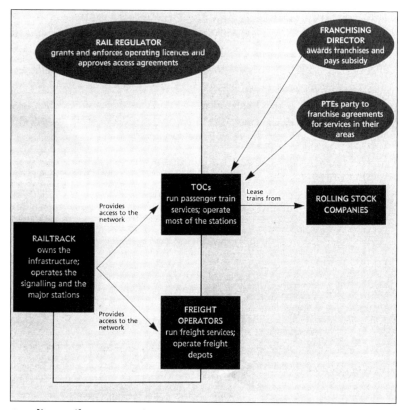

Anglia Railways Train Services Ltd

The core of Anglia's service is the old Great Eastern route from London Liverpool Street through Essex, Suffolk and Norfolk to the county city of Norwich. Electrification was completed in 1987.

Anglia provides the fast electric services under the InterCity banner between London Liverpool Street, Colchester, Ipswich, Stowmarket, Diss and Norwich; a few boat trains as required serve Harwich International (the former Parkeston Quay). Trains are made up of Class 86 electric locomotives, and mostly air-conditioned Mk 2 rolling stock. Driving van trailers enable operation in a push-pull mode. Service frequency is basically hourly, increased to half-hourly at peak times.

Maintenance of all locomotives and rolling stock is carried out at Norwich Crown Point.

Away from the main route, Anglia provides local services between Ipswich and Lowestoft, Felixstowe, Cambridge and Peterborough; also between Norwich and Great Yarmouth, Lowestoft and Sheringham. All are operated by diesel units and frequencies are usually hourly or, occasionally, two-hourly. In some cases, 'irregular' would be the only fair description. Services are provided over 348 route miles.

The Anglia franchise has been let to GB Railways Group plc for a term of 7 years 3 months. The company began operations on 5 January 1997. The support payable by the Franchising Director declines from £35.9 million in 1997/8 to £6.3 million per annum in 2003/4 over the length of the franchise as shown in the diagram.

Franchise plan commitments made by Anglia include:

- maintaining current train miles for five years
- introduction of through services from London via Norwich to Great Yarmouth, Lowestoft or Cromer by May 1998
- introduction of modern multiple-unit trains between London and Norwich, to be completed by September 2000
- investment of £2 million in station improvements
- stepped improvements of Passenger Charter standards.

In 1996/7, Anglia Railways provided a modest 3.8 million train miles per annum, but an average passenger journey length of 61 miles (the London-Norwich distance is 115 miles) shows how much the business is dependent on the InterCity element of its carryings. This is reflected in the revenue per passenger journey of £7.45. A measure of train loadings is passenger miles per train mile, or the number of passengers on average on a train at any one time. At 86 for Anglia, this is close to the national average.

The charter standards of 99% for reliability and 90% for punctuality had the following results in 1996/7. They, and those for other companies in this chapter, are assessed on a moving annual average basis, which smooths out any seasonal fluctuations.

All service groups exceeded the Charter Standards, with the notable exception of the Ipswich-Felixstowe branch, on both counts. This service 'maintained its unenviable position as the route offering the highest rate of cancellations on the network', as the Central Rail Users' Consultative Committee put it in their Annual Report 1996/7.

In competitive terms, Anglia Railways has the Great Eastern Railway providing local services to Ipswich and Harwich and on all the Essex

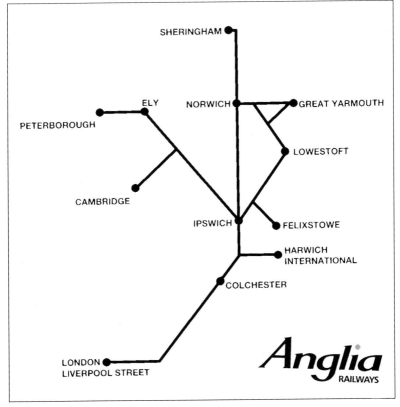

Area	Reliability	Target	Punctuality	Target
InterCity	99.7%	99.0%	92.0%	90.0%
Norwich-Sheringham	99.2%	99.0%	94.7%	90.0%
Norwich-Lowestoft	99.4%	99.0%	96.9%	90.0%
Norwich-Gt Yarmouth	99.6%	99.0%	96.5%	90.0%
Ipswich-Felixstowe	96.1%	99.0%	88.0%	90.0%
Ipswich-Lowestoft	99.1%	99.0%	91.6%	90.0%
Ipswich-Cambridge	99.5%	99.0%	94.0%	90.0%

Above:
Anglia Railways No 153335 takes the Felixstowe branch at Westerfield, the line here having just become two parallel single tracks on a working from Ipswich, 9 May 1996. Anglia is the one franchise which combines part of what was InterCity and Regional Railways operations.

branches, while Central Trains reach Norwich from Peterborough in the west, on the route via Ely and Thetford. The provision of 12-car platforms on the fast lines at Stratford as part of the GE resignalling operation will allow Anglia services to stop there as a matter of course.

Cardiff Railway Co Ltd

The Cardiff suburban and valleys services occupy but two platforms at Cardiff Central, the hub of the railway in the area and where connections are made with the InterCity services of Great Western trains and others. To the west of Central, the main route is south to Barry Island with a branch to Penarth, while the reinstated service via Fairwater to Radyr passes under the main line and then turns north.

Leaving Central to the east, the railway crosses the main lines to reach Cardiff Queen Street, in many ways a more satisfactory location for access to central Cardiff. Train services then split to reach eventually no less than five termini at Rhymney, Coryton, Merthyr Tydfil, Aberdare and Treherbert. Service levels are relatively intense, with half-hourly standard. This drops to hourly on the Fairwater-Radyr line, and north of Bargoed to Rhymney. The Aberdare and Merthyr branches also have an hourly service. On the other hand, the combined service between Pontypridd and Cardiff Central runs every 15min, with 3tph to both Barry Island and Penarth.

Additionally, there are four trains per hour between Queen Street and Cardiff Bay. Alternately, these start back from Caerphilly. Cardiff Railway is one of the smallest operations, covering a total of 86 route miles.

Maintenance of all the diesel units concerned is undertaken at Canton.

The franchise was let to Prism Rail plc for a period of 7 years 6 months. The company commenced operations on 13 October 1996. The annual support payments by the Franchising Director decline from £20.4 million in 1997/8 to £13.6 million in 2003/4.

Franchise plan commitments by Cardiff Railway are as follows:

- to operate at least the pre-franchise number of train miles for the life of the franchise;
- to introduce jointly with Wales & West new through services between Cardiff Railway and the Wales & West network, due from June 1998;
- to restaff Radyr and one other station for an experimental period of 12 months and equip five stations with CCTV evaluation. Radyr was staffed from 21 April 1997.

Annual train miles are 1.9 million, with the average passenger journey length of 10 miles. This is reflected in the low revenue yield on a per journey basis of no more than £1.07. However, usage appears to be rather less than the timetable would suggest, with an average of only 31 passengers on a train at any one time.

Operating performance recorded reliability as 98.8% against a target of 99.0%. Punctuality was 93.4% against a standard of 90.0%.

As with all busy suburban-type operations, Cardiff Railway makes heavy use of the infrastructure provided. As a traditionally self-contained operation, neither the scope for competition nor the means of physically accommodating it is immediately apparent. The letting of the franchise to Prism, as with Wales & West, offers perhaps the greatest opportunity for developing new through services beyond the confines of the valleys.

Investment in new signalling and the infra-

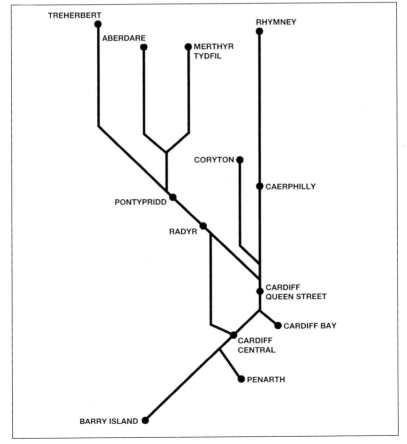

structure generally would be welcome, though this is at least as likely to take the form of service extension with light rail. The Cardiff Bay developers have long had a wish to see a new light rail system in the area; the various possibilities for integrating it (or otherwise) into the Cardiff valleys network still await resolution.

Central Trains Ltd

Central Trains is physically a large operation running from Birmingham to The Wash, and to central Wales as well. As such, it operates a diverse collection of services. These include the longer distance express services of the mini-InterCity type, a range of more local services in terrain as diverse as the Welsh hills and the Lincolnshire fens, and an intensive suburban service for the West Midlands Passenger Transport Executive, also known as CENTRO.

Alphaline services, provided by Class 158 'Express' units, operate between:

- Norwich, Peterborough, Nottingham, Sheffield, Manchester Oxford Road, Liverpool Lime Street (hourly)
- Cambridge, Peterborough, Leicester, Birmingham New Street (hourly)
- Birmingham New Street, Wolverhampton, Shrewsbury, Aberystwyth (alternate hours)
- Nottingham, Derby, Birmingham New Street, Gloucester, Cardiff Central (alternate hours).

Other longer distance services, but on a less regular service interval, include those between:
- Skegness, Grantham, Nottingham, Derby, Stoke-on-Trent, Crewe
- Grimsby Town, Newark Castle, Nottingham, Leicester, Coventry.

Both these service types reflect the operational advantages of longer distance journeys. Rolling stock and train staff utilisation is improved, while commercially they may be very attractive. Even with shorter distance passenger journeys, a change of train may be avoided. It may be noted that in these, as in other service descriptions, many intermediate station calls are omitted.

Central Trains operates rural services in Lincolnshire and in Nottinghamshire generally, including the Robin Hood line to Mansfield Woodhouse, the Ivanhoe line in Leicestershire and the Matlock branch in Derbyshire. North of Birmingham, it operates to Chester and, of course, everything west of Shrewsbury, to Pwllheli and Aberystwyth. It also provides local services on the West Coast main line. Some services are of a seasonal nature, and this is now the only type of operation to take Central Trains to Great Yarmouth.

However, in the West Midlands conurbation CENTRO is a major customer, and railway services have been developed in recent years to the extent that there are now three cross-Birmingham lines. These are:

- Coventry, Birmingham International, Birmingham New Street, Smethwick Galton Bridge, Wolverhampton (half-hourly)
- Lichfield Trent Valley, Sutton Coldfield, Birmingham New Street, Longbridge, Redditch (every 15min within the CENTRO area)
- Leamington Spa/Stratford-upon-Avon, Birmingham Snow Hill, Smethwick Galton Bridge, Kidderminster, Worcester Foregate Street, Hereford (mostly three or four trains per hour within the CENTRO area).

In addition, there are the other lines feeding into New Street, of which the only other local service is that from Rugeley via Walsall.

The Lichfield-Redditch service was made possible by electrification, while the 1995 opening of Smethwick Galton Bridge brought about a new service pattern. While direct New Street services are denied for most of the time to those on the ex-GW line to Kidderminster, the two-level interchange is the best alternative that could be devised.

Maintenance of all the diesel units concerned is undertaken at Central Railways' Tyseley depot or Norwich Crown Point. Electric units are maintained at Bletchley.

The franchise was let to the National Express Group plc for 7 years 1 month, and operations began on 2 March 1997. Annual support payments decline from £187.5 million in 1997/8 to £132.6 million in 2003/4.

In the franchise plan, Central Trains is to:

- run an additional 212,000 train miles for the length of the franchise, providing extensive new services
- improve Passenger Charter performance targets for punctuality and reliability by 1%-2%

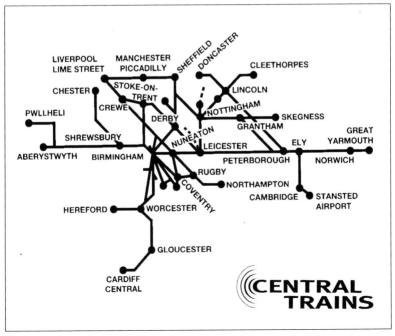

- invest £1.25 million pa for three years on improved security and accessibility at stations
- extend staffing at PTE stations.

As readers will have gathered, Central Trains is a large operation of 16.8 million train miles a year. The average fare paid is £1.77, for a journey of 22 miles average length. Train occupancy is 40 passenger miles per train mile, again relatively low. With all these figures, the diversity of the operation makes it difficult to draw worthwhile conclusions.

Reliability as measured for the Passenger Charter exceeded the charter target of 99.0% on all service types in 1996/7; punctuality was 94.6% in East Midlands and Lincs, 91.6% for inter-urban services and 93.0% in Mid-Wales and the Marches. All were against a target of 90.0%.

One of the operational problems of the area is Birmingham New Street which, since the growth of traffic due in part to CENTRO's activities, is regularly operating close to capacity. The re-establishment of Snow Hill, now once again a through station, goes at least part of the way to freeing up New Street and allows a new station to be constructed for the International Convention Centre on the ac lines north of the city centre.

The Ivanhoe and Robin Hood lines both have more work to be completed on them, and it is intended that the Walsall-Rugeley link should reach the Trent Valley station. Throughout the area, new stations are being proposed.

The first stage of the West Midlands light rail scheme serves Birmingham Snow Hill and stations northwards towards Smethwick, *en route* to Wolverhampton; for this also, National Express is the operator. There is also a scheme proposed for Nottingham. The direct effect of either on rail services is likely to be marginal.

Competitively, Central Railways runs parallel to other operators in a number of areas, most notably on the WCML in the Midlands. The interaction with InterCity West Coast in the Coventry-Wolverhampton corridor is a long-standing problem related to capacity as well as the fares policies of CENTRO. In the southeast of its operation lies Stansted Airport, to which more services are again being extended south of Cambridge.

Below:
The interior of the Class 323 units is characterised by 3+2 seating and a mixed face-to-face and face-to-back layout. Seats have excellent views, due to the narrowness of the window pillars.

Chiltern Railways Co Ltd

The Chiltern lines saw the first of the 'total quality' approaches under BR, in which investment moneys were concentrated on the line to effect a step change in the quality of service offered. Work included the provision of new trains, new signalling and upgraded stations. A healthy growth of patronage ensued, and this is continuing. There are but two lines in the franchise, with a connection between them. The whole is the result of agreements and co-operation between the Great Central, the Great Western and the Metropolitan Railways in the 19th century.

Services over the Aylesbury branch from Marylebone consist of a basic twice-hourly stopping service to Aylesbury via Amersham, with a journey time of about 56min for the 37.75 miles. These services, of course, have the Metropolitan Line services of London Underground running in parallel and then sharing the same tracks between Harrow-on-the-Hill and Amersham.

On the High Wycombe line, services from Marylebone run alternately to:
- Aylesbury via Princes Risborough;
- Birmingham Snow Hill via Princes Risborough and Banbury; and
- intermediate stations to High Wycombe.

It might be noted that the journey time for the 43.25 miles to Aylesbury, reached this way with a limited stop service, takes only about 5min longer than via Amersham. The Chiltern lines could

Above:
Marylebone station has been equipped with new style indicators on the concourse. This picture was taken on 12 November 1997. The calling pattern scrolls if necessary; the 11.45 to Snow Hill does not run nonstop to Solihull!

indeed compete with CrossRail, should that scheme ever be revived. The present Chiltern company operates over 168 miles of network.

All services are provided by the Class 165 'Turbo' units of mixed two-car and three-car varieties. Maintenance is undertaken at Aylesbury.

The franchise was let to M40 Trains Ltd for seven years, starting operation on 21 July 1996. Support payments, initially £14.4 million in 1997/8, decline to £3.3 million in 2002/3 in the last full year of the franchise.

The franchise plan commits Chiltern to:

- maintain service numbers, with additional peak and Sunday services from June 1997
- introduce new additional rolling stock for a London-Birmingham express service; orders were placed in August 1996
- invest £1 million in station improvements
- raise Passenger Charter punctuality standards to 93% from summer 1996.

The company operates 3.5 million train miles in the course of a year, with an average passenger journey length of 25 miles. This reflects the outer suburban nature of the operation, with services nearer London often provided by London Underground's Metropolitan or Jubilee/Central Lines. Average revenue per passenger journey is £3.24, and there is an average of 58 passengers on a train at any one time. Operating performance recorded reliability as 99.6% against a 99.0% target. Punctuality was 94.2% against a standard of 93.0%.

This is another of those largely self-contained railways, with a notably upmarket clientele. The introduction of express services to and from the Midlands offers exciting possibilities; these will be more attractive still when the West Coast main line modernisation gets under way. However, some uncertainty attaches to CrossRail which, if built as previously proposed, would result in the end of the Chiltern line service to Aylesbury in its present form. On the other hand, CrossRail could not be introduced within the present franchise period.

Connex South Central Ltd

This highly complex series of lines are largely those bequeathed to present generations by the London, Brighton & South Coast Railway. There are two distinct parts: the web of inner suburban services which form collectively the South London Metro lines, and the longer distance operations out to the Sussex coast. Both are made more difficult to comprehend by the width of London which confronts a railway approaching from due south, in that no single terminus can serve adequately both the City and the West End. Connex South Central's trains thus make either for the Brighton side terminal platforms at London Bridge (for the City) or for the Brighton side platforms at Victoria (for the West End).

As a further variation, a few Connex South Central trains cross to the South Eastern lines at London Bridge, to terminate eventually at Charing Cross. There is now an hourly Charing Cross to Horsham service, but such manoeuvres cannot be accomplished during rush hours.

On the South London lines, most services operate at 30min headways. There are a few exceptions: the Tattenham Corner branch is only hourly beyond Smitham, and so is its counterpart, the Sutton-Epsom Downs service. On the other hand, stations from West Croydon to Sutton enjoy three 30min services, one from London Bridge and the other two from Victoria, offering a (slightly irregular) 10min frequency.

Further south, frequencies tend to be nearer to hourly, whether on the Uckfield branch from

Left:
Connex South Central's new livery is appearing extensively; there are no paint warranties to worry about with older stock. Class 421/3 4CIG unit No 1722 is seen where the South Western lines (on the left) separate from the Brighton lines (foreground), south of Clapham Junction. The train is the 11.47 to Hastings via Lewes, on Sunday 28 September 1997.

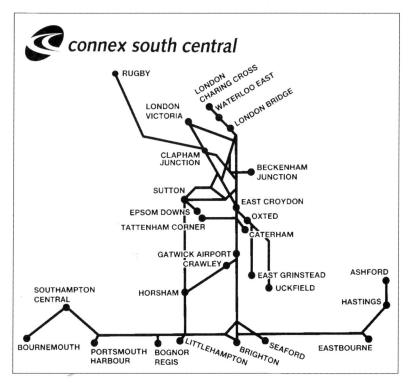

connex south central

RUGBY
LONDON CHARING CROSS
WATERLOO EAST
LONDON VICTORIA
LONDON BRIDGE
CLAPHAM JUNCTION
BECKENHAM JUNCTION
SUTTON
EAST CROYDON
EPSOM DOWNS
OXTED
TATTENHAM CORNER
CATERHAM
GATWICK AIRPORT
CRAWLEY
EAST GRINSTEAD
ASHFORD
SOUTHAMPTON CENTRAL
HORSHAM
UCKFIELD
HASTINGS
BOURNEMOUTH
PORTSMOUTH HARBOUR
BOGNOR REGIS
LITTLEHAMPTON
BRIGHTON
SEAFORD
EASTBOURNE

Oxted, or on services from London to the coastal routes, apart from Brighton itself. Thus, the following service pattern is provided every hour by Connex South Central:

- Victoria to East Croydon and Brighton only (Connex Express).
- Victoria via Gatwick Airport to Haywards Heath (train divides). Rear portion to Lewes and Eastbourne. Remainder to Hove, Worthing (train divides). Front portion to Barnham, Havant, Fareham, Southampton Central and Bournemouth, and rear portion to Littlehampton.
- Victoria to Brighton stopping service.
- Victoria via Gatwick Airport to Haywards Heath (train divides). Front portion to Lewes, Eastbourne and stations to Hastings. Rear portion to Hove, Worthing Central and West Worthing.
- Victoria via the Arun Valley to Barnham (train divides). Front portion to Havant and Portsmouth Harbour, and rear portion to Bognor Regis.

The local service along the coast supplements this:
- Hastings, Eastbourne, Lewes, Brighton
- Seaford, Lewes, Brighton, Worthing, Littlehampton
- Seaford, Lewes, Brighton, West Worthing
- Brighton, West Worthing
- Brighton, Worthing, Barnham, Havant, Portsmouth Harbour
- Littlehampton, Barnham, Bognor Regis
- Barnham, Bognor Regis

Omission of other station names is purely to simplify the illustration. The net effect is that several service frequencies are higher than they have been for many years past (three trains an hour to Hastings via Eastbourne!), while many more journeys are possible without change of train, particularly across Brighton.

The above illustrations concern solely the trains of Connex South Central.

Long distance services rely on the ageing 4CIG and 4VEP units; these are allocated to Brighton. Local services are mostly in the hands of Class

455 or 456 units of more recent years. Class 319 ac/dc units of 1987 are also leased to Connex South Central, being surplus to Thameslink's current requirements. All units are based at Selhurst.

The company operates over 444 route miles.

The franchise was let to Connex South Central for a seven-year term and commenced operation on 26 May 1996. Support payments decline from £74.7 million in 1997/8 to £35.9 million in 2002/3 the last full year of the franchise.

The franchise plan commits Connex South Central to:

- spend an additional £2.5 million on station refurbishment
- refurbish Class 319 rolling stock for Connex Express service; introduced from January 1997
- provide Sunday services at 2tph from London Bridge to West Croydon via Tulse Hill for at least 8hr/day for not less than two years; started May 1997
- improve Passenger Charter punctuality standards; delivered January 1997
- introduce and participate in multi-modal ticketing scheme in Brighton; started June 1996.

Connex South Central is one of the larger TOCs, with 14.0 million train miles operated per year. It does, however, have considerable volumes of short distance traffic, with a 15-mile average journey length for which the passenger pays £1.87. Average occupancy rate is 93 passengers; all of these statistics are very much in line with those of the other ex-Southern Region companies. Connex South Central operates in busy commuting territory, but other traffic includes that to and from Gatwick and the attractions of Brighton.

Service reliability was over 99% for both service groups (South London Lines and Sussex

Coast), target 99.0%, but punctuality was less satisfactory. For South London it was a respectable 92.7% against a target of 90.0%, for Sussex Coast 88.6% against a still relatively undemanding target of 87.0%.

As always with any commuter railway, its fortunes depend so much on the state of the local economy. Spare line capacity is available at present, but a return to 1989 travel volume levels could present a few problems.

There are always new ideas to be tried, and the example of the Hastings to Portsmouth corridor shows some interesting developments. In a bid for service extension, the company has introduced an hourly limited stop Gatwick Airport to Rugby service via Clapham Junction, the West London line and Northampton.

The next task is to make sense of the South London services for the average person in the street; sadly, Connex South Central decided it was necessary to reduce some service levels in September 1997.

Connex South Eastern Ltd

Connex South Eastern carries a very sizeable passenger traffic; in many ways it is the county of Kent's rail operator, at least for domestic traffic.

The network over which today's South Eastern operates still bears the scars of the 19th century clashes between the established and staid South Eastern Railway and the brash newcomer of the London, Chatham & Dover Railway. Historians refer to the inter-company relations as 'the feud'. Despite the efforts of the Southern Railway and subsequently British Railways' modernisation plan works such as the junctions at Chislehurst, it remains a complex network.

The London termini served are Charing Cross, Cannon Street, Blackfriars and Victoria. As with Connex South Central's services, this was a consequence of companies wanting access both to the City and the West End. However, here there were two companies which were both trying to do this.

Today's inner suburban services revolve around a 30min headway. From Charing Cross, on the mid-Kent line, there is a 2tph service to Hayes,

Left:
Connex South Eastern has a large fleet of Class 465/466 units, which today monopolises the inner suburban routes. No 465178 arrives at Waterloo East Platform C with a service to New Beckenham on 11 November 1995.

60

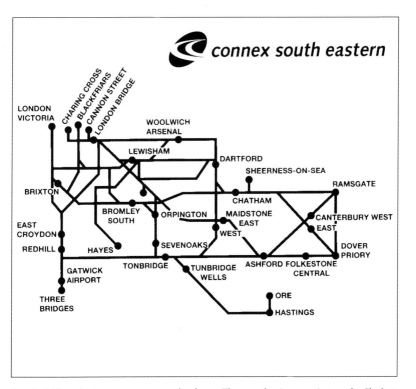

connex south eastern

though Addiscombe is no more as a result of Tramlink construction. On this is superimposed, in part, a Cannon Street-Orpington 1tph service.

Further east, there is a 2tph Cannon Street-Orpington service, but this time on the main line via Elmstead Woods. This is interwoven with a 2tph Charing Cross to Orpington stopping service, one of which continues to Sevenoaks. Bromley North is served by a 2tph shuttle from Grove Park, which connects alternately with a Cannon Street and a Charing Cross train.

Also, 2tph depart from Charing Cross for Dartford over each of the three routes, via Greenwich, via Kidbrooke and via Sidcup respectively. Alone, the Kidbrooke service is extended to Gravesend. Additionally, from Cannon Street there are services which fail to get to Dartford, being 2tph via Greenwich to Slade Green, and 2tph via Sidcup to Crayford. From Victoria, there are an additional 2tph via Kidbrooke to Dartford. On top of all this, there is a semi-fast 2tph Charing Cross to Gillingham service, which has a 2tph connection from Strood to Maidstone West.

There are few inner services on the Chatham side, but these include a 2tph Victoria to Orpington service via Kent House and 2tph from Blackfriars via Catford to Sevenoaks.

If the service patterns seem desperately complicated, then that is probably because they are. Take the case of Orpington: a 9tph service sounds very respectable but, in reality, this is made up of 5tph from Charing Cross, 2tph from Cannon Street and 2tph from Victoria. Even the stopping patterns vary between trains on what is ostensibly the same service. What the travelling public makes of it is another matter; compare this necessarily abbreviated description with the relative simplicity of travelling by London Underground.

The longer distance services from Charing Cross via Tonbridge consist of 2tph to Hastings and 2tph to Ashford. These latter are extended to Ramsgate via Dover Priory. But Tonbridge has two other hourly services, made possible by the electrification of the South Eastern line from Redhill. These are:

• Three Bridges-Gatwick Airport-Redhill, and

all stations to Tonbridge, Paddock Wood and Maidstone West;

- London Bridge-East Croydon-Redhill-Edenbridge-Tonbridge-High Brooms and Tunbridge Wells.

A journey time of 80min for the 40.75 miles between Gatwick and Maidstone is not perhaps record-breaking, but is nevertheless an interesting development, while Croydon is opened up as both a business and a shopping centre for Tonbridge and Tunbridge Wells.

Maidstone East enjoys an hourly Charing Cross to Ashford, Canterbury West and Margate train and 2tph from Victoria, one of which is extended to Canterbury West. The heart of the Chatham territory is the North Kent line from Bromley South via Chatham and Gillingham to Sittingbourne (2tph connections to Sheerness-on-Sea) and Faversham. From here, there is choice of routes to Margate and Ramsgate, or to Canterbury East and Dover Priory. Hourly services, stopping at those stations, are provided to each branch.

At Faversham, cross-platform connections into and out of a slow Victoria-Dover Priory service are provided from the fast Ramsgates and into and out of a slow Victoria-Ramsgate service from the fast Dover Priorys. Splitting and joining trains at Faversham is, once again, a rarity.

The total Connex South Eastern route network is 481 miles.

The franchise was acquired by Connex South Eastern and runs for a 15-year period, starting on 13 October 1996. The support of £114.6 million in 1997/8 falls eventually below zero, and there is a premium repayment to the Government of £1.3 million in 2010/11 the last full year of the franchise.

In its franchise plan, Connex South Eastern committed itself to:

- running at least the pre-privatisation mileage throughout the franchise term
- replace the entire Mk 1 fleet with new-build trains; Class 411 stock by 2000, Class 421/423 stock by 2006
- invest £25 million in stations, car parks and depots, including security measures
- introduce additional southeast London/Kent services
- improve Passenger Charter performance targets by January 1998.

Annual train miles by Connex South Eastern are a sizeable 17.5 million, putting the company in the top echelons as measured by production. Perhaps surprisingly, average passenger journey length is only 15 miles, bringing in £2.26; this may be an indication of the importance of the dense inner-suburban operation. An average train occupancy of 98 is encouraging.

All operations are over the electrified 750V dc network. A fleet of 97 four-car Class 465 and 43 Class 466 two-car Networker units provide the inner services from Slade Green, but the outer operations are still mostly the preserve of the ageing Class 411 4CEP Kent Coast Express stock. These date from around 1960 and are supplemented by some slightly newer Class 421 and 423 units. All these are based at Ramsgate. While a modest injection of 25 Class 365 Networker Express units is helping the situation by allowing some withdrawals, a comprehensive replacement policy has yet to be finalised. The Class 365 fleet offers hourly services from Victoria to Ramsgate via Chatham and to Margate via Ashford. To supplement the existing fleet, middle-aged Class 507 EMUs are returning south of the Thames from Merseyside.

The Kent Link inner services recorded service reliability at 99.1% for 1996/7 (target 98.0%), with punctuality at 86.3% against a target of 88.0%. Kent Coast's reliability was above the 99.0% target at 99.4%, but punctuality at 88.8% was only an improvement on the modest target of 83.0%.

The inheritance of competing lines from the Victorian era still has its effects on service patterns, to which another new player may be added. The Channel Tunnel Rail Link will be able to offer the capacity to carry 8tph at peak from both the Ashford and Northfleet (Ebbsfleet) areas; most, if not all, of these trains are likely to originate on the network presently served by South Eastern Trains.

This network is currently carrying both Eurostar passengers and Channel Tunnel freight services, both of which represent an element of capacity constraint. On the other hand, this is offset by the loss of boat train traffic, which is much diminished from past years.

The East Thames corridor offers regeneration prospects, which might bring a new rail crossing of the Thames in the Woolwich Arsenal area. This could link north Kent with the North London line and has been canvassed as being able to offer services through to Stratford and perhaps beyond.

In perhaps the shorter term, Thameslink 2000 is once again including Kent in its list of possible destinations. The combination of the above offers an interesting mix of opportunities and threats to Connex South Eastern.

Gatwick Express Ltd

The former Gatwick Racecourse station on the Brighton line, built in 1891 but rarely used since the outbreak of World War 2, was rebuilt, resignalled and renamed Gatwick Airport on 28 May 1958. Very soon afterwards, aircraft started to use the airport itself, built, so it was reported at the time[2], 'to relieve London Airport of Channel Islands air traffic and later, probably, of some cross-Channel services'.

Well, much has changed since those days, when the service provision from Victoria was a two-car unit detached every half hour from the back of a Bognor Regis train. Traffic growth produced first the economical 4VEG stock variations of the 4VEP trains with luggage racks substituted for some seats, but the overcrowding of the Network South Central commuter services was becoming unbearable. The economical solution adopted was to convert some surplus air-conditioned Mk 2f stock for use as trailers and, with internal layout changes, match them with a 2HAP driving motor car with its seats removed, plus a Class 73 — and there was Gatwick Express!

Gatwick Express services run between London Victoria and Gatwick Airport only; there are no intermediate stops and no service variations. Departures on a daily basis (this is the only TOC to advertise the same timetable every day of the week and every day of the year) are every 15min from Victoria from 05.00 until 00.01. Outside these times the frequency reduces to 30min and

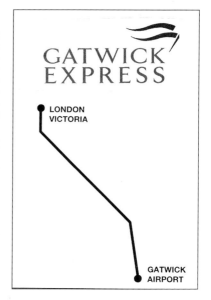

Below:
Gatwick Express services have been operating now for 14 years, still with the second-hand rolling stock with which they started. Here, No 73123 *Gatwick Express* leaves Victoria with the 11.00 to Gatwick Airport shortly after services began. The date was 24 May 1984.

then hourly in the darkest hours. Journey time is 30min for the 27 miles.

The Gatwick Express fleet consists of 13 Class 73/2 locomotives, 74 coaches made up into two- or three-car trailer sets of Class 488, and 10 Class 489 GLVs. All are based at Stewarts Lane. Even the coaching stock is nearly 25 years old, while the locomotives are nearer 30 and the GLVs older still.

The franchise was awarded to the National Express Group plc. It is for 15 years, conditional upon the delivery of new rolling stock. Operations under the new owners started on 28 April 1996. Alone among the franchises, there are no support payments, only premiums payable to the Franchising Director increasing from £6.21 million in 1997/8 to £23.1 million in 2010/11, the last full franchise year.

The franchise plan requires Gatwick Express:

- to maintain the pre-franchising level of service throughout the franchise term
- to provide additional early and late services (in place since March 1997)
- to provide an experimental hourly night service (in place since March 1997)
- to provide a new fleet of rolling stock (due 1 April 1999)
- to provide one on-board staff member for every three occupied vehicles, to be responsible for a refreshment trolley and answering queries (in place)
- to provide airline passenger and baggage check-in facility at Victoria (due 1 April 1998).

This is a modestly sized operation, with its annual 1.3 million train miles the lowest of any TOU, barring only the Island Line. Nevertheless, Gatwick Express average revenue scores at a remarkable £7.55 per passenger journey, given the fixed journey length. This works out at no less than 28p per passenger mile. Train loadings equate to a very average 74 passengers.

In the reliability stakes, 99.7% of services operated (target 99.0%), with punctuality recorded at 91.8% against a 90.0% target.

Competitively, Gatwick Express has to contend with Connex South Central, which has two fast trains per hour calling intermediately at Clapham Junction and East Croydon, taking 33min, and two calling also at Redhill and taking 36min. This is very similar to the 30min that Gatwick Express offers. Additionally, Thameslink provides four direct services per hour from London Bridge in 30min, or a little longer from Blackfriars or City Thameslink. So there are alternatives.

However, positive specific branding and the Victoria check-in facility are clearly on Gatwick Express's side. But what arrangements might any of the companies work out on the ticketing side, especially in conjunction with the airlines?

Great Eastern Railway Ltd

Shorn of its Cambridge interests and indeed those beyond Ipswich, the Great Eastern Railway of today is not the same as the pre-Grouping company. This is real commuter railway territory, albeit that it shades off into the lesser used parts of the system towards Sudbury or Harwich. Something like three-quarters of the company's income is derived from season ticket (or Travelcard) holders; the maximum single journey distance which can be travelled is a fraction over 70 miles. The company operation covers 164 route miles.

There is substantial peak supplementation, but the analysis which follows is confined to the inter-peak period. Even interval services here are the order of the day, and they dovetail neatly together. The service pattern of trains originating from Liverpool Street, in summary, is:

Above:
Great Eastern Railway inner services are provided by 45 Class 315 units. No 315802 was photographed at Stratford on 23 December 1997 on a Liverpool Street to Shenfield working.

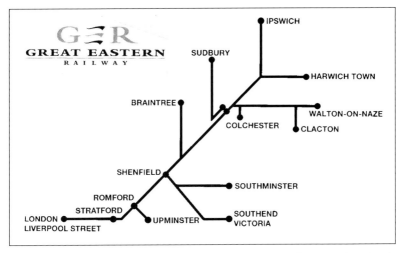

- All stations to Gidea Park   3tph
- Stratford, Ilford, Romford and all stations to Southend Victoria   2tph
- Stratford, Ilford, Romford and all stations to Southminster   1tph
- Fast to Billericay and then all stations to Southend Victoria   1tph

The Southend/Southminster trains fit together neatly to give as nearly as possible a regular 20min service on the Southend branch.

- Chelmsford, Colchester, Manningtree and Ipswich   1tph
- Shenfield, Chelmsford, Witham, Marks Tey, Colchester, Wivenhoe, Thorpe-le-Soken and Clacton   1tph

The Ipswich train connects into a 1tph Colchester, Colchester Town and all stations to Thorpe-le-Soken service, which itself then has cross-platform interchange at Thorpe with the Clacton train, before proceeding to Walton-on-Naze itself. The Ipswich train also connects at Manningtree with a 1tph Ipswich, Manningtree (reverse), and all stations to Harwich Town service. There is also a connection at Marks Tey from the Clacton train into the Sudbury branch 1tph shuttle and at Colchester into the 1tph Anglia service to Norwich. Finally, there are:

- Romford, Shenfield and all stations to Colchester Town   1tph
- Romford, Shenfield, Chelmsford, Witham and stations to Braintree   1tph
- between Romford, Emerson Park and Upminster only   2tph

The Great Eastern Railway example is given in some detail to show what can be achieved within a reasonably uncomplicated network and where only two operators are involved.

Inner suburban services are provided by the fleet of Class 315 units dating from 1980, while the outer services are the preserve of Class 321s (1989) and Class 312 (1978). All are based at Ilford.

The franchise was awarded to First Group plc for a 7 year 3 month period, and commenced operation on 5 January 1997. A support payment from the Franchising Director of £29.0 million in the first full year (1997/8) converts to a premium payment by the franchisee of £9.5 million in the last year (2003/4).

Great Eastern Railway train miles at 6.2 million pa are not huge, but the railway is very well used at 149 passenger miles per train mile. Revenue per passenger journey is £2.66, with average passenger journey length at 19 miles.

In performance terms, reliability at 99.6% is comfortably in excess of the 99.0% target, and punctuality at 92.2% better than the 88.0% charter aim. Railtrack's GE main line resignalling is now reaching fruition; this will allow further revisions to services in 1998.

Of perhaps greater import is the possibility of major investment schemes in the area. Among these is the Channel Tunnel Rail Link, for which an underground box would be constructed north of the present Stratford station and which might contain both an international and a domestic CTRL station. Then, for the GE services themselves, the CrossRail link in tunnel to Liverpool Street, Farringdon, Tottenham Court Road, Bond Street and Paddington, thence onto the GWML, still has a place in the in-tray. A Shenfield-Reading service would form part of the total proposed service, but how would this fit into the franchising regime?

In the 'definite' category is the 1998 Jubilee Line opening to Stratford, while access to Docklands is likely to increase further in importance.

Great North Eastern Railway Ltd

Although not the 'Premier Line' in the historical sense, the East Coast main line has nevertheless built up an enviable reputation for quality and speed over the years. The long-delayed electrification of the principal trunk routes was eventually completed in 1991. This encompassed Glasgow Central via Carstairs, Edinburgh and Leeds (and now Bradford Forster Square), but did not extend to destinations such as Harrogate, Hull, Teesside or Aberdeen. The result is that IC125 sets still make an occasional appearance at King's Cross. Most services are provided by the Class 91 locomotives, Mk 4 coaching stock and Driving Van Trailers, which together make up the 31 IC225 electric sets. All trains are fully reversible, so that remarshalling is not needed at any point.

The hourly interval pattern of the Great North Eastern Railway from London during the day usually consists of one Glasgow Central via Edinburgh train, one to Leeds and one to Newcastle or beyond, but up to six trains may leave King's Cross in the busiest hour. Other intermediate terminating points used are York and Edinburgh. Aberdeen has three through trains from King's Cross in the course of a day, as does Bradford Forster Square, while Hull and Inverness both have just one. Harrogate has one train via Leeds, but in the up direction only.

With stops at York and Newcastle only, the 15.00 Mondays to Fridays from King's Cross arrives at Edinburgh at 18.59 (fastest time in the public timetable). This equates to an average 98.7mph capital to capital speed. This is, however, with a maximum 125mph; the 225 km/h (or 140mph) capability of these trains has yet to be exploited.

Operation is over 920 route miles.

Maintenance and servicing for the GNER fleet is carried out at Bounds Green, Neville Hill, Heaton and Craigentinny.

The franchise was let for a seven-year period to

Above:
As part of a drive to increase the number of trains available for service, the unique Brush locomotive No 89001 was restored to full operational use. It is seen here at King's Cross on the 08.10 departure to Leeds on 8 November 1997. This locomotive is owned by Sea Containers Ltd and not a ROSCO.

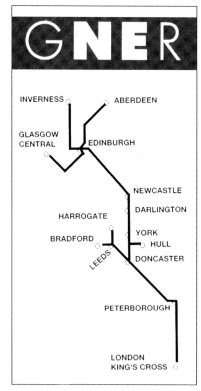

Great North Eastern Railway Ltd, part of the Sea Containers group. The handover was on 28 April 1996. The support payments from the Franchising Director decline from £55.0 million in 1997/8 to zero over the period of the franchise.

Franchising commitments made by Great North Eastern Railway as part of the plan include:

- run half-hourly services to Newcastle, York and Doncaster, and hourly to Edinburgh and Leeds for the period of the franchise
- improve Class 225 reliability
- refurbish the IC125 fleet to a higher standard of comfort
- for at least two years, run dedicated coach links to connect Bradford with Wakefield and for at least one year to connect Lincoln with Newark, four times a day, five days a week
- invest in station improvements including security and disabled access.

At 9.9 million train miles a year, service provision is similar in volume to that of Virgin Cross Country. Average journey length is 175 miles, the highest of any TOC and about the distance from London to Wakefield. Encouragingly, the revenue per journey is also a system high at £20.59 and so is train occupancy at 210 passenger miles per train mile.

Reliability was on target at 99.1% for 1996/7 (Charter 99.0%); punctuality nearly made it at 89.8% against a 90.0% standard.

The East Coast route does not enjoy quite the same number of commercial centres as does the West Coast, but both business traffic and tourism (notably York, Durham and Edinburgh) are valuable earners. North of Doncaster additional services are operated by Virgin Cross Country, while the Trans-Pennine services of Regional Railways North East join at York. On the northern part of the route there is thus some scope for competition, while Midland Main Line has always operated some service to Leeds via Sheffield—if only to reach its stabling point at Neville Hill. Still, two can play at that game; the 'Master Cutler' once reached Sheffield via Retford, while at Grantham there is a route to Nottingham. Neither, though, is electrified, and in all cases competition might have to be based more on price than on speed.

Great Western Trains Co Ltd

The name 'Great Western' is indelibly associated with I. K. Brunel, its illustrious engineer. Today's Great Western company provides InterCity services from its Paddington terminus westwards to Reading, and thence by a number of routes, to destinations in a wide arc from Worcester and Hereford in the north, to Penzance in the south. Apart from the sleeping cars, the entire operation is in the hands of IC125 units, which are based at Laira, Plymouth; St Philip's Marsh, Bristol; and Landore, Swansea. The sleepers are Laira-based.

One of the difficulties of operation on this route is the nature of the territory it serves. Except for South Wales and Bristol, there is a lack of large centres for which to aim. With the Bristol Channel neatly dividing its territory, Great Western has little choice but to run separate services over several routes. As a result, service frequency on each is perhaps less than could be justified were some combination of services possible. In turn, this makes future investment options such as electrification difficult to justify, due to the large number of track miles involved relative to traffic potential.

The principal services by Great Western are those running hourly from Paddington to Bristol Parkway, Cardiff Central and Swansea, and to Bath and Bristol Temple Meads. Usually, there is also a departure for Taunton, Exeter St David's and Plymouth, many of which are extended to Penzance.

Other services are of a more occasional nature; thus, there are four trains per day to Gloucester and Cheltenham, one of which continues to Worcester Shrub Hill. But Worcester also sees three Great Western trains which run from Paddington via Oxford and the Cotswold line. These all continue to Great Malvern and two of them on to Hereford.

Another occasional projection of London trains from Bristol Temple Meads is to Plymouth, perhaps diverting via Weston-super-Mare. Fishguard Harbour receives minimal service, in connection with Rosslare boats only. Other destinations served, such as Newquay and Pembroke Dock, are restricted to the summer months or summer weekends; Paignton receives a solitary through train from Paddington in the rest of the year.

The 'Night Riviera' sleeping car service between London and Plymouth/Penzance ran to and from Waterloo every night except Saturdays though it has now reverted to Paddington. The company operates over 850 route miles.

The franchise is for a period of 10 years, provided that rolling stock commitments are met. Great Western Trains started operation on 4 February 1996; with Stagecoach's South West Trains, these were the first franchisees. Over the franchise period, the support from the franchising

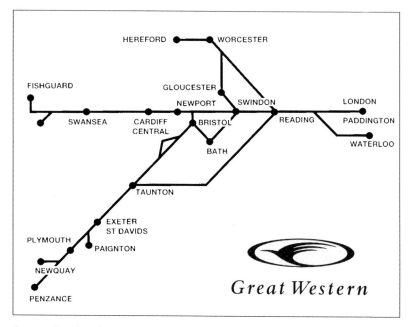

Great Western

director reduces from £58.7 million in 1997/8 to £34.2 million in 2004/5, the last full year of the franchise. The company is now owned by First Group plc

Franchising plan commitments include to:

- exceed the level of service in the pre-fran-chising timetable
- refurbish existing rolling stock by April 1999 (the first refurbished IC125 entered service in 1996)
- provide facilities for cyclists (IC125s are equipped with racks for six cycles)
- develop an integrated transport system (bus/rail links and through ticketing intro-duced in 1997 in Somerset, Wiltshire, Devon and Cornwall).

Half of Great Western's business is leisure related, with business travel accounting for a further third. This company is in the middle rank when it comes to annual train miles, recorded as 8.3 million. Average passenger journey length is 85 miles, rather more than the distance from London to Swindon. For this journey length, the average fare paid is £16.21. At 85, the average train occupancy is well above the network mean.

How does the service perform? Reliability was recorded as 99.5% for 1996/7 (target 99.2%);

punctuality was 90.4% against a 90.0% standard.

To the south of the Great Western main line lies Heathrow Airport, linked by the Heathrow Express Railway for nonstop trains to Paddington. With at least a chance that Terminal 5 will be constructed and Heathrow air traffic grow further, what role might there be for the railway in providing more surface access? The Great Western could indeed be an important player in this game, provided that line capacity is not too serious a problem.

There is not a need in itself to divert the main line through the airport, with all the extended journey times which this would entail, but it could be one of the possibilities. This would make elec-trification of the GWML a necessity, since diesel traction is not permitted on the airport's railway. Apart from any other factor, there are no suitable ventilation ducts.

Meanwhile, county councils in the West Country and South Wales would like to see the Great Western upgraded. They recognise that the IC125 fleet is now over 20 years old and that elec-trification schemes take time to plan and imple-ment, even if the finance is available. But deciding which of the rail routes could justify electrifica-tion, and whether it should be to their ultimate termini or stopping short (and, if so, where?), is

Above:
Paddington's Platform 2 sees Great Western Trains'
HST power car No 43016 ready for departure with
the 09.15 to Bristol Temple Meads on 16 October
1997.

another matter. To which, one might add: 'Don't
forget Birmingham.'

However, what they are likely to get, in the
shorter term anyway, is half-hourly services of
IC125s from Paddington to both Bristol and
Cardiff, throughout the day.

Island Line Ltd

The Isle of Wight network at its peak stretched to
55 route miles. As one commentator has
observed, 'with the wonderful benefit of hindsight, it now appears that much of the railway
expansion on the island was carried out with the
heart, rather than the balance sheet, as the main
raison d'être'. Closures started in 1952, and by
1966 the only railway left (apart from what is
now the preserved steam line) was the 8 mile 31
chains section between Ryde Pier Head and
Shanklin.

This line survives today, electrified and with its
second generation of electric rolling stock, albeit
that the latter is well over half a century old.
Formerly owned by London Underground, the ex-
1938 tube stock trains hardly look as though they
are in their element as they battle up the 700yd of
Ryde Pier in a stiff breeze. A force eight and water
coming over the tracks on the pier is enough to

stop them. This is a very limited operation; even
the newly extended Bluebell Railway in Sussex
has a greater route mileage, while some of its
rolling stock is actually newer!

Services operate at an irregularly spaced twice
an hour frequency over the length of the (now)

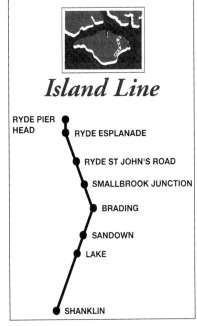

Island Line

RYDE PIER
HEAD
     RYDE ESPLANADE

       RYDE ST JOHN'S ROAD

        SMALLBROOK JUNCTION

      BRADING

     SANDOWN

    LAKE

   SHANKLIN

Above:
Island Line is a small franchise, depending on its
fleet of ex-London Underground 1938 tube stock for
passenger services. No 483004 is seen a little to the
north of Brading on its way to Ryde Pier Head in
June 1992.

mostly single-track line. Indeed, in the six miles
south of Smallbrook Junction, the only switch and
crossing work is that for the passing loop at
Sandown, where there are also a couple of sidings
for permanent way purposes. In itself, this is a
limitation on the maximum service which can be
run. Just for the record, the fastest end to end
journey time of 21min equates to an average
speed of 24mph, including stops. The two-car
Class 483 trains (as they are known to offi-
cialdom) are limited to a maximum speed of
45mph anyway.

Alone, Island Line remains a vertically integrated or unified railway, in the sense that the
infrastructure has not been split off from operations to a separate company. Its small size and
isolation from the rest of the network have
perhaps been the main reasons for the Island Line
being treated differently from the remainder. The
TOC is the infrastructure controller. Railtrack
owns the infrastructure, but Island Line leases it
from them and liaises closely with the South West
Infrastructure Maintenance Unit which has a
permanent way team on the island.

Likewise, Ryde Works, where maintenance
work is undertaken, remains part of Island Line.
The works is largely self-contained; only wheel

turning and major work on the traction motors
has to be sent away to the mainland.

The franchise was acquired by Stagecoach
Group plc on 13 October 1996; it is the only franchise for a period of less than seven years and is
for a five-year term. The support payments reduce
from £2.0 million in 1997/8, to £1.8 million in
the last full financial year of 200/1.

Franchise plan commitments by Island Line
are:
- to maintain pre-franchise train service mileage
  throughout
- to introduce enhanced public transport information at each station
- to introduce a local residents' travel scheme
  and test other discounted fares.

Train miles operated were 172,000 in 1996/7. The
average passenger journey length of five miles is
the same as that of London Underground, though
the average fare paid of £0.90 is less. A dispiriting
average train load of 19 passengers is the lowest
of any TOC, by some margin.

In performance terms, service reliability was
99.1% for 1996/7 (target 98.5%) and punctuality
was 96.5% against a target of 93.0%. One of the
problems of island rail operation is the desirability
of meeting Wightlink's catamaran from
Portsmouth at Pier Head. If the catamaran is
delayed, there is little point in the train departing,
but it can play havoc with the rest of the
timetable.

But there is another way for 'classic'—ie non
car-bound—passengers to cross from Portsmouth

to Ryde, and this is by hovercraft from Southsea Hoverport to Ryde Esplanade. This service is operated by Hovertravel.

Given also that minibuses are now allowed on Ryde Pier, the future of the Island Line looks less secure than perhaps it once did. The Isle of Wight enjoys relatively comprehensive bus service provision; it is much to be hoped that the railway can offer a worthwhile contribution to the travel needs of the island in the 21st century.

LTS Rail Ltd

The 'Tilbury' has always led a largely self-contained existence, even given its acquisition by the Midland Railway in 1912. Although freight usage to and from places like Dagenham, Purfleet and Thames Haven requires access to the rest of the network via Barking and Forest Gate, the passenger services rarely stray outside the local area.

This is real commuter territory, with the Fenchurch Street terminus receiving nearly 30,000 passenger arrivals in the morning peak. This is more than the combined totals of Euston, Marylebone and Paddington, and has to be absorbed by a four-platformed station consisting of two islands, with a (nowadays) twin track approach.

Off-peak, though, it is a different story, with little more than 3,000 arriving. Fenchurch Street is a fine destination for city workers, and with a walk to Bank LUL station can be used for access to the West End, but it is hardly ideally sited for the off-peak shopping or leisure traffic.

Service provision is correspondingly peaked; it is the off-peak basic timetable which is described here. This consists of 8tph from Fenchurch Street.

Of the four on the main line, two omit Limehouse, West Horndon, Laindon and Pitsea, but all run to Shoeburyness. The basic Tilbury service at 2tph now starts at Fenchurch Street and runs via Upminster, Ockendon, Chafford Hundred (for the shopping centre), Grays, then all stations to Southend Central. The 2tph service provides for the intermediate branch stations beyond Barking, and terminates in the bay platform at Grays. That is the complete service. It might be added that 20 trains leave Fenchurch Street between 17.00 and 17.59 on Mondays to Fridays, which is another measure of the peak period's domination.

The company serves a total of 80 route miles.

The franchise passed to LTS Rail Ltd for a 15-year term, conditional upon franchise plan commitments on rolling stock being achieved. The first day of operation was 26 May 1996; support was £27.7 million in 1997/8, declining to £11.7 million in the last full year of 2010/11 at the end of the franchise period.

The franchise plan commits LTS Rail to:
- run at least 95% of previous train mileage plus additional Sunday services
- replace the Class 310s and Class 312s by November 1999; the order was placed on 9 June 1997
- replace Class 302s with Class 317s
- install barrier gates at all stations; Barking completed 1997
- open new station at West Ham by December 1999
- raise Passenger Charter standards from April 1997
- invest £14 million in station improvements.

Annual train miles are 3.4 million, with an average passenger journey length of 16 miles. This brings in an average fare of £2.35 and an average

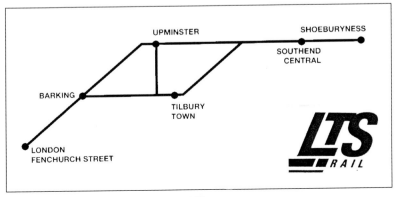

Above:
LTS Rail has undertaken to construct a new station at West Ham for interchange with the Jubilee and North London lines. This allows passengers ready access to Docklands, and perhaps even to the West End given the unsatisfactory location of Fenchurch Street. On 23 December 1997, a Class 310 unit running up line passes the construction site.

train loading of 98 passengers on what is primarily a commuter railway. This is helped by the importance of non-London destinations, such as Southend, Basildon and Barking for example; these and other stations have a considerable ability to attract both work and leisure traffic.

Trains, presently a mixed fleet of Classes 310, 312 and 317, are maintained at East Ham. All lines are electrified at 25kV ac. Performance on reliability was 99.0% in 1996/7 (target 98.0%) and punctuality 93.9%, comfortably above the 88.0% standard set.

The Tilbury has had its share of poor performance in recent years, with ageing signalling equipment and a 1960 build of trains both partially to blame. A further difficulty was the removal of LTS tracks on the London side of Limehouse in order to accommodate the Docklands Light Railway. The infrastructure problems are now on their way to a satisfactory resolution; replacing the trains had to take

account of the progress of new builds for other lines, as well as the domestic problems of the LT&S.

Merseyrail Electrics Ltd

The Merseyrail network has a variety of origins, the oldest part being the Mersey Railway which started electric working in 1903 between Liverpool Central and Rock Ferry. It was not until 1977/8 though that the 'loop and link' tunnelling scheme to unite the then electrified network under central Liverpool was completed, with the help of Merseyside PTE (Merseytravel). This brought together the lines to, respectively, Rock Ferry, West Kirby and New Brighton (the Wirral Lines, with a loop) and to Southport, Ormskirk and Kirkby, plus the reopened line to Garston (the link).

The system, electrified at 750V dc, was subsequently extended. Electrification reached Hunts Cross (1983), Hooton (1985), Chester (1993) and Ellesmere Port (1994). Merseyrail Electrics covers a total of 75 route miles.

The service pattern is intense, with a 15min frequency standard on all routes. In the central area of Liverpool and including the section under the river between James Street and Hamilton Square, the combined service reaches 12tph or a train every 5min. The 15min frequency falls to 30min only for the two sections beyond Hooton,

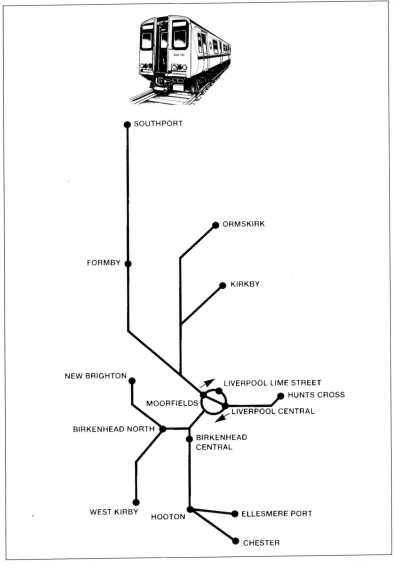

where Chester and Ellesmere Port both have a 2tph service. On the link line, the Southport trains are the ones projected to Hunts Cross; the Kirkby and Ormskirk services terminate at Liverpool Central. Peak supplementation is confined to the Hooton line, where services are broadly doubled.

Franchised operation started on 19 January 1997, with the new owners MTL Trust Holdings Ltd having been awarded a 7 year 2 month franchise. Support payments by the Franchising Director are £80.7 million in 1997/8, falling to £60.8 million in the final year of 2003/4.

The franchising plan contains commitments by Merseyrail Electrics to:

- introduce security enhancements, with help points at every station; rapid response teams were in place in mid-1997 and CCTV installed on 24 trains early in 1998
- modify train doors to allow on-train staff to check tickets and provide customer care on all units by 31 March 2000.

The concentrated Merseyrail Electrics operation provides fractionally more annual train miles than LTS Rail at 3.5 million, but the average passenger journey length is only seven miles. Fares income equates to £0.90 per journey. The average number of passengers on a train at any one time is 44.

The service is provided by the (almost) identical Class 507 and 508 units built around 1979; many of the latter are off-lease and 12 sets have now made their way to Connex South Eastern. The units are maintained at Birkenhead North.

Reliability at 98.5% (Northern Line) and 99.1% (Wirral Line) for 1996/7 was near the standard of 99.0%. Punctuality was rather better than Charter Standard at 93.4% and 92.2% respectively against a 90.0% target.

What of the future? The railway depends on Liverpool at least as much as Liverpool depends on the railway; the fortunes of one affect the other. The pre-franchising prolonged closure of the city centre rail tunnel due to the problems of

Above:
Merseyrail's fleet of 76 three-car units of Classes 507/508 was clearly much too generous for the services to be provided in the late 1990s, and some are presently being returned for service south of the Thames. No 507002 calls at Hightown on the Southport branch with a train for Liverpool in 1983.

the rising water table must have been relatively disastrous for the Merseyrail business, quite apart from its effect on the city transport system. Such problems have to be overcome without service withdrawal wherever possible; if passengers are forced to find alternatives, some at least will stay with them.

This railway operation also suffers from industrial action.

Further system expansion may be possible, provided that this does not overload the present infrastructure. The trains which presently terminate at Liverpool Central could be extended eastwards beyond Hunts Cross to Widnes and perhaps Warrington Central. Another possibility would be to revive the Edge Hill spur proposal, for which a header tunnel was built at Central in the 1970s, to offer a service to St Helens Central. But these are not short-term schemes. They involve varying amounts of civil engineering work and electrification. Then, 25kV ac and dual voltage stock, or 750V dc?

Midland Main Line Ltd

The Midland Railway was based in Derby, and in the company's mind everything radiated from there. For many years, in defiance of normal conventions, it was 'up' to Derby on the Midland, not to London.

Midland Main Line is presently the only railway operator using St Pancras, which has a sadly deserted air about it as a result. IC125 sets provide all the services; every hour on the hour there is a train from St Pancras to Nottingham and on the half hour to Sheffield via Derby. Leicester has the positional benefit of being served by both. In the busiest hours, the number of departures rises to four.

There is some origination of early services from north of Sheffield, since the 14 IC125 sets are all based at Neville Hill, Leeds. There is a similar extension of trains north of Sheffield in the evenings. Thus, the 18.30 St Pancras to Nottingham train reverses at Nottingham, to proceed via Alfreton (now shorn of its Parkway status) to Sheffield. It then runs via Wakefield Westgate to Leeds. Some services make a detour via Doncaster. Midland Main Line operates over 298 route miles.

The franchise was awarded to the National Express Group plc, who commenced operations on 28 April 1996. Payments by the Franchising Director were £8.2 million in 1997/8. This changes to a small premium payable by the oper-

ator in 2000/1 and a final premium of £10.2 million to the Franchising Director in the last full year of 2005/6. The franchise term is for 10 years, subject to the rolling stock commitments being achieved.

The franchising plan requirements to which Midland Main Line decided to commit the company are:

- to introduce in 1999 a significantly increased service frequency (10 more services each weekday to and from Derby, 10 each weekday for Nottingham and 22 for Leicester)
- procure new air-conditioned rolling stock to run additional stopping services and refurbish the IC125 fleet
- undertake a programme of station improvement
- subject to feasibility studies and obtaining planning consents, to build a new 'East Midlands Parkway' station south of Trent Junction, giving access to both the motorway network and East Midlands Airport.

This is a limited operation and the annual train miles at 3.2 million are much the same as both Merseyrail Electrics and LTS Rail. Journey length is much higher at an average 81 miles (London to Market Harborough). This elicits a revenue of £11.04, putting Midland Main Line behind only the GNER and Virgin West Coast companies. Average occupancy of the trains is 149 passengers. Leisure is recorded as the principal market, but business travel is also significant. There is also some commuting, notably from Leicester southwards to London, but also into Leicester itself.

The service quality measurement saw reliability of 99.7% for 1996/7 (target 99.0%) and punctuality at 91.3% against 90.0%.

Like other IC125 users, the question mark over their lifespan grows increasingly bigger. Does electrification, already in place for the first 50 miles to Bedford, have any appeal as part of an investment strategy? What other alternatives will there be?

Of perhaps more immediate consequence is the forthcoming use of St Pancras as the CTRL London terminal. This will permit easy interchange into Midland Main Line trains, and slightly less easy transfer to neighbouring King's Cross. It will also be made possible to access the WCML out of Euston for the provision of direct services. Of these three routes, it is the Midland which, conspicuously, is not electrified. While this does not in any sense prohibit interchange, there may be a market for direct European services from Midland territory. For that, electrification would be a necessary requirement.

Above:
The Midland Main Line services are provided wholly by HST sets. Power car No 43066 *Nottingham Playhouse* stands at the buffer stop end of St Pancras's Platform 5 on Friday 2 January 1998.

Little of this concerns the Midland Main Line business in the short term, but pity the writer of the OPRAF Passenger Service Requirement.

North Western Trains Ltd

The core of North Western Trains' operating area is the complex network of railways surrounding Manchester and Liverpool, but the company operates over 1,124 route miles. With a route network built primarily by the London & North Western and the Lancashire & Yorkshire companies, but with generous contributions from (what became) the Great Central and others, unification was never the name of the game. However, in the last decade, two important linking pieces of infrastructure have been built, and another major traffic source can now be reached by rail. These are as follows:

- The Hazel Grove chord, which allows trains from Sheffield via the Hope Valley to enter Manchester via Stockport, and to continue via Oxford Road if required with minimal obstruction of the station throat at Piccadilly.
- The 700m Windsor Link, which allows trains from Manchester Oxford Road to gain access to the L&Y lines from Manchester Victoria towards Bolton, at the new Salford Crescent station.
- The opening of Manchester Airport station,

connected initially by a facing junction to the Styal line towards Manchester, but with a south-facing junction towards Crewe added subsequently.

It might also be added that some conventional rail traffic was lost with the acquisition of the Bury and Altrincham branches for Metrolink. Nevertheless, the advent of these schemes has allowed a complete rethink of the means of serving Greater Manchester by rail, amongst which has been the substantial downgrading of Victoria station.

North Western Trains is the principal operator, whose interests stretch from Holyhead to the Cumbrian Coast, as well as the land east of the Pennines and south to the Midlands. Services may be divided into urban services, mostly the subject of agreements with Greater Manchester PTE or Merseytravel, longer distance services, and rural. Of these, the urban services are understood to account for well over half of North Western Trains' total revenue.

The PTE diesel services in Merseyside and all local services in the Manchester area are run to PTE specifications. Service frequencies are often 2tph or more, especially when several services run between the same points—as, for instance, between Manchester and Romiley. The longer distance services, mostly hourly, include:

- Crewe-Holyhead (with an interspersed service to Chester only)
- Manchester Piccadilly-Llandudno
- Liverpool Lime Street-Preston, then continuing to Blackpool North or Morecambe
- Manchester Airport, Piccadilly, Stockport,

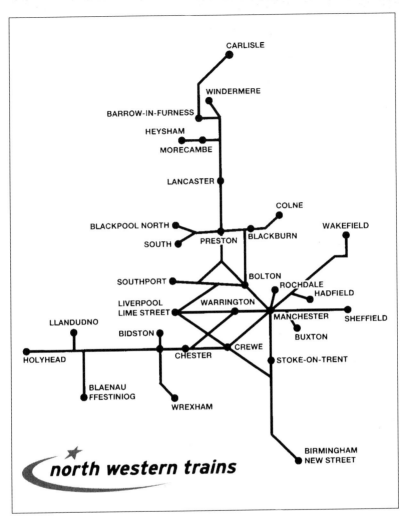

north western trains

Sheffield, Doncaster, Cleethorpes
- Manchester Airport, Piccadilly, Bolton, Preston, Blackpool North
- As above to Preston, then continuing to Barrow-in-Furness or Windermere.

The truly rural services include those between Llandudno and Blaenau Ffestiniog; Barrow-in-Furness, Whitehaven and Carlisle; and Oxenholme, Lake District and Windermere. Services such as Preston-Ormskirk also perhaps

come into this category. These routes are typified by the use of minimum resources to provide a service, the intervals of which often appear to owe as much to economical rostering of staff and diesel units as to passenger demand.

A feature of recent years has been the growth of longer distance urban services, longer in the sense of end-to-end journey times and distances rather than any noticeable affinity between the places at either end. Some of those operated by North Western Trains, all hourly, are:

• Southport and Chester	30 stations	83 miles	158min
• Buxton and Blackpool North	27 stations	75 miles	137min
• Blackpool South and Colne	26 stations	50 miles	109min
• Rochdale and Wigan Wallgate	12 stations	33 miles	70min

It takes little work with a calculator to show, that at around a 30mph average speed, how tedious such journeys are over longer distances. They may minimise the use of land in city centres and be cheap to provide, but such operations hardly show the railway at its best.

The North Western Trains' diesel unit fleet is a mixture of Class 142 Pacers and heavier duty DMUs of Classes 150, 153 and 156, plus some Class 158s. A few Class 101s still survive. The principal maintenance depot is Newton Heath. Class 323 electric units have superseded many of the Modernisation Plan units.

Franchising was effective with the handover to Great Western Holdings Ltd on 2 March 1997, with a franchise for 7 years 1 month. OPRAF support in 1997/8 was £184.9 million, reducing to £125.5 million in 2003/4 at the end of the franchise. The company is now owned by First Group plc.

Franchise plan commitments by North Western Trains are as follows:

• develop by June 2000 new long distance services from Rochdale and from North Wales to London

• introduce additional services between Liverpool and Manchester and between Manchester and Wigan/Preston via Bolton, by June 1998

Above:
North Western Trains operates services for Merseytravel, amongst others. Pacer unit No 142058 is about to leave for Wigan North Western on 22 November 1997 with the 10.12 departure from Liverpool Lime Street.

• replace entire Mk 1 rolling stock fleet with 70 new DMU vehicles by March 2000

• refurbish the whole of the Class 150 fleet and remaining Class 142s by December 1999

• invest £5 million in station improvements

• improve the existing Passenger Charter (compensation doubled to 40%).

North Western Trains runs a sizeable 14.7 million train miles a year, with an average passenger journey length of 18 miles. The associated revenue per journey is £2.17. Usage, however, in terms of train occupancy, remains depressingly low, with only 31 persons at a time on the average train. Service performance reached a low ebb a few years ago, which incurred the wrath of the Greater Manchester Passenger Transport Authority. By area, North Western Trains' 1996/7 results were as follows:

Area	Reliability	Target	Punctuality	Target
Cumbria	99.5%	99.0%	97.9%	90.0%
Lancashire local	99.0%	99.0%	94.9%	90.0%
Manchester local	99.2%	99.0%	93.2%	90.0%
Manchester long distance	99.5%	99.0%	95.1%	90.0%
North Wales branches	99.3%	99.0%	89.8%	90.0%
North Wales inter-urban	99.1%	99.0%	94.8%	90.0%

Whilst not perfect, they are now respectable.

There remains much to do in the area. The growing Manchester Airport originates a 5tph service northwards, but there are more potential destinations than there are train paths. In infrastructure terms, the congested link from Slade Green Junction (at the northern end of the Styal line), through Piccadilly to Oxford Road and Deansgate is perhaps the most restrictive element, but what other use might be made of further airport connections?

There are other TOUs who might well offer some competition, while electrification of any or all of the Trans-Pennine route via Huddersfield, the missing elements of the line from Manchester through to Preston (or Blackpool North), or more lines east of Liverpool Lime Street would again alter the range of services which might be provided.

Meanwhile, how might services in the Blackburn and Burnley areas be developed most effectively?

Regional Railways North East Ltd

Regional Railways North East covers the whole of the Yorkshire area and northwards to the border. Also within the area, of course, are the operations of GNER and Virgin Cross Country, while North Western Trains and Central Trains lie to the west and south respectively.

Historically, the northeast was a one-company area, the grip of the pre-1923 North Eastern

Below:
The Class 155 twin units have all been rebuilt to single units, excepting only the seven owned by West Yorkshire PTE but managed by Porterbrook ROSCO. They are operated by Regional Railways North East. No 155346 has just arrived at Leeds Platform 12 on the 09.18 Hull to Manchester Piccadilly. The date was 11 November 1997.

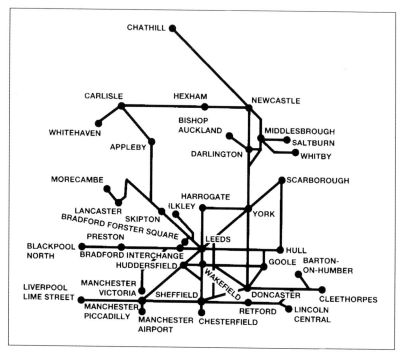

Railway being well known. Further south, the Midland penetrated to West Yorkshire, as did some companies from Lancashire, but the network complexities resulting from rival schemes have long been all but eliminated. It is now 30 years since Leeds and Sheffield both had more than one station.

There are a number of long distance services operated by Regional Railways North East (RRNE). These include the following hourly services, which together provide a 3tph fast service between Leeds and Manchester:

- Sunderland, Newcastle, York, Leeds, Huddersfield, Manchester Piccadilly, Liverpool Lime Street (alternately, trains start from Scarborough instead of Sunderland)
- Middlesbrough, York, Leeds, Huddersfield, Manchester Piccadilly, Manchester Airport
- Hull, Leeds, Huddersfield, Manchester Piccadilly

Other hourly services include:
- York, Leeds, Bradford Interchange, Burnley, Preston, Blackpool North
- York, Leeds, Bradford Interchange, Hebden

Bridge, Manchester Victoria (alternately, these trains start from Selby)
- (Middlesbrough), Sunderland, Newcastle, Hexham, (Carlisle)
- Wakefield Westgate, Huddersfield, Manchester Victoria, St Helens Junction, Liverpool Lime Street

And, at about a two-hourly frequency:
- Leeds, Skipton, Carnforth, Morecambe
- Leeds, Skipton, Settle, Carlisle
- Saltburn, Middlesbrough, Darlington, Durham, Newcastle
- Saltburn, Middlesbrough, Darlington, Bishop Auckland

The latter are additional to the local Saltburn to Darlington service.

RRNE provide urban services for three PTEs; West Yorkshire (METRO), South Yorkshire, and Tyne & Wear (NEXUS). Tyne & Wear's only supported service is that between Newcastle and Sunderland (4tph), while South Yorkshire's involvement has always been limited, due to the relatively small part of the railway system which lies within its boundaries. All lines heading northwards from South Yorkshire to Leeds have a joint involvement with METRO.

Leeds is in many ways the centre of the network. From here, local electric services now reach Wakefield Westgate plus Doncaster (1tph, but 2tph from Adwick into Doncaster), while Ilkley and Skipton have trains at 2tph from both Bradford Forster Square and Leeds. This gives a joint 15min service to each of those destinations!

Diesel units from Leeds offer 2tph to Harrogate and Knaresborough, one of which continues to York. An important service is that to Castleford, Wakefield Kirkgate, Barnsley and Sheffield. Hourly from Leeds, it becomes 2tph from Wakefield Kirkgate and 3tph from Barnsley with the addition of a train from Huddersfield via Penistone. Castleford benefits also from an hourly Leeds-Knottingley service, while Sheffield may also be reached via Moorthorpe.

Other services of interest to SYPTE include 3tph from Sheffield to Doncaster, one of which continues to Hull and another (ex-Manchester Airport), to Cleethorpes. Over the old Great Central network there is a 1tph service to Worksop and Retford, alternate services continuing to Lincoln Central.

Elsewhere on the network, Regional Railways North East runs an hourly local service between Scunthorpe and Doncaster and between Wakefield Westgate and Pontefract Monkhill. Hull to Bridlington has 2tph, reducing to 1tph or less thence to Scarborough. And while there is an hourly service from Newcastle to Morpeth, the service thence to Berwick-upon-Tweed is little more than residual.

Other very limited services are: that on alternate hours between Cleethorpes and Barton-on-Humber, the very occasional projections beyond Knottingley to Goole, York to Hull via Selby trains, the residual Sheffield to York direct, and the poor old Whitby branch from Middlesbrough. One has the distinct impression that these are very much PSR-induced services.

This is not a complete inventory. One-off services such as the 16.00 weekdays Sunderland to Whitehaven service always invoke incredulity, but they really do exist.

Regional Railways North East operates over 1,277 route miles, putting it a little ahead of North Western Railways.

Regional Railways North East became a franchised operation on 2 March 1997, for its new owners MTL Trust Holdings Ltd. The franchise period is 7 years 1 month. Support payments from the Franchising Director were £224.5 million in 1997/8, falling to £145.6 million in the last year of the franchise in 2003/4.

The franchise plan requires the following:
- pre-franchise train miles maintained for the length of the franchise
- introduction of 12 daily additional Trans-Pennine services from May 2000
- rolling stock improvements, such as replacing Class 308 units by December 2000
- investment of £0.5 million on station improvements
- investment of £0.4 million on station security in PTE areas.

How does Regional Railways North East compare with others? It operates as many as 20.5 million train miles a year and the average passenger journey length is 20 miles—but for a fare of only £1.86. On the other hand, the average train occupancy rate at 38 is similar to that of Central Trains, with whose operation that of RRNE is perhaps broadly comparable.

Rolling stock, a variety of Class 14x units and the more salubrious Class 15x diesel units, are maintained at Neville Hill (Leeds) or Heaton (Newcastle). Some of these units are owned by METRO, albeit that they are managed by Porterbrook Leasing Co. Electric units comprise a small Class 321 fleet of three and 21 Class 308s drafted in for the Airedale and Wharfedale electrification.

On performance, the Trans-Pennine services appear to be the least punctual:

Area	Reliability	Target	Punctuality	Target
Trans-Pennine Express	99.8%	99.0%	91.4%	90.0%
West/North Yorks long distance	99.5%	99.0%	92.9%	90.0%
South Yorks & Humberside long	99.6%	99.0%	96.0%	90.0%
Northern long distance	99.6%	99.0%	94.6%	90.0%
West/North Yorks short distance	99.3%	99.0%	96.1%	90.0%
South Yorks & Humberside short	99.1%	99.0%	94.7%	90.0%
Northern short distance	98.9%	99.0%	92.8%	90.0%

Of new developments in the area, both Meadowhall and Gateshead Metro Centre are out of town shopping centres which are reasonably close to an RRNE station. Clearly, RRNE could obtain considerable advantage from the implementation of Trans-Pennine electrification, especially if extended at the eastern end to York and perhaps also to Hull. Line capacity, though, is the key factor, given the intention to increase passenger services and the aspirations of English, Welsh & Scottish Railways Ltd (EWS).

Infrastructure problems include the Leeds area station layout and its signalling, both of which were, essentially, designed for rather lower rail traffic levels. And therein lies one of the principal benefits which local railways can bring: the relief of road congestion in urban areas. What is the best way to make use of this opportunity?

ScotRail Railways Ltd

ScotRail TOC is the nearest to a self-contained railway system on mainland Britain. Although companies from the InterCity stable in the form of GNER and Virgin Trains penetrate on occasion as far as Glasgow Central, Inverness and Aberdeen, ScotRail is largely its own master. Indeed, since assuming control of the Anglo-Scottish Sleeper

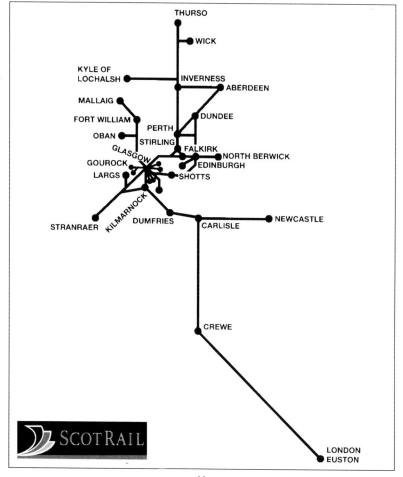

services, it has a toehold all the way to London via the West Coast route. ScotRail operates over 1,885 route miles.

Strathclyde PTE has the largest urban network outside London and is correspondingly important to ScotRail as a source of revenue and of business. The heart of Strathclyde's Glasgow operation is that of the former 'Blue Trains', the electrics which plied the network from 1960. The 'north side' electric services, as joined subsequently by the Argyle Line services to the south east, are displayed in Table 226 of the timetable. Suffice to say here that this whole network operates on a basic half-hourly frequency, save only the sections beyond Motherwell, both to Lanark and to Coatbridge.

Nearer to Central Glasgow, services combine to provide a joint frequency; this equates to 6tph through Glasgow Queen Street low level and 4tph through Central low level. Partick, where both lines join and which has interchange with the Glasgow Underground, has a splendid 10tph off-peak service.

Although not the size of London, Glasgow stretches a considerable distance for its catchments. Typically, cross-Glasgow journeys like Drumgelloch to Helensburgh, or Lanark to Milngavie are 35 miles or so in length, similar to the distance between Croydon and Stevenage. The 2tph frequency extends also to the 'south side' services which make up the Cathcart circle group, to Ayr and Ardrossan. Largs and Wemyss Bay have only an hourly service, though Gourock has 3tph. Diesel services, such as to Cumbernauld, Maryhill, Paisley Canal, East Kilbride and Barrhead, are also at 2tph, though services beyond to Kilmarnock are hourly.

Edinburgh's suburban services are much more limited: electric trains to North Berwick run hourly, as does the Bathgate service. The Fife circle to Dunfermline and Kirkcaldy runs hourly in each direction. The local service to Glasgow Central via Shotts is also hourly.

Longer distance services include that between Edinburgh and Glasgow Queen Street via Falkirk High, presently 2tph but prospectively 4tph. The main alternative is of course to travel Virgin via Carstairs to Central.

Both Glasgow Queen Street and Edinburgh offer an hourly service to Aberdeen, which gives 2tph north of Dundee. Of the eight daily Inverness services, Edinburgh has the majority, but other connections are available at Perth. ScotRail dominates the service provision, although other operators make an appearance.

In the Highlands, Oban, Mallaig, Kyle of Lochalsh and the far north line to Wick all survive on a basic three trains per day service. Wick can now be reached only via Thurso, adding a 13-mile round trip and half an hour to the journey times. Intrepid passengers for Wick may, of course, disembark at Georgemas Junction to admire the scenery while their train runs up to Thurso and back again. The last time the writer was at Georgemas, he envied a sheep which was seeking shelter under a stationary mineral wagon. The Aberdeen-Elgin-Inverness service runs alternate hours, with some small supplementation to offer a commuter service between Aberdeen and Dyce, 6.5 miles distant.

An interesting development is that associated with the former Glasgow & South Western routes. From Glasgow Central, both to Carlisle and to Stranraer, services run very approximately about every 2hr.

It is now possible to catch the 12.37 'Galloway Enterprise' from Newcastle to Stranraer, via Carlisle, Kilmarnock and Troon, to be deposited there 230 miles and 5hr 18min later. This leaves 35min to catch the catamaran operated at 18.30 from West Pier by SeaCat Scotland, arriving at Belfast Donegall Quay at 20.00. There are other direct links from Scotland to the Newcastle-Carlisle line, some of which appear to be geared to give access to the Gateshead MetroCentre station.

ScotRail's fleet consists of a handful of first generation diesel units of Classes 101 and 117,

while the remainder is formed from Classes 150, 156 and 158. These are based at Haymarket, Corkerhill and Inverness. The 25V ac electric units are of Class 303 (original Blue Trains), 305 (brought in for North Berwick electrification), 314 (Argyle Line), 318 (Ayrshire electrification) and 320 (Class 321 clones). These are maintained at Glasgow Shields and at Yoker. Sleeping cars and other coaching stock are based and maintained at Inverness.

ScotRail was the last British Rail Train Operating Company to enter private hands, doing so on 31 March 1997 when the franchise was acquired by National Express Group plc. This is a seven-year franchise; payments by OPRAF in the first year of 1997/8 were £280.1 million and will be £202.5 million in the last year of the franchise in 2003/4.

As a business, ScotRail tops the list of TOCs with 20.5 million train miles a year. Even so, the average passenger journey length is no more than 20 miles, which perhaps represents the importance of the urban services as a proportion of the total. Revenue per journey is also relatively low at £2.06. The average passenger occupancy per train is also well above the target at 38.

The franchise plan commits ScotRail to:
- introduce a 4tph service on weekdays Edinburgh-Falkirk-Glasgow from May 2000, using nine new three-car DMUs, by May 2000
- run an additional 80,000 off-peak train miles annually on Strathclyde PTE services, starting April 1998
- double off-peak frequency on Fife Circle route for at least two years from summer 1998
- introduce 38 new three-car EMUs for Strathclyde PTE by March 2000
- invest £1 million on station improvements by March 2000
- enhance standards on Anglo-Scottish sleepers between September 1998 and September 2002.

In performance terms in 1996/7, while reliability was close to target, punctuality was satisfactorily above the targets set:

Area	Reliability	Target	Punctuality	Target
Express	99.0%	99.0%	94.6%	90.0%
East	98.1%	99.0%	93.5%	90.0%
Central	98.1%	99.0%	93.3%	90.0%
Highland	99.7%	99.0%	95.8%	90.0%
South West	99.4%	99.0%	95.7%	90.0%

The development of ScotRail's Edinburgh-Glasgow Queen Street via Falkirk High service has already been touched upon. There are also a number of infrastructure investments under consideration, such as Glasgow's CrossRail north to south link over a reinvigorated Troon line, now freight only. Electrification of additional parts of the network, notably to Aberdeen, would also make a different range of service options possible. Around Aberdeen itself, there is some council pressure for a local service to be reinstated.

Particularly in the Central Lowlands, there is little spare railway capacity, which would make real competition difficult to achieve. So the railway must meet the needs of its passengers as best it can, economically and with regard to local transport planning aspirations. Who better to express these than bodies like Strathclyde PTE, who have to back their decisions with funding, and the local authorities in the Edinburgh area?

Silverlink Train Services Ltd

The 25kV ac electrification of the WCML to Euston in 1966 at last brought quality outer suburban service to the communities north of Watford. For years, they had endured irregularly spaced trains with gaps of up to nearly 3hr in the services to stations south of Bletchley.

Today, five Silverlink County trains an hour leave Euston. These are as follows:

1tph Watford Junction, Milton Keynes Central and Northampton only

2tph Principal stations to Milton Keynes Central, all stations to Coventry via Northampton, Birmingham International and, not always, Birmingham New Street

2tph Harrow & Wealdstone, Watford Junction and all stations

The peak service virtually doubles this service frequency.

And then there are the seven 'other' Silverlink Metro lines, whose total length is about equal to the distance between London and Rugby. These are discussed in turn.

Euston, Willesden Junction, Harrow & Wealdstone and Watford Junction (17.75 miles)

This, the so-called 'New Line' from its construction in the early years of this century and subsequent 1922 electrification, offers a basic 3tph. These are supplemented by the projection of

London Underground Bakerloo Line services from their usual Queen's Park terminus to Stonebridge Park or, occasionally, to Harrow & Wealdstone. Both systems are dc, but the fourth rail no longer extends beyond Harrow.

Richmond, Willesden Junction, Gospel Oak, Stratford and North Woolwich (22.5 miles)

A 3tph service is provided, which can be maintained despite the single track beyond Custom House to North Woolwich. Electrification varies between fourth rail dc for the District Line sharing into Richmond, third rail thence to South Acton (and also beyond Stratford), with 25kV elsewhere. This requires the use of the dual-voltage Class 313 units, which presently operate these services and those of the New Line. These two lines form the core of today's inner suburban operations

Willesden Junction and Clapham Junction (6.25 miles)

This 2tph service also requires Class 313 units, due to the change from overhead to third rail at the entrance to the Eurostar North Pole International depot.

Watford Junction and St Albans Abbey (6.5 miles)

Electrified at 25kV ac, this line has seen stations added at Garston and then How Wood. This is a one-train operation at a 45min headway, to suit the single journey time of 16min. There are no through workings off the branch.

The Croxley Green branch presently has its one train each way per day replaced by a bus service.

Gospel Oak and Barking (12.25 miles) and Bletchley and Bedford (16.75 miles)

These two lines, one urban and one largely rural, remain outside the electrified network. They are condemned as a result to services provided by first generation DMUs. Services are half-hourly and hourly respectively. Traffic on both may euphemistically be described as 'light'.

The fleets of both diesel and electric multiple-units are allocated to Bletchley.

The Silverlink Trains franchise passed to National Express Group plc on 2 March 1997 for

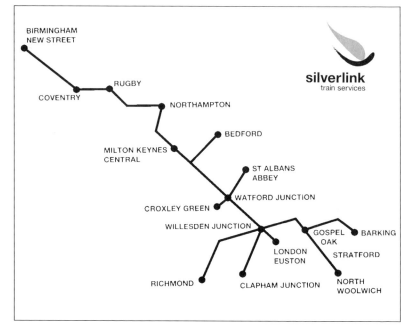

a 7 year 6 month period. Support from the Franchising Director was £48.6 million in 1997/8, falling to £15.8 million in the last year of the franchise of 2004/5.

The franchising plan commits Silverlink as follows:

- to run the pre-franchising train mileage for the length of the franchise
- to replace all slam-door DMU stock within two years
- to introduce a Watford-Gatwick service and operate additional morning and evening services on the core Euston-Birmingham route
- to reintroduce a 3tph service on Watford dc lines (achieved)
- to improve Passengers Charter punctuality on orbital service to 88% from September 1997.

Silverlink runs 5.4 million train miles a year over a 200 route mile network. The average passenger journey length is 16 miles. This is worth £1.68 in operator income. Occupancy per train is 81, close to the TOC average.

Performance statistics showed a mixed picture:

Area	Reliability	Target	Punctuality	Target
Northampton	99.1%	99.0%	86.7%	90.0%
Watford Locals	98.4%	97.0%	92.0%	90.0%
Orbitals	96.9%	97.0%	93.7%	90.0%

The Northampton lines performed adequately for service reliability, but punctuality was decidedly poor. The London orbitals failed to meet a very modest reliability target; the Watford locals were better. Punctuality in both cases was around the mid-range of all TOCs.

Connex South Central is presently operating its Rugby service from Brighton, and this will result in Silverlink seeking alternatives to their commitment to the Franchising Director to introduce a Watford-Gatwick service. In any event, this is competition north of the Thames for Silverlink's prime market; Virgin Railways also compete for some of the longer distance traffic.

Silverlink, too, will have to endure the upgrading work to be carried out on the WCML. But the further expansion of Milton Keynes may bring further traffic to the railway, though some of this will be shared with others. In the Department of Transport's view, Watford, Milton Keynes and Northampton are all important business centres attracting significant off-peak travel, but there are few tourist attractions in this route's corridor.

South West Trains Ltd

South West Trains (SWT) is in many ways still the London & South Western Railway, shorn of everything west of Exeter and a few of the branches. It still has the same uneasy relationship with the Brighton company to the east. This is a 584-route-mile operation.

Today, the inner suburban services via Wimbledon virtually all run at 2tph, as indeed do the Windsor line services. The only exceptions are where 1tph stops short, such as the Waterloo to Weybridge service at Staines, or the 2tph fast Epsom services which are projected to Dorking. These connect at Epsom with SWT's West Croydon to Guildford service. The Hounslow loop service is again reinstated to run as such.

In the outer suburban area, regular interval services are also commonplace, with variations such as one of the Alton services terminating at Farnham, and half the Guildford-Aldershot-Ascot service at Aldershot. But change is appearing, in that there are now four trains per hour between

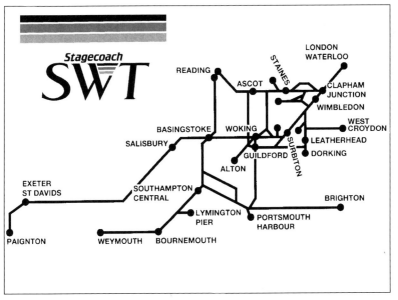

Above:
South West Trains 4VEP unit Class 423/0 No 3417 approaches Clapham Junction on the up slow line, 28 September 1997. The train is the 09.20 Alton to Waterloo. A Plasser and Theurer tamper stands on the up fast line, awaiting some reballasting to be completed.

Waterloo and Reading. These have different stopping patterns, and one is routed via Hounslow.

On the Portsmouth main line, a 3tph service mix of fast, semi-fast and slow has an additional stopping train beyond Guildford to Haslemere only. On the West of England main line, departures are hourly, but some trains terminate short at Gillingham or Yeovil Junction, whereas a few are projected to Paignton.

The Bournemouth line sees an hourly Weymouth, an hourly Poole and an hourly Southampton operation. These are filled in with two stopping trains to Basingstoke, one of which is extended to serve intermediate stations and forms a service to Portsmouth Harbour via Fareham. Other trains serve intermediate stations between Winchester and Brockenhurst alternate hours, while the self-contained Lymington Pier branch has a 2tph service. There is also an hourly Brockenhurst-Wareham service.

Other railways use parts of the Bournemouth line, whether from Victoria and along the coast to Bournemouth as with Connex South Central, or to gain access from the Midlands like Virgin Cross Country. An innovation by SWT was a 1tph Brighton, Worthing, Havant, Winchester, Basingstoke service, some of which are extended on to Reading.

Service provision is in the hands of Class 455

units for the inner services and, apart from the Class 442 Wessex Electrics, elderly CIG, BEP and VEP stock for the outer electric operations. The Exeter line has the Class 159s, based at their own Salisbury depot; electric stock is based at Wimbledon, Fratton and Bournemouth.

The franchise was let to Stagecoach Holdings plc for seven years, with the new owners starting operations on 4 February 1996. Subsidy from the Franchising Director was £63.4 million in 1997/8, down to £45.2 million in 2001/2, the last complete year of the franchise.

The Franchise Plan of South West Trains requires the company:
• to improve Passenger Charter reliability by 1% and punctuality by 2%
• to introduce dedicated bus feeder services with through ticketing; links are operating Bordon-Liphook and Romsey-Winchester
• to combine rail and bus information services
• to invest in station improvements and security measures.

South West Trains runs an extensive service which requires a hefty 19.6 million train miles a year. The intensity of suburban use is reflected in the 18 miles average journey length, worth £2.94 in passenger revenue. Train occupancy rates at an average of 104 people are good.

Main line service reliability was 99.2%, better than the target 99.0%, but punctuality was 88.3% against an unexciting target of 89.0%. The suburban services achieved service reliability of 98.7% (target: 99.0%) and punctuality was 91.6% against a target of 92.0%.

Annual figures conceal the four-weekly results: in early spring 1997, South West Trains' reliability dropped to the point that over 5% of suburban services were being cancelled. Too many drivers had enthusiastically accepted a redundancy package. OPRAF issued a draft enforcement order, but performance quickly improved.

The indigenous commuter traffic for both inner and outer services is characterised by a mature and prosperous ABC1 market, while Haslemere has the highest number of first class season ticket holders in the country. Such, anyway, are the conclusions of the Department of Transport. One can almost hear the slamming of the doors on the VEP units.

Commuting is augmented by both business use and leisure traffic, with attractions such as Windsor Castle, Winchester, Salisbury and Portsmouth among the destinations reached. The railway also serves some major shopping centres at Guildford, Kingston and Southampton.

While SWT has launched a modest offensive against the Brighton line in the West Croydon-Epsom-Leatherhead-Dorking corridor, the Bournemouth line with its access to Reading seems more likely to produce new service patterns. Line capacity is one restraint; this particularly affects the number of trains which can access Waterloo at busy times.

Heathrow Airport is also near the line between Feltham, Ashford and Staines. There is, as they say, scope for a more productive rail involvement, with or without Terminal 5. In the shorter term, this will result in a rebuilt Feltham station with a dedicated bus link.

Thames Trains Ltd

Thames Trains runs at the London end of the Great Western main line, and makes extensive use of the relief lines which continue as far as Didcot. This is not inner suburban traffic; the destinations served are as far afield as Bedwyn (66.50 miles from Paddington), Hereford (149.75 miles) and Stratford-upon-Avon (121.50 miles). These are sizeable distances, for which the high specification Class 165 series units are reasonably suitable.

The hourly service pattern from London is as follows:

- 2tph to Greenford, via Ealing Broadway
- 2tph Ealing Broadway and all stations to Slough
- 2tph principal stations to Reading, alternately extended to Oxford
- 1tph stations to Bedwyn

Together with a 1tph all stations service from Reading to Oxford and 2tph Reading to Basingstoke, this covers most of the main line. There are also the self-contained services on the branches to Windsor & Eton Central (2tph) and Marlow (1tph). For Henley-on-Thames (1tph), off-peak services run through to Reading.

A further group of services is provided towards Gatwick Airport from Reading. An hourly fast service is supplemented with an hourly stopping service to Shalford, one station beyond Guildford. A further service on alternate hours calls at intermediate stations from Guildford to Redhill.

Thames Trains' long distance 'Turbo Express' services leave Paddington at xx.48; all proceed to Oxford. From there, successive trains in the midday period continue to Hereford, Banbury, Great Malvern and Stratford-upon-Avon. The last of these is a five per day service, and provides most of the trains over the Leamington Spa to Stratford-upon-Avon line. The last train back to Paddington leaves at the innovative time of 23.15, arriving in the London terminus at 01.24. Interestingly, on Saturday nights, this service is provided by a bus which is actually 3min faster to Oxford, arriving at 00.16, but gets into Paddington at an even more dismal 02.35.

The Thames Trains fleet consists of a mix of two- and three-car Class 165/0 and 165/1 units, plus the Class 166 build of 21 three-car air-conditioned sets. All are based at Reading.

The company operates over 363 route miles.

Below:
Thames Trains operates Networker Turbos, some of which, like this example, are fitted with air-conditioning and used on the longer distance services. No 166203 will be departing from Paddington to Oxford in this October 1997 view.

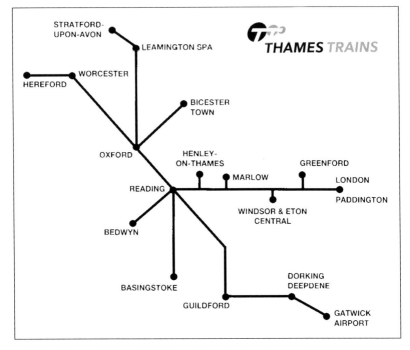

The franchise was let for a period of 7 years 6 months to Victory Railway Holdings plc, and took effect from 13 October 1996. The company is now wholly owned by the Go-Ahead Group plc. Support from the Franchising Director falls from £34.2 million in 1997/8 to zero in 2003/4, the last year of the franchise.

The Franchise Plan submitted by Thames Trains requires the company:

- to run at least the pre-franchising train mileage for 2.5 years minimum
- to increase the weekday Oxford-Paddington service to half-hourly in 1998, to provide additional services between Thatcham, Theale, Newbury and Paddington, and additional Paddington to Maidenhead off-peak fast services from 1999
- to invest £4 million on station facilities including security and information systems, for completion in 1998.

Thames Trains runs a substantial 7.5 million train miles a year, with an average passenger journey length of 17 miles for which a fare of £1.94 is paid. The mean occupancy level is 63 passenger miles per train mile.

Service performance in 1996/7 found reliability at 99.3% (target 99.0%) and punctuality at 93.7% against a target of 91.0%.

The operator of a suburban service always has the opportunity to extend its geographical area of interest. Thus, Turbo Express to Hereford can be quite competitive in overall timings with an IC125 to Newport and changing trains there. Again, neither Bedwyn, Basingstoke nor Gatwick is at the end of their respective lines.

On the other hand, Reading is accessed by other operators, who also provide services over links such as those to Basingstoke and Leamington Spa, and beyond at each end.

Perhaps the most interesting future opportunities will come from infrastructure investments. Potentially, three major developments are in the offing: first is the Heathrow Express Railway, especially if Terminal 5 is built and the severe capacity constraints anticipated in the short term within Heathrow can be alleviated; second are the possibilities represented by CrossRail, should that scheme resurface; and the third is the potential of the Great Western main line for upgrading.

Thameslink Rail Ltd

Thameslink grew out of the foresight of the Greater London Council, which commissioned a detailed study of the case for the reopening of the Snow Hill tunnel between Farringdon and Blackfriars. The project came to fruition in 1988. Today, we have Thameslink, operating from Bedford and Luton, through central London and on to destinations such as Gatwick Airport and Brighton. The route network is 140 miles.

Linking together two separate railways has its own problems, not least the level of traffic already in existence south of the Thames. Today's Thameslink is constrained unduly by capacity limitations in general, and junction limitations in particular; the Thameslink 2000 scheme hopes in due course to overcome these. What does Thameslink presently offer?

The single most serious limitation at present is the inability to find train paths through London Bridge in the peak, involving as it does access from Blackfriars and then crossing to the Brighton lines on the flat in the London Bridge area. The

Below:
Farringdon Junction at the east end of the station has platforms extending a little beyond it. Seen here is the line to Moorgate (left) and to Blackfriars (right), with a Class 319 unit disappearing towards the latter. Also, there is a steep downhill gradient at the western end of Farringdon station, to allow Thameslink trains to pass below the Metropolitan. It is this shortage of available space which makes it necessary to close the Moorgate branch with the Thameslink 2000 plans if 12-car trains are to be accommodated.

alternatives for trains from the Midland lines, both of which are used, are either:
- to divert to, and terminate at, Moorgate, or
- to run via Tulse Hill and reach the Brighton line at Streatham Common.

Trains southwards can of course start their journeys at London Bridge.

The peak service at present thus bears only a limited relationship to that at other times. During the day, Thameslink offers 8tph:
- 2tph run from Bedford via London Bridge to East Croydon, Gatwick Airport and Brighton
- 2tph run from Luton to Brighton
- 2tph run from Bedford to Sutton, via Wimbledon
- 2tph run from Luton to Sutton, direct.

Trains approaching Sutton direct continue on the loop back by the 'other' route to Blackfriars and beyond, and vice versa. The services shown have a variety of stopping patterns, with trains from Bedford running nonstop between St Albans and King's Cross Thameslink. Best publicly advertised journey time over that section is 19min for the 20.18 miles.

All services are provided by a fleet of 40 Class 319/0 and 26 319/1 dual voltage units; only the latter have first class accommodation. This does make stock working more difficult, and while the Brighton trains might be expected to have first class, the timetable shows that some do not. This would seem to make first class travel something of a lottery, even assuming that units do not stray from their booked workings. All units are maintained at Selhurst, which is also the home for the Class 319 units leased by Connex South Central.

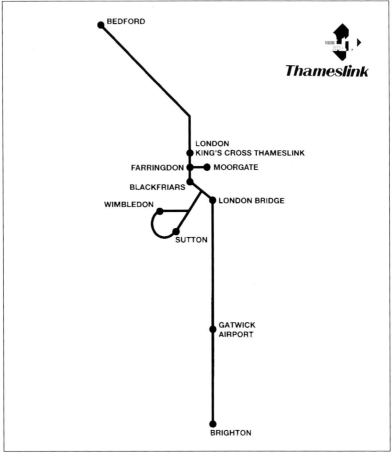

BEDFORD

Thameslink

LONDON KING'S CROSS THAMESLINK

FARRINGDON — **MOORGATE**

BLACKFRIARS

WIMBLEDON — **LONDON BRIDGE**

SUTTON

GATWICK AIRPORT

BRIGHTON

The franchise was awarded to GOVIA plc for 7 years 1 month which began operations on 2 March 1997. In the first full year of 1997/8, the Franchising Director was paying a subsidy of £2.5 million, but this quickly becomes a premium to be paid by the operator. This reaches £28.4 million in 2003/4, the last year of the franchise.

The Franchise Plan provides for Thameslink as follows:

- to operate at least the pre-franchise train miles for the length of the franchise
- to introduce a new fare for groups
- to undertake an internal upgrade of the rolling stock
- to integrate bus and rail services at Brighton,

Luton and St Albans and provide a bus feeder Dunstable-Luton

- to invest £0.9 million on station improvements and passenger security
- to introduce Passenger Charter upgrade, with punctuality rising from 89% to 92% by 2003.

Thameslink runs 6.2 million train miles a year; average passenger journey length is 21 miles. This is worth £3.04 in revenue and the passenger occupation rate at 93 passenger miles per train mile is close to the national average. In Charter terms, service reliability was 98.7% for 1996/7 (99.0% target) and punctuality was 88.1% against a target of 89.0%.

Thameslink 2000 plans envisage the feeding in also of Great Northern services from stations to Peterborough and to King's Lynn, while in the south services will be projected as now, plus as far east as Ashford and as far west as Littlehampton. The maximum throughput of the T2000 central section through City Thameslink is put at 24tph.

Operations will be severely disrupted as and when T2000 work takes place, while the construction of the Channel Tunnel Rail Link may also bring increased traffic to the Midland line and competition in Kent. There are provisions for early termination of the Thameslink franchise, depending on construction timescales.

Virgin Trains (Cross Country)

The Cross Country service network is essentially what was the non-London InterCity business, built around what were once the locomotive-hauled northeast-southwest services such as Newcastle-Bristol, plus later additions like Manchester-Poole. Essentially, all were (and are) centred on that linchpin of the railway network, Birmingham New Street.

Today, Cross Country services originate on both the East Coast and West Coast main lines, sometimes from as far north as Aberdeen or Glasgow. South of Birmingham their destinations include Swansea, Penzance, Poole and Brighton, as well as Paddington and, surprisingly, Ramsgate! This last justifies its inclusion by being the destination of a summer Saturday service from Birmingham New Street and return, operating on six occasions a year in July and August.

Service provision resembles a four-pronged web, with services reducing in frequency as distances from Birmingham increase. Starting from New Street, the main thrust is to Sheffield and Newcastle, with about half the total service operating via Wakefield Westgate and Leeds rather than via Doncaster. North of Newcastle, the service is in the residual category, since

Edinburgh trains are mostly routed via Preston.

The WCML operation, to Glasgow and Aberdeen as well as Edinburgh, divides to run a couple of services via Manchester, but most continue on the electrified main line via Crewe and Warrington. Some services terminate at Liverpool Lime Street, and rather more at Manchester Piccadilly.

To the south of Birmingham in the southeasterly direction, apart from a few trains which terminate at Birmingham International, all reach Reading. Rather more than half the services reverse, to continue to Bournemouth or Poole. Others finish up at Paddington, apart from a couple for Brighton. On the line to the southwest, a third terminates at Bristol Temple Meads and most of the remainder at Plymouth, though a few workings reach Penzance. Other destinations reached via Bristol are Paignton and Swansea, but both for a single daily train only. Summer Saturdays are a different matter, as already suggested, with destinations such as Newquay featuring. The total number of trains per day is around 15 from Birmingham New Street on each of the main corridor groups, apart from a rather heavier service to Manchester Piccadilly.

As always with an operation where the infrastructure used is electrified only in part, and not even all on the same system at that, the choice is between locomotive-hauled stock and time-consuming traction changes, and diesel operation throughout. The need for en route reversal, or otherwise, is another factor. Virgin Cross Country operates a fleet of InterCity 125 trains plus Class 47 diesels and Class 86 electrics for the hauled stock.

Further Cross Country services are those to and from Manchester Airport, from Edinburgh. These, operated by one of Virgin Cross Country's five Class 158 Sprinter Express units, run via Carlisle. Occasionally, these services are combined

Right:
Virgin Cross Country has the most widespread network of any TOC. HST power car No 43063 *Maiden Voyage* is at the rear of the 'Wessex Scot', the 09.10 Edinburgh-Bournemouth on 22 November 1997. Despite the advertising of a recommended but decidedly West Midlands product on the nearby pub, the location is Wigan North Western.

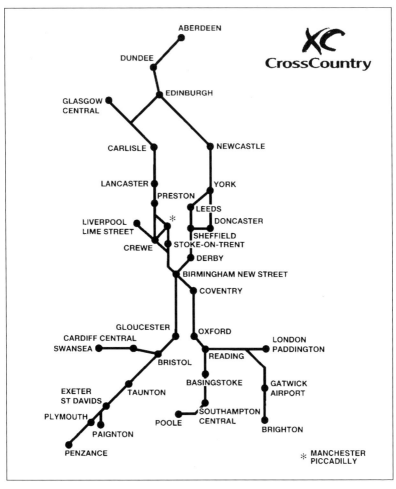

CrossCountry

ABERDEEN
DUNDEE
EDINBURGH
GLASGOW CENTRAL
NEWCASTLE
CARLISLE
LANCASTER
YORK
PRESTON
LEEDS
DONCASTER
LIVERPOOL LIME STREET
*
SHEFFIELD
CREWE
STOKE-ON-TRENT
DERBY
BIRMINGHAM NEW STREET
COVENTRY
GLOUCESTER
OXFORD
CARDIFF CENTRAL
LONDON PADDINGTON
SWANSEA
READING
BRISTOL
BASINGSTOKE
GATWICK AIRPORT
EXETER ST DAVIDS
TAUNTON
PLYMOUTH
POOLE
SOUTHAMPTON CENTRAL
PAIGNTON
BRIGHTON
PENZANCE
* MANCHESTER PICCADILLY

with those of North Western Trains (NWT). Thus, the 12.03 Virgin service from Edinburgh combines with the 14.00 NWT service from Barrow at Bolton, from where they depart as one train to Manchester Airport. Bicycles cannot be conveyed on the Virgin portion according to the timetable, but there is no restriction on the NWT unit!

There is a token Virgin service diverging at Wigan for Liverpool Lime Street. Total Cross Country operation is over 1,657 route miles.

The franchise was awarded to Virgin Rail Group Ltd for 15 years on 5 January 1997, the extended period being in recognition of the company's substantial commitments made as part of its Franchise Plan. Support from the Franchising Director of £115.9 million in 1997/8 will decline to zero by 2009/10 and will result in a premium payment by the franchisee of £5.1 million in 2010/11, the last full year of the franchise.

The Franchise Plan commits Virgin Trains to:
- establish dedicated low cost telephone central reservations and a sales facility (completed in April 1997)
- introduce a pilot group fare for two or more

people travelling together, established initially between Birmingham and Manchester in either direction
- improve passenger information at 100 stations served
- procure an experimental university bus link
- replace by May 2002 existing loco-hauled stock with a brand-new flexible fleet of 128 high speed DMU vehicles, and by May 2004 the current IC125 rolling stock with 24 high quality seven-car DMUs.

The Cross Country fleet operates about 9.2 million train miles a year, from that measure making Cross Country about an average size Train Operating Company. However, as might be expected from a business which includes the longest continuous runs on Railtrack such as the 704 miles between Penzance and Dundee, the average passenger journey length is a healthy 100 miles. Trains also have a reasonably high occupancy rate of 131 passengers on average, while the revenue per passenger is £9.82. Although this is less than for the top-earning companies, Cross Country has virtually no opportunity to tap the London business market, albeit that it is well placed to benefit from Birmingham traffic. The consequential lack of first class traffic depresses earnings, and the company's IC125 fleet has only one first class trailer car. The main business is long distance leisure travel, plus some modest commuting flows.

Operating performance for reliability was recorded as 99.5% in 1996/7, better than the 99.0% target, but punctuality at 86.7% (89.0% target) put the company at equal 59th out of the 62 routes in the league. Virgin Cross Country does of course have to interwork with many other passenger companies; there is also freight and, as the Department of Transport has delicately observed, 'there are many individual freight flows on the InterCity Cross Country routes'. Whatever the reason, punctuality in 1996/7 clearly left a lot to be desired.

As to the future, Virgin Cross Country operates over a wide range of routes. Together, these allow plenty of development scope, with the possible additions of other destinations such as those which are served during the summer period only. On the other hand, most routes are at least in part covered by the services of other operators; inter-availability of tickets is likely to be an important requirement.

The rolling stock replacement programme is bound in with that for the West Coast main line.

Virgin West Coast Trains

The first main line terminus in London was Euston, opened in 1837 as the terminus of the London & Birmingham Railway. The original station would not be recognisable today, after the massive 1960s-style rebuilding undertaken as part of the electrification of much of the network radiating from it.

Yet the priority given to the West Coast main line in the massive investment programme outlined in the 1955 Modernisation Plan was surely right. This is a main line railway, whose owners were not much interested in suburban traffic; there was more profitable business to pursue. Indeed, commuting has never reached the epic proportions enjoyed (if that is the right word) by the south and east of London.

Today, Euston's major traffics are with the West Midlands and the north. The hourly midday service pattern offers the following, principal calling places only mentioned:
- xx.00 Manchester Piccadilly, via Stoke-on-Trent
- xx.05 Liverpool Lime Street, via Stafford
- xx.15 Birmingham New Street, via Coventry and Birmingham International
- xx.35 Preston, via Crewe; alternate trains extended to Glasgow Central
- xx.45 Wolverhampton, via Coventry, Birmingham International and New Street

During the business peaks, some additional trains are run, but supplementation is kept to a minimum. Additional services are those to Holyhead in connection with boat sailings. Services operate over 676 route miles.

The principal rolling stock consists of a mixture of Class 86/87/90 locomotives and coaching stock of the Mk 2 and Mk 3 air-conditioned varieties.

The franchise was let to Virgin Rail Group Ltd for a period of 15 years and started operation on Sunday 9 March 1997. The support profile shows a £76.8 million payment by the Franchising Director in 1997/8, turning into a small premium in 2002/3 and rising to as much as £202.2 million in 2010/11, the last full year of the franchise.

The Franchising Plan of Virgin West Coast Trains is extensive in its commitments to:
- invest approximately £500 million in high speed tilting rolling stock by 2002
- significantly reduce journey times
- refurbish Mk 2 and Mk 3 rolling stock
- provide integrated train-taxi facilities, a dedicated sales centre and Internet bookings.

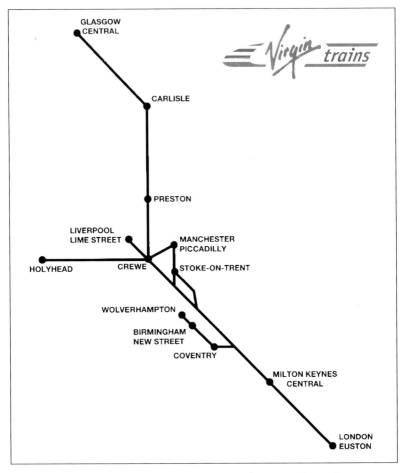

Virgin West Coast Trains cover 10.3 million train miles a year. The other indicators show a similar pattern to GNER, in that the average passenger journey on Virgin West Coast is 137 miles, for which the average fare paid is £16.85. Train occupancy rates are an average of 176.

Performance has been less than satisfactory. Results for 1996/7 are broken down as follows:

Given that trains in the InterCity category are defined as punctual if they arrive up to 10min late, the records show that travellers on the North West and Scottish services had a 20% chance of being more than 10min late. This is compiled after around 10min 'recovery time' has been added to the timetable for the final 17 miles between Watford Junction and Euston for up trains.

Area	Reliability	Target	Punctuality	Target
West Midlands	99.2%	99.0%	86.0%	90.0%
North West	99.6%	99.0%	80.8%	90.0%
Scottish	99.8%	99.0%	79.1%	90.0%

The CRUCC commented that 'the average annual figure on this route conceals some truly awful performances early in the year', though acknowledging that there was a sustained improvement in later months and that the overall result was better than in the previous year. Virgin West Coast Trains came bottom of the punctuality league.

On the WCML, there are outer suburban services parallel to the Virgin West Coast services to Birmingham. London to Birmingham itself, which includes Snow Hill, is of course possible by a number of routes, all of which are beginning to offer different fares. Further north there are also other operators whose services can or do impinge on Virgin Trains' operation; be it not forgotten that the Scottish sleeper traffic now brings ScotRail to Euston.

Wales & West Passenger Trains Ltd

The West Country has always been a difficult area for rail, split between the Great Western and London & South Western companies, and without any real industrial base. In South Wales, all becomes very rural once Swansea has been passed.

In Wales & West's territory, there are no PTEs, while the Cardiff valleys have been franchised separately. There is thus much more emphasis on

Above:
Virgin Rail hires five Class 158 units for services from the north of Preston bound for Manchester Airport. No 158748 arrives at Carlisle on 11 November 1997 with the 12.03 from Edinburgh. This service combines at Bolton with the 14.08 from Windermere, operated by North Western Trains.

the inter-urban and rural operations. Indeed, urban work is confined to minor routes such as the hourly Severn Beach branch (partly replaced by bus beyond Avonmouth), the 2tph on the Exeter St David's to Exmouth line and the relatively recent Cardiff Central to Maesteg and Bridgend to Swansea services, both at 1tph.

Some inter-urban services are marketed under the Alphaline banner, which offers a Class 158 with trolley service, reservable seats and card telephones:
• Cardiff Central, Bristol Temple Meads, Salisbury, Southampton Central and Portsmouth Harbour
• Cardiff Central, Hereford, Shrewsbury, Crewe and Manchester Piccadilly

Other services include:
• Bristol Temple Meads, Westbury and Weymouth
• Cardiff Central to Weston-super-Mare, some projected to Paignton, Plymouth or Penzance
• Swindon, Gloucester and Cheltenham Spa
• Swansea, Carmarthen, thence to Milford Haven or Pembroke Dock

97

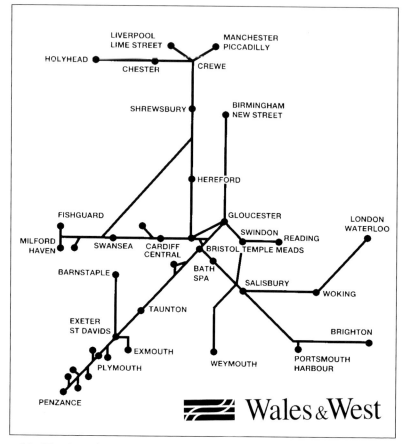

- Bristol Temple Meads, Weston-super-Mare, some projected to Taunton
- Exeter Central to Barnstaple
- Exeter Central to Paignton
- Shrewsbury to Crewe
- Swansea, Llanelli, Llandrindod and Shrewsbury

But service frequencies are often low, with 1tph at best in this last group, and in the case of the Central Wales line, only four trains per day.

Other limited services do run, such as the 06.02 (weekdays) Carmarthen to Waterloo, in connection with Eurostar services, the 06.00 Portsmouth Harbour to Liverpool Lime Street via Cardiff (Mondays to Fridays) and the 14.51 (Sundays) Holyhead to Carmarthen.

Perhaps the most remarkable of these services is the 07.59 Manchester Piccadilly to Waterloo via Newport and the 15.17 back. This return service avoids Newport by use of the direct curve.

Noticeably, there are only what might be termed 'fill-in' services by Wales & West beyond Plymouth, in the gaps left by Great Western and Virgin Cross Country services. Here, the main role of Wales & West is to operate the five branches, whose Monday to Friday winter service is shown below.

Service intervals are not regular, principally because of the importance of connecting with main line trains, in both directions if possible, at the junction for the branch. Most branches are, effectively, self-contained. The main exception is St Ives, where the unit makes alternate trips to and

• Plymouth and Gunnislake	8 trains/day	14.75 miles	44min
• Liskeard and Looe	10 trains/day	8.75 miles	25-30min
• Par to Newquay	4 trains/day	20.75 miles	52min
• Truro to Falmouth	13 trains/day	12.25 miles	22min
• St Erth to St Ives	16 trains/day	4.25 miles	10-13min

from Penzance rather than only to the junction station of St Erth.

Wales & West operates over 1,568 route miles of network.

The franchise for Wales & West was let to Prism Rail plc for a period of 7 years 6 months, with operations starting on 13 October 1996. The subsidy profile shows the company receiving £72.9 million from the Franchising Director in 1997/8, reducing to £39.2 million in 2003/4, the last year of the franchise.

The Franchise Plan key commitments are:
- to operate at least the pre-franchise train miles for the whole franchise term
- to refurbish the whole of the 78 vehicle Class 158 fleet by April 1999
- to restaff selective stations (delivered at Newquay, Falmouth Town, Filton Abbey Wood, Severn Tunnel Junction, Ludlow, Leominster, Tenby, Whitland)
- to equip nine stations with CCTV and develop Park and Ride at three of them by October 1998.

At 11.7 million, Wales & West operates rather more train miles than does Virgin West Coast. With a substantial 35 miles as the average journey length, the fares changing hands are an above average £3.71. At 39 passenger miles per train mile, this measure is the same as Central Trains.

Services are operated by the usual mix of modern diesel units. This includes the Class 143 Pacer units used on the services sponsored by the former Mid-Glamorgan and West Glamorgan County Councils and owned by them. Maintenance is carried out at Cardiff Canton.

Reliability is generally slightly above target, and only in Avon did punctuality fail to reach the required level.

Area	Reliability	Target	Punctuality	Target
Western Express	99.2%	99.0%	92.8%	90.0%
South Cotswold	99.6%	99.0%	93.3%	90.0%
West and Central Wales	99.0%	99.0%	94.5%	90.0%
Avon	99.2%	99.0%	90.3%	90.0%
Devon	99.5%	99.0%	95.0%	90.0%
Cornwall	98.3%	99.0%	97.7%	90.0%

Wales & West operates services to Maesteg, seen here on 10 October 1992 with No 150219 and the 11.20 arrival from Cardiff Central. Car park usage is quite impressive, but there is also a nearby supermarket.

Much of the operation is clearly seasonal, which is a constraint in itself. However, the urban traffic problem remains, whether in the larger cities served by Wales & West or the smaller ones. There is much to be gained by making the maximum use possible of an existing infrastructure to provide services into the towns of the area, and several station openings have been commissioned in recent years.

Perhaps the greater problem for Wales & West is the priority which it can expect when train paths in areas like Bristol are being allocated and, in the more rural parts of its operating area, how its services should relate to those of the InterCity companies. Are main line connections more important or less important than local travel needs? Whose business gains (or suffers)? Who is really in a position to resolve any insoluble differences of opinion, with no British Railways Board to bang heads together?

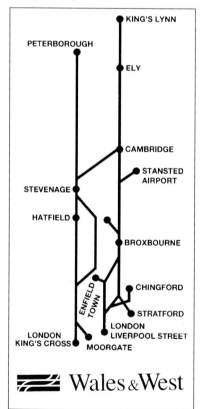

West Anglia Great Northern Railway Ltd

The West Anglia Great Northern (WAGN) is a combination of the less glamorous side of Liverpool Street's operations and the more limited suburban operations on the GN out of King's Cross and also Moorgate. Unlike the situation south of the Thames, the use of three London termini is not accompanied by extensive interconnections between the lines approaching them.

Services mostly operate on a half-hourly frequency, thus:

From Liverpool Street:
• Enfield Town
• Cheshunt via Seven Sisters
• Chingford (3tph)
• Hertford East via Lea Valley
• principal stations to Bishop's Stortford via Lea Valley, with 1tph extended to Cambridge
• Stansted Airport, calling at Tottenham Hale and, alternate trains only, also at Bishop's Stortford

From Moorgate:
• Welwyn Garden City
• Hertford North, with 1tph extended to Letchworth

From King's Cross:
• Cambridge, nonstop   1tph
• Cambridge, nonstop and stations to King's Lynn   1tph
• Finsbury Park, Stevenage and principal stations to Peterborough, alternately principal stations to Cambridge   2tph
• principal stations to Hitchin, extended alternately all stations to Peterborough or Cambridge   2tph

WAGN's outer suburban services in particular are tightly timed. Pride of place must go to the King's Cross to Cambridge services, which cover the 58 miles in 49min, but King's Lynn and Peterborough both have services timed at an average 60mph. This has benefits for the operators as well as passengers, since stock and staff utilisation can be that much better.

The Stansted SkyTrain takes 41 or 42min for the 37.50 miles from Liverpool Street to Stansted Airport.

Inevitably, inner services have a less sparkling performance. For instance, to travel the 10.75 miles from Liverpool Street to Enfield Town, calling at all 14 stations, takes 30min. Moorgate to Enfield Chase takes 1min less. This points,

Above:
The Class 365 Networker Express units are dual electrical power systems, although not as yet used as such. Operating on West Anglia Great Northern, No 365526 arrives at Ely on 8 November 1997 with the 09.28 King's Lynn to King's Cross.

perhaps, to the economics of inner suburban operations compared with the longer distance journeys. Asset utilisation is poorer, costs increase due to the greater number of stations which need to be maintained and, probably, staffed as well, while revenue yield per passenger is relatively modest. Of course, if there are lots of passengers...

The whole of the 257 route miles operated are electrified, including the 99.25 miles out to King's Lynn. There is a third rail section from Drayton Park to Moorgate, for which the dual voltage Class 313 sets are used. All operation is in the hands of multiple-units based at Hornsey. This comprises some of Class 317 for the outer suburban services and parts of Classes 313/315 for the inner operations. There are also the five Class 322 Stansted Express units, and the 25 new Class 365 Networker Express units with dual voltage capability.

The West Anglia Great Northern franchise was awarded to Prism Rail plc for a period of 7 years 3 months and commenced on 5 January 1997. Support from the Franchising Director, £54.9 million in 1997/8, falls to zero and results in a premium payment by the franchisee of £25.5 million in the last year of 2003/4.

The Franchise Plan key commitments include the following:

- to operate pre-franchise train miles for the first three years of franchise and Cambridge Cruiser service throughout
- to invest c£14 million in station facilities,

information systems and rolling stock refurbishment
- to offer discounts on Peterborough-London tickets (delivered)
- to raise Passenger Charter targets to 93% reliability and 99% punctuality from April 1998.

With annual train miles at 10.2 million, WAGN actually exceeds Great North Eastern Railway. But there the comparisons stop; WAGN's passengers travel no more than an average 18 miles and spend £2.66 in the process. Average train occupancy at 91 is in the same league as operations such as Thameslink Rail or Thames Trains.

In performance terms, service reliability for Great Northern was 98.8% for 1996/7 (target 99.0%) and punctuality was 89.3% against a target of 91.0%. On the West Anglia side, reliability was 99.3% (target 98.5%) and punctuality was 94.4% against the same target of 91.0%.

The WAGN Railway faces substantial change in the medium to longer term. This is as a result of factors as diverse as:

- the traffic which might be generated by the Channel Tunnel Rail Link at St Pancras
- the construction of Thameslink 2000, into which some (but only some) of the GN trains could be diverted; and
- the growth in the use of Stansted Airport.

The general view seems to be that WAGN has a relatively stable market, which expanded in the last decade following the King's Lynn electrification and that of the ECML to Peterborough. High commuting growth is likely to occur due to the recession ending.

1 British Railways Board Annual Report and Accounts, 1993/4.

2 *Trains Illustrated*, July 1958 p382

The Freight Railway

While the passenger railway may have broadly maintained volumes over the years, rail freight certainly has not. In 1996, the total freight traffics forwarded by rail were roundly 100 million tonnes. Compare that with the early days of British Railways when, in 1948, traffic levels were nearly three times greater. The commodity mix then looked as shown in the table below:

For those who wonder about the tonnage of livestock, the report conscientiously informs the reader that the tonnage equivalent of the number of horses, cattle, sheep, pigs, etc is computed on a standard basis, although this is not disclosed.

But, even when converted into volumes as expressed in ton kilometres, the average length of rail haul in 1948 at 115km was only a little shorter than that of the 133km today. Meanwhile, road freight has expanded tremendously, now exceeding rail tonne/km volumes by a factor of 10.

Industrial changes are at least partly to blame, notably the significant restructuring in the traditional core businesses of coal and steel. This itself reflects the changing importance of these businesses to the British economy, as well as the railway's market share. Rail's past dependence on these areas is illustrated by the 1948 results. As a commodity, coal on its own in 1948 accounted for half as much again as the total freight tonnages carried by rail today.

The method of operation has of course undergone enormous change. While the late 1950s and early 1960s saw the building of numerous large marshalling yards to speed the movement of freight wagons, the businesses themselves were opting more and more for movement by trainload. In this era the merry-go-round (mgr) movement of power station coal from pit head to power station was introduced, as was Freightliner, while wagon load traffic continued to decline.

Local goods yards and many private sidings were closed. The wagon fleet was equipped with continuous brakes, while their individual size and capacity of the wagons increased with new builds.

The Speedlink wagon load business was closed in 1991, and the British Railways Board's freight activity from then was managed through two separate organisations. Trainload Freight, itself subdivided into the four profit centres of coal, metals, construction and petroleum, dealt essentially with bulk loads from private siding to private siding traffic.

Ideally, such freight flows should meet the following requirements:

- volumes should be significant, typically above 100,000 tonnes a year;
- trains should run from source to destination with no intermediate marshalling;
- loading and unloading should take place at fixed origin and destination points;
- movements should be regular, ie daily or even several times a day; and
- full use should be made of locomotive power, to maximise the train's carrying capacity.

Trainload Freight customers include National Power, British Steel, AMEY Roadstone and Shell UK. Their commitment and that of others to rail has included investing £1.5 billion in terminals and over £500 million in wagon fleets.

The other company, Railfreight Distribution (RfD), catered for longer distance general freight. Notably, this included containers, automotive traffic and international freight services. RfD included the Freightliner operation, although this was subsequently separated out before sale.

Intermodal services operate in two distinct spheres. Deepsea is concentrated on the ports of Felixstowe, Southampton, Liverpool and Tilbury, and distributes over 400,000 deepsea port

Freight Train Traffic Originating, 1948[1]			
	'000 tons	%	av length of haul (km)
Merchandise Minerals (bricks, iron ore,	54,780	19.8	187
limestone, pig iron, roadstone)	59,280	21.5	122
Coal and coke	161,145	58.4	88
Livestock	912	0.3	na
Total	276,117	100.0	115

containers a year, or around 35% of the market. The other is the UK/Irish business, centred on the Port of Liverpool, operating a road/rail combination which links with daily sailings to Ireland. Intermodal services are justified where volumes are insufficient to support trainload services, or are physically impossible. Typically, road or ship will bring containers to terminals, where they are trunked to other terminals for distribution.

Importantly, compared with trainload, intermodal terminal handling operations represent a significant element of the total movement and therefore of its cost. Also, they necessarily carry a time and reliability penalty. The combination of these factors suggests that a trunk movement of 320-400km is needed to overcome this competitive disadvantage.

To which may be added the Channel Tunnel, which greatly enlarges the directly served markets and the distances required to make intermodal a success. Manchester to Munich represents a 40hr rail journey, compared with 54hr by road over a distance of (roundly) 1,570km. There are no hauls within Britain of anything like that distance; even London to Glasgow is a mere 640km.

The subsequent restructuring of the railfreight businesses into a number of new businesses at Government behest was intended 'to increase the opportunities for competition, lower entry barriers, and focus operations more closely on the needs of the customers and localities served'.[2]

Consequently, during 1994/5 the Trainload Freight business was split into three. This was broadly along geographical lines. The three companies were:
- Loadhaul (based on TLF North East)
- Mainline Freight (TLF South East)
- Transrail Freight (TLF West).

These companies also absorbed part of the domestic non-container business of Railfreight Distribution, as well as taking responsibility for the provision of all rail services in support of BR Infrastructure Services (BRIS). Although based initially in defined areas, all of these businesses were able to operate anywhere in the country. This amounted to an 11,600 track mile network.

The result of the geographical split was that Loadhaul had the benefit of petroleum traffics from refineries on Humberside, Mainline Freight inherited substantial aggregate traffics, while Transrail Freight had the South Wales steel traffic. All shared in power station coal movements; the location of the power station rather than the originating point of the coal determined the initial allocation between companies.

The new freight structure was, however, short lived. All three companies were sold together in February 1996 to English, Welsh and Scottish Railways Ltd (EWS), who had already bought Rail Express Systems (RES) in December 1995. This was to be followed by the sale of Railfreight Distribution to EWS, although this sale was to be protracted as a result of intervention from the European Commission.

English, Welsh and Scottish Railways Ltd is a sister company to Wisconsin Central (USA), Algoma Central (Canada) and Tranz Rail (New Zealand). Ed Burkhardt, EWS Chairman, has already made great play of the lessons which each of these companies can learn from the other. He has stressed, too, that this is not a one-way flow and the company is interested in achieving the best international practice. For instance, in a lecture to the Chartered Institute of Transport: 'We found Tranz Rail to be light years ahead of Wisconsin Central in use of single person train crews and radio-controlled shunting operations.' He also praised the Kiwis' equipment utilisation, door-to-door transit times, and their road/rail intermodal transfers. But Burkhardt does not underestimate the difficulties: 'The Tranz Rail ideas involve changes to managerial philosophy, marketing orientation and customer relations. Change in these areas is much more difficult to achieve than finding a better source of locomotive repair parts.'[3] The aim of EWS is to triple rail freight's market share in the next 10 years.

This left Freightliner alone to be bought by another rail freight company. Freightliner was sold to MBS Ltd, a management buy-out team who acquired the company in May 1996.

The table overleaf shows the structure of the freight industry in rolling stock asset terms, as it was in 1992:

It may be noted that the BR-owned wagon fleet was recorded as having reduced to 13,379 as at 31 March 1995. The comparison with the 1,165,166 wagons which it took to move the traffics of 1948 referred to earlier is quite remarkable.

The EWS fleet also includes locomotives and

Locomotive and wagon fleets by freight sector, July 1992				
Sector	Locomotives		Wagons (traffic vehicles only)	
	Main line	Shunters	BR owned	Privately owned
TLF Coal	220	42	9,987	200
TLF Construction	76		236	2,000
TLF Metals	95	107	3,610	500
TLF Petroleum	79		6	6,750
RfD Contract services			1,268	
RfD Other	254	226	42	4,000
Freightliner			1,336	
RES	109		796	—
Totals	833	375	17,281	13,450

wagons for internal user traffics, which are used for railway infrastructure materials handling. Services include resourcing and managing train operation, hauling materials from source to destination and transporting spoil and waste materials in specialist rolling stock. Also available are long-welded rail and cable-laying trains, and track inspection trains. EWS also handles the BR Telecommunications contract. BRT has its own fleet of Bescot-based Class 20 locomotives and wagons. These are maintained by EWS, who also undertake the planning and control of all BRT train movements throughout the country.

EWS thus had to reintegrate the three TLF companies and RES, with RfD still to come. Efforts have been concentrated on negotiating deals which are aimed at greater staff productivity and a new track access deal with Railtrack. Under this, EWS makes a minimum annual payment to Railtrack which is similar in total to the previous charge. A fixed charge makes up about three-quarters of this, with a charge per gross tonne mile after that.

The objective is to enable EWS to quote spot rates readily to customers for new freight flows. These could be priced at the margin should EWS so wish. Mail and what used to be called internal Civil Engineer's traffic are excluded from this arrangement.

Also in the news was the decision by the company to order an extensive new fleet of loco-motives and wagons. Somewhat disenchanted with the reliability of the locomotive fleets which they had inherited, EWS decided to order 250 new locomotives of Class 66 and 2,500 wagons. The Class 66s are close relations to the General Motors Class 59s already in service, since EWS have better things to do than spend much time on Railtrack certification. Delivery has been taking place from early 1998.

The wagons are being constructed by Thrall Europa at the reopened York carriage works, previously owned by Adtranz. In the first two years of the six-year agreement started in 1997, some 1,100 wagons will be bought. The first 200 are steel carriers, but the remaining types will be specified later according to the developing requirements of the freight business. All will be bogie wagons.

A further fleet of 30 Class 67 locomotives is being constructed in Spain by General Motors in partnership with GEC Alsthom. These 90-tonne locomotives are intended for 125mph operation and may be used on EWS's contract with Royal Mail. However, EWS confirm that they will be suitable for passenger operations. The Class 67s feature two-axle bogies and are fitted with electric train heating; delivery is expected from the end of 1998.

In traffic growth terms, much effort has been put into Enterprise, the less than trainload service pioneered by Transrail in 1994. In that year, Enterprise carried over 100,000 tonnes, and by 1997 this had risen to over 1 million tonnes. With the hoped-for future integration of RfD's Connectrail services to Europe, volumes will double. The number of terminals will have risen from 40 to 250.

By the end of 1997, EWS was moving 90 million tonnes of freight annually and running over 1,000 trains per day for 120 customers. A total of 830 locomotives and 19,000 wagons were wholly owned, without the involvement of leasing companies.

The services operate from 40 depots and 340 sidings and terminals. Like all statistics, though, there is always more to the story. Thus, on a lightly used line such as Dingwall to Kyle of Lochalsh, Railtrack has allowed loading to take place on the main line between trains.

What other opportunities exist? The development of transhipment points, not necessarily on quite such a small scale, may be used to support the terminals such as Corby, Daventry, Doncaster and Hams Hall. These four were all added to the network in 1996/7. Urban locations will be especially useful, allowing goods to be brought by rail into the heart of cities and towns.

The question of new terminals, the level of facilities required, what is essential and what is not and requirements for both rail and road access, need to be understood by all concerned. This includes planning authorities as well as site developers, potential users and operators.

The Freightliner business, loss making to the tune of £22 million annually at the time of its acquisition, has also been dependent on an attack on costs and volume growth. The business is firmly focused on the distribution of deepsea containers. The company operates around 88 trains per day, each of which has a capacity equivalent to around 60 HGVs.

The 13 terminals are located as follows:
- In the southeast at Barking, Felixstowe, Southampton, Thamesport and Tilbury
- In the Midlands and north at Birmingham, Cleveland, Leeds, Liverpool, Manchester and Seaforth
- In Wales and Scotland at Cardiff and Coatbridge.

There are also Freightliner facilities at Belfast, Dublin, Eastleigh, Ipswich and Mossend.

Operation is in the hands of Class 47 diesels, plus Class 86/6 and 90/1 electrics. The company has 72 locomotives, plus 1,046 container wagons. The first 'pocket' container wagons to carry 40ft x 9ft 6in containers are now in service.

RfD continues to be responsible for the international intermodal services via the Channel Tunnel and the automotive freight businesses. RfD has a mixed diesel and electric fleet, including some diesel shunters, while wagon ownership includes 450 Euro-twin wagons in its intermodal fleet and 60 new five-car sets of articulated automotive carriers.

Rail Express Systems' principal customer is the Royal Mail. The following description indicates the size and scale of the investment which is being undertaken by the parties.

The Princess Royal London Distribution Centre (LDC) at Wembley is the key to the long-term 'Railnet' contract between RES and the Post Office, for the carriage of mail by rail. This contract lasts until 2006.

For this, a fleet of 16 100mph electric four-car Class 325 Parcel Units has been built by Adtranz at Derby. These are owned by Royal Mail; consequently, there are no hire charges associated with their use. Operation and maintenance are contracted to EWS, who employ the train crew. The Class 325s have roller shutter doors and are based on the Class 319 Thameslink vehicles. The Class 325s thus have dual ac/dc capabilities, but are also designed to be hauled by diesel traction when their duties take them away from the electrified network.

Conventional locomotive-hauled trains also remain in Post Office use. All mail is carried in dedicated trains; passenger services are no longer used.

The LDC opened for business on 20 May 1996. The Park Royal industrial estate site is 16.5 acres, 0.5 miles long and the rail part of it has seven platforms. The choice of site was influenced by ease of access to the M1, the M40 and the national rail network—particularly the WCML.

The rail building is 27,000sq m, which is bigger than two football pitches. The steel structure has won awards; there are no central columns supporting the roof. The rail platforms are each 263m in length and hold 12 cars. Being level with the floors of rail vehicles, external vehicle doors

Left:
Stacking containers saves space, as being demonstrated here at the Railfreight Distribution seminar at the National Exhibition Centre on 4 September 1992.

must open inwards, if they are not fitted with shutters as with all Royal Mail rolling stock, or sliding doors.

The sorting hall is 14,000sq m. It is to standard warehouse specification, so it could be sold for alternative use later! This is the largest dedicated rail terminal in Europe and the biggest station built in England this century.

The automatic mail sorting machines are computer controlled for volume and speed; there are 21 outlets each using a chute, each then segregated into 10 flows. Bags are labelled by a three-digit code for sorting; each destination has a unique code. All is controlled from the operations room nerve centre.

A total of 550 road vehicles per day use the centre, each with a turnround time of about 30min. Between 21.00 and 23.00 is the busiest time. About half the mail comes in ready sorted. There are 16 million items of mail per day through LDC, or 20% of *all* UK mail. This includes Streamline (junk) mail. If Streamline is excluded, LDC handles 65% of mail volumes. Bags are loaded into York trolleys. All mail is now moving to full containerisation; train floors are being refurbished for strength and retaining straps fitted.

The Propelling Control Vehicles (PCVs, former Class 307 driving trailers) are used on the WCML and GWML trains as there is a need for services to go south from the LDC before they can proceed north or west, respectively. The driver in the front cab tells the locomotive driver what to do; type approval took a long time. Other vehicles are converted General Utility Vans or Gangwayed Brakes.

The first wave of services in mid-afternoon is for second class mail, followed by a mid-evening wave of first class. Travelling Post Offices are still used on the late evening wave of overnight services; most come into the LDC. Only first class mail is sorted on board. TPOs are needed to places like Truro, to ensure next day delivery in relatively remote areas. Simplified and much less extensive terminal facilities have been constructed at a number of other locations.

RES is thus essentially a network business, operating over a wide area and primarily for a single external customer—the Royal Mail.

RES also has a contract to move locomotives and stock to and from repair points on behalf of the rolling stock leasing companies, since it has the unique asset among the operating companies of a track access agreement with Railtrack which covers the whole of the network.

Consequently, RES is also the provider of non-

timetabled operations such as private charters and the movement of the Royal Train.

There are also likely to be new entrants to the railway industry. Both Foster-Yeoman Ltd and ARC Ltd as the constituent companies of Mendip Rail have a small fleet of Class 59 heavy-haul locomotives from General Motors, to which must be added National Power. The latter company purchased six Class 59 locomotives and 106 hoppers for use from an operating base at Ferrybridge. However, pricing deals on coal transport and the prospect of more effective stock utilisation have resulted in their sale to EWS from April 1998.

Another intending newcomer is Eddie Stobart, a Carlisle-based road haulier, who plans to start operations on the new Daventry International Freight Terminal-Mossend corridor in 1998, subject to the successful conclusion of freight facilities grant applications from the Department. The company envisages 20/23 wagon trains making one round trip a day hauled by a hired pair of Class 37 locomotives.

While these fleets have been acquired for stated specific purposes, there is no reason to assume that these companies and, indeed, others will not seek to expand. Thus British Nuclear Fuels have acquired some Class 20s, through their subsidiary Direct Rail Services. The traffic consists of the following movements:

• Irradiated fuel from Barrow to Sellafield
• Low level waste from Sellafield to Drigg
• Nuclear waste from Drigg to Sellafield
• Nitric acid from Ince to Sellafield
• Caustic soda from Ellesmere Port to Sellafield.

More recently, the company have purchased six surplus Class 37/6s from Eurostar (UK).

Assuming that they are not going to subcontract the operation to an existing operator, the new operator on the railway has to:

• obtain safety case approval from Railtrack through risk analysis
• satisfy the Regulator that insurance cover is available
• obtain a licence from the Rail Regulator
• negotiate an access agreement with Railtrack
• lease or purchase locomotives and rolling stock
• secure depot and maintenance facilities.

It might be added that he will also need suitably qualified staff for the various tasks involved.

Track access agreements of course have to be entered into by all freight operators, although agreements made for previously existing traffics

Above:
To transfer containers between Freightliner rail flats and an HGV trailer one need not employ a gantry crane. The portability of the arrangement shown here is patent, and it opens up the possibility of inter-modal operations for infrequent services by bringing in cranage only when required. This was photographed at the Railfreight exhibition at Cricklewood in 1989.

are not subject to the approval of the Regulator. Normally, the Regulator will need to be satisfied that the proposed agreements are not framed in such a way that represent the abuse of a monopoly position, create undue discrimination between users of a facility, or unduly limit competition in the provision of railway services. Nor must the agreements be woolly; rights and obligations will need to be clearly specified and also scrutinised to check that they are legally robust.[4]

However, there is also the matter of the charges to be made by Railtrack. Here, the Rail Regulator has published a policy statement.[5]

Given that it is still early days and much is still to be learned, the Regulator intends to apply the following criteria:

- charges should be greater than or equal to the avoidable costs incurred by Railtrack as a direct result of carrying that particular freight flow;
- charges should be less than or equal to the stand-alone cost which would be incurred by a notional efficient operator;
- charges should not be higher or lower, after allowing for specific factors relevant to each case, than those for other operators or users to such an extent that they risk significantly

distorting competition between rail freight operators or users; and
- the structure of charges should broadly reflect the value to users of access to the rail network, and should enable Railtrack to recover its total freight-specific costs plus any expected contribution to the shared common costs of its passenger and freight services.

In short, the aim is to stop Railtrack making charges which are excessive, which distort competition between freight operators or which result in cross-subsidies. These last might be between individual freight users, or between freight and passenger services.

The Regulator's success, or otherwise, in achieving his objectives will become clearer as time progresses.

Railtrack is introducing a code of practice which sets out the company's key commitments to promote the development of the rail freight industry. Specifically, it contains a commitment by Railtrack to provide information on the capability and capacity of the network to handle freight traffic, and about its actual use for carriage of freight. The strategy will be reviewed and confirmed each year in the Network Management Statement, which will give details of:

- the current capability of the network and some key indicators of its condition;
- the progress made in the previous year in implementing the network development and routeing strategy for freight traffic; and
- Railtrack's future plans, including information on forthcoming projects proposed by Railtrack or its customers.

Railtrack will also ensure that consideration of

network developments will include the requirements of freight, and that changes will be implemented with minimum disruption to current traffic. Operating costs will be published and reductions will be shared with the rail freight industry by reductions in access charges.

Another matter for consideration by those in the freight business is the potential of some financial help from the Government, in the form of:

- An expanded freight facilities grants scheme, which may provide Government grants for capital expenditure on railway facilities. This now includes all railway equipment, including locomotives, and takes account of reductions in rail traffic on motorways and inter-urban dual-carriageway roads (s139, Railways Act 1993). The eligible road mileage saved is valued at 20p per mile. Typically, 50% of costs are payable.

- A grant of up to 100% to contribute towards track access charges levied by Railtrack, where the traffic would otherwise move by road and there are environmental or other wider benefits to be gained (s137).

Under the previous Government, the grant's budget of £43 million over the three years until 31 March 1997 for the two schemes combined was substantially underspent. A simplified scheme was announced in August 1997, together with 12 grant awards totalling over £8.5 million.

The Department offers this example of a grant to Manchester Airport plc: the proposed construction of the second runway at Manchester Airport involves the transport of 1.45 million tonnes of limestone to the site. Transporting the stone by road would necessitate 70,000 lorry journeys a year on already congested roads between Buxton and Manchester.

Manchester Airport plc applied for a Freight Facilities Grant towards the cost of providing a temporary rail facility for the delivery of these materials. The proposal was judged to bring widespread environmental benefits to the Peak District by sparing the roads a considerable increase in freight traffic as well as bringing relief to the congested outskirts of Manchester. The project was therefore awarded a grant of £2.191 million.

By comparison, grants under the Railways Act 1974 were running at £2-3 million a year.

There are many calls to use railways more for freight; the following is perhaps typical. 'The Government wants to see more freight on rail as a contribution to reducing congestion and pollution on our roads, and to making better use of existing resources'.[6] Perhaps the most outspoken in recent times was the Royal Commission on Environmental Pollution's report of October 1994. This called for rail's freight market share to rise from 7% to 20% by 2010, which broadly means restoring the 1948 position with which this chapter began. Is this realistic, and what action would be needed to turn this into reality? As already related, Railfreight today is doing around a third of the business of nearly half a century ago, during which time the total freight market by all modes (including road, water and pipeline) has broadly doubled.

The Rail Regulator commissioned a report into the prospects for rail freight, and this was published in October 1997. The report identifies the main determinants of demand by commodity group, and suggests how changes in the railway industry might affect the outcome.

The core freight business of rail over the years has been the large scale bulk movements of coal, steel, aggregates, petroleum and a few other products such as chemicals and automotive. This has been supplemented by the non-bulk market, represented by intermodal and international services.

The bulk movements have suffered the worst in volume terms. There are two principal matters affecting the present market. First, what is the transport demand for the commodity in question? Second, what share of that total does the railway capture? Taking each bulk flow in turn, the report analyses the present situation with reference to goods moved in billion tonnes/km.

- *Coal:* The most precipitous decline in both the volume and market share of rail has occurred in the carriage of coal and coal products. In the early 1980s, rail carryings at around 6 billion tonne/km were almost twice as high as road. By the mid-1990s, rail carryings had fallen by almost a half. What is more, by 1995 rail was only just the majority carrier.
- *Iron and steel:* Rail traffic increased during the 1980s, although not as rapidly as road volumes. During the 1990s both rail and road carryings have fallen, and there has been a continuing though modest erosion of rail's market share.
- *Oil and petroleum products:* There has been a slow but fairly steady decline in rail traffic and a steady growth in road traffic, so that the rail share of the road plus rail market has fallen from nearly 40% to less than 25%.
- *Construction:* In construction and aggregates traffic, there has been a small net increase in rail traffic volumes between the early 1980s and the mid-1990s, with only limited erosion of market share.

Rail movement volumes of other types of traffic, including unitised and international traffic, declined between the early 1980s and early 1990s. Recently, traffic of this kind has increased strongly, especially since the opening of freight services through the Channel Tunnel.

Rail has high fixed costs, but relatively low variable or distance-related costs; the railway also has advantages at higher demand levels due to the size of wagons and the capacity of a train. High volumes and/or longer distances are where rail scores.

What about break-even distances? Mgr traffic has no terminal transfer problems, and no time or cost penalties associated with it. But the penalty of collection and/or delivery by road when necessary, coupled with quality of service differentials, suggest that the break-even distance before rail becomes truly competitive can be as high as 700km. This would rule rail out for a lot of traffic.

The disappearance of many private sidings and the relocation of manufacturing industry to places more accessible to the road network have not helped. Some attention is given to Government policies and fiscal measures. These include vehicle dimensions, with larger articulated vehicles replacing smaller rigid ones in recent years. Dense traffics such as coal and aggregates are responsive to weight limits, but with less dense goods the payload space is filled before the weight limits are exceeded.

But does the railway provide the quality of service that the shipper wants? Discussions elicited the response that in bulk goods the dominant factor in modal choice is price, with speed and reliability rather less important. Investigations suggested that the operating costs of road vehicles had declined at between 3% and 4% per year for the previous 10 years. However, the non-bulk market is relatively price insensitive. Here, the key issues are matters such as punctuality, reliability and flexibility, if rail is to make any headway into new markets.

Coal consumption has declined steeply with the 'dash for gas' in power stations, and in the other lesser markets for coal as well. Two shafts of light were identified:

- A significant proportion of imported coal movements are handled by rail; for instance, Avonmouth to Didcot and Liverpool to Fidlers Ferry.
- The average length of haul has increased, partly due to the imported coal but also to the concentration of both coal production and electricity generation on fewer sites.

British Steel's demand for trainload freight movements arises at three stages:

- Imported iron ore and coking coal, and some limestone
- Bulk steel semi-finished products

- Finished products to inland break-bulk sites, to final consumers or to ports for export.

Further metals flows by rail include scrap to Sheerness for Co-Steel and traffic for British Aluminium and Allied Steel and Wire. Some semi-finished products have recently returned to rail as a result of more competitive pricing; more rail use for finished products is hampered by smaller volumes and a lack of rail connections.

In petroleum, the demand for rail freight has fallen, following changes in the organisation of production and distribution of oil products. Rail construction traffic has broadly followed trends in the industry's output which has fallen in the 1990s.

While the railways lost 3.4 billion tonne/km of bulk traffic between 1992/3 and 1995/6, they gained 1.0 billion tonne/km of non-bulk traffic. Overall, though, the report concludes that 13.1 billion net tonne/km of rail freight in 1995/6 is likely to fall to a mid-range expectation of 12.3 billion net tonne/km by 2005. This base case assumes that no improvements are made in the rail industry's performance.

So, what can the rail freight businesses do? The report suggests action in the following areas:

Lower rail freight charges as a result of:
- EWS cost reductions from new equipment, more flexible working practices and rationalisation
- Railtrack cost reductions, to the extent these are passed on.

Improved reliability as a result of:
- EWS's use of new locomotives and wagons
- Railtrack investment in infrastructure, especially for freight capacity and co-operation over new connections.

More flexibility as a result of:

- Development of EWS's 'Enterprise' service and other markets not served traditionally by rail freight
- Railtrack infrastructure investment to alleviate loading gauge limitations on key parts of the network.

Enhanced customer service as a result of:
- Railtrack's new track access agreement with EWS
- EWS's intention to offer a 'one stop shop' to freight users.

The report calculates that the combined effect of these measures could result in a 30% reduction in Railtrack's and EWS's costs by 2005, with service quality improvements equivalent to a further 20% cost reduction. The result? A growth in rail freight traffic of virtually 40% above the base case considered above. Expressed by commodity sector, this appears as shown in the table below:

The report stresses that the near doubling of domestic non-bulk and international traffics 'is critically dependent on significant improvements in both prices and service quality'. Cost reductions would reduce the journey lengths over which rail is competitive with road for intermodal traffics. Road competition will not go away.

Such results would require all the actions outlined above, and the report also suggests actions to be taken by the Rail Regulator. These actions fall under the headings of:
- Regulating Railtrack
- Network enhancements
- Lowering entry barriers so that the threat of competition can be maintained
- Monitoring the industry
- Encouraging the now enlarged Department of Transport to make freight grants more available
- Supporting the European Commission to

Rail freight industry projected volumes by 2005 Net tonne/km (billion)	1995/6	2005 base case	2005 with key improvements
Coal	2.9	1.7	1.8
Metals	2.1	2.4	2.9
Oil and Petroleum	1.7	1.3	1.6
Construction	2.1	2.4	2.9
Domestic intermodal	2.5	2.5	4.0
International	0.8	1.2	2.0
Others	1.0	0.8	2.0
Totals	13.1	12.3	17.2

make open access more of a reality in continental Europe.

The report does not refrain from telling a few home truths, but it does show how the prospects for rail freight might be improved dramatically. Whether it lives up to some of the expansionist ambitions of the rail freight industry, and what the results will be, time will tell.

Besides the Channel Tunnel and the CTRL link, what other new opportunities are there? Domestic waste is a growing market for rail as the easier nearby sites are exhausted, but what about piggyback technology?

Piggyback means carrying road trailers on rail wagons, without tractor units or their drivers. It is common in North America, where flat wagons can be used, and is also found in continental Europe. However, bridges and tunnels are lower in Europe and special 'pocket' wagons with a wide space between the frames have been used. Cranes pick up the trailer and place it on the wagon so that the wheels drop into the 'pocket', where the tyres are only 330mm above the running rails. Could the limitations of the even more restrictive width and height of the British loading gauge be overcome? The Piggyback Consortium thinks that they can. This group of 37 freight transport operators, port and terminal operators, rail track authorities, local authorities and others, is dedicated to studying the feasibility of piggybacking 4m-high road semi-trailers through Britain on specially designed wagons. An initial study concluded that:

- rolling stock could be built to carry the semi-trailers past British platforms;
- the cost of upgrading the spine route from the Channel Tunnel to Ireland/Scotland via the WCML and Holyhead/Heysham/Stranraer was about £70 million; and
- there is a worthwhile market for piggyback.

The Thrall Eurospine piggyback prototype wagons are running trials. Freightliner intend to invest £10 million in piggyback trailers. The first operations are with special reduced height road trailers within the British loading gauge; Railtrack are considering gauge enhancements.

Meanwhile, Direct Rail Services began trials in mid-1997 of a daily Penrith to Cricklewood milk train. This was operated for Milk Marque by Tankfreight, using four Tiphook intermodal wagons and carrying a 29,000-litre tanker.

The road tanker used the 44-tonne weight exemption for transfer to and from intermodal terminals. The milk was collected from Cumbrian farms and transferred to the Penrith base, and was subsequently taken by road to Chadwell Heath for unloading.

By comparison, Tranz Rail in New Zealand sees two daily milk trains of about 15 wagons each and carrying 1.5 million litres of milk between them on a 6hr transit. This new traffic started in August 1997. As the New Zealand railway press said: 'If trains can successfully tackle sensitive traffic such as this (in the sense of hygiene, speed and reliability), is there anything they can't do?[7]

Upgrading of rail routes for freight and ensuring that capacity is available is the subject of feasibility studies by Railtrack. The routes include Channel Tunnel to Glasgow via Redhill, where reversal is presently necessary, the Reading East link beneath the GW main line and the West Midlands. Other routes are from the ports of Felixstowe and Southampton to the Midlands and north, and freight access to Cardiff and Avonmouth. Gauge clearances are being looked at in southwest England and northern Scotland, and general capacity requirements across the Pennines.

Can the rail freight market be expanded as suggested? The problem is not confined to Britain. European Commission statistics show the modal split of freight to rail declining from 31.7% in 1970 to 14.9% in 1994 over EU countries as a whole. At the same time, rail tonne/km have gone down by 22.3%. It is not a happy picture.

Yet the idea of transferring freight from road to rail has everything going for it, including public opinion. Many of the obstacles to progress have been identified. To raise rail freight volumes by a third would undoubtedly be a hard task, but we cannot say that 'it can't be done'. That is the task for the rail industry and its customers, with judicious support from Government.

The enemy of rail freight in Britain is not other rail companies, but the road freight businesses.

1 British Transport Commission Report and Accounts, 1948, p370
2 'New Opportunities for the Railways', Cm2012, 1992
3 'Using Best International Practice to Serve the Rail Customer', Edward A. Burkhardt. Paper published in *Proceedings of the Chartered Institute of Transport UK*, vol 6, no 2, June 1997
4 'Criteria and Procedures for the Approval of Freight Access Agreements', p7. Office of the Rail Regulator, December 1994
5 'Framework for the Approval of Railtrack's Track Access Charges for Freight Services'. Office of the Rail Regulator, February 1995
6 'Developing an Integrated Transport Policy', DETR, August 1997
7 *Rails*, January 1998, Vol 27, No 6

Other Organisations

Rolling Stock Companies

The three rolling stock companies (ROSCOs) are Angel Train Contracts Ltd, Forward Trust Rail (formerly Eversholt Leasing Ltd) and Porterbrook Leasing Co Ltd. Together, they own about 11,000 passenger vehicles and locomotives, which are leased to the Train Operating Companies. The leasing system means that capital costs are no longer a factor to be contended with by the TOCs; they get what they pay for on a long-term contract. Whether this is precisely what they want, in quality or quantity, at the price which they judge they can afford, is perhaps another matter.

For the time being, anyway, only home-grown rolling stock is suitable for use within the restrictive British loading gauge, while any new stock added to the overall fleet is likely only to result in the withdrawal of locomotives and units built in the 1960s or even earlier. Fleet shortages do not, of course, manifest themselves uniformly across all rolling stock types, while there are also new technical requirements to be met. Fire safety regulations restrict severely what can (or cannot) work into Heathrow Airport, while opportunities for through workings which link Clapham Junction and the south with Willesden Junction and the north will put a premium on dual voltage EMUs. Similarly, the advent of the Robin Hood and Ivanhoe lines, together with expansion in Strathclyde, increase the requirement for diesel units.

If, though, you should want a Class 141 Pacer of the first 1984 build, step this way! Initial leasing periods were set at four years for short-term vehicles and eight years for the remainder. With later franchises, these were extended to six and 10 years respectively. The leasing charges reflect both the capital value of the asset and the life costs of heavy overhaul and maintenance. This is where the 'Mean Equivalent Asset Value' came in, valuing the vehicles as if they were new, albeit making allowance for their being of older design. This way, it was argued, there would be an industry incentive to renew an ageing fleet.

When a vehicle comes 'off lease' it can be bid for by other TOCs, or sold. Sixty-three former BR Mk 2d/e coaches have recently been acquired by Tranz Rail New Zealand (another Wisconsin Central company), where they need new 1,067mm gauge wheelsets and bogies; other BR coaches may be found in regular traffic in Ireland and Israel. Despite the limitations of the British loading gauge, is there more scope than may have been thought for international trading—in either direction? At home, a few Modernisation Plan vehicles are still in service, with replacements only tentatively in sight. And then the IC125s will not last for ever...

Such problems are for the leasing companies, perhaps in conjunction with the rolling stock manufacturers, to sort out. It is also the ROSCOs' responsibility to finance their businesses and pay for such heavy maintenance as may be required. The TOCs are not, however, bound to obtain any extra rolling stock that they might need from the ROSCOs, if they can find another source.

Each Train Operating Company has entered into a Master Lease with one or more ROSCOs. These contain the basic lease conditions, as opposed to the detailed ones for each fleet concerning the rentals and the lease length.

The following are some of the obligations of the TOC:
- payment of rent to the ROSCO;
- carrying out running repairs and maintenance;
- use of the rolling stock only in accordance with its permitted use;
- securing and paying for third party insurance;
- fault rectification; and
- return of rolling stock at the end of the lease in the condition specified.

The corresponding obligations of the ROSCO are:
- supply of the rolling stock in an agreed condition;
- allowing the TOC to use the stock without let or hindrance;
- procurement of heavy maintenance and repairs;
- paying for any mandatory modifications; and
- securing property damage insurance, which is recharged to the TOC.

Of the three ROSCOs, Porterbrook has been sold on to South West Trains franchisee Stagecoach Holdings plc, and Eversholt has passed into the ownership of Forward Trust, the leasing arm of HSBC Holdings. Both commanded high premiums for their previous management buy-out owners. Angel Trains was sold at the close of 1997 by Nomura to the Royal Bank of Scotland.

Association of Train Operating Companies

The Association of Train Operating Companies (ATOC) has been set up as an unincorporated association by its members to administer essential inter-operator commercial activities and become the trade association of the passenger rail industry. All 25 TOCs are members, as is Eurostar (UK) Ltd.

ATOC's principal objectives are to facilitate the development and operation of commercial arrangements between passenger operators and to promote the use of the railway network (including, in particular, the making of journeys which involve the services of more than one operator). The agreements have been put in place for the following reasons:

- to enable participants to offer network-wide products to passengers;
- to fulfil licence or franchise conditions imposed to safeguard passenger interests; and
- to perpetuate elements of the BR organisation which would otherwise be under threat with the disaggregation of the passenger rail industry.

The ATOC schemes cover a number of areas:

- The offering by passenger operators individually and collectively of new and existing fare types, Railcards and reservations and, in addition, goods and services provided by third parties, including travel on London Transport services. Fares may be for travel only on the trains of a single passenger operator or may be inter-available and/or through fares.
- The honouring of fares, Railcards and reservations by carriers, and the carriage of passengers subject to the national conditions of carriage.
- The retailing of these products by passenger operators and third parties, including travel agents and providers of other means of transport.
- The provision of passenger information through the operation of Telephone Enquiry Bureaux.
- The provision of staff travel facilities, comprising reciprocal rights between the passenger operators themselves and with certain third parties as well as non-reciprocal rights with some third parties.

- The allocation of revenues between passenger carrying operators and the payment of commission to both retailing passenger operators and third parties.
- The settlement of sums due between passenger operators and to and from some third parties through the mechanism of the Railway Settlement Plan.

Membership of ATOC is obligatory, in view of the functions which the organisation carries out. It is the official voice of the entire passenger rail industry.

ATOC is also involved with other key players in the passenger rail industry, including the Department of Transport, major suppliers such as Railtrack, the rolling stock leasing companies, and the Passenger Transport Executives. ATOC is funded by members' subscriptions, scheme participation fees and from specially commissioned work for members.

ATOC's mission is 'to carry more people on more trains, more reliably—this year, next year and every year'.

Heathrow Express Railway

Heathrow Express is a company wholly owned by BAA plc. This is a private Train Operating Company which also owns the railway infrastructure within Heathrow Airport. Ownership starts clear of the flyover which provides access between the five-mile Heathrow branch and the Great Western main line at Airport Junction. The BAA-owned section is mostly underground. There are presently two stations at Central Terminal Area (CTA) and Terminal 4.

The whole is electrified at 25kV ac, which also required electrification to Paddington. Services are run by a fleet of 14 air-conditioned 100mph Class 332 four-car electric multiple-units. These cover the distance from London Paddington in 16min to CTA and a further 5min over the single track projection to T4. A 15min frequency is provided from 05.30 to 23.30.

This limited operation is expected to carry 6.2 million passengers in the year 2000, rising to 7.8 million by 2015. Expansion plans include services to St Pancras via Acton and Cricklewood; this would require some further electrification and line upgrading. The Terminal 5 inquiry, if it rules in BAA's favour, will result in a further £85 million westward extension from CTA to T5, and connections perhaps to both the GWML and the Windsor lines in the Staines area. It may be noted, though, that the existing infrastructure is in part

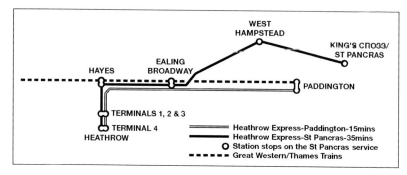

single track. Substantial growth in service provision will need a corresponding enlargement of the existing railway within Heathrow Airport itself.

British Transport Police

The first persons to be responsible for railway safety in a practical sense were the railway police, men recruited by the companies and organised and modelled on the lines of the then recently formed Metropolitan Police force. According to the Great Western Rule Book of 1841: 'The duties of the Police may be stated generally to consist in the preservation of order in all the stations and on the line of railway.' In those early days, the police were signalmen, enquiry officers, permanent way inspectors, messengers and policemen all rolled into one, but the ancillary tasks soon became the responsibility of others.

The railway, however, is a specialist environment. It requires considerable knowledge of railway operations and procedures, especially if police work is to have a minimal effect on its operation or on railway customers. It is also geographically widespread, in itself a justification for a national police force.

The Transport Act 1947 finally combined the company forces into a single force responsible for law enforcement throughout the whole of the newly created British Transport Commission's jurisdiction, of which by far the greatest parts were that of British Railways and London Underground.

The business of the British Transport Police is to police Britain's railways as effectively as possible. This puts the force squarely in the mainstream of British policing, dealing with the same crimes and responding to the same public and political priorities.

The force serves primarily the people who use, work on and manage the railway system, as well as the wider community. Statistically, its policing population is assessed as three million people, who expect a safe comfortable journey or working environment, and it is the force's business to help ensure that that is what they get. This can only be achieved in conjunction with operators, Railtrack and others. Working closely with BT Police is a safety case requirement.

The Police Services Agreement spells out the core services that BT Police provide as:

'to maintain law and order, and include (without limitation) services undertaken in relation to safety, anti-terrorism, the prevention and detection of crime, the keeping of the peace, the bringing of offenders to justice and rendering support to the victims of crime'.

Specialist areas receiving attention include:
- trespass and vandalism, which can be dangerous for both the individuals concerned and third parties;
- riding on the outside of trains, or surfing;
- safety programmes, taking the safety message to local communities;
- misuse of level crossings by road vehicle drivers; and
- contingency planning procedures, training and live exercises.

Whatever the ownership of the railways, they remain public space. They need to be protected by a publicly accountable police force which has the powers necessary to carry out its duties properly.

HM Railway Inspectorate

The Inspectorate, the origins of which go back to the Railway Department of the Board of Trade in 1840, is now part of the Health and Safety Executive. The Railway Inspectorate's objectives are to ensure the continued safety of Britain's railways by the following means:

The Issue of Guidance for Railway Operations on the Design, Construction and Operation of Railways

The 'Railway Safety Principles and Guidance' has recently been republished in two parts. Part 1 sets out the principles and gives an indication of the factors to be taken into account in implementation. Part 2 consists of eight separate sections dealing with specific aspects of railway construction and gives examples of good practice. These sections are:

A   The Infrastructure
B   Stations
C   Electric Traction Systems
D   Signalling
E   Level Crossings
F   Trains
G   Tramways
H   Heritage Railways

Prior Inspection and Approval of New Lines, Rolling Stock and Equipment

Proposals are considered by the Inspectorate. New infrastructure can range from minor platform lengthening or track layout revisions to the construction of Ashford International station, Sheffield Supertram or the Channel Tunnel Rail Link. The Inspectorate gives type approval to new locomotives and rolling stock, including track maintenance machines.

The Monitoring of Safety Procedures on Existing Lines, to Ensure Compliance with the Health and Safety at Work Act and Relevant Statutory Provisions

The Inspectorate has powers to investigate any notifiable accident or dangerous occurrence, inspect premises and issue notices in respect of potentially dangerous procedures or breaches of legislation.

The Investigation of Selected Accidents, and the Study of Accident Trends to Identify Priorities for Improvement

The Inspectorate has investigated accidents from 1842, although it did not have the formal powers so to do until the Regulation of Railways Act 1871. It issues reports and makes many recommendations. An annual report is issued, containing many statistics and accident records.

These are perhaps the traditional areas of interest of HMRI, within a unified railway. The job is changing and the following principles (abridged) have been agreed as fundamental for railway safety:

- Any system must not lead to any diminution of current safety standards, should be practical and able to deliver appropriate and effective control of risk;
- the prime responsibility of ensuring safety must rest with the party who has control, to the extent that they actually have that control;
- the degree of statutory control shall be the minimum consistent with the need to ensure adequate and cost-effective levels of control of risk and to secure public confidence;
- any arrangements should be demonstrably fair to all parties involved; and
- legislation pertaining to railway safety should be administered by a single independent safety regulator, the HSE.

From these, other principles have been derived:

- Safety systems on the railway must address technical, operational and organisational issues;
- duties and responsibilities must be adequately defined;
- within the limits of their control, the infrastructure controllers will bear primary responsibility for the co-ordination of measures to control risk on the railway; and
- there must be effective co-ordination and co-operation between all parties and individuals.

This is not a treatise on railway safety, which is a subject in its own right. Suffice to say here that all train and station operators have to submit a safety case to Railtrack under the Railway (Safety Case) Regulations 1994. This demonstrates that an operator has the systems in place to manage operations safely and meets required safety standards. It includes a safety policy, a risk assessment, a description of safety management systems, and the safety side of maintenance and operational arrangements.

Every railway operating company must present written documentary evidence on how it will operate and maintain its system and equipment, from the point of view of both its staff and its passengers. This documentation is assessed by Railtrack who can, of course, either accept it, reject it or require alterations. Without such acceptance, the company cannot operate. The documentation has to cover every aspect of the railway's function, right down to the most menial office tasks. Everything has to be covered and everything has to be accepted. The Railway Safety Cases will also be regularly monitored.

Railtrack's own RSC must be validated and accepted by HMRI, who also view other operators' safety cases to ensure that they are properly considered by Railtrack.

HMRI is also concerned with the standards for safety-critical staff under the Railway (Safety Critical Work) Regulations 1994. These require that all staff are competent and fit to undertake those tasks associated with the safe movement of trains. HMRI is responsible for enforcement.

Eurotunnel

Eurotunnel plc is the owner of the Channel Tunnel, which opened in May 1994. Eurotunnel's operating licence has now been extended to the year 2086 (previously 2052). The tunnel itself is 31.4 miles in length and consists of two large-diameter running tunnels, with a much smaller central service tunnel. The running tunnels are interconnected at two intermediate points with high speed crossovers. These divide the tunnel into three portions of equal length and allow maintenance work to be carried out while services continue to run.

The company operates its own 'Le Shuttle' services, using a fleet of single-deck and double-deck carrier wagons. These provide facilities for private cars, motorcycles, coaches and HGVs. Services operate between Folkestone and Calais and are designed to carry accompanied road vehicles only.

Eurotunnel also sells train paths to passenger and freight companies on the European railways. These are used principally by Eurostar (UK) and Railfreight Distribution, an EWS company. Journeys through the tunnel itself take about 25min for a train occupying a 'standard' path, defined in relation to Le Shuttle speeds. Faster or slower trains consume more track capacity, the fast trains because they have to leave an extended headway before entering the tunnel, and slow trains because it is longer before they can be followed without causing a delay. (It should be stressed that this is a capacity and not a safety issue.) Eurotunnel charges to operators reflect the track capacity used.

The 'flighting' of trains in groups of slower and faster ones helps minimise the total capacity used.

Eurostar (UK)

This is the British company running Eurostar, a service provided jointly by the railways of Belgium, Britain and France. European Passenger Services Ltd was set up by the British Railways Board. In April 1994, ownership was vested in the UK Government, and in May 1996 the company was sold to London & Continental Railways Ltd, the organisation created to design, build and operate the Channel Tunnel Rail Link. L&C is effectively a holding company with two subsidiaries: the operator runs the trains as Eurostar (UK), while the construction arm is Union Railways. London & Continental shareholders include the National Express Group and Virgin Group (17% each), which between them subsequently became the franchisees of seven TOCs.

Eurostar Services commenced on 14 November 1994 between the five-platformed Waterloo International and Paris Nord or Brussels Midi, with a journey time of 3hr to Paris (308 miles) and 3hr 15min to Brussels (237 miles). Service levels since have been increased progressively, with 17 weekday trains in each direction to Paris and 10 to Brussels in early 1998. Service provision is marginally less on Sundays. Intermediate calls are made, on a limited number of services, at the privately funded and built Ashford International, Calais-Fréthun and Lille. It is anticipated that full

Below:
UK Eurostar set No 3014 passes through Vauxhall with the 07.53 Waterloo to Paris Nord on 23 November 1995.

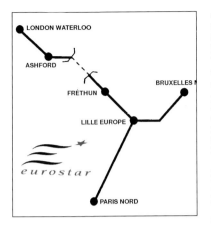

LONDON WATERLOO

ASHFORD

FRÉTHUN

BRUXELLES

LILLE EUROPE

eurostar

PARIS NORD

operation will see two international trains leaving London every hour.

From December 1997, journey times to Brussels were reduced to 2hr 45min, following completion of the new Belgian high speed line. There are also limited services to Paris Marne-la-Vallee (for Disneyland) and to the French Alps.

Onward TGV connections are available directly from Lille, while Brussels provides connections to Amsterdam, Frankfurt and Berlin. At home, IC125 services from Waterloo to the East and West Coast main lines and to the West Country were short lived. Remaining in operation are the Penzance sleeper run by GW Trains and services to Bristol and South Wales run by Wales & West. These, however, are run independently of Eurostar services, in the sense that they do not operate under a contract to that organisation.

International services are provided by 31 Eurostar sets of Class 373 stock at a cost of around £24 million each, divided into 11 UK-owned, 16 French and four Belgian. An operational train set consists of two identical nine-coach half sets and a power car on each end. These 18-car sets are articulated within themselves. Trains contain 210 first class seats and 584 second class seats, totalling 794, and are 393.48m long. First class accommodation thus accounts for 26.5% of the total.

In Britain, 11 Eurostar sets are maintained at North Pole International, reached via the West London line. Longsight depot in Manchester has been equipped to look after the North of London sets.

The follow-on order for seven shorter North of London Regional trains has two vehicles omitted from each half set. This makes them 14-car sets

overall. All are British-owned. The 1997/8 timetable shows three daily services to Paris from Glasgow via the ECML, from Manchester via Birmingham and from Manchester via the Trent Valley. Only the last runs on a Sunday. These are very much out and back workings, timed for early departures from Britain and arriving home late. All vehicles need to return to Longsight as their home depot on a regular basis. Alternatively, could the train sets find a productive (or more productive) use with Virgin Trains, still operating from Longsight but on domestic services to London Euston?

The bill for the station at Waterloo International was £130 million, with that for North Pole International Depot £85 million. The private sector Ashford International station builder, John Laing plc, is remunerated by a toll from each of the annual two million or so passengers using it, payable by the international train service operators.

Half of Eurostar's passengers are British, with the French and Belgians together accounting for another 35%. The 15% balance is from other countries, notably North America and Japan. Around six million customers used the services in 1997. Eurostar services help to provide London & Continental with what has turned out to be an inadequate revenue stream to help fund the construction of the CTRL. Effectively, this will create a vertically integrated operation, in contrast to the domestic scene of Railtrack, Train Operating Company and ROSCO.

Union Railways

Union Railways Ltd was created in 1992 as a wholly owned BR agency company to plan and design the proposed high speed rail link between London and the Channel Tunnel. In March 1993, the Government announced its choice of a northern route to an expanded St Pancras station and that the project would be developed as a joint venture between the public and private sectors. Union Railways is now a subsidiary company of London & Continental.

The 109km (68-mile) route is designed to provide additional line capacity, reduce journey times and to promote economic regeneration of the East Thames corridor. An intermediate station, for both international and domestic traffics, is now in place at Ashford, which requires a small diversion from what is to become the CTRL main line. Other stations, again international and domestic, are planned to be built at Ebbsfleet and Stratford.

Junctions with the existing railway, besides those at Ashford, may be made south of Ebbsfleet where a link to Swanley and Waterloo is to be engineered, and at Ebbsfleet itself with a junction from the North Kent line, Northfleet and Gravesend. Freight traffic would leave the CTRL at Ripple Lane, while onward connecting lines would be available in the immediate area of St Pancras. For rolling stock purposes, a London-facing junction would be provided at Stratford to allow access to a new servicing and maintenance facility on the Temple Mills marshalling yard site.

Speeds of up to 185mph are envisaged, but provision will be made for freight. The CTRL is considered capable of reducing the London to Paris or Brussels journey time by half an hour, while Ashford might gain commuter trains to London taking 40min to St Pancras instead of the present 75min to a London terminus. Similar journey time reductions would be achieved from Folkestone and Canterbury West and, to a lesser extent, from the Medway towns eastwards.

The Channel Tunnel Rail Link Act received Royal Assent on 18 December 1996, clearing the way for London & Continental to build the line subject to raising the necessary finance.

The Railway Forum

The Railway Forum's aim is to be the voice of the many companies working to provide rail services in Britain, setting out the benefits of rail and ensuring that the rail option is fully considered in the policy-making and planning process.

The principal objective is to promote policies which will encourage the development of the business and trading opportunities for rail-based transport and to be the authoritative voice of the railway industry. Its aims are:

- to provide a forum for members to share information on political, economic and commercial opportunities;
- to analyse and respond to European Union and British Government policy and legislative proposals affecting the competitive position of rail, and to influence such policy;
- to ensure wider appreciation of the industry's achievements and innovations;
- to raise awareness of the social, economic and environmental benefits of rail transport; and
- to press for optimisation of the organisational and financial framework of the railways.

Membership is mainly from the railway supply industry and infrastructure companies, with little representation from operators.

European Legislation

A key European ideal is mobility through freedom of movement, in which transport is obviously a central issue. Other concerns on which transport has a bearing are employment, economic development, social exclusion (people should not be excluded by poverty, disablement or even lack of a car), environmental impact and global warming. However, there is a prejudice towards the benefits of opening up markets to expose them to more competition.

At present, mobility, social exclusion and the environment are high on the agenda. Public transport is seen as vital, and European policy recognises its role. However, European legislation has not fully embraced the needs of the public transport industry.

In part, this is perhaps due to the system of 23 more or less autonomous directorates, of which perhaps eight are involved in matters which impinge on the transport industry besides DGVII Transport. The directorates are all part of the European Commission, which is the only body that can propose legislation. Proposals are often first discussed informally. The present EU Transport Commissioner is Neil Kinnock.

The European Parliament gives opinions on and proposes amendments to the Commission's proposals, but the decisions are taken by the Council of Ministers.

There is a lobby to improve the function of public transport. This may be seen in the Citizens' Network Green Paper, which looks to removing obstacles to public transport use and a higher quality product altogether. Present work by the Commission is defining what is meant by public transport quality under no less than eight main headings, 26 sub-headings and 96 individual items. It all makes the judgement of franchisee performance by OPRAF look a little limited!

An outline of the principal European legislation relating to railways may be found in Appendix 1.

There are, of course, many other organisations whose businesses depend largely on the railway industry. Some, such as the former British Rail Engineering Ltd, have been in the private sector for several years. Others, such as Business Systems or BR Telecoms, have only recently made the change, while a third group includes firms, such as Pandrol Rail Fastenings Ltd, which have never been in the public sector.

Space consideration has dictated that only the major players can be discussed here, but the omission of the rest does not in any way seek to minimise their contribution.

Have the railways been managed inefficiently? The British Railways Board recorded the following table (below) in their Annual Report for 1994/5:

In production terms, train km per member of British Rail staff at 56% above the Community of European Railways (CER) average was decidedly commendable, but production of train km is of little value if they cannot be sold. Here, BR appeared much weaker; the average passenger train load on BR at 83 compared very unfavourably with the CER figure of 130. Freight was hardly more flattering at 267 tonne/km per train, compared with the CER's 319. On the other hand, in proportionate terms much less public finance went into the railways of Britain; perhaps, one might argue, you get what you pay for.

Crudely, it would seem that operations were relatively efficient, but that the volume of passenger service provision in particular was over-generous for the traffic actually on offer. Alternatively, one could take the view that both the passenger and freight traffic was there, but that the railway was not good at selling its wares. The steadily declining railway market share, which has continued for many years, gives support to such a conclusion.

Whatever the reasons, it is difficult to avoid the feeling that 'we could do better'. What can the railways do most usefully and most successfully in the future, for the benefit of the nation as well as themselves? This is not a question about matters of ownership or competition, which are relatively peripheral. Rather, it is addressing the long-term aims of GB Ltd's overall strategy, and the political willingness or otherwise to dedicate the necessary level of resources. For, whilst railways may and perhaps should meet their operational costs through revenue from customers, the meeting of major investment costs can be all but impossible. There is a clear need for a statement of aims, to be supported by a general framework for decision-making, and associated with both political and social vision. It is areas such as these that the new Strategic Rail Authority will need to address.

Few would suggest that there is any place for a low quality, bargain basement railway in the 1990s and beyond. The industry can do much better than that. However, it is the prerogative of the politicians to decide what sort of railway they want to see in the future, and for the professionals to foster the debate and help them to achieve their political aims. But, for progress to be made, there does need to be agreement on what the fundamental questions and issues really are.

The Problem Areas

What are the main transport problems facing Britain? According to the Department of Transport, these include:

- Overall passenger mileage by all modes, which is now running at three times 1951 levels, but is satisfied mostly by private cars.
- Growth of car ownership, from 14% of households in 1951 to 66% in 1989. At 374 cars per 1,000 population in 1990, this compared with 417 in France, 490 in the former West Germany and 648 in the USA.
- Forecasts of continued traffic growth, related to GDP, with demand in the range of 83% to 142% of 1988 levels by the year 2025.
- Growth of traffic congestion, which cannot be met by any conceivably acceptable road building programme, least of all in cities.
- Growth in personal mobility, trade, resourcing of industry and retail distribution, with an increasing dominance of out-of-town locations for leisure and shopping activities.
- Environmental considerations, including noise, infrastructure impact, air pollution and global warming.

BR International performance indicators (1993/4 year)		
Comparison	British Rail	Average, other CER railways
Train km per member of staff	3,463	2,220
Average passenger train loading (nos)	83	130
Average freight train loading (tonnes)	267	319
Support from public funds as % of GDP	0.18	0.59

There is a limit to the contribution which even the most effective railway can make to such a range of problems, but a necessary precursor is to find a sensible form of railway organisation to meet the challenge. What does the railway presently achieve?

Market share by different passenger transport modes, 1996	Passenger km (billions)	% of total
National Railways	32	4
other railways	7	1
Buses and coaches	44	6
Cars, vans and taxis	620	86
Motorcycles	4	1
Pedal cycles	4	1
Air (domestic)	6	1
Total	717	100

(Source: Transport Statistics 1997, Department of Transport)

The extent of the eclipse of public transport modes is thus quite overwhelming; the national railway system now accounts for a mere 4% of the total passenger miles, or little more than a quarter of the 15% achieved in 1952. Actual levels of rail volumes have changed little. This is unlike the bus industry over the same period, which has declined remorselessly, albeit now showing signs of stabilisation. The key change is in the growth of private road transport.

From these figures, various conclusions can be drawn:

- First, National Railways with 4% of the market can hardly be held to exercise general monopoly powers. That said, rail is dominant in the Central London commuter business and in some corridors in other cities, while it is said to have up to 40% of some long-distance markets.

- Second, road traffic cannot continue to grow at the rate evident in the post-World War 2 years. This is not a political statement; merely it is a reflection on the infrastructure resources which would be needed to sustain that growth

and the environmental consequences, in the widest sense, which would follow.

- Third, it is evident both from its continued level of usage over the years and the general affection which rail holds in the public's eye that a smartly run, well promoted and modernised rail system is the principal contender to take a higher proportion of market share. The British people have always loved railways, but never the companies which run them.

- Fourth, there is scope for sizeable increases in freight traffic. This requires the railway to get its unit costs down, with prices to reflect this, and also to get its service quality right for the markets concerned.

It follows that, if the positive technical attributes of rail can be harnessed, exploited and developed, a new railway age might be at hand.

Rail is in all respects an integrated *system*, in which colossal numbers of potentially conflicting movements are being made all the time over large geographical areas. The actions of each train operator thus impinge directly on many others, a situation to which only the system controller can bring order. This affects both the planning stage and actual day-to-day operations. Unlike other modes of transport, the British Rail we knew had service provision, operational control and infra-structure engineering under a central body, albeit devolved latterly to a series of businesses. As recorded above, BR productivity compared well internationally with that of other administrations.

But, on its own, this is not enough. Like any other business, the railway needs to be orientated primarily towards the purchasers of its products: its customers. In the end, the present and the potential customers are more important than the operations managers and the engineers on whom the railway depends to make it all happen.

This is not, in any sense, to decry the contribu-tions of the latter. Effective and efficient produc-tion methods, with quality control, are immensely

Right:
This view is of the sorting arrangements at the Royal Mail's London Distribution Centre; mail descends from the high level conveyor on the right and is placed in the appropriate York containers. These are removed at up to six at a time in the trucks seen at the bottom left and taken to the trains.

Above:
Royal Mail's London Distribution Centre sees Royal Mail-owned No 325002 on the right and a Propelling Control Vehicle on the left on the evening of 23 September 1997.

important. The rail businesses, passenger and freight alike, cannot sell what they cannot deliver. The aim is to keep unit costs down, but also to explore and exploit technical advances.

There is no reason to doubt that private sector organisations can run the railways of Britain well; in 170 years of history, the railway has been in private ownership for 70% or so of that period. Both the nationalised and private periods have had their successes and failures. This is not to say that the railway has been devoid of state controls. The Railway Department of the Board of Trade from 1840 was an early manifestation, while there is a long legislative history preceding the Railways Act 1993. The major Acts of recent times may be found in Appendix 1.

The main concern today is whether the situation we now have will meet the needs of 21st century Britain and the European Community to which this country belongs, as well as the technical and operational requirements of a railway system.

Investments as part of the Franchise Plans of the TOCs have been mentioned under the headings of each; at the end of 1997, the score as far as rolling stock is concerned looked something like this:

Franchise Plan Commitments

These total about 1,730 passenger vehicles. Orders for EMUs/DMUs identified for 12 of the 25 TOCs, with contracts awarded or signed for six of these.

Outside Franchise Plan

These total approximately 140 passenger vehicles, 280 freight locomotives and 2,500 wagons. Orders for EMUs identified for two TOCs, contract signed in one case. Orders for diesel locomotives and freight wagons signed for EWS, and a further order for 200km/h diesel locomotives expected to follow.

Delivery is spread over several years. Most new rolling stock should be available by the end of 2000, but delivery of some of the vehicles for Virgin is timed to coincide with the West Coast main line requirements, after the modernisation scheme is complete.

There is clearly much, much more to be done, though there are encouraging signs around. For instance, Richard Brown of National Express Group Trains Division to the Railway Study Association:

'90% of the population outside the southeast don't use trains and have a low awareness of services on offer. We intend to offer targeted marketing with a constant stream of improvements and continuous promotion. Above all, we need to be talked about and create a buzz. Hence the 4-Sight ticket for two, three or four people travelling together.'

This ticket is available between Midland main line stations Leeds to Wellingborough inclusive, and St Pancras. It must be booked three days or more in advance and (free) reservations are compulsory. The return fare in all cases was initially £29.00, for up to a car-load of people.

Or, take the Great Western Vision as expounded by Brian Scott: 'The Great Western experience is the first choice for millions of customers.' This was backed up by the customer service mission:

> 'Information is accurate, timely and easily accessible.
> It is easy to buy the right ticket for my journey.
> It is easy to find my train.
> Stations and trains are clean, comfortable and enjoyable.
> Trains are fast, frequent, direct and on time.
> I am safe and secure when travelling with Great Western.
> All this delivered by staff who are courteous and helpful.'

And Ed Burkhardt of English, Welsh & Scottish Railways:

> 'Foremost among the many British contributions to the world are railways. It seems fundamental to me that the land where railways were born should now lead the way toward a resurgence of rail transport, free of governmental controls...restored as an important part of a free enterprise society. We will do all we can to meet that challenge.'

But nobody pretends that this will be easy. Burkhardt again: 'I know if we have any future at all, it will come from productivity, tight control of costs, competitive pricing and a strong service orientation.' Passenger operators, too, have pressures, as succinctly put by Richard Etherington of Great North Eastern Railway: '80% of costs are fixed. The subsidy in year 1 is £70m, declining to £0 in year 7. Revenue must grow!'

And then there is the infrastructure, and its adequacy or otherwise. If the railway is to expand its carryings to the extent that at least some of the businesses think achievable, if not downright essential, some serious work is required here. There are some well-known pinch points; the line between Manchester Piccadilly and Oxford Road is one; the West London line is another.

Expansion or resignalling is not the end of the matter, either. How is the capacity allocation between would-be users to be made, and how should Railtrack determine the access charges? What quality is required, in terms of axle loads,

Above:
At Oxenholme, a pushchair is following a bicycle onto the 12.45 Manchester Airport to Windermere, formed of No 156459. The service is operated by North Western Trains, the date 11 November 1997.

train lengths, maximum permitted speeds, ride quality, loading gauge clearances and so on? What will be the relative priorities for freight, express passenger and local passenger services? Questions which need attention include:

- What exactly, in technical terms, should be done?
- Who will promote it?
- What timescale is achievable, given the likely need for legal powers?
- How will the capital costs be paid for and by whom?
- What constraints or opportunities will the package place on operators?
- What benefits will it bring, over what period, and for whom?

To resolve such problems satisfactorily will perhaps represent one of the greatest tests of the efficacy of the post-1993 Act railway. What, one might ask, are the answers to such problems to do with letting competitive seven-year operating franchises? The Strategic Rail Authority may prove to be an all-important player.

The railway we need will have the capacity to carry the traffics for which rail is best suited, and it must provide what people want. The new railway age, if indeed that is upon us, needs to work within a framework of competition, a political and public concern for the environment, and the European Community. To that, one hopes, may be added the benefits of a supportive government.

Meanwhile, it is up to those in the rail transport industry to do everything in their power to make the new system work, for the mutual benefit of the railway businesses, their customers and their staff. Let us hope that a climate has been created in which the railway businesses can grow.

Appendix I: Principal Acts of Parliament and European Legislation

Domestic Legislation

The Acts listed, together with their major objectives, are those which directly affected the railways from nationalisation onwards. The annual private acts promoted by the British Railways Board and its predecessors, mainly for the authorisation to carry out new works, are omitted.

1947 Transport Act

Nationalisation of the railways, London Transport, road haulage, docks and inland waterways. Creation of the British Transport Commission (BTC) with the Railway Executive as one of its subsidiaries.

1953 Transport Act

Disposal of the Road Haulage Executive; abolition of the Railway Executive.

1962 Transport Act

Abolition of the BTC and creation of the British Railways Board (BRB) and others. Deficit grants for BRB. A formalised passenger service closure procedure, with ministerial decision after consideration by the Transport Users Consultative Committee.

1968 Transport Act

Establishment of the National Freight Corporation, Passenger Transport Authorities and Executives, the National Bus Company/Scottish Transport Group. Grants for unremunerative railway services.

1974 Railways Act

Writing off debts of the British Railways Board and introduction of freight facilities grants. 'The British Railways Board shall from 1 January 1975 operate its railway passenger system so as to provide a public service which is comparable generally with that provided by the Board at present' (directive by the Secretary of State for Transport).

1987 Channel Tunnel Act

Construction of the Channel Tunnel, but including limitations on the contribution of public moneys towards the funding of a Channel Tunnel Rail Link.

1992 Transport and Works Act

To provide a mechanism for the Secretary of State to grant statutory authority for activities which previously required private Acts of Parliament. Thus an order may provide for, amongst other things, the acquisition of land or rights over land—whether compulsorily or by agreement—for a project, the payment of compensation, incidental or ancillary works, policing and the making of bye-laws.

1993 Railways Act

Separation of rail infrastructure from operations, passenger services to be provided by franchised operators, overseen by a regulatory body, rolling stock-owning companies created and the general privatisation of the various aspects of the industry.

1995 Disability Discrimination Act

Makes provision for disabled persons, including those in wheelchairs, to gain access to and be carried safely in, rail vehicles constructed after 31 December 1998 (unless specifically exempted).

1996 Channel Tunnel Rail Link Act

Parliamentary powers to permit of the building of the rail link from Folkestone to St Pancras on the defined route. This includes sections underground, with intermediate stations at Ebbsfleet and Stratford.

European Legislation

Note that the two digit figure represents the year to which the item relates.

Council Regulation 1191/69

As modified by Regulation 1893/91. Definition of scope for establishing public service requirements and the obligations of public authorities to compensate operators for providing public transport services. Action by member states concerning the obligations inherent in the concept of a public service in transport by rail, road and inland waterway.

Council Regulation 1192/69

Common rules for the normalisation of the accounts of railway undertakings.

Council Regulation 1107/70

Rules on the granting of aid for road, railways and inland waterways transport.

Council Regulation 1108/70

Introduces an accounting system for expenditure on infrastructure in respect of transport by rail, road and inland waterways.

Council Regulation 2830/77

Measures to achieve comparability between the accounting of systems and annual accounts of railway undertakings.

Council Regulation 2183/78

Lays down uniform costing principles for railway undertakings.

Commission Recommendation 922/82

Definition of a higher quality, international rail passenger transport system.

Council Directive 91/440

The development of the community railways. Separation between the infrastructure and operations, at least in accounting terms. Management autonomy, a sound financial structure, and access to the infrastructure for combined transport and international railway groupings.

Council Directive 95/18

The licensing of railway undertakings.

Council Directive 95/19

The allocation of railway infrastructure capacity and the charging of infrastructure fees.

Council Regulation 2236/95

Rules for financial contributions to Trans-European Networks, for all modes.

COM(95) 337 final of 19 07 95: Future Measures to Develop the Railways

Extension of access rights to all freight services, domestic and international, and for international passenger services, without the need for groups as in 91/440.

COM(95) 601 final of 29 11 95: The Citizen's Network (Green Paper)

Public transport should ideally be open to all citizens in terms of accessibility, affordability and availability in terms of service coverage, and offer a real alternative to the private car. Networks should fit together, making interchange easier—whether from train to train, or train to bus, car, bike or tram. This applies to long distance and local networks.

COM(95) 691 of 20 12 95: Towards Fair and Efficient Pricing in Transport (Green Paper)
Discusses the conditions of competition between modes, and the extent that the prices paid by users do not necessarily affect external costs such as congestion, pollution and accidents.

Council Directive 96/48
Sets out the requirements for interoperability and technical standards of high speed rail network.

COM(96) 421 final of 30 07 96: A Strategy for Revitalising the Community's Railways (White Paper)
The strategy is designed to reverse the severe decline in rail's share of passenger and freight markets. It proposes that the railway of the future should first and foremost be a business with an independent management, and exposed to market forces. Railways need a sound financial basis, open access for freight, market forces introduced for domestic passenger services, and international operability.

Omitted from this list are more general matters such as Regulations on rules for the use of the European Development Fund (ERDF) or the European Social Fund (ESDF). Further Directives relate to the procedures for procurement by public bodies, or employment, environmental or other legislation which may have an effect on railways.

Appendix II: Objectives, Instructions and Guidance for the Franchising Director

A summary of the main points in the 'Objectives, Instructions and Guidance', irreverently known as OIG. This document was tabled on behalf of the Secretary of State for the Environment, Transport and the Regions before both Houses of Parliament on 6 November 1997.

1. 'Your principal objectives are:
   - to increase the number of passengers travelling by rail;
   - to manage existing franchise agreements in a manner which you consider promotes the interests of the passenger; and
   - to secure a progressive improvement in the quality of railway passenger and station services available to railway passengers'.

2. 'You should therefore:
   - stimulate the development of railway services by promoting high levels of cost-effective investment in the network;
   - protect passenger network benefits by the strict application of existing contractual obligations, and seek to enhance their effectiveness;
   - support the development of railway services and facilities which make it convenient and cost-effective for passengers to make journeys involving more than one mode of transport;
   - promote the personal security of passengers travelling by rail;
   - promote the enhancement of facilities for disabled passengers;
   - encourage efficiency and economy in the provision of railway services'.

3. Franchising is now complete, for the time being. However, 'you are to consult me (the Secretary of State) before taking steps to re-tender any franchise'.

4. On investment issues, the Franchising Director is to prepare an annual report with an assessment of the type and level of services the network should provide; this should include a critique of Railtrack's Network Management Statement. Budgetary implications will be included. It remains to be seen how this will fit in with the duties of the Strategic Rail Authority.

   Promoters are to be encouraged. 'You are to offer clear and well publicised guidance and assistance, primarily to local authorities, on the mechanisms for developing, and securing finance for, investment in the restructured railway industry'. The net social and environmental benefits of schemes are to be maximised.

   The Franchising Director must give advice on future service levels to Railtrack and others. However, he must consult the Secretary of State before giving significant guarantees to potential investors.

5. Franchise management by OPRAF must concentrate on protecting the rights and interests of passengers. A quarterly bulletin is to be published on franchise operational performance.

6. Ticket interavailability between different franchisees is to be maintained, but this is slightly qualified by the condition 'where you believe the benefits of doing so will outweigh any benefits that might arise from greater price competition and service diversity'. However, the Franchising Director must consult the Secretary of State before taking such action.

7. Multi-modal travel schemes (including the London Travelcard which gets a specific mention) are to be preserved, and new schemes promoted.

8. Besides policies on passenger transport, 'you should have regard to the Government's policies on the environment and railfreight'.

9. The Franchising Director is instructed to maintain effective liaison with other key bodies. This includes the Rail Regulator, who must 'have regard to your financial position. You should supply him with such financial information as he reasonably requested to enable him to do so'. Other consultees to be kept informed include local authorities, and most of the bodies who appear elsewhere in this book.

10. On service levels, the Franchising Director is to 'secure that minimum levels of service remain at least broadly comparable to those specified in the current Passenger Service Requirements'. It is recognised that operators may wish to adjust services over time to match changing demands.

11. Finally, at the end of the franchise, 'you must take all reasonable steps to ensure there is no disruption to railway passenger services'. The Franchising Director is even reminded of the sections of the Act (27, 30, 51-53 and 86) which give him the necessary powers to secure continuity.

    Compared with previous versions, instructions on how to set about franchising have been removed. This included references to vertical franchises (discouraged), details to be considered in service specifications, and control of fares levels. There is no mention of open access services, which may be provided outside franchising agreements.

Right:
Automotive products (new cars to you and me) have proved to be an enduring traffic for RfD. Here a trainload of new cars leaves Longbridge on 22 October 1997 behind a Class 47. The Cartic-4 vehicles combine double-stacking of private cars with articulated wagons. These rail vehicles feature protective side barriers.

Appendix III:
Passenger Service Requirement

Extract fromThames Trains PSR. It is stressed that this is the extent of the *requirement*; the operator may provide more extensive services if he so wishes.

Maidenhead to Marlow

1 **Weekdays Service Pattern**
    1.1.1 An hourly service shall be provided between Maidenhead and Marlow calling at Furze Platt, Cookham and Bourne End

1.2 Maidenhead Departures
    1.2.1 An eaely departure no later than 0645.
    1.2.2 A late departure no earlier than 2330.
    1.2.3 Maximum Journey Time 23 minutes.

1.3 Marlow Departures
    1.3.1 An early departure no later than 0630.
    1.3.2 A late departure no later than 2300.
    1.3.3 Maximum Journey Time 22 minutes.

1.4 Additional Services and Variations
    1.4.1 An additional service from Marlow to Maidenhead calling at stations specified in paragraph 1.1.1 shall operate on Fridays only, departing one hour after the late departure shown in paragraph 1.3.2 above.
    1.4.2 Departures from Maidenhead at or before 0730 may omit to call at Cookham.
    1.4.3 Departures from Maidenhead or Marlow at or before 1815 and btweeen 1745 and 2000 may terminate short of destination provided that a connection within 20 minutes is provided for through passengers.
    1.4.4 One additional service in each direction shall be provided between Bourne End and Maidenhead and shall be extended to and from London Paddington during the Morning Peak and to depart from London Paddington during the Evening Peak. Connections to and from Marlow shall be provided within 10 minutes. These services shall call at stations specified in paragraph 1.1.1 and the maximum Journey Time between Bourne End and London Paddington shall not exceed 41 minutes in each direction.

2 **Saturdays Service Pattern**
    2.1.1 An hourly service shall be provided between Maidenhead and Marlow calling at Furze Platt, Cookham and Bourne End.

2.2 Maidenhead Departures
    2.2.1 An early departure no later than 0700.
    2.2.2 A late departure no earlier than 2330.
    2.2.3 Maximum Journey Time 23 minutes.

2.3 Marlow Departures
    2.3.1 An early departure no later than 0730.
    2.3.2 A late departure no later than 2400.
    2.3.3 Maximum Journey Time 22 minutes.

3 **Sundays Service Pattern** These are also specified.

Readers are invited to consult Table 120 of the Great Britain Passenger Railway Timetable to see how this works out in practice. It may be noted that through trains to Marlow must reverse at Bourne End. This station has two platforms on what is otherwise a single track formation. It is thus possible to run an independent shuttle service between Bourne End and Marlow, with separate through services between Paddington/Maidenhead and Bourne End only. There are more restrictive train length limits on the Marlow portion of the line.

Appendix IV:
Principal Names and Addresses

Franchised Train Operating Companies

Anglia Railways Train Services
15-25 Artillery Lane, London E1 7HA

Cardiff Railway Co Ltd
10th Floor, Brunel House, 2 Fitzalan Road, Cardiff
CF2 1SA

Central Trains
PO Box 4323, Stanier House, 10 Holliday Street,
Birmingham B1 1TH

Chiltern Railway Co
Western House, 14 Rickfords Hill, Aylesbury
HP20 2RX

Connex South Central
Stephenson House, 2 Cherry Orchard Road,
Croydon CR9 6JB

Connex South Eastern
Friars Bridge Court, 41-45 Blackfriars Road,
London SE1 8PG

Gatwick Express
52 Grosvenor Gardens, London SW1 0AU

Great Eastern Railway
Hamilton House, 3 Appold Street, London
EC2A 2AA

Great North Eastern Railway
Main Headquarters Building, Station Rise, York
YO1 1HT

Great Western Trains Co
Milford House, 1 Milford Street, Swindon SN1 1HL

Island Line
Ryde St John's Road Station, Ryde IOW PO33 2BA

LTS Rail
Southend Central Station, Clifford Road, Southend-
on-Sea SS1 1AB

Merseyrail Electrics
Rail House, Lord Nelson Street, Liverpool L1 1JF

Midland Mainline
Midland House, Nelson Street, Derby DE1 2SA

North Western Trains
PO Box 44, Rail House, Store Street, Manchester
M60 1DQ

Regional Railways North East
Main Headquarters Building, Station Rise, York
YO1 1HT

ScotRail Railways
Caledonian Chambers, 87 Union Street, Glasgow
G1 3TA

Silverlink Train Services
65-67 Clarendon Road, Watford WD1 1DP

South West Trains
Friars Bridge Court, 41-45 Blackfriars Road,
London SE1 8NZ

Thameslink Rail
Friars Bridge Court, 41-45 Blackfriars Road,
London SE1 8NZ

Thames Trains
Venture House, 37 Blagrave Street, Reading
RG1 1PZ

Virgin Trains
Meridian, 85 Smallbrook Queensway, Birmingham
B5 4HA

Wales and West
9th Floor, Brunel House, 2 Fitzalan Road, Cardiff
CF2 1SA

West Anglia Great Northern Railway
Hertford House, 1 Cranford Street, London
EC1V 9GT

Other Bodies

English, Welsh & Scottish Railway
310 Goswell Road, London EC1V 7LL

Eurostar (UK) Ltd
Eurostar House, Waterloo Station, London SE1 8SE

Eurotunnel PLC
Cheriton Parc, Cheriton High Street, Folkestone
CT19 4QW

Freightliner Ltd
The Podium, 1 Eversholt Street, London NW1 2FL

Heathrow Express
Cardinal Point, Newall Road, Hounslow TW6 2QS

Office of Passenger Rail Franchising
Golding's House, 2 Hays Lane, London SE1 2HB

Office of the Rail Regulator
139-142 Holborn, London EC1N 2SU

Railtrack PLC
Railtrack House, Euston Square, London
NW1 2EE

George Jeffreys –
A Ministry
of the
Miraculous

E.C.W. Boulton
Editor – Chris Cartwright

Sovereign World

Sovereign World Ltd
PO Box 777
Tonbridge
Kent TN11 OZS
England

ISBN 1 85240 196 6

This Sovereign World book is distributed in North America by Renew
Books, a ministry of Gospel Light, Ventura, California, USA. For a free
catalog of resources from Renew Books/Gospel Light, please contact your
Christian supplier or call 1-800-4-GOSPEL.

Typeset by CRB Associates, Reepham, Norfolk.
Printed in England by Clays Ltd, St Ives plc.

Endorsements

'George Jeffreys was an outstanding evangelist in the early twentieth century. This book challenges and inspires us as we pray for revival today. It is shocking that this wonderful story is largely unknown – it is one of the great treasures of Pentecostal literature.'

Dr Patrick Dixon

'George Jeffreys is one of the few Christian leaders of Great Britain that spiritually owned the nation during his life. He filled to capacity the auditoriums of Great Britain and had notable miracles that are still being talked about today and in many parts of the world.

His life is one that future ministers should study to see what caused such a great anointing and how George Jeffreys' life of ministry came to conclusion. I believe one who reads this book would see what caused him to rise and some of the challenges that he faced.

I am very proud of this book coming back into print again for the present generation to learn from one of the great Pentecostal healing evangelists of the 20th century. May God give Great Britain many more just like him!'

Roberts Liardon

Acknowledgements

This book is very much a team effort. From the moment I presented the idea of a re-print I have had much encouragement from Wynne Lewis and Derek Green of Elim. To my mentor in ministry, Colin Dye of Kensington Temple, I owe a debt of gratitude, not merely for his friendship and advice, but for modelling the ministry of the miraculous to myself and the whole of his team. Under his leadership at Kensington Temple, I looked back at Pentecostal history with, I trust, a new humility, gratitude and faith. To my colleagues on the team at Kensington Temple's International Bible Institute and the many students who gave me an opportunity to hone and shape my own thinking, I say thank you. To the congregation of Cardiff City Temple, one of George Jeffreys' key church plants, and now my congregation, I look forward to years of reopening the wells.

My publisher Chris Mungeam of Sovereign World has been a source of constant encouragement. This project has been fulfilled very much through his persistence. Thanks also to those who have typed the manuscript and helped with research: to Alistair Sanders, Jean Jones, and particularly Myra Harris.

To my wife Annie and my children Jordan and Alexandra, I thank God for the adventure of our lives together and thank you for your constant love and support. To my parents, particular thanks: my father Desmond Cartwright has a knowledge of British Pentecostalism which is unsurpassed and his enthusiasm for research has convinced me that we have not just a rich Pentecostal history, but a destiny that is still to be fulfilled.

Contents

Preface

In preparing this volume the writer has endeavoured to keep a threefold purpose before him. In the first place, that God whose arm hath wrought these wonders might be duly magnified amongst His people. Secondly, that before the Christian public might be put an authentic account of a work which has suffered much at the hands of those who have sadly misunderstood both its message and its methods. And lastly, that the members of our own churches might be furnished with a reliable record of that which God hath done amongst us in these days. Many of our own people are to a great extent ignorant of the early history of the work with which they are identified, and therefore we feel confident that from this quarter it will meet with the warmest appreciation.

We submit that in these days of spiritual declension and departure from the Divine pattern, when the fire of faith burns so low upon the altar of Christian consciousness and when perhaps in some directions it is threatened with utter extinction, this volume will bring a most timely message to many of God's people, awakening new and stronger desires for the return of revival and restoration of true Pentecostal power to the Church of God as a whole.

These pages are full of the clearest and most convincing evidence of the renewal of that miraculous *dunamis* which characterised and energised the ministry of the Early Church. The miracles recorded bear the stamp of the Divine. These 'signs and wonders' reveal that a new era of spiritual possibility is opened up to God's children – at the very threshold of the Church stands a mightily Holy Ghost outpouring waiting to deposit its wealth of power upon the

Laodicean-like conditions which obtain in so many religious circles today, transforming many a frigid fraternity into a warm and genial fellowship in which faith, hope, and love are found to flourish.

Within the covers of this book we see how George Jeffreys with the rod of the inspired Word fearlessly smote the waters of an incredulous and invasive modernism, opening up a passage by which many others might pass. He dared to breast the waves of popular religious opinion, thereby exposing himself to a fierce cross-fire of criticism from most sections of the Christian Church. In the very face of this, God enabled him to achieve triumphs which must for all time adorn the annals of evangelical enterprise. His example should wield a wide influence and provide an abiding inspiration to many, both within and without the circle of his own workers.

E.C.W. Boulton
Elim Woodlands, Clarence Road
Clapham Park, London, SW4
September 1928

Introduction

The remarkable life of George Jeffreys remains largely unknown outside of the British Pentecostal Churches. Yet George Jeffreys was one of the most significant pioneers of the world-wide Pentecostal Movement, and has been viewed as the most successful British evangelist since John Wesley. For almost a quarter of a century, Jeffreys blazed a trail throughout Britain. He moved with his crusade team from town to town and city to city, with little or no advance publicity, and often beginning in the smallest halls. Time and again his meetings were characterised by dramatic conversions and powerful miracles of healing and, as the word spread, crowds flocked to hear and see what God was doing. It is no exaggeration to say that cities were shaken and large churches birthed in what was seen as a wave of revival and restoration. As such, Jeffreys stands alongside his contemporaries Smith Wigglesworth, Aimee Semple McPherson and John G. Lake, as a man who influenced the spiritual life of multitudes and reached a generation for Christ.

This book tells the story of the early years of George Jeffreys' ministry. Written by one of his co-workers E.C.W. Boulton, a true Christian gentleman, it takes the story from the early days of ministry in Ireland through to revival scenes at the Royal Albert Hall in London in 1928.

It is clearly a period piece. A product of its time. E.C.W. Boulton's intention in writing the first biography of George Jeffreys was not so much to chronicle mere facts, but to reflect the dynamism of what he saw as a movement of God's Spirit through the ministry of an apostolic and highly charismatic leader. There is a sense of praise and thanks to God that runs through these pages. There is also an attempt to provide an authentic account of a work which, Boulton was aware, had suffered 'much at the hands of those who had misunderstood both its message and its method'. There was also a more practical reason for writing. E.C.W. Boulton, a former Salvation Army officer, was writing in 1928 as a minister of the Elim Pentecostal Churches. The denomination which had been founded in the slip-stream of George Jeffreys' evangelistic ministry was, by now, flourishing. Boulton writes so that the early Pentecostals, many of them having come to faith in Christ through the ministry of George Jeffreys, would be informed of the early history of the work with which they were now identified.

At times the book is overly sentimental. I have attempted to edit with a feel for the biographer's clear intentions, yet I have found it necessary to remove occasional anachronisms and a few purple passages. The original book was written for an audience which warmly awaited its publication. It refers in part to churches and leaders who were still in the very places spoken of. In such cases, I have simply removed the more personal references while seeking to maintain the thrust of the narrative. The focus at all times in this revision, is upon the miraculous ministry. Historical details of the future development of the Elim denomination and George Jeffreys' later ministry are dealt with elsewhere. Notably, Albert Edsor, long time associate of George Jeffreys and his crusade pianist and Revival crusade secretary for many years, has written from a personal perspective. Desmond Cartwright, in his book *The Great Evangelists* (Marshalls), and recently Malcolm Hathaway, in his chapter in *Pentecostal Perspectives* (Paternoster Press), provide the basis for a wider study.

At the close of a century which has seen the Pentecostal Movement grow from a small group of eager Bible students in Topeka, Kansas, who experienced the Baptism of the Spirit with speaking in tongues on the first day of the new century in January 1901, to a world-wide revival movement with more than 400,000,000 members, many are finding that these early days of Pentecost this century have a relevance to our own times. Events at Toronto, Sunderland and Pensacola have stimulated a great appetite for revival and revival literature. The roots of Pentecostalism provide many lessons for leaders and believers in the current move of God's Spirit. Certainly this story contains much that will fuel the faith of all those seeking to move in the current of God's Spirit today. I have added in this introduction the brief biographical details and the context for the ministry of George Jeffreys which is largely left out of the original biography, and I have sought to take the story from 1928 into what were undoubtedly the most successful years of George Jeffreys' ministry. Here we can only hint at the 'glory days' of crusades in cities like Cardiff and Birmingham, but even the briefest of detail will help to give the reader a fuller picture of the man, the methods and the ministry.

George Jeffreys – the Early Years

Born in South Wales at 24 Metcalf Street, Nantyffylon, Maesteg, on Thursday, 28 February, 1889, George Jeffreys was the eighth child and sixth of the eight sons of coal miner Thomas Jeffreys (1848–1895) and his wife Kezia (1851–1929).

He was named George after a brother who had recently died. Almost as soon as he was born, his brother Stephen, aged twelve, left school to join his father in the coal mine. These two brothers, from the relative obscurity of the Lynfi Valley, South Wales, were to have an impact on a whole nation and to affect the lives of thousands of people between two world wars. The effect of their ministry was to have repercussions across Europe and as far as New Zealand, Australia, South Africa and the USA.

George was converted with his brother Stephen in November 1904 in the first weeks of the period generally acknowledged as the beginning of the Welsh Revival. George and Stephen were present on Sunday morning 20 November, when the minister of Siloh Independent Congregational Church, Rev. Glasnant Jones, preached. Stephen had been under conviction for some days and he accepted Christ as Saviour along with fifteen-year-old George.

George immediately busied himself in the life and work of the chapel. The minister took a special interest in the young George and recognised that the hand of God was upon him and that he was 'a chosen vessel'. George worked for a while in the local co-operative store. Yet God had another path for him to follow.

By 1910, a fresh wave of blessing was blowing across Britain in the form of the emerging Pentecostal movement. From Sunderland in 1907 where T.B. Barratt had preached 'the Baptism in the Spirit' in Alexander Boddy's All Saint's Church, Monkweaworth, the message of a subsequent experience of the baptism in the Holy Spirit evidenced by speaking in tongues had spread to many parts of the nation including South Wales.

Stephen's son, Edward, returned from holiday having received a definite baptism of the Holy Spirit where he had spoken in tongues. George had spoken against the Pentecostal manifestations when they had first appeared in the area, but when he saw the positive effect this experience had upon his nephew, Edward, he became more open. Soon afterwards, in Duffryn Chapel before the start of the Sunday morning meeting, George and Stephen confessed their fault and that same morning George began to sing in tongues and praise God.

George had always felt that he would be a minister some day. Even as a boy he would play at conducting services. Yet there seemed many obstacles in his way. He was frail and sickly. A facial paralysis pulled his muscles to one side and he had a speech impediment. One morning, while praying, he received a wonderful touch of God's power. He described it as if his whole body had been connected to a powerful battery. He was totally healed. In later years when he proclaimed Jesus Christ to be the healer of the body as well as saviour of the soul, he could back up his words with his own powerful testimony.

The next few years saw George Jeffreys embark upon a course that would propel him into a ministry of pioneer evangelism that would place him in the mould of men like Wesley, Whitefield and D.L. Moody.

In 1912, he applied to the Pentecostal Missionary Union for ministry training and was recommended to go to Thomas Myerscough's Bible School in Preston, England. He was 'set apart for the regular work of ministry', sent off from his home town of Maesteg and sponsored by Cecil Polhill, a wealthy squire from Bedford, one of the Cambridge Seven who had gone together on missionary service to China in 1885. George Jeffreys was at the Bible school only for a few months when his brother called for him to help in an extraordinary mission in Cwmtwrch, near Swansea. Stephen had been preaching without a break for weeks with converts at almost every meeting. He was exhausted. George joined him and the meetings lasted seven weeks in total with 145 converts, with many speaking in tongues and some dramatic healings.

Urgent invitations flooded in for the brothers to minister across Wales. Soon George preached at the great Sunderland convention of 1913 and began to see increasing numbers of remarkable healings in his meetings. His preaching at the Sunderland convention led to his being invited to Northern Ireland by William Gillespie of Belfast.

It is here, in Monaghan, that the Elim Evangelistic Band was formed, that the first Elim church was opened in Hunter Street, Belfast, and that George Jeffreys was launched fully into the apostolic and evangelistic ministry that would occupy the rest of the his life. It is here also that E.C.W. Boulton begins to tell the story of the rise of one of God's generals.

City-Wide Conquests

As E.C.W. Boulton unfolds the story of the ministry of George Jeffreys up to 1928, a clear pattern emerges of a move of God's Spirit through a chosen instrument. Jeffreys proclaimed a powerful gospel message. Increasingly it was expressed as the foursquare Gospel (Jesus the Saviour, Healer, Baptiser and Coming King). Moving from town to town and city to city, all of Britain was opening up to the message of the foursquare Evangelist. Dramatic miracles of healing were attested to in many of the meetings and the national press were often keen and fair reporters of all that went on at Jeffreys' meetings.

Yet, the greatest and most successful 'crusades' were ahead. In September 1929, George Jeffreys held meetings at the Cory Hall in Cardiff, South Wales. Beginning on Sunday,

22 September, Jeffreys spoke to only a 'handful'. After three days, numbers grew and the first three decisions for Christ were recorded. Three weeks later there were 500 converts with no sign of things slowing down. The meetings went on for 51 days with what Jeffreys described as 'a real revival atmosphere'. At the end of the meetings they had recorded over 2,400 converts and were using the largest church in Wales, Wood Street Congregational Church.

From Cardiff, George went to Swansea. Beginning with an audience of 100, the meetings went on for a month with thousands packing the halls. One reporter from the *Daily Express* who had reported on the Welsh Revival 25 years earlier compared George Jeffreys to Evan Roberts. Swansea saw an outstanding miracle of healing. Glyn Thomas, a young hump-backed newspaper seller, known throughout the town, was instantly healed after George Jeffreys laid hands upon him and prayed for him. The jacket hung limp upon his shoulders as God removed the huge hump. The local newspaper confirmed the healing and many in the town who knew him were profoundly affected.

In the following years, George Jeffreys continued to blaze a trail across Britain. From place to place he preached the foursquare Gospel with wonderful effect. Up to 1939 and the outbreak of war, George Jeffreys pursued his evangelistic vision with incredible zeal and left many thriving churches behind him, and he regularly called Pentecostal people together for mass rallies in the largest halls in the land, including the Royal Albert Hall and the Crystal Palace.

The most powerful of all his series of meetings was in Birmingham in 1930. A few hundred gathered in a Congregational church in Steelhouse Lane, Birmingham, on Wednesday, 26 March, 1930. The meeting was not a great success with some confusion when Jeffreys called people forward for prayer for healing. George wrote 'they rushed out like wild Indians'. Within days, however, dozens had accepted Christ and within a week the church was full with long queues outside. After a month, they hired the Town Hall for four days of meetings. This too was packed out, so the largest ice rink in Europe seating 8,000 was used. For four weeks this was filled until finally, Jeffreys hired the Bingley Hall Exhibition Centre with a capacity for 15,000 people.

George preached 26 times in the Bingley Hall. Thousands responded to the gospel appeal. Recorded conversions went from 600 in the first few weeks to well over 10,000. Moody and Torrey had used the same halls years earlier with the support of many local churches. George Jeffreys had filled them for weeks with no such support.

George sensed Birmingham was ripe for revival and this drove him on to go through the 'door for effective witness' that God opened in the city before him. In addition to the large number of converts, over 1,000 were baptised in three services and well over 1,000 testified to having been healed by the power of God.

A Legacy or an Inheritance

George Jeffreys died on Friday, 26 January, 1962, at the age of 72. Over a lifetime of ministry, he had personally planted hundreds of churches, led multitudes to Christ and seen thousands healed and restored.

George Jeffreys had a singular evangelistic anointing. A full biography of this great servant of God is yet to be written. Certainly it will contain many lessons for future generations.

In Britain, Jeffreys had a far greater impact than that apostle of faith, Smith Wigglesworth. George Jeffreys, though more orthodox and conventional than Smith Wigglesworth in his methods, shared the same faith in a supernatural God. They were co-workers whose paths crossed from time to time in ministry but who each had their own contribution to the time and season to which they were called. George Jeffreys was so highly thought of amongst his contemporaries in the world-wide Pentecostal movement that, upon the disappearance in 1926 of Aimee Semple McPherson, Mother Kennedy (Aimee's mother) cabled George Jeffreys to come and look after Angelus Temple, Los Angeles.

At that time, Angelus Temple was possibly the most famous church in the world. He didn't go, but responded politely by assuring her of his prayer and stating that the work that God had called him to in Britain constrained him.It took a certain and definite call of God to say no to such an offer.

One final story is told more fully by Colin Whittaker in his biography of Reinhard Bonnke, *Reinhard Bonnke – A Passion for the Gospel* (Kingsway). Weeks before George Jeffreys' death, he received a visit at his Clapham home from a young German Bible College student. The young Reinhard Bonnke knocked at the imposing residence and asked if he could see George Jeffreys. The housekeeper was about to send him away when a voice from inside called him to come in. He entered the room where the ageing evangelist was and after some time, George Jeffreys laid his hands upon Reinhard's head and prayed for the power of God to come upon him. There are a number of unexpected but significant meetings in church history. This was one such meeting. Reinhard Bonnke has since placed on record his belief that God orchestrated that meeting and that in some way, the baton was passed from one generation to another.

It would be a fitting tribute to the ministry of George Jeffreys if, in reading this book, a new generation of Spirit-filled people would be stirred up to reach the Nations with the Gospel of Christ in the power of His Holy Spirit.

Chris Cartwright
Cardiff City Temple, 1998

Chapter 1

Another Pentecost

The story which we have to tell flows out of what was designated the Pentecostal Movement in the British Isles as it emerged in 1907; a Movement which, though undoubtedly and indisputably the creation of God, has been the object of much misunderstanding and malignity. Like other and similar movements of the Spirit of God, the Pentecostal outpouring was quickly thrust out of the camp of religious recognition: orthodox and organised religion soon hailed it to the bar of judgement, and an unreasonable and unrestrained prejudice speedily pronounced its verdict of condemnation.

The Welsh Revival of 1904–5 had left a wonderful aftermath of blessing. The tidal wave of revival which had risen in the valleys of Wales had exceeded the expectation of those who were prominent in its promotion. In a comparatively short space of time it had penetrated far beyond the borders of Wales, its billows of blessing reaching out to many a dry and derelict district, where no rain had fallen for years.

One of the characteristic features of this awakening was the enrichment of the spiritual life of numbers of church members. Thousands, who for years had wandered in the wilderness of uncertainty regarding their personal acceptance with God, now entered into full assurance of salvation, and found their lives flooded with a fullness of joy which completely revolutionised their Christian outlook. To some it apparently brought permanent soul satisfaction, yet at the same time within the heart of many Christians, representing all sections of the church, there was left a desperate hunger for a deeper and fuller life in God, a baptism of power which would make their work and witness more effective in the field of evangelism. Within the consciousness of these longing disciples was the conviction that in the recent revival the Divine depths had not been fathomed, that the outpouring of 1904 had but brought them to the verge of a still larger place in the purpose of God. They had been brought to the place where the waters were 'to the loins'; now they longed to go on to a place of yet greater fullness. On every hand gatherings were being held especially to plead for a further and even more fruitful and wonderful manifestation of Divine energy. People gave themselves up to this quest for that which they realised the Word of God offered and the hand of God held for them. We are not surprised to find that within the next decade a response to this widespread cry came from on high, in the shape of a most remarkable and phenomenal outpouring of the Holy Spirit, which in a few years had practically spread throughout the whole world.

It was in the year 1907 that the first showers of this 'Latter Rain' revival fell upon a small company of God's people, in Sunderland in the North of England. Rev. A.A. Boddy was at this time the Vicar of the Anglican Church of All Saints, Monkwearmouth. It was to this consecrated man of God that the Holy Ghost came. For some time, along with other children of God, he had been seeking an enduement of power from on high, but it was not until the latter part of 1907 that the outpouring actually took place. In the Parish Hall, Fulwell Road, might be seen a 'deep cut stone near the entrance' commemorative of the glorious baptism of fire then experienced; on which are inscribed the following words:

SEPTEMBER, 1907.
WHEN THE FIRE OF THE LORD FELL
IT BURNT UP THE DEBT.

The eyes of these devout and desperate believers had been anointed to see that an outpouring of Pentecostal power, similar in manner and measure to that promised to and possessed by the early church, was now available for them; that God was pledged and prepared in the twentieth century to grant them such a visitation and vision of heavenly virtue that was more than sufficient to meet the need of their lives and the land. It was not long before faith was rewarded, and the fire fell, mantling them with a glory and grace hitherto unenjoyed. In answer to their importunate prayer, the heavens had opened to pour forth a flood of power. Much of the Word of God which, prior to this, had been entirely unintelligible, now found fullest expression in their lives. The report of this remarkable return of pentecostal fullness quickly reached other centres and cities, being followed by similar signs. Those who for months, and in some cases years, had been thirsting for spiritual plenitude and prosperity, with rekindled desire and determination fell to their knees, soon to find themselves the subjects of a glorious immersion in the Holy Ghost, so abundant as to exceed their highest hopes. Thus from church to church and from district to district the stream of spiritual life and power flowed on its cleansing, conquering course, transforming lives, making them luminous with love and fragrant in holy sweetness. Higher and higher rose the waters of this wonderful downpour.

Soon hundreds could claim an experience analogous to that of the early church, corresponding in almost every detail to that which befell the one hundred and twenty in the upper room at Jerusalem. The revival being of such an unusual character and without precedent in the religious life of the period, encountered much in the form of opposition from those who, perhaps, assailed it before thoroughly understanding it. The chief objection raised by the opponents of this movement, was to the miraculous manifestations by which it was accompanied and distinguished. Like every other heavenly awakening, it became the target of bitter criticism. The denominational doctrinal experts pronounced its teaching to be nothing other than a system of error to be eradicated – a noxious growth which must be uprooted at all costs and by any means. What perhaps, to a great extent, influenced current Christian opinion and at once put a veto upon its acceptance, was the fact that it bore no sectarian stamp: had it appeared in the garb of orthodoxy then it would have been credentialled. How often we discover that the best way to ensure the permanence of a work is to oppose it; amid the clash of conflict it thrives and triumphs. So it proved in this instance. In spite of the fierce and sometimes organised opposition which surrounded the movement at this time, we find that it continued to spread to various parts of the country, fresh fires being lit, sometimes in most unlikely localities and with unexpected results. The winds of adversity but fanned the flames, making them take a stronger hold. As the official voice of the ministry of established church life was almost altogether silent, except when raised in denunciation concerning this new and phenomenal outpouring of the Spirit, it became necessary to convene special central gatherings at which teaching could be given bearing upon the subjects relevant to the revival which was then visiting the country. And at this time we find, here and there, in suitable centres, generally during national holidays, conventions being arranged which became the occasion for the concentration of Christians who had either received the baptism in the Holy Ghost or were seeking that enduement. It is worthy of note that a few of those in the regular ministry of the denominations had themselves become the recipients of this wonderful baptism of power, but for the most part, these were entirely fastened up in their respective churches and consequently unable to devote the needed attention to the rapidly developing work which was growing up around them. As a result the oversight of small companies of baptised believers often found its way into the hands of inexperienced and unqualified workers. Though possessed of a maximum of zeal, they frequently enjoyed a minimum of knowledge. That they were earnest and devoted is true, but these qualities alone do not necessarily qualify for leadership in the church of God. We are happy to add that even at this juncture, the movement owned a few men of calibre and capacity calculated to fit them for the direction of this Spirit-born undertaking, men who had suddenly found themselves cut adrift from their old religious moorings.

Within six years of its introduction into Great Britain, the Pentecostal revival had assumed such proportions as to necessitate the creation of some form of scriptural organisation. To observant minds it was evidence that unless some stable, scriptural government was established, the whole thing would become unwieldy and unmanageable, and much of the rich results reaped during those early years would fail to be conserved. But here stood a difficulty calculated to tax the resources of those who felt to some extent responsible for the future well-being of the work which God had wrought, and which in some cases they had been instrumental in commencing. In many instances the people had withdrawn from a cold church ceremonialism; they had thrown off the trammels of a dead traditionalism. The new spiritual stimulus given by this Pentecostal outpouring left them completely out of harmony and sympathy with a merely mechanical ministry. Others had seceded from a rigid religious legality, and having succeeded in freeing themselves they now swung to an opposite extreme, regarding with distrust any attempt to produce unity of church policy or practice, in some cases going so far as refusing to recognise any and all human government. This was regarded as opposed to the idea of guidance and government by the Holy Spirit, an idea which had taken deep root in the minds of many. Obviously the truth of Christian liberty was being misinterpreted and misapplied by some very sincere and saintly people. A false emphasis was being given to spiritual impulses in the direct and discipline of personal and church life, some passages of Scripture bearing upon this subject being so grossly misunderstood as to become the basis of a distinctly revolutionary and reactionary movement. It seems a tremendous swing of the pentecostal pendulum to go from luke-warmness to lawlessness, and yet that was what was actually taking place within this God-raised movement.

This distorted presentation of a glorious truth constituted a serious challenge to the progress and prosperity of the work, and also represented a menace to its future usefulness. Thus it was not long before a most undesirable and unscriptural condition existed among many of these groups of earnest but misguided believers. Restraint was resented – teaching on moderation in the exercise of spiritual gifts gave offence. As occasion offered, here and there a voice would be raised in warning, pointing out the peril of this trend towards lawlessness. But it would quickly be drowned by a chorus of disapprobation. During the first few years, several efforts were made to bring together into a cohesive and co-operative whole, what was at that time nothing less than a host of scattered companies. Each attempt however, only met with more or less disappointing results, until at last, growing up side by side throughout the country, were several small bodies known as Pentecostal people, each more or less controlled according to their varying shades of conviction.

In the midst of all this, is it to be wondered that things of more vital importance were lost sight of? Issues that affected the whole of the movement were veiled by the insistent demands of some small sectional interest. The danger of stagnation was growing greater the longer this condition continued. Many were so engrossed in the defence of their doctrinal position and democratic demands, as to preclude the presence of that apostolic aggressiveness and enterprise which should have characterised a work of this type at this stage. Halls were often located in most out-of-the-way places, which made access most difficult. Congregations were small, sometimes dwindling to a mere handful, and little if any attempt appeared to be made to improve the general situation. It almost seemed as though the movement was suffering from the paralysis of passivity. When objection was sometimes raised about this state of things, one would not infrequently be met with the argument that it was the Lord's business to bring the people. If the believers simply went on with God what more could be done? The success of the church or the birth of a soul did not depend upon the fleshly activities of assemblies. And was not the work of ripening the church for the rapture of greater importance than the evangelising of a whole district? Could not this work be left to other less spiritual though more evangelical bodies of Christians? Had not this outpouring of the Holy Ghost been sent for the specific purpose of gathering out a company of choice and chaste souls who in turn should be prepared for the imminent advent of the Bridegroom? This and other kindred ideas and ideals gripped the mind and absorbed the energies of many of these disconnected companies of Pentecostal believers. Why worry about the absence of converts if here and there a few saints were being baptised in the Spirit? That these little gatherings were often characterised by much spiritual fervour and feeling cannot be denied; that they experienced times of refreshing from the presence of the Lord is also admitted.

Many hearts at this time were deeply stirred. There were those who realised that the purpose for which God had so copiously and graciously poured out His Spirit was not being fulfilled, that the river of blessing was slowly but surely being diverted from its appointed course, and that unless some definite steps were taken it would eventually lead to the withdrawal of the power. In many quarters, the tide of revival had visibly receded. But who would take the essential initiative? Who would be prepared to take any action which would incur the censure and criticism of the majority?

In 1912 the founder and leader of the Elim work came into the picture. George Jeffreys, a young man who had recently received a mighty baptism of the Holy Spirit, whose heart burned with holy ambition and throbbed with passionate purpose, lived and laboured away in the Welsh valleys. He was brought up in the Welsh Congregational Church 'Siloh', Maesteg, whose minister, the Rev. W. Glasnant Jones, took a decided interest in the young lad, privately coaching him for a future ministry. Writing of George Jeffreys, he eloquently testified to the religious zeal that burned in the heart of the young disciple.

> At the open-air revival services I always found young Jeffreys at my side. I was privileged to give him his early religious tuition and a splendid scholar he was. Superior to other lads there was character in his face: I knew he was a 'chosen vessel'. When I left 'Siloh', Maesteg in 1907 young Jeffreys was in business, and had he remained in that calling, I am convinced he would have become a merchant Prince.

Although having reached a position of some responsibility and trust in the business world, he was conscious that the Divine call to be a regular minister of the Gospel of Christ was about to be realised. The conviction that God had called him to the Christian ministry had been his since childhood.

How to enter the regular ministry seemed problematical as there were many difficulties in the way. The few doors that seemed open began to close when his faithful testimony to the baptism of the Holy Spirit with signs following was maintained. Then again as an unmarried son, the responsibilities of the home began to weigh upon him. At what appeared the darkest hour, Cecil Polhill, one of the famous Cambridge Seven, came forward and supplied the financial support to undergo a course of Bible training under the auspices of the Pentecostal Missionary Union of Great Britain. Thus was the door opened through which George Jeffreys passed into a ministry and a work that is today world-renowned. In the furnace of trial he had borne within him an undying purpose to see doors opened into the ministry for others who were similarly placed as he himself had been.

His teacher, when at the Preston Bible School, was one beloved by all. The name of Thomas Myerscough stands in many Christian circles as a synonym for sound, sane and scriptural exposition of the Word of God. George Jeffreys' fellow students included W.F.P. Burton and Jimmy Salter, the God-honoured pioneers of the Congo Evangelistic Mission, Percy N. Corry, Dean of the Elim Bible College, and E.J. Phillips, the Secretary-General of the Elim Alliance. None would ever have dreamt of the potentialities and possibilities of that student class; in it were those whose influence has penetrated the whole world.

Within the heart of this Welsh youth were latent those qualities which, when properly harnessed make for powerful and successful leadership. Unseen and unknown, the hand of God was at work, moulding a vessel in which He could place the utmost confidence, and to whom could be entrusted responsibilities. Silently and surely Divine forces were in operation shaping circumstances and creating crises which were to have important bearing upon the future of this 'Latter Rain' awakening in this country.

As the young prophet-to-be looked out upon the conditions of the day, he was conscious of a great cry being borne within him for something to be done that would transform things. He saw that if this Heaven-given movement was to serve the Divine purpose, it must be freed from fanaticism and purged of many of its extravagances. And yet how to accomplish this presented a staggering difficulty. Little did he realise at this time how the Lord would lead and how wonderfully He would work out His sovereign will. Farthest from the mind of this young Christian disciple was the thought that he was destined to be the Nehemiah who should play such a large part in the re-building of the walls of this modern Jerusalem. The succeeding chapters of this book will show how, through the instrumentality of this chosen channel, God has been pleased to establish a work which has become a living demonstration of Divine power, expressed in well-ordered and properly organised churches throughout the land.

It was whilst all this was going on in the heart of one of the sons of Wales, George Jeffreys, that an incident occurred which proved to be a vital link in the chain of circumstances which was drawing him to Ireland. He was first introduced to Ireland by William Gillespie, who with his brother, George, eventually became the sponsors of the new movement called Elim. William had met George Jeffreys who was one of the speakers at the great International Pentecostal Convention in Sunderland in 1913.

One day a letter arrived, which, when opened was found to contain three ten shilling notes (£1.50), being the amount necessary to cover the travelling of the Evangelist to Ireland. This money was sent by William Gillespie of Belfast, who with his brother faithfully stood by George Jeffreys during those early days of struggle. It was the support of these two brethren that made it possible for the pioneer and his workers to carry on their work, throwing their home open and supplying much needed hospitality at a time when friends were few.

What times these were! Supplies often ran out and frequently the next meal was uncertain; letters would remain unposted for days as sufficient cash to purchase stamps was not forthcoming. And yet no appeals were made for funds from those outside. It was always to the Lord that they took their needs. These were days of character building – God was tempering the steel in order to make trusty weapons for future ministry.

Chapter 2

The Stream at its Source

A survey of church history shows how small have been the beginnings of many a mighty work. In Jerusalem we see a handful of trembling disciples, waiting for the promise of the Father; later on we see Luther, single-handedly facing the furious forces of Rome; whilst later still we find Wesley with his little group of inspired, but despised and discredited Methodists; and yet again, William and Catherine Booth with their tiny band of untrained and untutored workers seeking to evangelise the East End of London. In the light of such triumphs as those represented in the lives of these men and women of God, who can probe the possibilities of that which, though as 'small as a man's hand', has its genesis in God?

The story of the commencement and early development of George Jeffreys' ministry and the Elim work which he founded, reveals the humbleness of its beginning, the almost insuperable difficulties which it encountered and surmounted, the steady acceleration of growth and accession of strength, the ever-expanding area of influence, and the unflagging faith and zeal of the pioneers. The vision, which at first is seen to be largely local and limited, gradually assumes wider proportions, each new triumph adding to the ever-extending horizon.

Elim was the name given to the Foursquare Gospel Movement founded by George Jeffreys in the North of Ireland in the year 1915. It is taken from Exodus 15:27 where it is recorded that the children of Israel encamped after a long weary march. They sat in the shade of its seventy palm trees and drank of its twelve wells of refreshing water. Thus it signifies a place of refreshment, the most appropriate symbol of this glorious work.

That the North of Ireland was divinely destined to be the particular scene where this glorious work should have its birth, seems most fitting. Ulster had been the birthplace of the greatest revival of the nineteenth century, and thus it had become immortally endeared to those who remember that wonderful 1859 awakening. During this revival the Spirit of God fell in pentecostal power, with many remarkable physical manifestations. One writer, whilst surveying some of the work achieved by George Jeffreys and his band of evangelists, asks the very pertinent question, 'Is it that the prayers and tears of bygone days have hallowed in a peculiar way that soil, and are still being held in remembrance by God?'

By the year 1914 the young Evangelist had gained some prominence by reason of the success attending his campaigns in various parts of the British Isles.

Many remarkable things had taken place in the campaigns which he had conducted. At Emmanuel Baptist Chapel in Plymouth a wonderful wave of revival was experienced. Many were saved. Other were baptised in the Holy Ghost with signs following. A Christian worker who was privileged to attend this particular campaign, and who received the baptism in the Holy Spirit in these very services, gives his witness in the following words:

The evening meeting began with singing. Oh, how near we seemed to get to God! The place seemed to be charged with the mighty power of God, and we were lost amid the rapture of His presence. The church was filled with people that night, the preacher taking for his text, Luke 16:19–31. The power of God descended upon me, and my whole being was filled with the glory of God. From my innermost being flowed streams of praise. I was filled with an overflowing joy, and 'spake in other tongues, glorifying God'. George Jeffreys was, of course, interrupted in his preaching, and thinking that it was someone who had already received the baptism of the Holy Ghost, and should therefore keep silence until the address was over, he turned and placed his hand on my shoulder, only to discover that it was God witnessing to his ministry, and 'confirming the Word with signs following'.

Edwin Bacon, minister of the Baptist Church where these meetings were being held, says:

Sinners of deepest dye have been saved, drunkards, lovers of pleasures, and religious journalists and hypocrites have wept their way to Calvary and families have been re-united in the bonds of love. Hallelujah! Tobacco pouches and pipes and many other idols have been given up and consumed by fire. Some of the ungodly have been struck down in the meetings as dead, whilst others tremble from head to foot under the power of the preached Word. In some of the meetings Acts 10: 44 has been repeated, and numbers have been baptised into the Holy Ghost with the Bible signs, and came through 'speaking with new tongues'. In one meeting we counted over twenty who received in this way, and the glory of God was so great that both of us could do nothing but sit down and praise Him. Christians of all denominations are being brought into the blessing, baptised and builded together for an habitation of God through the Spirit. The number who have received during the Mission is upwards of forty, and the work is still going on – the revival fire is spreading.

At Coulsdon, in Surrey, a powerful campaign had been conducted, when great blessing had been experienced. Souls were saved, backsliders reclaimed, and many baptised in the Holy Spirit with Bible signs. The ministry of George Jeffreys at this time was described as 'mighty in God to the breaking down of the strongholds of Satan'. In one of the meetings Obed Miles attended with his wife and the power of God fell upon him, knocking him clear off his seat across the floor. The Lord saved him that night. His testimony is of interest. He says:

God did a marvellous thing for me at that mission. After some months of struggling against conviction, I was at last made willing to accompany my wife to the services. During the meeting on that glorious night I felt the power of God forcing me to the floor – I tried to resist it, but it was too strong for me. When I rose from my face, I know that I was wonderfully saved. So full of joy was I that the remainder of the meeting was entirely lost to me. I had something within that was continually urging me on to higher things. Smoking and drinking had ceased. Though I had five or six gallons of home-made wine in the house at the time of my conversion, yet this all found its way down the sink. Pipes and pouches were burnt. Thus all the bridges were burnt behind me.

News of the young Revivalist's successful ministry had filtered through to some brethren in Monaghan who were deeply interested in the evangelisation of Northern Ireland, and who after much prayer decided to send an invitation to George Jeffreys to contact a mission in the district where they resided. The revival campaign was arranged to be held in the town of Monaghan where it was felt a great need existed for the proclamation of the full Gospel. The Monaghan mission yielded some excellent results which fully justified the effort thus put forth, and also further revealed that, though facilities were few, opportunities were many for an aggressive full Gospel work.

Writing from Monaghan at this time George Jeffreys says:

Monaghan is a place situated almost in the heart of Ireland, where John Wesley was imprisoned for preaching the same Gospel which I am now privileged to proclaim. Although many years have gone since then, the Gospel which that saintly man of God loved and preached with such remarkable results, is still proving itself to be just as powerful in the convicting and saving of precious souls these days in the very same town. From the first of the meetings God has been saving souls, and sinners have been trembling under conviction of sin. One young man was stricken down from his seat by the power of God, was saved and immediately delivered from sin. Next morning he burnt a number of cigarettes, although no one had spoken to him about them. People come from great distances, and the hunger for revival is such that people come from miles around and the cry is everywhere, 'Come over and help us'. The young men who organised this campaign are on fire for God, and have received quite recently the outpouring of the Holy Ghost which first fell at Sunderland some seven years ago. Since then, many dear saints have held on to God for Ireland and, praise His Name, their prayers are now being answered. God willing, early next summer, I purpose going through some of the Irish districts, as I feel the need so much. For this purpose I am purchasing the Bangor Tent. Many the need of Ireland be laid upon the hearts of God's people for prayer.

At this early stage of operations it was clear that God had His hand upon George Jeffreys and that he possessed exceptional soul-winning capacities. Moreover, by this time he was becoming aware that God had a more ambitious plan than that of holding isolated and independent evangelistic missions in different parts of the country, a conviction which was also gradually taking shape in the hearts of those who were associated with him in this early enterprise on Irish soil. Deep down in their heart was the feeling that God had brought them together at this specific time for some special purpose, that His Spirit was constraining them to some, as yet, unrevealed endeavour.

And so, in the early part of January 1915, we find a little band of Christian brave-hearts assembled in solemn conclave in Monaghan, to discuss the best means of reaching Northern Ireland with the Foursquare Gospel. The vision was confined to Ireland; it constituted their Jerusalem, and as such was laid heavily upon their hearts – Judea and Samaria might come into the perspective later, but the burden of the present was Ireland for Christ and the Foursquare Gospel.

It was an hour pregnant with possibility and charged with commission. And yet how little they realised that that day the foundation of a work was being laid, whose ramifications should, in days to come, stretch forth in ministry to thousands of souls then unborn.

The most important decision which was arrived at that day, and which is recorded in the minutes of that meeting, was the determination to co-operate with the Revivalist, George Jeffreys, in the establishment of a permanent Pentecostal work in Ireland, and that a centre should be chosen by him in which to establish a church from which other preachers should be sent to evangelise the surrounding towns and villages. A further minute records the agreement of all present to the hire of a tent for the purpose of conducting special revival services. Before the year closed, God had put into the possession of His servant a tent suitable for campaign work. The expenditure of £20, which was the purchase price of their first tent, represented a large sum in those days when financial supplies were so small. Within its precincts many a well-fought battle issued in glorious victory. On the sawdust-covered ground of that tent sin-fetters were snapped by the score, and the victims of sin's seductive snares found the freedom for which they longed.

The minutes of the Monaghan meeting record:

> We agree that God promises to supply the temporal needs of every Evangelist that may be called by Him into the work, and that through prayer and faith in His promises, He will prove Himself to be Jehovah Jireh to each one.

From this memorable meeting at Monaghan, led by their dauntless leader, they went forth to carry out the commission which they were honoured to bear. It has been said that 'Christianity began as one sublime, incredible adventure'. It was in this spirit that these exponents of the evangel of emancipation went out to achieve exploits in the name of their Master, in several instances surrendering comfortable and remunerative positions in secular life. They reckoned and relied upon God, hence their triumph. Oh for more of this flaming faith! This robust religion! This vigorous vision! – that enables men to count not their lives dear unto themselves.

While the events just recorded were taking place at Monaghan, a few men in the City of Belfast were also being much exercised concerning the evangelisation of Northern Ireland on similar lines. God was working in different places at the same time, forging links that in His own time should be made into a glorious chain of blessing.

Shortly after the commencement of the work in Ireland, a lady, Mrs Jane Rees, in the north of Wales who had been greatly blessed through George Jeffreys' ministry, being anxious to do something for the promotion of a cause in which she took a deep interest, made a will in which she made him residuary legatee. Had this will been executed according to her wishes the work would have been benefited by several thousand pounds. However for quite a few years a legal conflict went on which absorbed much of the original legacy. Finally only a few pounds found their way into the treasury of the growing Elim movement. This naturally proved a great disappointment at this time, as money was so much needed for the development of the work. What a pity that a legacy of this character should have been largely lost to the work of the Lord!

Five months later, in the June of 1915, definite plans for the acquisition of suitable premises in which to establish a church were submitted and discussed. The district selected in which to carry on this work was in the Donegal Road area of Belfast. A hall having been found in Hunter Street, it was now decided to proceed to secure the lease, George Jeffreys being unanimously asked to accept the pastorate.

It is significant that at this meeting a resolution was passed prohibiting proselytising, deprecating any attempt to induce members of other assemblies to withdraw from their own fellowship with a view of membership in the Elim Church, a resolution which we believe has ever since been faithfully adhered to. Another interesting decision reached at this gathering was for the Pastor to prepare a statement of church belief, which eventually was printed in leaflet form, and adopted as a basis of belief by the Hunter Street Church, in Belfast. Though the building was humble and primitive yet within its walls God wrought many a wonder of grace.

In the five months that had elapsed since the last informal meeting at Monaghan, God had been blessing the ministry of the Revivalist in various parts of Ireland. Many souls had been saved and brought into blessing. He had also experienced much opposition in the districts where he had ministered.

Exactly one month later we find another conference of workers in progress. Again George Jeffreys is the central figure and around him are gathered those who are pledged to the cause so much at heart. The minutes of this meeting furnish us with the information that the first two full-time workers were definitely dedicated to the ministry. From the Minute Book we make the following excerpt:

> Pastor George Jeffreys informed the meeting that God had already answered prayer, and had given a definite call to Mr R E Darragh and Miss M Streight of Bangor, Co. Down, to work in connection with the Band of Evangelists, which we had claimed by faith for the Pentecostal Movement in Ireland.

As we move on 'step by step' in the unfolding of this story of blessing, once can see the work growing. As the months pass new ventures are made and fresh opportunities seized for the extension of the Kingdom of God in needy Ireland. The frequent meetings of the workers at this stage of the development of the work, provide interesting and illuminating insight into what was being accomplished and show the advances which were steadily being made and maintained. Here was no flash-in-the-pan movement – no mushroom growth which would wither under the first blighting test of trouble. God had vouchsafed a living vision which gripped its chosen founder and leader to such an extent that withdrawal was never entertained. Again and again during these early days of struggling we find this little company meeting together to discuss their difficulties, to face their problems and form their plans, always seeking fresh guidance and grace from Him who had set them apart to this holy calling. The goal was never lost sight of. This work owes much of its success to the possession of a leader who was capable of inspiring his followers with a spirit of unquenchable and unconquerable zeal. Like a true commander we see him in times of discouragement and disappointment, when perhaps faced with some temporary set-back, rallying his forces and turning what looked like certain defeat into splendid victory.

A few months after the church at Hunter Street had been established we discover the people rejoicing that, under the ministry of George Jeffreys, many souls had been saved and accepted into membership, whilst lives and homes had been transformed by the grace of God. Galway had also been visited and the report of God's blessing upon his tour of that part of Ireland was received with much thankfulness by the Lord's people.

The close of 1915 saw the ministry making good headway, in spite of strong seas of opposition. That year had been a year of preparatory work – of excavation and foundation laying, making ready for the superstructure which was destined to follow. Early in 1916, a new centre was chosen in which to commence operations. A town situated some thirty miles to the north of Ulster's Capital, Ballymena lies in a neighbourhood which figures prominently in the religious history of Ireland. Rev. Thos E. Hackett, MA reminds us that it was here almost 1,500 years ago, and on the adjoining slopes of Mount Slemish, a young captive and slave boy of sixteen, later the great apostle of Ireland, Saint Patrick, poured out his heart night and day in prayer to God, seeking His converting grace for himself and the mighty power of the Holy Ghost for the conversion of Ireland, still almost entirely pagan, to the faith of Christ, to which even then during his six years of captivity he was led to dedicate himself. How touching are his own works as found in his confession, or autobiography, to be found in the Book of Armagh: 'In a single day I have said as many as a hundred prayers, and before daylight used to rise to prayer in snow and frost and rain, and I felt no harm nor was there any sloth in me, because, as I now see, the Spirit was burning within me.'

It was in the February of 1916 that George Jeffreys commenced the work in this town, where a really remarkable awakening took place. Within five weeks one hundred and twenty souls were won for Christ; twenty-three were baptised in the Holy Spirit. It is recorded that the day after the Gospel tent was taken down, people were found weeping on the spot where it had stood. One lady wrote:

I do praise God for answered prayer. About seven and a half years ago I paid a visit to England and stayed at a place called Whitley Bay. During that time I heard of great blessing in a Vicarage at Monkwearmouth, Sunderland, and was very anxious to meet with those who were the recipients of the blessing. Praise God, the way was opened, and I found myself in the midst of the happiest band of saints that I had ever met in my life. They had received the baptism of the Holy Ghost, and were praising God. I recognised immediately that the Lord was doing a new thing in their midst, and oh, how a longing came into my heart that the blessing might reach my home in the North of Ireland. I made known my desire to the vicar and his wife, and we knelt down together and asked God to send the blessing to Ballymena. Ever since then I have kept on believing that He would answer those prayers, and although it seems a long time since then, I do praise God because I am privileged to see the answer.

Another Ballymena eye-witness adds:

For over five weeks the tent (in which we have seating accommodation for 275 persons) has been packed every evening, and in some of the meetings we have seen three persons sitting upon two chairs, while others are standing around where ever there is room to be found. On Sundays the wall of the tent have to be taken down that the people outside may hear. From the country districts around people come from some distances, and return filled with the power of God.

We have up to the present witnessed one hundred and twenty conversions and still they come in. Hallelujah! This again proves the statement some people make that Pentecostal Christians do not reach the unsaved is wrong. The desire to see souls saved is intensified in the experience of those who receive the blessing mentioned in Acts 1:8. Many have received the Baptism in the Holy Ghost with signs following in Ballymena, and they all testify to the power that they have received to witness for God. One sister was baptised on the street after leaving the meeting one evening, while another received during the dinner hour in her business place. Some who have been faithfully Christian for years are now seeking and are very hungry for the fullness.

It is wonderful to hear of how God is working in some of the homes. The workers are being sent for to deal with cases under deep conviction of sin, while other convicted ones come to the place where we stay seeking deliverance from the guilt of sin. The spirit of prayer seems to be given to the young people. One young man since coming to the camp meetings said he had been compelled by the Spirit of God to rise at five o-clock in the morning to pray.

I have spoken to many of the old inhabitants who were in the revival of 1859, and it is a real treat to listen to their testimonies. They speak of seeing many at that time prostrate under the power of God, while others would lose the power of speech for many days, and also of seeing lights and visions in the heavens; and oh, how they praise God for a touch of old time power! On Wednesday evening about one hundred and fifty Christians publicly testified that they were consecrating themselves afresh to God that they might receive the Pentecostal Baptism. One of the favourite hymns of the Camp meetings is 'Ireland for Christ!'

Among the early experiences of these times were many wonderful exhibitions of God's power. During one of the services, shortly after the Ballymena work had been commenced, whilst at prayer, the whole congregation was swept by the power of the Spirit. Fifty or sixty of the converts were literally mown down as the power of God poured itself into the meeting. On this occasion the glory of God was so great as to render further ministry impossible in that service.

A newspaper report of a subsequent convention held in the Ballymena Town Hall shows how much the town was gripped by the Foursquare Gospel Message. The hall was filled before the announced time to commence. So eager were the people to procure seating accommodation that at 7.30, some were standing in every available place, and numbers were turned away unable to gain admission.

Thus we see that at this early period God was drawing numbers of people together under the ministry of His servant.

Just prior to this, two more brethren William Henderson and Fred Farlow, became members of the Elim Band, and were added to the work. Another departure is indicated as taking place during the summer of 1916 when it was decided to invite Mr John Leech, MA, KC, of Dublin, and Rev. T.E. Hackett, MA, of Bray, to become advisory members of the Evangelistic Council which had been formed with a view to the general direction of the work. Both accepted the invitation, and became definitely associated with the work of the Evangelistic Band. It was at this time that the four evangelists working under George Jeffreys first of all adopted the title 'Elim Evangelistic Band'.

All these changes denoted progress, and marked fresh stages in the general growth of the work. Each new departure demanded fresh and fuller reliance upon God; the increasing responsibilities meant that more supplies of men and money must be forthcoming if advantage was to be taken of the opportunities which were continually presenting themselves. Hence the need for faith to be ever enlarging. Each new advance brought its additional burden of oversight. The new position captured must be consolidated; the new converts made must be shepherded; the believers brought into fresh blessing must be fed. And all the time the work was gathering responsibility, God was graciously pouring out that sufficiency of strength which made those youthful workers equal to the tasks imposed upon them.

Chapter 3

Widening and Deepening

During the next two years, 1917 to 1919, the work grew in all the centres where it had been established. Within this period the band of evangelists had been busily engaged in campaigning in some of the country districts of Ulster.

On 18 July, 1917, the first official Ordination Service was held under the auspices of the Elim Alliance. The number of preachers joining the work was rapidly increasing, and the burden of leadership was beginning to be realised by the one who was himself directly responsible for the direction of the work. That some authoritative ordination of the leader was necessary was becoming apparent in view of the fact that he himself would soon be called upon to officiate at the ordination of those of his followers who were called into the regular ministry. Therefore, the deacons of Elim Christ Church, Belfast, invited Rev. Moelfryn Morgan, an ordained minister of the Welsh Congregational Church, to perform this ceremony. Rev. Morgan was at this time co-operating with Stephen Jeffreys in a revival campaign at Belfast. So there under the roof of the great Canvas Tabernacle, which had been specially erected for the campaign, gathered deacons and ministers at the ordination of one, who in God's plan, was destined to ordain many others to the work of God. The ordination service marked a stage in the life and ministry of George Jeffreys which still further singled him out as the chosen and anointed of God.

This event coincided with Stephen Jeffreys' first visit to Ireland and also his first introduction to the Elim work. He had been invited by his younger brother to conduct a revival campaign in Belfast, under the auspices of Elim, Stephen

Jeffreys being at that time the minister of the Island Place Church, Llanelly, South Wales.

In the October of 1918 it was decided to call the general work the Elim Pentecostal Alliance, this title to include the three different branches of work then in operation, Elim Churches, Elim Evangelistic Band and the Elim Missions. Thus the three sections were co-ordinated for the common purpose of extending the Kingdom of Christ in Northern Ireland. It was in the same year that the 'Elim Pentecostal Alliance Council' was formed and legally incorporated for the purpose of holding the Alliance property in trust. The founder of the work decided on the formation of this council so that, in the event of his home-call, the property would be safeguarded and preserved for the Lord's work. The idea of making money or holding property for any selfish ends was foreign to George Jeffreys' mind.

Meanwhile, the church worshipping in the Hunter Street Hall had grown to such an extent that towards the close of 1918 it was found that the existing building was too small to accommodate those who gathered to hear the Gospel week after week. This presented a perplexing problem which to all appearance would heavily tax the limited temporal resources of those who had been responsible for the formation of the church and who were so anxious for its expansion. Furthermore, the lease of the building then occupied had nearly expired, which made removal imperative. Here once more, as we follow the history of this work, we shall see God's hand making a way for His people where no way appeared possible.

It had been resolved that the need of another hall should be made known unto God, and so again we find this band of believers on their knees before the Lord, asking Him to open a door and secure for them a suitable sanctuary for the work at this stage.

Every part of Belfast had been searched in vain in order to find premises which might be converted into a place of worship. All avenues of hope seemed closed – every means of escape from this difficult position seemed cut off. What was to be done? Soon after this an old derelict Picture House was discovered in Melbourne Street, which had originally been a Methodist chapel. When making enquiries respecting this building, one old lady who had been resident in the district for many years volunteered the information that she remembered it in the times when it had been filled with God's people and praises. Little did she dream that so soon the departed glory was to be restored!

But though the building was suitable in size and situation, yet the figure asked for it represented a sum which made a heavy demand upon the faith of those who were anxious to purchase but who possessed no earthly account upon which to draw. Here was a splendid opportunity for advance! It was only because of the Spirit-breathed conviction that possessed them that they ventured to step out and pay the deposit which secured the premises.

Shortly after the purchase of the property, the caretaker, a burly Irishman, chancing one day to meet George Jeffreys, remarked: 'I hope you are not going to turn my wife and me on to the road.' 'No,' replied the Pastor, 'You shall not be turned out of your dwelling.' Not long after this, the opening prayer meeting was held in the minor hall which had such an effect upon both man and wife that they suddenly developed a desire to leave the premises and as a result made their departure under the cover of midnight darkness, and were not seen again. Evidently the atmosphere created by that first prayer meeting was by far too warm for them, and so they beat a hasty retreat.

It was early in 1919 that the Melbourne Street building actually came into the possession of the Elim Alliance. Few, at that time, had the prophetic vision to foresee the stream of souls that would find deliverance within its walls or had the power of perceive that it would become a veritable Pool of Bethesda.

Though the brethren had consecrated themselves to the higher calling of transforming lives, yet when occasion demanded they could vigorously apply themselves to the work of transforming a temple of bricks and mortar, so that it might become a fit sanctuary in which to worship the Lord. And so with the assistance of a local contractor, the one time Picture Hall speedily changed its appearance and became ready for the occupation of those who wished to do business for God within its consecrated walls.

Having completed the necessary renovation and decoration the opening day eventually arrived. What a day it was! There, with wide open doors stood the beautiful Elim Tabernacle, a tangible testimonial to God's faithfulness – incontrovertible proof of His power to provide for His people. The opening of the Tabernacle in Belfast, which actually took place in the July of 1919, certainly marked a decisive and distinctive epoch in the progress of the work. From this point it seemed to grow still more rapidly.

Combined with the opening services was the first Midsummer Convention held in connection with the work in Ireland. This was my first introduction to the Elim movement. I had the privilege of being the first preacher to minister within the sacred walls of this prayer-possessed temple. The other special speakers on this occasion included John Leech, KC, of Dublin, Stephen Jeffreys, and James Salter of the Belgian Congo, with George Jeffreys being the Convenor.

Again and again during those days the congregation was swept with the creative breath of the Holy Spirit. These special gatherings were more particularly arranged for believers, yet quite a number of souls were saved at this time. One young man, who became one of the most well-known Elim Evangelists, gave his heart to Christ during these meetings.

Such gatherings in a wonderful way justified the bold move which had been made, and were in themselves a splendid foretaste of future blessing. On all sides were signs that God was indeed with them, honouring their testimony.

Seven years later in the same city, a second tabernacle was reared to the glory of God – described as 'another magnificent Elim Tabernacle'. So great had been the strides made in this period that it became necessary to erect a building capable of holding the large convention and campaign crowds which gathered in the City of Belfast during the year. The opening of this splendid and spacious tabernacle proved another striking triumph of and tribute to the power and faithfulness of God. From the first meeting every available seat was occupied, in addition to which the throng simply 'besieged the three big doors'. Each of these opening services was made memorable by the things which happened and the signs which followed the preaching of the gospel. The great platform was crowded with young men – all radiant in redemption's resplendent robes – the 'inspiration and admiration' of all present.

For several years now George Jeffreys' growing number of large campaigns, which took him all over the British Isles, had necessitated his absence from Ireland for long periods at a time. It became imperative, owing to the growth of the work, to transfer the Headquarters from Belfast to London. It goes without saying that the dear Irish saints felt the priority of claim upon him. However, realising that it was part of the price of progress that they were called upon to pay, they gladly suffered the sacrifice, knowing full well that their loss would mean gain to the Alliance work in general.

But with the constant spread of the work an ever-increasing need was arising for more labourers. Already it was becoming a serious problem how to man the missions and supply the centres with regular workers. Here was a handicap that promised seriously to impede the progress and retard the growth of the work. It was becoming imperative that other full-time workers should be forthcoming to help in the harvesting of precious souls for Christ. But where could they be found? The fields were white and ready for the reapers. Once more we find this valiant company claiming from God the sadly needed reinforcements. He had the disposal of all hearts in His hand, and therefore could constrain other young lives to a similar consecration of their all to His service. And so they 'prayed through' each difficulty as it arose, conscious that it presented yet another opportunity for God to prove Himself strong on their behalf. Before the year 1919 closed the number of Band members was considerably augmented. During this year it rose from seven to seventeen. Eight more, including two married couples, having obeyed the call to leave all and follow Christ as fishers of men.

If some of these preachers lacked the polish of the more professional ministry, and in the estimation of their critics did not always appear to advantage in the pulpit, yet the fruit which they bore in transformed lives and homes and the splendid spiritual absorption which possessed them, formed an excellent apology for any scholastic or social deficiency from which they might appear to suffer. At times they gave their message with faltering tongues, but always with flowing hearts. It is men and women of this stamp who have, in every age, left the Church a legacy of glorious experience and example.

Another new opening had taken place during 1919. Bangor, the popular Irish seaside resort, about twelve miles distant from Belfast, now possessed its own established church under the permanent pastorate of one of the Elim ministers. The Church at Ballymena also at this time had its first pastor, Robert Mercer having been appointed to this charge.

One illustration shows something of the personal evangelisation that was being undertaken. An Elim Evangelist, whilst cycling to an appointment, on passing through a small town, found the annual Fair in progress. The sights and sounds which are common to such occasions impressed him with the fact that the scene of sinful pleasure through which he passed contained no witness for God. This thought so laid hold of the preacher's mind that after leaving the town he was constrained to dismount, and there in the quietness of the country road he gave himself to prayer. That prayer took the form of a request for guidance, and from the young evangelist's lips went up the cry, 'Lord, what woulds't Thou have me do?' Soon he was on his way back to the scene of revelry armed with a bundle of tracts with which to face the ungodly crowd. Nor were the labours of that hour without their fruit. As he moved about amongst the crowd speaking to each one personally about Christ, three young men voluntarily took off their hats and there in the midst of the busy market surrendered to the Lord. The following year, this evangelist paid another visit to the same Fair, and a young lady, a farmer's daughter, was spoken to about her soul with the result that she was unable to retire to rest without first of all giving herself to Christ. In this way was the Foursquare Gospel being carried from place to place, and souls were continually being brought into saving contact with the Lord Jesus Christ. Sometimes such incidents as those described above resulted in the formation of small companies of believers who in turn became the nucleus of country churches where regular services were held.

Chapter 4

Going Ahead

Though still in its infancy, the Elim movement, under the leadership of George Jeffreys, was spreading out to many of the more important districts of Northern Ireland. One by one new centres were being added to the list of those which stood for the Foursquare Gospel. Like most pioneer efforts, much of the work at this stage was of an uphill character – in fact as we review the work of those days, what was actually accomplished appears all the more wonderful and creditable. Contemplated in the light of the well-nigh insurmountable difficulties, one marvels that so much was so successfully undertaken. In those days friends were few, funds were scarce, whilst enemies were many. And yet in the face of all this George Jeffreys and his band of workers persevered and prevailed.

The close of 1919 saw the appearance of the first issue of the *Elim Evangel*, at that time edited by a young Cambridge man, E.W. Hare, BA, who had joined the Elim Evangelistic Band. Appearing at this time as a quarterly magazine, the little green-covered messenger proved a welcome and necessary adjunct to a growing evangelical work such as that which it represented. The ever-increasing number of revival campaigns in connection with the Elim Alliance and the ever enlarging circle of friends, demanded an official channel through which teaching could be given and reports could be circulated. The *Elim Evangel* met this demand. Its pages became the medium of spiritual instruction to those who had been brought into blessing through the various agencies of the Alliance.

In its early days it was quite an unpretentious periodical.

Its primary purpose was to facilitate the spread of the Gospel in its fullness. That it met with a very hearty reception is revealed by the editorial of the second number, which states that 'it is a matter for real encouragement to know of the kindly welcome given in so many quarters to our first issue'. In the same editorial the spirit of its ministry was expressed in the desire 'that God will own and use our little magazine to the deepening of many Christian lives'.

After two years' service as a quarterly paper, so successful had it been and so great was the demand for it, that it was decided to convert the magazine into a monthly. Later on we find yet another transformation taking place, when in the January of 1925 it appeared in a new and enlarged form as a fortnightly. So great has been the success which the *Elim Evangel* has enjoyed that, at the close of 1927, its publishers were able to record an increase in its circulation for the year of 55,000 copies, bringing that particular year's total sales to nearly a quarter of a million copies.

By 1928 the Elim Foursquare Gospel Alliance publications numbered no less than four regular productions, including one weekly, two monthlies and one bi-monthly paper. Back in 1919 readers were few indeed compared to the thousands who now peruse the pages of our periodicals.

The reports from some of the country campaigns at this period furnish splendid proofs of the unique power of the Cross. Early in 1920 we learn that work was being carried on in many of the country districts. Meetings were being held in old schoolrooms and Orange Halls, where the people would gather night after night, sitting on backless forms, drinking in the message of life, often resulting in a real ingathering of souls. At Tullynahinion, a country district not far from Ballymena, a gracious visitation of Divine power had taken place. Robert Tweed, another Elim preacher, had undertaken a mission here, but had found the ground so terribly hard that he was driven to his knees for a season of fasting and prayer. The victory evidently came in this way, for almost at once a wave of revival broke over the place. The meetings were held in a large farm kitchen, where over forty were saved, mostly young farmers, whose lives had been most wicked. At night, when the meetings had closed and the people had gone, the kitchen would gradually refill with the young men who had returned to talk over the things of the Kingdom. There they would sit talking and praying till far into the night. The whole countryside was affected by this movement of the Holy Spirit.

During the year convention meetings were held in Bangor and Ballymena. Into the ears of the hundreds that thronged the Bangor promenade and foreshore was poured the glad tidings of redemption. Stirring appeals were thus made in the open air to the godless crowds, more than one definite result being registered.

Amongst other happy memories of those convention days was the picturesque scene witnessed on the seashore, when a number of believers were publicly immersed. Most of those who thus followed their Lord gave an unhesitating testimony of the power of Divine grace to save.

During those convention services many were filled with the promised power of the Holy Ghost, returning to their homes to tell of the Lord's doings in their lives.

One visitor at the conventions tells of the wonderful way in which the Lord seemed to control the meetings, and the marvellous spirit of praise and prayer that found expression in so many different forms, and through so numerous a company of Christians. Sometimes the blessing of the Lord would fall upon the assembled congregation like a shower of 'Latter Rain', and then again it would descend like the dew from Heaven, each and all being enveloped in a veritable glory-cloud, which seemed for the time being completed to shut out all earthly sights and sounds, and shut them in with God.

It is impossible to calculate the actual results of these conventions or rightly estimate the important bearing that they must have had upon the formation of Christian character and spiritual usefulness. That they were a source of strength to the movement is obvious. Think of some of those tired and tried workers, facing mountainous obstacles, often for months together; labouring alone in some lonely and difficult out-station. What must these annual central gatherings have meant in spiritual stimulus to such? With what gladness of heart they would wend their way to the feast which they knew awaited them in the house of God. With what renewed energy would they return to their appointed post to spend and be spent in the cause of Christ. And then again, frequently to such services as these, the worker would have the opportunity of bringing some converts that they might learn the way of God more perfectly, and be more thoroughly grounded in the things of God. Amid such an environment many a young believer would be deepened in the Divine life and drawn into closer communion with his Lord.

The summer of 1920 also saw the town of Lurgan invaded by a few of the Foursquare Gospel evangelists. Once more the Gospel tent was in service and figured prominently in a campaign which yielded some excellent and gratifying fruits. A report of this mission reveals that a very gracious work of the Spirit was soon in progress in this place. A large and attentive congregation was drawn to the tent, to whom the Word of God was proclaimed in the demonstration of the Spirit and in power. A great conviction speedily fell upon the people, many of them surrendering to Christ. A most encouraging feature of this campaign was the fact that decisions for the Lord were not only made in the meetings, but also in the homes of the people.

The tent soon proved too small to contain the crowds who sought entrance night after night, and so a larger meeting place became necessary. The Town Hall was eventually secured, accommodating over 1,000. To this hall George Jeffreys came and conducted a fortnight's special services for Christians. Even this hall soon became too small to hold those who came, numbers being turned away.

Some time after the close of these special services an Elim Hall was erected on the very site where the tent had first stood, and a church was formed which became in turn a real centre of fruitful ministry in the neighbourhood. It was estimated that over two hundred souls sought Christ for salvation during the campaign held in Lurgan. These were a happy portent of that wonderful stream of souls that have since found Jesus as Saviour, Healer and Baptiser in our campaigns all over the land! These were the days of comparatively small things, when the cloud was as a man's hand in size, but behind it was the irresistible energy of God. Stage by stage the Spirit of the Lord led His people on to more remarkable achievements, until the day in which we write these lines witnesses souls being won by the thousand.

Another new advance which distinguishes this year was the opening of a permanent work in the town of Armagh, a city rich in historical and religious associations. From its earliest days Armagh has been the centre of Irish religious life. For some time meetings had been held in some of the surrounding villages, but the time was now deemed ripe to commence in Armagh itself. Once again the tent was brought into action, but unfortunately on the very first Sunday night a storm of wind and rain came on which flooded the field, and in spite of strenuous efforts to prevent it, the tent was blown down and damaged to such an extent that it was impossible at that time to re-erect it. The disappointment was great, and all the harder to bear by reason of the severe criticism of those who opposed our work, and who regarded the storm as a kind of judgement from God to drive us from the district. However, in the teeth of all this God was working, and preparing to provide for His people in a manner which revealed His wisdom. Shortly after, the Lord opened the way for the renting of a church in one of the main thoroughfares of Armagh, a building admirably suited for the proclamation of the Foursquare Gospel.

At this point we again find George Jeffreys conducting the opening services of this, another Elim Hall, remaining for a seven-day mission which gave the new church a splendid send-off into the future. God greatly blessed the meetings which he conducted, and a considerable amount of healthy interest was aroused in the district as a result.

During the year 1920 several new members had been added to the Elim Evangelistic Band, thus strengthening the personnel of this Gideon-like company of Christian witnesses.

The close of 1920 finds churches formed in various districts where permanent work had been established as a result of the activities of the Elim Evangelists. Everywhere George Jeffreys campaigned large crowds assembled, some of the biggest halls in the North of Ireland being packed to suffocation.

Twenty-one workers had by this time entered the regular ministry under the auspices of the Elim Alliance. Thus the little group of Christian labourers to whom we are first introduced in 1915 is seen to have increased to several times its original number. The borders had certainly been enlarged in the short space of five years far beyond the hopes of the Lord's servant.

One instance may now be given of a particular test through which these pioneers were called to pass, a test which took every member of the Elim Band to their chamber of prayer. Robert Tweed, a most promising young evangelist, had been attacked by tubercular trouble, and hope of his complete recovery was, humanly speaking, small. It looked as though a valuable ministry was to be cut short. However, let him tell in his own words the story of his healing through faith in the Living God:

> I do praise the dear Lord for this glorious privilege of declaring the wonderful things He has done for my body, as well as my soul. There are many who can testify to instantaneous healing, but I cannot do that. For over six months I could scarcely walk, owing to pains in my legs and back. Also on my left side there was an abscess. As I believed the Lord could heal me, I called upon the dear saints to pray for me, and anoint me according to James 5:14. This was done three times without any apparent result. My lameness just seemed to increase, so that I could only walk with the aid of a stick. The Devil told me there was no hope for me, and that the Lord did not care how much I suffered. But the Word of God says:
>
> > *'For the mountains shall depart and the hills be removed, but My kindness shall not depart from thee, neither shall the convenant of My peace be removed, saith* **the Lord that hath mercy on thee.'**
> > (Isaiah 54:10)
>
> Praise Him! He did know my weakness! So one morning, while I was sitting all alone, a little distance from the house where I was staying, I realised His presence coming very near to me. As the Lord drew near the words of Mark 11:24 (RV) seemed to come to me:
>
> > *'What things soever ye desire when ye pray* **believe that ye have received them** *and ye shall have them.'*

I saw that I must put my feelings on one side and simply trust the Word of the Lord. I then arose from where I was sitting and uttered these words: 'Satan, I resist thee in the Name of Jesus Christ', and though the pain still lingered I still kept praising the Lord for healing me. Thank God He soon made it a reality! In a very short time I was completed healed.

Bless His Holy Name, though it is about a year since that took place, I am still completely delivered. Hallelujah! So if there is anyone who reads this testimony who has been prayed for in the same way but without result, I would like to say to them: 'Cease to depend upon other people's faith, and in the Name of Jesus Christ begin to walk by faith in His Word. Even though death itself should threaten you in the attempt, keep praising the Lord, and in a short time you will find yourself wondering where the trouble has gone to'. He is still the same Jesus.

Many years have rolled away since our brother thus proved God's power, and today he is still labouring in our ministry occupying the pulpit of one of our largest London churches.

Chapter 5

Entering Wales

And now the scene moves from Ireland to Wales. Wales with its fascinating and thrilling past; the land of so many mighty enthusiasms and deep emotions; a people capable of such intense pathos and feeling. As a nation the Welsh possess a remarkable record of religious revival. Again and again has the Divine breath blown upon its national life, until the mountain slopes and the verdant valleys have resounded with the songs of revival, and the purifying fire of the Holy Ghost has burnt its way throughout the length and breadth of the land.

In the soil of a national consciousness peculiarly suscept-ible and responsive to religious influences and impulses, God has from time to time sown the seed of His eternal Word, which in turn has yielded rich harvests of revival.

From the womb of the Welsh nation have sprung some of the mightiest of preachers, in whose ministry might be found a wonderful blend of prophetic and poetic passion; seers whose eyes had caught the glory of the eternal and from whose lips pealed forth the message of life with Divine authority.

Adjoining the town of Merthyr Tydfil is the thickly popu-lated district of Dowlais, with its large iron works and coal mines. It was in this district in the year 1920 that the Foursquare fire broke out first of all, and the fire here quickly spread to other centres, speedily making its presence felt as an aggressive force for God.

Pastor Stephen Jeffreys had been conducting special services here with remarkable success, the whole place being mightily moved by the revival which resulted. Hundreds of souls were saved and many wonderful cases of healing were recorded. Meetings had been held in various halls in the town, but eventually the Ivor Street Independent Church was rented and became in turn the centre of most enthusiastic meetings. In this building, afterwards to become the first Elim Tabernacle in Wales, great blessing was experienced. The crowds that assembled were all aglow with revival fervour and fire, and before long this building was thronged with those in quest of greater spiritual freedom and fullness.

At the close of this campaign George Jeffreys was invited to go and take over the work and to establish Elim for the first time in the land of his birth. In response, he crossed over from Ireland and conducted a remarkable series of services. Night after night the crowds of thirsty souls drank in the Word of God. The Ivor Street Church was at this time purchased by the Elim Alliance, Stephen Jeffreys accepting the pastorate, relinquishing the oversight of the Island Place Assembly Llanelli, of which he had been the minister for some years. Under his powerful ministry the Dowlais Church enjoyed several years of prosperous activity.

Speaking of those early days when Elim was being born in Wales, and when God was making her the instrument of awakening to the 'land of song', one privileged participator says:

> After a devastating way, and after the failure of the organised churches to meet the colossal need everywhere, there are breezes blowing from Calvary over the land of song, among the furnaces of Dowlais, and in the sweet Valley of Aberdare. The sick are being healed. Diamonds are being polished from the mines. The North of Ireland is being linked to South Wales. The Lord is doing a quick work. The Cross is being preached as the only refuge from sin, and the Holy Spirit as the sole Director and Energiser in the spreading of the true Gospel. The Resurrection power of our Risen Saviour is being experienced in the meetings. Visions have been vouchsafed. People are speaking in tongues. Paeans of praise are going up to the throne of God. Soul-stirring messages are being delivered. The flimsy trappings of Churchism are being laid bare, shams are being exposed, and Jesus revealed in all His wondrous beauty and glory.

The Elim work enjoyed a most hearty reception from these dusky toilers whose labour took them daily into the bowels of the earth. They were quick to realise the presence of God in their midst, and not slow to respond to His call.

Later than this and subsequent to the purchase of the church premises at Ivor Street, we learn that 'God continued to save, heal and baptise in His Holy Spirit'. The people were hungering for teaching that would satisfy their souls, and this was gladly given, resulting in numbers being brought into blessing that completely transformed their Christian living and thinking.

It was during George Jeffrey's visit to Dowlais that Mr Cyril Taylor, BA was ordained and set apart for work in the Congo mission field, Pastors George and Stephen Jeffreys officiating at this beautiful service.

The following year the Jerusalem Chapel, Merthyr, was acquired, and in time became a centre of revival power and blessing.

Chapter 6

Invading England

Until 1920, the Elim work had confined its operations to Ireland the land of its birth, but now God was opening a wider door and admitting to a larger ministry. Many urgent appeals had been received by George Jeffreys begging him to come over to England and commence something similar to that which had been established in Ulster.

Some sought to discourage any thought in this direction by reminding the Pastor that he would find England difficult to move, that the English temperament was far less impressionable and responsive to revival influences. Would it not be wise to seriously consider the big risks involved in any attempt to introduce Elim to England? Its native soil was Irish – to try to transplant it might mean disaster.

However, it has ever characterised the founder of this work, that when the call of God comes, however difficult and apparently impossible, it must be obeyed. God knows best! 'Nothing is too hard for the Lord' is a sufficient answer to all the threatening things that stood like mountains in his path. This is the spirit which prevailed in every crisis through which the work passed. 'God is able' was the war cry of these warriors of the Lord as they sallied forth to the fray. It was under the constraint of such a conviction that the first English stronghold was approached.

The place which claims the distinction of being the first to have the Elim Alliance flag unfurled is Leigh-on-Sea in Essex. George Kingston, a consecrated Christian gentleman, and his devoted wife, had both experienced a gracious baptism in the Holy Spirit, and for some time had been holding drawing-room meetings in the district. But it soon became evident that a building was necessary in which to establish a permanent work on full Gospel lines. A suitable site having been secured, a splendid hall was soon erected thereon. And so it is in the summer of 1921 that we find the Revivalist conducting the official opening services of England's first Elim Hall.

During these initial gatherings many souls were saved, backsliders restored and Christians of many years' experience re-consecrated their lives to God. It was at this time that he ordained George Kingston to the pastorate of the newly formed church. One who was present at this ordination service describes it as 'most impressive, and one not easily to be forgotten'. For eight days God's power was poured out upon those who filled the freshly opened sanctuary.

The same year witnessed a much more formidable undertaking, and one which made a far greater demand upon the faith of the Founder and his followers. The district now chosen for this new venture of faith was in one of the south-western suburbs of London. A disused Methodist Chapel had been located not far from Clapham Common, and though in anything but a habitable condition, was regarded as a likely centre in which to campaign for Christ. The roof of this building was far from being rain-proof and the interior sadly needed renovation. In fact as it then appeared it was described as a 'miserable-looking, tumble-down building, on which the boys of the neighbourhood had chalked in large letters: "The haunted church".' But nothing daunted George Jeffreys and his noble band of assistants prepared to tackle what seemed like a hopeless undertaking. They quickly worked such a speedy transformation that one interested onlooker said the building seemed to rise from the dead. An old issue of the *Elim Evangel* tells of 'Pastors and Evangelists, like Nehemiah, taking part in the building, with trowel, hammer and paint-brush'.

Negotiations had been entered into with the trustees, and eventually arrangements were made to rent the Chapel for twelve months, with the option of purchase at the termination of that period.

These earnest evangelists in the midst of a strange district were preparing to break up new ground for the Foursquare Gospel in England's Capital. They had not even the smallest nucleus with which to commence their effort. Many weeks of plodding, painstaking ministry followed, with congregations of a most discouraging character, and supplies so small as often to leave the evangelists with barely sufficient to meet their temporal needs. In fact the resources of these pioneer preachers seemed pitifully inadequate to the task in hand. How easy it would have been for them to have lost heart and retired baffled and beaten from the field. And yet God brought them through to glorious triumph.

At last the longed-for break came. The breath of the Spirit had blown upon the dry bones and the river of revival was soon in full-flood. Writing of this early campaign in the Clapham Tabernacle, Henry Proctor, FRGS, says:

> Many of the dwellers around this district have waited long and prayed for a real Pentecostal revival. Thank God we are now seeing the answer to our prayers. For the past month meetings have been held every night in the Park Crescent Church, Clapham, the preacher being Pastor George Jeffreys. Night after night the message of God is given to professing Christians. At one time the hammer of the Word is brought with crushing and irresistible force upon empty profession, and at another the Word is opened up in such a marvellous way that heights of attainment, hitherto deemed impossible, have been made plain to many a longing heart, and never without results. Conversions, healings, and baptisms in the Holy Spirit have followed at every meeting. Souls have been saved even at the open-air meetings. The large hall in the rear of the building is frequently filled, and sometimes over-crowded with anxious souls.'

The following press reports will demonstrate the general effect of the meetings upon the minds of the public:

IRISH REVIVALIST AT CLAPHAM COMMON

The Revival Meetings conducted by George Jeffreys, of Belfast, in the old church at Park Crescent, are attracting much attention. By the testimonies of the converts who claim to have derived benefit from his ministrations, it is evidence that a Revival of the most apostolic type is in progress. Not only are they claiming to be relieved of burdened consciences, but publicly testifying to being healed of diseases through the faith cures. By the intense fervour of the worshippers one would conclude that the Revival is being enthusiastically supported by the congregation, which is composed of men and women of all classes and creeds.

HEALING IN CLAPHAM

A building, from the outside looking as if it belonged to a bygone age, yet viewed from within, bright with glowing lamps. Such is the setting for the strange scenes which are being enacted in a church in Park Crescent, Clapham Park Road, where George Jeffreys, of Elim Tabernacle Belfast, is preaching. The meetings are decidedly strange and in many ways reminiscent of early Methodist Revivals, for one can hear the Hallelujahs and Amens resounding on all sides as the address is given. Many of those who claim to have received good at the meetings believe the preacher has been sent in answer to the prayers of the old Methodist saints, who in years gone by had reverently prayed and worshipped God within its walls. The old church has been converted into a real apostolic centre, where people claim to have received miraculous gifts through the ministry of the Scriptures. Most remarkable testimonies have been given, including deaf people hearing suddenly. Some who were diseased prior to the application of the olive oil, which is lavishly used by the Pastor, now give glowing testimonies of faith healing. Conversions of a most striking type are reported daily as the irresistible power of his sermons penetrates the stoutest hearts. That a Revival is in progress no one can doubt.

I have had personal dealings with each of the following cases, and others just as remarkable are of constant occurrence:

A sister was healed of deafness after ten years' suffering. A brother was healed when anointed for deafness so that he could hear the ticking of a watch. A seventy-eight-year-old Christian lady, who had six cancers, was so overjoyed at the glorious result of the anointing that she is testifying everywhere of her deliverance from pain and suffering. A young man who came from Scotland on purpose to attend the meetings, and who described himself as 'a physical wreck', testified that he had received the baptism of the Spirit, and perfect healing of body, all within a week. The evening on which this brother received the baptism will be remembered by all present. It was Acts 10:44 repeated in this twentieth century. While taking notes of the preacher's message the power of God came upon him, and like Paul, he was prostrated. Every part of his being seemed charged with supernatural power and his face shone with ineffable light. Those about him gave the following testimony: 'We heard him speak with tongues and magnify God'.

But now the time allowed in which the Clapham premises could be purchased was rapidly drawing to an end. Was this building so admirable adapted for aggressive Foursquare Gospel work, to pass out of the hands of those who would use it solely for the spread of the truth? And yet from whence could they expect such a sum as that which was required to purchase the church? Once more in their extremity they turned to God for help. He had not led them this far to permit disappointment to overtake them now. He would find a way! And so it proved, for before the twelve months had expired the Park Crescent premises because the property of the Elim Alliance. A note in the *Elim Evangel* of November 1922 records:

> Friends will be glad to know that the church buildings at Park Crescent are now in the possession of the Alliance, those in charge having decided that the substantial amount of the purchase price that came in sufficiently indicated the mind of the Lord for them to proceed with the purchase.

How wonderfully those Clapham Christians gave! Nearly £2,000 in one evening! Great indeed has been the reward of these hearty souls, as they have watched the progress of the Clapham Church, and witnessed its growing fruitfulness. Ever since it was opened it has been a centre of blessing from which lasting good has streamed to other needy districts, and it has become the parent of many other Elim churches in London and its environs.

Though the chapel in Park Crescent had been closed several years previously by the denomination to which it belonged, yet there still lingered one or two faithful souls in the neighbourhood who secretly prayed that one day its doors might be re-opened, and that its walls might once again be filled with a company of those who loved the Lord. How far from their thoughts was such a fulfilment of their hopes and prayers as that which actually was realised in the times that followed. Doubtless it was their cry to God that resulted in George Jeffreys being constrained to that particular locality in which to commence the Elim work in London. 'God moves in a mysterious way, His wonders to perform.' Bless the Lord! The faith of those few believing souls fastened the doors of that derelict chapel against the speculative builder and the cinema promoter. Some holier purpose was destined for that house of the Lord.

Less than three years later at the annual church gathering, we discover that the Park Crescent Tabernacle possesses a splendid membership having by this time grown from a mere handful to a healthy spiritual church numbering nearly five hundred members. During the time since its opening, hundreds of Christian believers have been immersed in the baptistery which had been built, and scores have been baptised in the Holy Ghost.

This all gave an added stimulus to the work, putting fresh courage into the hearts of those who had so unselfishly poured out their lives in sacrificial giving and had thus made this praiseworthy performance possible.

Some twelve months after the commencement of the meetings in the Park Crescent building, we find a very interesting retrospective review and report given, in which reference is made to the character of the work which had thus entered London, showing how solidly and steadfastly it stood upon the bed-rock of Scripture, and revealing what an aggressive agency it became.

Just a year ago the Elim Pentecostal Alliance entered into the possession of an old disreputable building in Clapham, which had been going to rack and ruin for years. Some slight repairs were made and bright services were begun under the leadership of the Revivalist.

But, best of all, souls were saved nearly every night; on one occasion five surrendered to God in the open-air meeting. Many received a definite baptism of the Spirit, with the sign of tongues. A continuous work of healing has been kept up throughout the year; and many diseases have been healed through anointing and laying-on of hands as in apostolic times. People have come from great distances; not only from the North of England, but from Wales and Scotland, and many from distant parts of London, for the Pentecostal Baptism and for healing; and some have given ringing testimonies that they desires have been fulfilled beyond all their expectation.

But as the building had been hired for one year only, it was necessary to decide at the end of September as to the purchase. Much prayer for guidance was offered, and the Revivalist was definitely shown that it was God's will that the glorious work should continue. The response to appeals for the necessary funds was delightfully spontaneous and joyful. No sale of work, bazaars or concerts were even suggested, but the church seemed full of cheerful givers such as the Lord loves. Then a transformation began to be effected and the dirty old building, which was a disgrace to Clapham, has become 'a thing of beauty and a joy for ever.'

During the month of December we have held three baptismal services at which more than seventy have been baptised, each one after giving clear testimony to the new birth. An old gentleman who was present, testified that in all the sixty years since his baptism, he had never seen anything like the joy and enthusiasm with which these testimonies were given.

After forty-two years of Christian experience, the writer can affirm that he has come into contact with no church where the Scriptures are so definitely adhered to in every detail. Moreover, every kind of extravagance, which has marred so many revivals, has been strictly excluded here. Pastor George Jeffreys is a level-headed man, extremely logical and thorough in his discourses, founding all his doctrines upon the 'Impregnable Rock' of Holy Writ. At the same time there is none of that deadly dullness which is the hall-mark of so many 'orthodox' churches but every visitor is impressed with the happy look on the faces of all the people, young and old alike.

At some of the meetings there have been stirring episodes, when we have seen people who come in bath-chairs enabled to walk home without them. Persons who have been deaf for thirteen, eighteen, twenty-two, and twenty-five years have been enabled to hear the ticking of a watch. Mrs Mansfield, from Cardiff, especially was healed of two cancers, and on returning home, her miraculous healing was so noised abroad that twelve people came from Wales during the following week for healing. Some glorious meetings have also been held for the send-off of missionaries, among whom were Mr Capper of the PMU, for China, Miss Henderson for the Congo, and Dr and Mrs Slocum for the Punjab, with a view to entering Afghanistan later, when the door should be opened.

The growth of the Church has been as steady as it has been phenomenal, for at the Sunday morning service nearly all the congregation signified their desire to be admitted to permanent membership, and this in a field which another Christian body had given up as absolutely barren and hopeless. A Sunday school has also been formed, under the supervision of Mr Bonner, to which the children of the district are invited.

Other incidents indicative of the effective and infectious evangelism of these times might be given, enough however, and more than enough, has been written to reveal the character of the work which God was doing.

Chapter 7

Glorious Triumphs

The same year that the work in London was commenced saw another fresh field added to the ever-extending battle-front. This time the scene of action is transferred to the north-east of England, where two remarkable campaigns were conducted at Grimsby, Lincolnshire, and Hull, Yorkshire. By this time the Elim Revivalists were become more and more famous in the world of Christian evangelism, and much attention was being drawn to the revival services which they were holding up and down the country. Such earnest evangelism as they displayed was bound to win recognition, and was also calculated to arouse considerable opposition.

Of the campaign at Grimsby, one, whose wife was miraculously healed, says:

> When it became known that the Gaiety (which has in turn been used as a cinema, skating rink and boxing booth) was being taken to continue the Revival Campaign of the two Elim Revivalists, Pastors Stephen and George Jeffreys, a feeling akin to consternation seized the people. Imagine it! A place that would hold five thousand people, that had only once before been used for anything but secular objects: and then for the Palestine Exhibition. Whatever were they going to do with a big place like that! But, glory to God, He just know all about it and sent along the congregations; and those walls which have from time to time resounded with cheers for worldly attractions, now re-echoed with loud shouts of 'Hallelujah', 'Glory to Jesus', and 'Praise the Lord' from hearts the Lord had touched, hearts full of thankfulness to God for His wonder-working power.
>
> To the people of God and also to the poor sufferers the meetings specially held for Divine healing have been most

precious. Cripples and invalids have been carried or wheeled into the hall, and God has so touched them that in some cases they have wheeled their own carriages home. Some have travelled many miles to receive God's touch, and they have found that the Great Physician was waiting ready to heal them. One woman travelled over six hundred miles for healing, and the Lord graciously met her. Blind people have received their sight, paralysed folk have walked – used all their limbs and gone home praising God. Deaf people have received hearing; dumb people have spoken, invalids have felt God's healing virtue and consumptives have been healed.

The people of Grimsby are not likely to forget the month of April and the early part of May, 1922, and the old Gaiety Skating Rink will never be the same again.

One finds it difficult to know where to stop, for God has set Grimsby on fire for Himself; almost everybody seems to know about the Revival, and wherever one goes, night or day, one hears some of the revival choruses or hymns being sung. One is sorry to have to touch upon unpleasant memories, but still we cannot forget the aloofness of the Christian ministers and leaders of religious denominations in the town. In some cases they have even said that the work was of the Evil One and advised their people to keep away, but in spite of this the Lord is drawing hundreds to Himself.

No one can prophesy what will be the outcome of the meetings at the Gaiety; we are sure that God can heal and bless without being in an elaborately decorated Cathedral. Even the tram conductors have christened some of the trams 'Jeffreys' Cars'! The name of Jeffreys will ever be associated with the wonderful miracles of Jesus Christ which have been performed during these weeks of blessing. One of the chief officers of the Grimsby police force has said: 'If this thing is a fake then it is the best-staged and cleverest imposition that has ever been practised upon the public. If it is genuine, then the two thousand years since the beginning of Christianity have been swept away and we are again in touch with the Healer who did these things many times over.' Praise God hundreds of people can prove it is no fake, but truly genuine.

SCENES AT THE GAIETY

On Sunday afternoon last the walls of the Gaiety resounded with shouts of 'Praise the Lord' and 'Hallelujah' of the many people who packed the old skating rink, and, although the notices as to skating hung on the walls, one was reminded by the hallowed influence in the place as the services were conducted by Pastors Stephen and George Jeffreys. One woman spoke of complete deliverance from a nine-year-old rupture; another spoke of being able to walk without the aid of a stick, and her rheumatism had gone. An old man of sixty-seven testified to have been cured of heart disease, and said he was now better than he had been for forty-two years. A nurse spoke of having been healed of nervous debility. Another woman had been healed of catarrh in the head, nose and nerves. A dumb woman (dumb from birth) rose up and thanked God for giving her power to speak. Another woman said she had been healed of anaemia and failing eyesight; now she could read the smallest print. Another was unable to do her own work through rheumatism, now she could do her own housework, and all traces of rheumatism had gone. One woman suffered from heart disease and could not even poke the fire; now she could go upstairs at a run and do all her own work. One man spoke of his little baby having been ruptured from birth and now he was completely healed, requiring neither truss nor doctor. Pastors George and Stephen Jeffreys also conducted a morning service at Welcome Hall, when five hundred people took part in the weekly Communion Service. They also conducted a meeting at night in the Gaiety, Pastor Stephen preaching to a crowded audience, almost every seat being occupied. People are coming from far and near bringing invalids and cripples to the meeting.

What shall we say of the closing scenes at the old skating rink? On the last Saturday evening of the powerful and persuasive appeal made by Mrs Kingston, of Leigh-on-Sea (who with her husband – both Elim preachers – has been assisting the pastors for the past fortnight), after the eloquent and heart reaching address and the pressing invitation to sinners to come home to Jesus by Pastors Stephen and George Jeffreys? And then the sight of sinners weeping their way to Calvary, one will never forget. Then on Sunday afternoon, even with the shadow of our pastor's departure hanging over us, Jesus met with His people and a glorious time was experienced. God came very near to us as first one and then another gave testimony to God's saving and healing power.

At the last service in the Gaiety a huge congregation gathered, and Pastor George Jeffreys gave a beautiful Bible Study on Calvary and what it means to us, concluding his address with a most earnest appeal to all to come to Calvary and get rid of their load of sin. To set a seal to this most remarkable campaign, over twenty souls sought and found salvation at this never-to-be-forgotten evening service.

Before leaving the story of the Grimsby Revival it would be interesting to say that the Elim Alliance succeeded in securing a suitable hall in the town, which had for some years previously been connected with a sound evangelical mission. George Jeffreys had the joy of establishing the church in their newly-acquired hall and appointing a pastor to shepherd the flock that had been brought to Christ during the campaign.

From Grimsby, the Revivalists crossed the Humber to the City of Hull, only to discover that the fire had already preceded them, and expectations were running high for a great triumph.

Monday, 8 May, 1922, will long be remembered by many in Hull as the day which commenced what proved one of the most remarkable Revival Campaigns which this city has experienced. It was with some measure of trepidation that the campaign was launched, and the use of a hall acquired at a rental of £30 per week, but the same Lord who inspired the confidence to take this step of faith also supplied every need as it arose. These meetings were truly apostolic in character, for from the very commencement God set His seal to the proclamation of His Word.

On the first evening of the campaign about two hundred of those whom God had so wonderfully blessed during the Grimsby meetings came over to assist in launching this new venture of faith in Hull. What a soul-stirring sight it was to watch this band of jubilant soldiers of Christ, with radiant faces, marching from the pier to the hall, singing as they went! From the first meeting, the platform was filled with a number of men and women eager to witness of all that God had wrought in their lives. How one's heart filled with praise to God as one listened to the testimonies of those whose physical fetters had been snapped; one after another they rose to tell in glowing terms of how Jesus had healed them through the ministry of His servants, each testimony adding to the weight of evidence that Jesus Christ is the same yesterday, today and for ever. Whilst so many are seeking, in these days of unbelief, to discredit the Word of God, for the past month God has been graciously and conclusively proving His Divine power to alleviate the sufferings of the afflicted and oppressed.

As the meetings progressed so the interest increased; night after night without any cessation, the hall was thronged with people eager to hear the message of life, conscious that God was speaking with authority and effect in their midst.

What wonderful scenes were witnessed at the Divine healing services! Long before the doors were opened the sick and suffering ones would assemble, all so anxious to secure a place amongst the number of those who were to be anointed and prayed with in the Name of the Lord. What disappointment was written on the faces if those who, owing to the great crowed of sick, were unable to be dealt with. Hour after hour passed away, and still they came. Frequently the singing would cease and silence reign whilst some healed one told of what the Lord had done in his or her body, told of how deliverance had come after years of pain.

One woman told of nineteen long years of suffering through paralysis, but when anointed by the evangelists she was completely healed; continuing to describe her experience, she added, 'It was just like a thrill of life coming over me, but I know very well it was the touch of Jesus, and now I am perfectly whole.'

Another sister related how after four years of suffering from hip disease, during that time having undergone no less than four serious operations, also being laid in irons for over three years, her case pronounced as absolutely hopeless by the physicians, God stepped in and marvellously delivered her. Now as a result she is able to do her own housework and whereas life was a misery to her, it has now become a joy. Others who for years had not been able to hear, had their hearing completely restored when anointed.

One sister who had been stone deaf in one ear for several years, came to the services and, whilst listening to the Word of God, suddenly became conscious that the power of God was falling upon her, and there and then, as she sat in the congregation, she was instantaneously healed. In this case, no one had approached this sister about healing, neither had hands been laid upon her, but there, as she sat under the ministry of the life-giving Word, God performed this miracle. Again another was brought in a bath-chair, suffering from a spinal complaint, and this one after being prayed with was able to leave the meeting without her bath-chair. There must have been many deaf ones healed during these services, the writer again and again coming in contact with those who had received their hearing.

Another sister told of her remarkable deliverance. For sixteen years she had never left her house except in a bath-chair; three times was she operated upon, and an invalid for nineteen years. The doctors pronounced her case as incurable. For twelve years her husband had to carry her upstairs to bed, and in this helpless, hopeless condition she sought to be healed. She told of how when Jeffreys anointed her she felt the power of God go through her from head to foot with a mighty thrill. Her bath-chair was dispensed with and, to the astonishment of her friends and neighbours, she walked home unaided – the first time for sixteen years. To quote her own words: '... and I have been able to more housework these last eight weeks than I have done all my married life.'

Perhaps one of the cases which excited most interest was that of a young man who, in the early days of the campaign, was brought from a distance to be prayed with; his condition was pitiable in the extreme: paralysed in almost every limb, and unable to speak intelligibly; he was as helpless as a child. What a change was wrought in this young man! I remember so well the evening when, full of new life flowing through his hitherto helpless body, he swung his arms above his head, and then in the exuberance of his joy jumped again and again from his feet, demonstrating the reality of that which had been accomplished.

These are but a few of the many whose lives have been changed, and whose bodies have been healed during this month's campaign in Hull. Truly the Lord hath done great things! Things which have closed the mouth of many a disputer and turned many a critic into a Christian.

In the after-meetings, night after night people flocked forward. Sometimes as many as forty or fifty kneeling at the front together surrendering themselves to God.

One wonders what was the secret of such glorious results? Was it the eloquence of the preachers? Was it the excitement and emotion of the moment? Or was it some strange mysterious influence which swayed the people? Undoubtedly it was the power of God. One was conscious of a tremendous attraction God-ward which few could resist. Men and women knew that God was speaking, and many realised the solemn responsibility of hearing and obeying the Divine message.

Whilst we are not in a position to quote exact figures, yet we may safely say that hundreds of souls have been led to Christ during these services. Many and wonderful are the cases of healing, and numbers of believers who were living on a low level of Christian experience have been raised to a high life in Christ.

The month's revival services were brought to a fitting conclusion with a four-day Convention, the Sunday's meetings being held in the spacious City Hall, a splendid building with a seating capacity of three thousand.

The Wednesday evening meeting – the final gathering – when nearly two thousand people were assembled! The glorious climax to such a series of services saw at least fifty souls at the Communion rail giving themselves to Christ.

Time has failed to erase the glorious impression which this revival made upon the life of Hull. Ever since those memorable meetings of 1922, the writer has had the privilege and pleasure of ministering to the church which was formed as a result. Eternity alone will disclose the amount of good which was wrought in those days. Today the church at Hull boasts its own premises and continues to flourish as an evangelical force for God.

Chapter 8

Appreciations

While all this was going on in the north of England, the work in London, Ireland and Wales was steadily moving on, and reports of new openings, increasing congregations, and many souls being born again, were continually coming in. Fresh calls for campaigns were always arriving, but the perennial difficulty was now to meet the demand made upon the already heavily burdened staff of Elim workers. There can be no doubt that but for the earnest and enthusiastic example of their indomitable leader, the ever-increasing strain would have broken the spirit of this brave little band. His unflagging zeal served as a stimulating incentive to renewed devotion. And so, though often beaten to their knees under the accumulating burden, they rose again to engage in some fresh enterprise for God. Such was the spirit in which they toiled through to inevitable triumph. To them defeat was impossible. God was on the throne – hence all would work out well.

A fairly comprehensive appreciation of the work in Ireland at this time came from Donald Gee, who at this time was ministering in Edinburgh. Under the heading 'A Visit to Elim,' he writes:

We had met unexpectedly in Glasgow, this brother returning to his charge of an Elim assembly in Ireland, and myself; and our hearts were full of joy at the Heavenly Father's love in thus providing fellowship on the journey. Is it any wonder that it was nearly 1.30 am before we could tear ourselves away from the beautiful scene and seek our berths below?

Early next morning we arrived at Belfast, and were quickly escorted to 3, University Avenue, where breakfast and the warmest of welcomes awaited us, and plans for a brief tour of some of the Elim assemblies were discussed. It was to be a busy ten days or so in very deed!

As it was Thursday, we had our first introduction that evening at the usual meeting for Bible study in the Elim Tabernacle; and a blessed time it was! The fine building was well filled, and the happy faces of old and young, the bright singing, and the splendid company of young people, all made one rejoice at what Jesus can do when He is allowed to have His way in hearts and lives. The next day was occupied with a short run down to Bangor. One could not but appreciate the natural beauty of the place – but after all, the chief centre of attraction for us was the 'upper room' in the evening where the earnest company of Pentecostal believers met together. The taste we had of fellowship with them made one desire a week, but next morning saw us hurrying back to Belfast for the week-end.

On Saturday night the streets of the city were crowded. Thank God for evidences of the Revival on every hand; especially noticeable to a visitor from elsewhere were the large crowds that would stand and listen to the Gospel message. Hundreds gathered round the faithful band of Elim workers in Arthur Square, as one after another, some straight from their work, mounted the little platform to tell 'more about Jesus'. When the leader appealed for decisions at the close, it was good beyond words to see a response right out in the open-air; praise the Lord!

And then Sunday at the Tabernacle! Some were expressing sorrow that our visit was too soon to embrace the Easter Convention: personally, we were the more glad to see the work under normal conditions and in the ordinary stride. The building was nearly full for the breaking of bread service on Sunday morning – and what refreshing liberty! The touch of God came on us all as we worshipped, and from the song of praise there broke forth the still sweeter singing in the Spirit that has been such a wonderful feature of this Pentecostal revival all along. He whose presence makes Heaven itself what it is, became a reality in our very midst; Hallelujah! And then what appetite, what appreciation, as we closed our time of fellowship with a meditation on Jesus in the days of His flesh as revealed in the written page. The Gospel meeting in the evening saw the place completely full; every seat was occupied and some extra ones had to be brought into accommodate the large and inspiring congregation. Testimonies occupied the after-meeting, and it was the joy of one brother to testify that a soul saved that night was one of his own workmates.

We have recorded the visit to the Belfast Assembly in detail, as it largely describes what we found in other assemblies the following busy days when Lurgan, Armagh, Portadown, and Ballymena were visited, and where – as in Belfast – we were welcomed both in the assemblies and in the house of God's children with a delightful warm-heartedness that made us feel instantly 'at home'.

Between two and three hundred must have gathered at Lurgan. At Armagh also we would fain have stayed longer, but before leaving we had a glimpse of the situation that makes work very difficult there when a hurried visit was paid both to the ornate Roman Catholic Cathedral and also the Protestant Cathedral, situating in striking proximity in this comparatively small town. We found the humble hall at Portadown that night much more to our taste, and the sweet fellowship there was a time to be remembered.

The closing week-end was spent at Ballymena; on every hand we had been assured of a good time here, and we were not disappointed. From the very first, when we had a brief time of prayer before the open-air meeting on Saturday evening, right through the meetings on Sunday, there was a rare sense of His presence. A glowing word through the gifts of tongues and interpretations raised us to the very courts of Heaven in the morning, and in the afternoon the large company that had assembled found wonderful comfort in study of the Scriptures. The assembly at Ballymena is solid and stands firm through all opposition and difficulties; later on we were told of the wonderful way in which the hall was acquired – truly God alone brought it to pass – but that is another story!

We came away from Ireland with the warmth of sunny fellowship in the Spirit lingering in our hearts, and an impression gained of a truly beautiful and healthy work of God. It was a privilege to meet the different workers all happily busy in the Master's service, and to have seen a work thoroughly and primarily evangelistic and soul-winning, yet at the same time remaining loyal and out-and-out for the truths and experiences God has made so wonderfully real these last years in the 'Latter Rain' outpouring of the Holy Spirit. We saw every reason to believe that the manifest blessing of God resting on the Elim work will continue and increase, as we believe it is doing. To God be the glory!

From the foregoing we gather how healthy the work was at this juncture, and how wonderfully God was bringing to pass the vision of those who pioneered and piloted things thus far.

During the summer of 1922, George Jeffreys travelled with his brother Stephen to the Continent, to take part in the annual Swiss Pentecostal Convention, which was held at Goldiwil. A very precious time of fellowship in service and ministry of the Word was spent at that time. During the visit to Switzerland the George and Stephen Jeffreys and party were the guest of Mr and Mrs Reuss, whose loving hospitality added much to the deep enjoyment of those days spent on foreign soil. Whilst in Switzerland George Jeffreys officiated at a baptismal service at Berne, when seventy believers were immersed in the swift flowing of the River Aare.

From Switzerland, the party crossed over the frontier to Italy, a pleasure as great as it was unexpected. But perhaps it would be best to let George Jeffreys himself describes something of the joy of this visit to Rome:

> Little did we think as we crossed the Straits of Dover for the first time, that we would be privileged to see Rome ere we returned. It was indeed with joy that we responded to the request of our beloved brother Mr Reuss to accompany him on a trip through Italy, after the Convention at Goldiwil would close. The eight days spent in the midst of that bright and happy company of saints, gathered together with their leaders from different parts of Switzerland, will long be remembered by us. Although speaking by interpretation, we found it easy to minister. The crumbs were devoured by men and women whose hearts were hungry for the Bread of Life.
>
> Having said good-bye to the saints at Goldiwil, our little company (Mr and Mrs Reuss, Miss Peyer, Mr Darragh, my brother and myself), set out on our journey. We reached Milan the same day, and having a few hours to spare visited the great Cathedral. We then pushed on to Genoa, and finally reached Rome. I know the first question many will ask will be, 'What did you see in Rome?' We saw great church buildings which were like prison houses, altars, statues, vestments, and everything that the carnal mind could devise in order to obscure the light of the Gospel. All that we saw, if built upon the poor fisherman of Galilee, i.e. enough to ensure that he (Peter) will never take part in any resurrection. We saw as never before how far men had drifted

away from the simplicity of the Gospel as preached in apostolic days.

There were other things that claimed our interest and attention more than these. As we passed along the Appian Way we could not help but picture the little company that came out from the city to meet the Apostle Paul almost two thousand years ago. Yes! somewhere on this dusty road, the meeting took place. It was here they welcomed one who was a prisoner for the sake of the Gospel. I must confess I allowed myself to take flights of imagination. I could see the happy faces, over which rolled tears of joy. I could hear the 'Hallelujahs' and 'Praise the Lords' as they burst forth from hearts overflowing with gratitude. I could see the old warrior straightening himself and taking courage. What comfort he derived from the meeting cannot be expressed better than in the words of Scripture:

> *'They came to meet us as far as Appii Forum, and the three taverns; whom when Paul saw, he thanked God, and took courage.'*
>
> (Acts 28:15)

Our visit to the Colosseum reminded us of the dark days of persecution. This old building which was completed by Titus in 80 AD was used for gladiatorial exhibitions. It has the form of an ellipse, the outside being nearly a third of a mile round. In days gone by fifty thousand spectators looked on while brave men and women walked with firm tread through the valley of the shadow of death. Imprisoned within the iron bars that covered the openings of their dens, they were accustomed to hear the roar of the half-starved and half-maddened beasts on the other side. Yet they have fearlessly stepped forth by the thousands, ready, and happy to seal their testimony with their blood. They have gone into the presence of their Lord through the arena in this old building. As they heard the last roar of the lion, they have heard the first note of the Heavenly Anthem. They have been transported from the scene of hatred and abuse to a scene where they are admired by angels.

Our visit to the catacombs (the general name given to the underground cemeteries of the early Christians) will never be forgotten. When we arrived at one in the Appian district, the caretaker gave each member of our company a taper, and led us into the long narrow passages. Occasionally we would come across galleries which crossed one another at various angles. In some cemeteries we were told there were often five stories of them. Here and there we could see the little chambers called crypts, for the sepulchre of a whole family. Here too would lie the bodies of the martyrs awaiting the day when they shall be called forth to receive a martyr's crown. The lineal measure of all the catacombs yet discovered is calculated at about five hundred and sixty miles. They served during the time of the fierce persecution, as secure places of worship and refuges for the early Christians. Here, where no ray of the natural sun could penetrate, they communed with their God. Here the Sun of Righteousness caused the dark places to be flooded with supernatural light. Separated they were from the world and its people, but they were linked up with the inhabitants of Heaven. If ever they lived in the suburbs of the Celestial City it was when the fire of persecution had driven them into these old catacombs. We were shown the Baptismal Font, in which they had been baptised in water, thus following the example of the Lord they loved. It was no inviting place to the natural. The candidates had to descend a number of steps before coming to the Font, which was a hole made in the earth. One could not help but contrast the conditions under which these early Christians followed the Lord, with those of today. As we passed along we saw an old communion cup which was used by them at the breaking of bread service. How they must have valued the time spent around their Lord's table! Through the pathway of suffering they had come to remember His death, and to meditate upon His Word.

Time and space will not allow me to dwell on other places and things we were privileged to see. We were in the Vatican, which has eleven hundred rooms and twenty-four courtyards. In it there is a marvellous collection of the masterpieces of art. As we looked upon the grandeur, we could not help but picture the first Bishop of Rome (if ever he was so) with his fisherman's coat and heavy boots, who lodged with one who made his living by tanning skins in a little cottage. From Rome we went to Naples, and saw Vesuvius which at the time was not in eruption, except that it gave forth dense volumes of smoke. We called at Venice on our return journey, a most beautiful city built upon the water. It was so strange to be taken from the railway station in a gondola, in the dead of night, right up to the door of the place where we were to stay. In St Mark's Church we saw eight marble pillars which once were in the Temple at Jerusalem. Our journey was one of great interest, and our experiences will be of service to us in the future. To God be all the praise for opening up the way.

Chapter 9

Blessings Abound

We now come to the year 1923, a year full of gracious tokens of God's guiding presence. Throughout the whole of the work, which was now established in England, Ireland and Wales, could be found evidences of expansion. Churches were thriving; campaigns were increasing; the number of converts doubled and trebled. The total number of regular ministers also showed some splendid additions, whilst many other hopeful signs gave cause for much thankfulness, and constituted strong incentives to the leaders to push ahead with their God-given undertaking.

During this year halls had been opened at several places in England and Ireland, giving to the churches in these centres an added impetus and stimulus. George Jeffreys found a demand for his presence at the opening services of these new sanctuaries, and great blessings were witnessed on such occasions. Many received the baptism of the Holy Ghost, others would be saved, and healed, the work throughout every section experiencing gracious revival.

The work in Wales had also enjoyed no little blessing, conventions were held during the holidays which commanded large crowds, who came from most of the valleys. The year also included in its programme two remarkable conventions at Hull and Grimsby, where large companies of Christians assembled for conventions which have been described as the 'most powerful, praiseful and fruitful gatherings yet held in that district'. The climax of the convention was reached on the last night when the spacious building, seating nearly one thousand people, was filled with an eager crowd of seekers after truth. It was a never-to-be-forgotten meeting throbbing with life. Over and over again, like the anthem of some celestial choir rang out the familiar words, 'Love lifted me', 'Since Jesus came into my heart', or 'Saved by His wonderful grace'. Many during these convention days were saved, healed, and baptised with the Holy Ghost as on the day of Pentecost.

Amongst other places where campaigns were conducted in 1923 was the Garden City of Letchworth in Hertfordshire. This delightful residential district seemed a most unlikely place for anything like revival fire to break out. It boasted so many beautiful places of worship; its life moved on in a steady stream, unaccustomed to anything approaching the extraordinary. To disturb the religious complacency of this select retreat would most surely provoke a storm of mis-understanding and misrepresentation. But here it was that the Revivalist commenced what proved to be a substantial work for God. The only building that could be found in which to hold the services was a large, draughty, wooden building that had recently been occupied by an engineering firm – empty even of seats – but in a good position.

Loving hands speedily transformed the shed into some-thing different, and from the very first service it became, to many who gathered there, the gate of Heaven. Speaking of those memorable services, a local resident said:

> Never before has the whole truth of God been so fearlessly proclaimed here, and as night followed night the sense of awe deepened, and sin, formality and "Churchianity" withered up under the burning searching truth turned upon them. Then, when husbands and wives knelt together at the penitent form, and dear young people sought and found the Saviour, the songs of joy pealed forth. 'Saved by His wonderful grace' and 'How I love Him' were sung with full hearts. The campaign was arranged for three weeks, but at the request of the converts and others it was extended to a month. During that time over fifty souls found Christ, while many others were remarkably healed; some after years of suffering.

It was during the autumn of 1923 that George Jeffreys in company with his brother and two of the Elim Evangelists, paid a visit to Sweden, Germany and Holland. From the reports which he gave of that visit we gather that he was most favourably impressed with what he saw and heard of the Lord's work in Sweden. Specially was he impressed by the character of the men who were responsible for the leadership of the pentecostal churches in that land. In his letters he makes reference to the splendid spirit of unity which obtained amongst these dear Scandinavian saints, and the wonderful way in which they all, without a single exception, co-operated to accomplish the Lord's will.

During their tour many places of repute were visited, including Stockholm, Oslo, Gothenburg, Malmo, Berlin and Amsterdam. At Stockholm a very helpful mission was conducted which, in spite of the language difficulty, resulted in much blessing, and served to cement the hearts of the Swedish and British brethren in the unbreakable bonds of Christian fellowship. George Jeffreys writing of this particular occasion says: 'It was a short visit, but a sweet one. The services were inspiring, and we felt quite at home in delivering the messages.' He adds later, 'A tour such as we were privileged to take cannot help but deepen our lives, broaden our minds, and inspire us to attain greater things for our Lord in the homeland.'

Chapter 10

A Publishing Office and a
Bible College in Answer to Prayer

The spring of 1924 brought a much-needed development in the work. The continually increasing circulation of the *Elim Evangel* and the growing demand for Foursquare Gospel literature had made the establishment of a publishing office imperative. For four years the *Evangel* had been printed at Tamworth by Frederic B. Phillips, but the rapid expansion of the Alliance made it necessary to remove the printing plant to London, where in the early part of the year, the foundations of the new building were laid.

Thus at 12.30 pm on Easter Monday, 21 April, 1924, God opened another avenue of blessing through which He might pour His love and grace upon thirsty, needy souls. Who can estimate the power of the printed word, reaching countless hearts and homes where the voice of the Gospel preacher can never hope to penetrate?

Before long four gospel periodicals were being regularly printed on our own press, one of these being a weekly publication. Thus from its small beginning the Elim Publishing Office and Printing Works grew side by side and year by year. In 1927 the Publishing office secured more centrally situated premises in London's Clapham Park Road, which enabled them to cope more freely with the rising demands made upon them.

In the November of 1924 we have the first reference to the subject of a Bible School for the training of young men and women for the ministry of the Foursquare Gospel Church. For eighteen months prior to this the matter had been under consideration, and much prayer had been made along this line. However, the need had become so acute and the burden so pressing that it was decided to venture out in the name of the Lord. The readers of the *Elim Evangel* were asked to pray definitely and desperately for three things. Firstly, that suitable premises might be acquired. Secondly, that funds might be forthcoming, and lastly, that special guidance might be given in the selection of a suitable staff for the School.

At the same time that this appeal appeared George Jeffreys himself was so stirred in his own soul regarding the need of qualified labourers, that we find him making a further and supplementary appeal in which he says:

'Send forth labourers!' These are words that are stamped indelibly upon my heart, that ring in my ears, as I seek to pen this appeal for support to open a much-needed Bible Training School for eleventh-hour labouring messengers. Since the commencement of our ever-spreading Elim work, we have managed to carry on without such an institution, but now it is almost impossible to open up new fields and to respond to the various needs by sending out preachers without a certain amount of training. The midnight hour of this dispensation is almost striking, and hundreds upon hundreds of large cities and towns, to say nothing of the countless villages in our beloved British Isles have never been reached with the news of this present-day outpouring of the latter rain.

To these multitudes we, as Spirit-filled men and women, are debtors, and we must endeavour to meet our obligations before it is too late. Like the woman who obeyed the command of the old time prophet, we must go and borrow vessels that they might be filled to overflowing, and thus pay our debt. Yes! There are vessels beyond number waiting to be gathered in. Human vessels that should be filled with the same Holy Ghost as we have received. The one thing needful is that they might be gathered. The command to do so has been given by the greatest of all prophets and the method of procedure mapped out in the greatest of all books. It is by training and sending forth Spirit-filled preachers with the marvellous message of full Salvation for spirit, soul and body. There are souls like diamonds in the dust, waiting to be picked up. There are perishing ones all around that need to be rescued.

To saved parents who are praying for the conversion of their own boys and girls, the call comes. Will you not do something to assist in sending deliverance to other parents' children? While praying for your own, remember the drooping heart of some mother, some father, that you can cheer. In helping to send the blessing to theirs, you will surely command a blessing upon your own.

To parents whose children are saved, the call comes also. You of all should express in a most practical way your gratitude to God for their salvation, by assisting to send the delivering Word to the children of others.

To one and all, I say, see that you redeem the time by doing all in your power to cover the land with Holy Ghost messengers. Pay your debt to your neighbours in the British Isles.

Time, which is more precious than rubies or diamonds, is slipping by, and your opportunity will soon be gone. Look at that poor wretch grovelling in the mire of sin: he needs to be told of the power of God to save. Look at that dear saint agonising in the languishing bed of sickness; she needs to hear of the power of God to heal. Look at that Christian young man who is conscious of his lack of power for service. How thankful he would be if he were informed of the latter rain outpouring! Think of what the message would mean to one and all alike! Friend, pay your debt by helping to send forth those that will gather vessels for the glory of God.

To expedite this work we need a Training School, a place where the study of the Word of God can be combined with the practical side of evangelism. Our progress has been greatly handicapped during the past few years through the lack of such an institution. It has been impossible to accept more than a few into the work at a time, because there has been no means by which to train them and thrust them forth.

The need is great, and we must forge ahead. Suitable premises must be secured for the purpose of making it possible to speed up and take advantage of the soon-passing privileges. The call for training comes from those in all spheres of life. It demands our attention, and we should supply the answer in the most practical form by procuring a Training School that stands four-square on the Word of God. As I look back over the past, I cannot but feel grateful to God and our Elim friends for their faithfulness in prayer and practice. I have been more than encouraged at the measure of their support that has been given when I have deemed it necessary to appeal for a forward movement. In this again I know my word will not fall upon deaf ears.

It was an hour of supreme joy to George Jeffreys when the doors of the new Bible College were thrown open and an opportunity was thus given for young people to devote themselves to the Lord's work. For years he had cherished the hope of establishing a centre where labourers could be trained and from which a constant stream of workers could be sent to preach the Foursquare Gospel. And now the vision had been fulfilled, and there stood that substantial structure, proof positive of God's unchanging faithfulness and un-limited ability. How wonderful are all His ways! Who can measure them?

It was not until the latter part of 1925 that the Bible College came into the possession of the Elim Alliance. For some years it had been a Roman Catholic Convent and to pass into the hands of such an aggressive evangelical body as the Elim Foursquare Gospel Alliance was surely but little short of a miracle. And yet we are not surprised since prayer must prevail over the most stubborn resistance. That these doors have been opened in answer to living faith is certainly true. In the place where the mass had been often celebrated and where probably many an aching heart had poured out its pent up bitterness in the confessional, was now to be heard the sound of joyous praise issuing from lives immersed in the fullness Divine. What a contrast! Its gloom now gone; no longer the ghostly shadows of a medieval monasticism hover over that stately structure. It is almost as though it has experience a new birth – out of the dismal past has emerged the glad laughter of a new dawn.

It was most fitting that the personality around whom the Elim work had grown up, and upon whom its administration chiefly depended, should retain the Principalship, and one can easily understand the attitude of the Elim Alliance Overseers in prevailing upon their trusted leader to acquiesce in this.

News of the wonderful work that God was doing through His servants had reached Canada and the USA and requests for them to pay a visit to these lands had been coming in for some time. The question of crossing the Atlantic had been under consideration for many months, but owing to the demands of the work in the Homeland, it had been deemed wise to defer departure. However, in the early part of 1924, plans were made for the formation of a small party to proceed to Canada and the States.

Chapter 11

A Transatlantic Tour

When it became know that George Jeffreys and his party had definitely decided to visit Canada and the States, he was inundated with requests for revival campaigns. From most of the large cities of the Eastern and Western States came calls for campaigns. The majority of these invitations we were unable to accept.

The primary purpose of the tour was educational. It was with a view to the acquisition of experience and knowledge in certain directions that the project was first of all proposed. Then again the shortage of workers coupled with the growing demands of the work in the Homeland made it imperative that the tour should be as short as possible. It would be hard to spare a band of five experienced brethren for any considerable length of time. As a consequence the campaigns that were conducted were brief in duration.

It was on 21 June, 1924 that the evangelistic party embarked from Southampton on the *SS Empress of Scotland*. It proved a delightful day for departure! A cloudless sky and a sea as calm as a mill-pond. As the large liner gracefully glided out from the quayside – such a deep, sweet sense of the Divine sufficiency possessed us. Each heart was supremely conscious that He had gone before to prepare the path and make it plain. It seemed as though, with invisible hand, the Holy Spirit had painted in characters of gold across the rapidly receding stretch of homeland, that one significant word, 'Emmanuel' God with us! And so it proved! For throughout that nearly fifteen thousand miles journey over sea and land one was gladly and deeply aware of His unfailing guidance and control.

Seven days at sea saw us once more with our feet upon terra firma as we set foot upon Canadian soil. Our voyage of over three thousand miles contained many pleasing incidents. Opportunities for witnessing of Christ were numerous, and each member of the party was only too glad to seize such chances of dealing personally with souls.

Quebec was the point of disembarkation; a most impressive sight are those wonderful heights of Abraham which greet the eye from the deck of the incoming liner. Five hours railway journey brought the party to Montreal where the first meetings had been arranged to be held. A very cordial reception came from our Canadian host and hostess, Pastor and Mrs Baker, whose heart and home were thrown open to the English visitors.

Speaking of the experiences of that time, one of the party remarked how 'all sense of strangeness speedily disappeared' as we felt ourselves part of a glad family group with Jesus Himself in the midst. Three weeks fruitful and fragrant fellowship passed all too quickly, during which time meetings were held daily, and much profitable ministry was given. In one sense everything seemed so new and novel in the methods employed by our hosts, and yet beneath all this was found the same spirit to which we were so accustomed in our own work. During these meetings a steady stream of souls made their way to Christ, and a healthy atmosphere of revival prevailed.

Perhaps the most unfavourable season of the year had been chosen for anything like a prolonged series of services – the heat of the Canadian summer is so great that to a stranger it is almost unbearable – therefore to command a crowd of any really great size at such a time is difficult. However in spite of this drawback the crowds came, and over them was cast the spell of the Good News. More than one remarkable case of healing took place during the Montreal meetings. One was painfully surprised at the awful wantonness and wickedness of this great Canadian City, presenting as it did such a strange mixture of Arcadian beauty and Athenian idolatry: so completely given up to pleasure and profligacy that it would not be an exaggeration to describe it as a modern Sodom and Gomorrah – every conceivable allurement and attraction being offered for the indulgence of the sinful passions of the ungodly. It was a real joy to find such a splendid company of the Lord's people thriving in the midst of all this corruption and crime, holding forth the Word of Life with unflinching courage, standing like a brilliant beacon, throwing out its welcome, warning rays across the dark and angry waters that surge around.

The last night of the campaign at Montreal was in every sense of the word a fitting finish to what had undoubtedly proved a period of delightful and fruitful service of the Master. A large crowd gathered to listen to the final messages of the Evangelists. What a glorious service it was! So replete with the freedom of the Spirit, so full of the joy of Jesus, so pregnant with the power of God. During the brief stay of the party many had received blessing both in soul and body, and their faces bore traces of the deep appreciation which filled their hearts in that farewell service. From Montreal the party moved on to Ottawa where only a week was spent, but this was packed with precious proofs of Divine power. How much God can do in a short time! Though so short, yet this brief campaign yielded well. The congregations that gathered were just swept into surrender – swept by the strong, swift current of God's love and grace into a place of freedom and fullness. The Ottawa meetings chiefly took the form of Bible Readings, and were in the main devoted to the enlightenment and edification of believers.

Toronto, city of a thousand charms, and perhaps one of the most British cities in Canada, was the scene of the next special services. Whilst here we had the privilege of attending a large conference of Pentecostal brethren, their annual meetings coinciding with our visit. We thoroughly enjoyed the time thus spent in devout discussion of some of those problems which confront all Foursquare Gospel ministers in their work for the Lord. We were glad to find such a splendid body of ministers, and to find them thus united in teaching and testimony and welded together in love, at the same time wielding a wide influence for God in the area.

On the second Sunday morning at the Conference, a special service was arranged for the ordination of several brethren who had been called by God to the work of the ministry and who moreover had already given unmistakable proof of the genuineness of their call. G.A. Chambers, the able and devoted president of the Canadian Presbytery, presided, and George Jeffreys preached the ordination sermon, which took the form of a dual charge to preachers and people. The candidates were earnestly entreated to avoid those things which tend to discredit and dishonour the ministry to which they were devoting their lives. To those who were ordained and to all who were privileged to attend this service, it must ever remain a very precious and hallowed memory. From commencement to close the meeting was enveloped and encircled in a Spirit-laden atmosphere. How sweetly the fragrance of the presence of the Lord filled the place as hands were laid upon these 'chosen vessels' and they were set apart for the Master's service! Lives that had been laid upon the altar – burnt offerings which were proving and should yet prove in greater measure that 'good and acceptable and perfect will of God'. How the fire fell upon each as they were definitely committed to God. There was not one who did not realise a new anointing, a fresh inflow of the Divine Spirit!

Those Toronto days were really glorious; God did indeed make the ministry of a full-orbed Gospel draw the people to Himself. The altar was often thronged with seekers. Before the Toronto campaign closed George Jeffreys conducted a special baptismal service, some of the candidates having been born again and baptised whilst the meetings were in progress. The same hands that had led them to the Cross now led them down into the waters of baptism, there in figure to identify themselves with Christ.

The whole of the last days of the special services were a seemly climax to the campaign. The 'best wine' had certainly been reserved for 'the last great day of the feast'. The sanctuary resounded with the 'song of the Lord', and the 'glory of the Lord' filled the house, so much so that the priests at times found it difficult to minister. The people also united in psalm and song to make melody unto the Lord, realising that Jehovah had visited them with salvation; that having brought the tithes into the storehouse, the windows of Heaven were now opened and upon them was falling in unexpected fullness the much-needed showers of refreshing from the presence of the Lord.

The next city to be visited was in the West of Canada – Winnipeg.

Winnipeg was reached at last after a train journey of almost 40 hours, and another series of special services was soon in full swing. These dear Canadian brethren were intent on taking full advantage of the presence of five British preachers. To them it was a golden opportunity. And they seized it too! Those Winnipeg meetings resulted in the formation of many precious fellowships. God's hand was upon us during these days.

On the Monday evening the service was devoted to the baptism of a number of believers who were anxious to obey the Lord's command and be baptised in water. Prior to the actual immersion of the candidates, in the course of a concise and convincing address, George Jeffreys pointed out that water baptism was part of the Divine plan for the New Testament Church; that it was just as much an integral part of that plan as the laver was part of the Divine specification for the construction of the Tabernacle. A large number passed though the waters, and at the close of the service thirty more rose to their feet to signify their readiness to follow their Lord in this way.

On the last Sunday of our stay in Winnipeg a splendid and powerful communion service was held, when about four-hundred of God's people were gathered around the Lord's Table, many of them sitting there for the first time, newly-born souls admitted to this precious ordinance because of the redeemed relationship which now existed 'twixt God and them; taking their place of privilege at this blessed memorial feast. How gladly the King welcomes such guests to His table! There were also present on this happy Sabbath morning those who had but lately taken Jehovah as their Healer; whose bodies, so recently racked with pain, now pulsated with Divine life. Like Lazarus of old they had been called from the power of death unto resurrection life, and they were now sitting in blessed fellowship at the table of their Deliverer.

Before the party reached the scene of their next meetings there now lay a tremendous trip. Nearly three thousand miles of ceaseless travelling through four great Canadian Provinces and two large American States. The early part of the journey took us over hundreds of miles of rolling, trackless prairie land, the outlook being occasionally relieved by some straggling townlet or isolated cattle ranch. We went on what seemed an endless journey, until we reached the picturesque city of Vancouver, which is described as the 'commercial metropolis' of British Columbia, with its lovely coastal scenery and splendid seascapes.

From Vancouver the party took a boat to Seattle, and here we first touched American soil. Then on down the Pacific Coast through Portland, to San Francisco, the scene of that terrible earthquake in 1906. Some two hours journey from San Francisco brought the party to San Jose where a campaign was conducted in a large tent, which bore the proud designation of 'Canvas Cathedral', with a seating capacity of nearly three thousand. Dr Towner a godly and gifted minister of the Baptist denomination, had invited us to hold some special meetings, and so in response to his invitation the party spent a couple of weeks, and many souls were saved during these meetings. This series of services was amongst the most prolific in result, of any that were held during the tour.

One could not listen to Dr Towner's touching tribute to the work which had been accomplished without being amply rewarded for the service rendered. His words revealed the depth of his appreciation and the intensity of his feeling. Many were the beautiful testimonies given by those who had received blessing for soul and body – testimonies which bore the hall-mark of sincerity and simplicity, and which perhaps were the most eloquent emolument that evangelists could possibly receive.

The next place of call was Fresno in the San Joaquin Valley, where we stayed for several days and held some glorious gatherings. From a natural viewpoint one could not find more congenial environment; the character of this country undoubtedly answers to the scriptural description of the Promised Land. It is a land that is rich and fertile, upon which the sun smiles for twelve months in the year. The choicest fruit grows in profusion. The supply of oranges and grapes is simply prolific. In fact, it is known as 'God's Land' by the people who are privileged to live there.

The Fresno meetings terminated triumphantly – the whole congregation seemed to rock under the power of the Holy Ghost as the Word was delivered. It was found very hard to bring these services to such an early close, but circumstances demanded that the party should move on.

From Fresno a day's journey brought us to Los Angeles, where a few days of restful, recuperative fellowship were spent with some friends from the 'Old Country'. It was very hard to resist the urgent appeals to tarry here and conduct some special meetings, but to have responded to all these pressing invitations would have meant extending our tour and remaining another twelve months at least.

We could not leave Los Angeles, which might be termed the Mecca of the Pentecostal Movement, without paying a visit to the beautiful Angelus Temple, of which Mrs McPherson is the gifted pastor. It was a most impressive sight to see that large auditorium filled with people and to witness the great number of souls seeking the Lord at the close of each service. It was the intention of the party simply to visit one of the meetings at the Angelus Temple without making our identity known, but the keen eye of Pastor W. Black quickly detected our presence and insisted upon introducing us to Mrs McPherson. Thus first of all George Jeffreys came into contact with this great woman evangelist.

From California the party continued its journey eastward across the States, a distance of about three thousand miles, passing through Salt Lake City, Chicago, past the famous Niagara Falls, to Buffalo and New York. How wonderfully God had undertaken! A few days in New York and then, on 8 October, we set sail for home in the *SS Aquitania*. A pleasant voyage followed and we reached Southampton safely after having been absent from England for four months. Thus we returned to our own beloved work with an enlarged vision of the possibilities which are ours in God, and with an intensified determination to extend the Kingdom of God in our own land.

Chapter 12

Revival Streams in East London

The year 1925 was destined to be one of much progress; plans were laid for a series of campaigns in various parts of the provinces, and also in some of the Metropolitan districts. The time had arrived for a united offensive on a larger scale than previously. Consequently before the year was very far advanced, campaigns were in progress in the north and east of London. Barking and Hendon were soon experiencing remarkable revivals, and hundreds of people were flocking to the Foursquare Gospel standard. The capacity of the enquiry rooms was over-taxed by the large numbers who sought Christ; scores of prisoners were captured in the very teeth of the enemy, whose rage knew no bounds.

It should here be observed that Barking had been especially laid upon the heart of George Jeffreys, and so when passing through that populous district he booked the Baths Hall for a revival campaign, which his brother, Stephen Jeffreys, was appointed to conduct. A most remarkable series of revival services took place, as the following extracts from the local press of that period will show:

THE GREAT REVIVAL AT BARKING

PASTOR JEFFREYS' CLOSING MEETINGS

The fourth and final week of the revival and Divine healing campaign conducted at Barking by Pastor Stephen Jeffreys will conclude on Sunday. Each week the crowds have grown in numbers and the interest in the mission has become more intense, till in the closing stages hundreds of people have, in the interest of public safety, had to be denied admission to the Baths Hall by the stewards and police.

The pastor appears to have drawn the people to the meetings by some magnetic power, and, as if caught in the wave of a great religious power, hundreds have stood in the assemblies and professed conversion. A large amount of attention has been paid to the healing part of the mission, but in all his addresses it is the spiritual side which is specially emphasised by the missioner.

Great meetings have been held in the afternoons and evenings throughout the week, and the scenes witnessed have been absolutely without parallel in the life of the town. At each service people have sought admission long before the time of commencing. In some cases people who have attended in the afternoon have brought their tea with them and remained till the evening meeting. Many have been quite content to stand at the back of the hall throughout the services.

A case which aroused a good deal of interest was that of a woman who has been suffering from rheumatoid arthritis for many years and has been wheeled about in a chair. She was taken to the mission on Monday night, and after seeing the pastor she walked round the hall and stood, without assistance, talking to her friends, telling them of the great benefit she had received.

(*Barking Advertiser*, 14 February, 1925)

A local Christian gentleman writing of these particular meetings says:

From the first meeting, when about 100 gathered to hear the Gospel, the Lord's presence has been with us mightily. The numbers have grown rapidly, so that we are no longer able to accommodate all who come along, and it is general to see a crowd standing outside the hall, endeavouring vainly to get in. Our greatest joy has been in seeing the dear ones giving themselves to our Saviour, and, Praise His Name, many have seen beauty in Him, and as many as forty or fifty as one service have yielded to His claims. It is blessed indeed to see converts of a few days bringing along their friends to the meetings, and eventually leading them to the enquiry room, where there are workers anxious to lead them to Jesus, and make quite clear God's plan of salvation. Not only have we seen this, but also many of God's children are being led into a deeper life in Him, and crying out for the continuance of the full Gospel teaching. Our hearts bubble over with joy when we see many who have hitherto been opposers of this work coming to every possible meeting, and enjoying with us the Word as it is faithfully preached.

The Divine Healing Services have been wonderful indeed, as we have seen paralytics and cripples healed, the blind receiving their sight, the deaf hearing, tumours and cancers dispersing, and many other diseases fleeing at the Name of Jesus. Who would not praise God to hear a young mother given up by doctors to die of consumption, a few days ago examined, and told that the tubes to her lungs were wasting away, and then after a touch from our Jesus, the doctors again examine her, and cannot find a trace of consumption. Hallelujah!

Another woman who had been blind for five years has again received her sight. It was touching to see a woman of 44 years who had never walked, walking round the hall unaided. Children have been brought in unable to walk, some on crutches, others being carried, but when they have come into contact with our Jesus, they have walked away unaided. Many critics say the healings will not last, but we know that our Lord does His work thoroughly. To Him be all the glory!

Many more cases of healing could be mentioned, but these name suffice to show that He is just the same, yesterday, today, and for ever. Glory to His Name!

This splendid campaign was continued with increasing power, gathering spiritual momentum under the ministry of George Jeffreys, whose messages were confirmed in an amazing manner by the miraculous signs that followed. The campaign conducted in the large hall was crowded in every part, many people waiting in the street for hours in order to gain admission, hundreds more accepting Christ as their Saviour and Lord.

With a remarkable tribute to the solid character of the work accomplished, to discover, after months of almost continuous meetings, there was not the slightest sign of the abatement of the outpouring. The results were, if anything, increasing in number; at every service between thirty and forty souls would be found at the front seeking salvation. And then the cases of healing also were quite as numerous as at the beginning, diseases of all kinds yielding to the touch of Christ.

One may gather some idea of the magnitude of the meetings from the fact that during one afternoon service conducted by the Revivalist in the Public Hall, a crowd of people were already in queue formation outside another hall waiting for the evening service. In fact, so great was the crush that it became necessary for the police to guard the doors and regulate the anxious throng who clamoured for admittance.

Many experienced Christian workers regard London as one of the most unyielding fields in which to labour for the Lord. They will tell you that the Metropolis is 'Gospel hardened', and yet it was right there in the centre of all these obstinacies that God poured out in such an apostolic manner His Spirit.

To form any adequate idea of what has actually been wrought it would be necessary to get behind the scenes and come into close contact with some of those wonderful trophies of grace, and let them tell in their own language the story of what the Lord has done for them. What tales we should hear! Lives whose tragedies have been transformed in glorious triumphs of grace! Here is a lady who is apparently simply overflowing with a gladness which is too full to contain. What is the cause of her joy? After eight years of agony completely healed, so that life is now a pleasure, and, a greater than this, gloriously saved, so that her home is now like heaven.

What an atmosphere of suppressed enthusiasm prevails as the preacher rises to his feet to proclaim the Gospel of Jesus Christ. Hundreds of eyes are focused expectantly upon the speaker as he announces his text, 'Christ hath appeared to put away sin by the sacrifice of Himself'. The air is electric – one feels that one is in the presence of God – conscious that something is about to happen – instinctively one realises that the power of Jehovah is to be displayed in that meeting. The large congregation is swayed by the searching truths which proceed from the lips of the preacher. The appeal has barely been made before numbers are making their way to the altar; a few moments more, and the front is lined with seeking souls crying to God for mercy. It is as though the touch of God has wooed these souls to Himself, and they have risen in response to the thrilling call of this God-breathed message.

The revival fire soon spread from Barking to East Ham, and speedily took a firm hold of the whole district. The town Hall had been taken for the campaign, but even this spacious hall was all too small for the throng that sought admission. The *East Ham Recorder*, 10 April, 1925, in a somewhat lengthy but graphic article, describes some of the remarkable scenes which took place at this time:

FAITH HEALING

FERVENT SUNDAY SCENES
RHEUMATIC LADY'S DANCE OF JOY

East Ham Town Hall has never been filled with such an enthusiastic body of men and women as assembled there on Sunday evening, when Pastor George Jeffreys, who has recently been heard of in connection with faith healing at Barking, held a healing service.

At 2.30 in the afternoon there were people waiting outside the building although the service did not commence until 6.30, and at 4.30 there was a long queue, which grew until it extended from the Town Hall doors to the Central Hall.

When the doors were opened, crowds streamed in until there was no seating accommodation and very little standing room left. In the end, the hall was packed almost to suffocation and the doors were shut, leaving a large number outside.

Within the hall the audience, compassed of members of every Christian denomination, whiled away the time before the Pastor's arrival by singing Elim Revival hymns with intense fervour and feeling, while the crowd outside gradually swelled.

There were many people walking with the aid of crutches and sticks; blind people were led to seats in the hall, and bath chairs and other vehicles of a similar nature were brought in bearing the lame. In one corner of the hall near the platform a mother carrying a sick child stood next to an aged man who walked slowly with the aid of a stick.

CRIPPLES AND CONSUMPTIVES

A cripple in a wheel-chair was assisted by a man evidently in the throes of consumption, and a blind girl sat near by. All joined in the hymns, which had a lilting refrain and were apparently well-known by all the audience.

People had come from all parts of London, and our reporter was told that several had come from the Elephant and Castle district, some from Leytonstone, and some from as far distant as Erith.

The scene was an impressive one as the sight of such outward signs of religious fervour in an audience composed of all the extremes of life must be. There were young and old, well and unwell, rich and poor mingled together, and the chief topic of conversation was the Faith.

People who had been healed were telling those who desired to be healed, of their experiences. There could be no doubt of the extraordinary intensity of their love for their faith. One young man told our reporter that he had been cured of stuttering after 20 years suffering with the affliction, and all around could be heard similar tales.

THE PASTOR ARRIVES

When Pastor George Jeffreys put in an appearance he made his way through the hall to the platform, and the service commenced immediately with a hymn which was followed by a prayer delivered by a deacon. The prayer was spoken with extraordinary volubility and a fervour which is not often heard. It was punctuated with sighs and remarks of 'Praise the Lord', etc. from the audience, many of whom were openly in tears, before the need of the prayer came and brought in its wake another hymn, which was sung with the same earnestness as heretofore.

Pastor Jeffreys then gave his address on the subject of 'A Lawyer's Perplexity'. He is a dark man, evidently Welsh to judge from his slight accent, with very dark eyes and crisp, curly hair. He is young-looking and has clear-cut features, while he gives the impression of possessing enormous vitality. His address was given with the same deep fervour that marked everything connected with the service. As he spoke he walked about the platform and gesticulated at times furiously. He had a trick of suddenly leaning over the table in front of him and pointing at the audience, speaking in rapid tones the while. He was lucid and voluble, and was never at a loss for a word. At times he would speak of the Bible, or the portion from which he took his text, and at another he would speak scathingly of certain present-day habits.

INTENT AUDIENCE

The audience listened as if entranced and followed him with intent eyes as he moved about the platform.

At the end of the address the Pastor asked those who wished to 'be saved' to hold up their hands. Several did so and, as he urged them in language that exceeded even his address for fervour, more and more held up their hands and were asked to go into a room adjoining the platform for enquiries. A long stream of people of all descriptions filed into the enquiry room and emerged a little later with smiling faces.

HEALING SERVICE

Then following the healing part of the service. A queue of people suffering from a variety of complaints went slowly up to the platform with their faces lit by a fervent hope. Mothers carried babies and were followed by old ladies walking with crutches and sticks. Several were helped up by attendants, and a blind girl was led to a seat.

The Pastor commenced healing immediately. A middle-aged woman suffering from an internal complaint was the first to be dealt with. The Pastor stood in front of her and said something and then placed his hands on her face. The woman immediately fell backwards as if unconscious into the arms of two deacons and was laid on the floor, when the Pastor and two deacons laid their hands on her. After a few minutes she rose and stepping to the front of the platform, announced to the audience that although she had been in pain for many years, the pain had entirely disappeared. The announcement was greeted with applause and cries of 'Hallelujah' and 'Praise the Lord'.

After a similar ceremony another lady suffering from pneumonia in one lung said she was cured.

PARALYSIS CURED

One of the most extraordinary cures effected was that of a lady who had suffered for six years from paralysis of the arm. After she had been touched by the Pastor she was observed to lift her arm quite freely and move her fingers easily.

Another remarkable case was that of a boy who had come up to the platform suffering from blindness in one eye. He was 'touched', and then walked to the edge of the platform and announced that he could see perfectly with the defective eye.

OLD LADY'S JOY

A pathetic scene occurred when an old lady who had with difficulty walked on to the platform with a stick was so completely cured that she dropped the stick and walked with ease. She jumped up and down in her delight and hugged one of the lady attendants.

There were several people who were not cured, but there were very many who were.

Interviewed after he had been cured, Mr Thorogood, of 145, Grange Road, Ilford, told our reporter that he had been suffering from a complaint that had caused him a great deal of inconvenience but was entirely cured after the Pastor had touched him.

About this time a large, disused Baptist Chapel, situated near the Elephant and Castle, and known as the Surrey Tabernacle, had been rented by the Elim Alliance. It was in this central building that the annual Eastertide Convention was held in 1925 which was by far the largest Foursquare Gospel Convention that had, up to that time, been held in the British Isles.

Throughout the Convention several notable cases of healing occurred each afternoon, among them one who had been paralysed from birth, who jumped up and down on the platform; a young man who had been blind in the left eye from birth, testified that the sight had been restored. He could see everyone. He said in a loud voice: 'The Lord has **done** it!' A little boy who had been blind from three years of age, could see the text over the pulpit and walked all round the Tabernacle. Of the deaf who received immediate hearing, one had been deaf 30 years. All glory to the Holy Name of Jesus!

What splendid strides the work had made in the ten years since its birth at Monaghan. Who would have even dreamt that such progress could have been possible in such a short space of time? How wonderfully God had vindicated the faith of those pioneer evangelists and their Spirit-led Leader! The horizon had now outgrown their farthest expectations. And yet even this was not to be the limit of what the Lord could do through those who would 'trust and obey'. Yet greater things were in store for these daring souls.

Perhaps one of the most impressive baptismal services held in the Surrey Tabernacle during the period that it was in the hands of the Elim Alliance was on the occasion when Pastor George Jeffreys baptised no less than 152 believers. After having immersed this large number, in response to the appeal for others who would signify their willingness to follow Christ through the waters of baptism, another 128 put up their hands. It would prove most interesting to know the actual number of those who were immersed in the Surrey Tabernacle baptismal pool. Certainly to our knowledge over one thousand passed through those waters, baptised by the Pastor himself.

A Baptist minister, who was privileged on various occasions and at difference places to come into close contact with the work and its leaders, pays a glowing tribute to the Elim Alliance at this time. He says:

> It is to the credit of the Elim Alliance that they seek to work in the most needy places, and, according to Apostolic precedent, they do not trespass upon other men's labours (2 Corinthians 10:6).
>
> A movement is usually judged by its leaders – it is what they make it. We were impressed by the leading personalities of the Alliance whom we met in Ireland. Pastor George Jeffreys seems to be not only a fine character, but one who inspires confidence and has the ability to lead. He has gathered around him a noble band of workers, who seem to regard him not only as their leader, but as a friend and brother.

During the summer of 1925, the new church at Barking was opened. Scenes of wonderful enthusiasm characterised this happy event. Years of fruitful service have followed under the able care of Elim ministers, during which much has been done to consolidate the results of the magnificent revival which gave birth to this work.

1925 also witnessed a wonderful campaign at Forest Hill in the south-east of London. The following is a press account of the meetings:

FOREST HILL REVIVAL SCENES

PASTOR JEFFREYS' MISSION

In these days when the trend of public thought is what is generally termed rationalistic or materialistic, it is a thing of much surprise to the matter-of-fact man in the street to discover the great interest that is being created in London, and particularly in the quiet, residential district of Forest Hill, in a revival campaign conducted by Pastor George Jeffreys in the Trinity Church, Perry Vale.

'What time is it by God's Clock?' was the subject dealt with before a crowded congregation on Sunday evening. A panoramic view of the dispensations of providence was dramatically depicted, and although the sermon lasted over an hour, there was rapt attention throughout. The Bible was likened to a time-piece which gave unmistakable signs denoting the close of a dispensation of grace. Some of the preacher's sentences seemed to pass over the congregation with the velocity and power of a cyclone, while others, given in low musical tones, hushed them into semi-consciousness. Describing the signs of the time, he would startle his hearers by such statements as: 'This world as a stage is being set for the bloodiest of all dramas, whilst the orchestra of materialism, modernism, and higher criticism is playing the lullaby of peace. The outlook is dark, but the uplook is bright. While the dark clouds are gathering, we, as Christians, can look up, for our redemption draweth nigh. We are about to witness and take part in a scene surpassing in prodigy and splendour anything that has already taken place on earth – the personal return of Christ in clouds of glory, and the translation of living Christians to meet Him there.'

As the sermon proceeds, it is punctuated at intervals with various ejaculations from a congregation which evidently greatly appreciates the pastor's messages. On the termination of his address, Pastor Jeffreys makes a stirring appeal for converts, who pass though an ante-room to receive further instruction. At this stage of the proceedings the order of the meeting is changed, and the Pastor invites those ailing in body, who desire what he terms 'Divine Healing' to come forward to the platform to be prayed for. Immediately sufferers from almost every conceivable kind of disease and infirmity press forward in a pitiable procession. The Pastor prays with each sufferer and lays his hands on their head, and usually the person prayed for seems to stiffen out and fall prostrate, lying on the ground in a state of semi-consciousness.

Many of those dealt with in this way testify to receiving healing. One lady eagerly told before the congregation how she had suffered from sugar diabetes and acute rheumatic pains since 1923, the suffering occasioning great loss of sleep. She stated that since being prayed for she has had complete healing and is now quite free from pain.

Another stated that since being prayed for she had been healed of internal trouble, necessitating constant medical treatment, also of defective eyesight.

Another woman claims to have been healed of septic tonsils, noises in the head, and also an internal trouble.

Several other testimonies given to healing received were: one from duodenal ulcer, another from infantile paralysis which occasioned the wearing of leg-irons and surgical boots, she is now able to walk about without these things, and her leg is now almost normal.

Many others dealt with on previous occasions claimed to have been healed; some from deafness, tuberculosis, partial blindness, and one who had been a deaf mute could now hear, and also pronounce a few words.

As the sick were being ministered to, occasional scenes of what could only be adequately described as of a supernatural order were being enacted. Several persons in different places in the congregation could be seen to shake or tremble violently, and others with loud sighs would apparently be prostrated; usually those so affected would eventually break out into ecstatic utterance, which after a few seconds would become extremely voluble and bear remarkable resemblance to what might be a foreign language spoken with great rapidity. Pastor Jeffreys explained this to be what he terms the baptism of the Holy Ghost, and he claims that these occurrences are identical with certain phenomena of a similar nature recorded in the Bible, particularly the instances spoken of in the Acts of the Apostles as being the descent of the Holy Spirit on the Disciples; this, it will be remembered, is generally recorded to be accompanied by a manifestation of speaking in foreign tongues. During these strange happenings, a remarkable influence, or some eerie mysterious power, seemed to manifest itself all over the meeting and a spirit of intense worship was created, thus preserving remarkable order where one might have expected to find chaos.

The meetings are generally brought to a close after about three hours' duration, most of the large congregation remaining all the time.

These revival meetings are conducted under the auspices of the Elim Alliance, a society founded by this young pastor is Northern Ireland a few years ago, and its churches are found throughout the United Kingdom.

(*Dulwich and Peckham Echo*, 25 September, 1925)

Two other new districts were now added to the growing list of places where the Foursquare flag was flying, Canning Town and Ilford proving as vulnerable to the power of the Gospel as the other centres had done, and yielding almost as prolifically in revival results. Writing of Canning Town when the campaign had been in progress for some little time, a Mr H. Proctor says:

The Latter Rain of the Spirit has continued here with increasing velocity. The fountains of the Great Deep have been opened and rivers of living water are flowing out in floods upon the dry ground. Hundreds of new wells have been opened and filled to overflowing.

High water mark was reached on Sunday, when 114 souls surrendered to Christ. 76 of this number yielded at the testimony meeting held at the Primitive Methodist Chapel. The testimonies included healings of consumption, heart trouble, defective eyesight, paralysis, mastoids, phlebitis and neuritis. Some occurred months ago, denoting permanence, while others were up-to-date. One that very afternoon had regained the use of hands and feet.

On the Thursday 68 more prisoners were set free and on the following Sunday 106 decided for the Lord. During this series of services the local Methodist ministers displayed a splendid spirit, and co-operated in every way possible.

At Ilford, God graciously bathed the assembled crowds in a real Holy Ghost revival, which for weeks created quite a stir in the neighbourhood. Many and varied were the explanations and interpretations of this remarkable movement of God. Some foolishly attributed the wonderful results to hypnotism and mesmerism, others described it as spiritistic. But in spite of what men 'thought and said' the outpouring continued, a perfect 'blizzard of spiritual power'.

The *Ilford Recorder* of 6 November, 1925, furnishes us with an illuminative description of these services:

18 YEARS' DEAFNESS CURED

HUGE CROWDS AND WONDERFUL SCENES AT TOWN HALL

Pastor George Jeffreys, the Elim Revivalist, held healing services at the Town Hall on Thursday.

At half-past four in the afternoon a dozen or so had lined up, and at six o'clock the crowd was being controlled by half-a-dozen policemen, it extending half-way down Oakfield Road. Men arrived with children held lovingly in their arms, with bandages on their heads, hands and legs. There also were cripples, and others who obviously were suffering acutely from maladies of divers forms.

A few minutes past six the crowd immediately outside the hall in the high road began humming a Revivalist hymn, and before long there was a chorus of voices singing 'All my sins are blotted out'.

Lined up as they were, the crowd resembled a cinema queue. Before seven o'clock there was a like crowd standing on the other side of the road, watching the crowd which was waiting for the doors to open.

At 6.40 pm, well over a thousand people were waiting, and from all directions came others in streams.

At the end of the line were two policemen. As another bunch took their places, one of them observed casually: 'A lot here, aren't there?' to which one of the policemen replied optimistically: 'Oh, no – another 3,000 to come yet.' It was obvious that the 7.15 contingent would never see the inside of the Town Hall.

THE MAN DESCRIBED

Well-built, with powerful shoulders, the Elim Revivalist makes a striking figure on the platform. His deep-set eyes and prominent forehead, surmounted by a thick crop of luxuriant black curly hair at once attract attention.

His arms work and his fists are constantly clenched, but he never strikes the table, behind which he is constantly moving. There is the difference between him and many ministers of other denominations – he is active, and he makes his words active. His sermon is alive, and he creates an atmosphere of spiritual fire.

After repeated singing of Revivalist hymns, Pastor George Jeffreys began healing the sick.

A woman of 35 years of age came before the Pastor. He put his thumbs on her ears, and his fingers at the back of her head and held them there, once shouting 'Hallelujah'.

A few seconds went, and then the woman fell back stiffly, showing every sign of losing consciousness. A minute passed, and there rang through the hall three screams. She had been cured of deafness, and the noise which she had heard, although almost nothing in volume, was enough to cause her acute pain.

'It is very strange to hear my voice,' she told me afterwards. 'I have been cured of deafness after 18 years. I cannot believe it.'

Others were healed, and the meeting closed with testimonies given by men and women who had been cured at previous meetings.

All the foregoing was only made possible by unceasing prayer combined with untiring consecrated effort. The splendid record of miraculous manifestation is but a further proof that 'the story of every great Christian achievement is the history of answered prayer'. 'God gets His way with man in the upper room', and this makes all things possible.

Chapter 13

Signs and Wonders
in the Provinces

1926 opens with a brilliant campaign in the south-west of England. Eleven years had now elapsed since Pastor George Jeffreys conducted his last special services in Plymouth. The presence of many of those who had been so richly blessed and healed in the 1915 meetings bore eloquent witness to the enduring character of the work then wrought.

Although in the first place the purpose of this visit to Plymouth was to consolidate the work already in existence, yet it soon became evident that a glorious Foursquare Gospel Revival was in full swing. Almost at the very onset many souls were being saved, bodies healed, and others filled with the power of the Holy Spirit.

The secular press gave glowing reports of the campaign as it proceeded. To read the press reporters' observations sounds like a modern repetition of the Day of Pentecost. These reports are full of indisputable facts, revealing that Pastor George Jeffreys' contention that 'Jesus Christ is the same today' is true. Here is a man who bases his belief on the whole of the Word of God, and emphatically affirms his confidence in its miraculous energy. Such dogmatism might certainly expose a preacher to severe and searching criticism, but when such startling assertions are substantiated by demonstrations of Divine power which result in dozens of remarkable physical healings, what objection can remain? His conclusions, opposed as they appear to natural laws, are supported by concrete cases of deliverance from incurable disease which leave no room for further argument. The following report is only one of a number of eloquent press tributes:

FAITH CURES

PASTOR JEFFREYS TREATS THE BLIND AND DUMB

Not since Charles II summoned his afflicted subjects to the old Church of St Andrew's to be cured of the 'King's Evil' by the touch of his royal hands, has Plymouth witnessed such scenes as have occurred at the faith-healing mission conducted by Pastor Jeffreys, a young Welsh revivalist.

The culminating point was reached at a meeting held in Plymouth's historic Guildhall, situated but a few yards from where Charles officiated as a faith healer many centuries ago. The sick, halt, blind and lame flocked from over a wide area, charabancs even being run from Cornwall, to participate in the streams of healing power which are declared to flow from the pastor's hands.

Such wonderful things have been claimed that many ministers were included in the vast congregation, and medical men were also numbered among those who had been attracted there by curiosity.

The healing was not performed until the end of the service, which was characterised by great earnestness occasionally rising almost to the heights of typical Welsh revivalism. Pastor George Jeffreys is 'powerful in prayer', as he would be described in his native Wales, and his Gospel addresses are charged very fully with that cascade-like eloquence and picturesque idiom which marked Evan Roberts and all his successors in religious revivalism.

A woman, bed-ridden for thirty-eight years with an internal complaint which necessitated the wearing of instruments, presented herself on his platform to thank him publicly for what he had been able to do.

'I am cured,' she said to him, 'but what am I to do about the instruments?' The revivalist replied, 'The faith which cured you disease can also remove the instruments,' and the woman went home fully believing. That night she slept as she had never slept before for thirty-eight years, and in the morning, so it is declared, she found the instruments on her bed when she woke.

Even sceptical policemen, whose duty it is to regulate the throng, have been swept off their feet by what they have seen and heard. One night two girls, one blind and the other dumb, inquired their way to the service of the officer nearby.

An hour or so later he was amazed when the couple returned to him, literally dancing for joy, the dumb girl speaking and the blind girl seeing.

A young woman tells how a serious affection of the eyes was banished by the Divine power wielded by the Pastor, and dozens of others relate stories of how he cured them by like means of weak lungs, gastric troubles, bronchitis, catarrh, and neuritis, as well as many other complaints.

Faith and prayer are the two great ingredients of the missioner's prescription. Those who have visited his extraordinary services say that they are pervaded by an atmosphere that is too elusive to be pictured in words.

(*Birmingham Sunday Mercury*, 31 January, 1926)

It is questionable whether the metropolis of the south-west has ever been privileged to witness scenes such as those which characterised this campaign. The whole district was fairly shaken and swept by a glorious Latter Rain storm. So great were the results that after urgent appeals had been made, the Pastor consented to cancel his other engagements in order to continue at Plymouth.

So rapidly was the revival developing that no building was capable of seating the eager crowds which came. There was but one hall remaining to be taken, and everything indicated that if possible this should be acquired, and that was the great Military Drill Hall, a building which one noted evangelist has described as 'a field with a roof on'. This hall had on one or two occasions been engaged for religious services, but then only under circumstances which practically ensured success. Both Dr Torrey and Gipsy Smith had held missions in it, but in their case they had the whole weight of the Free Church influence behind them. Pastor George Jeffreys had no such support; in fact, he had considerable opposition from this quarter. But in spite of all this the Drill Hall was taken, and, large as it was, it was packed with people. At some of these meetings as many as eighty, ninety, and one hundred souls accepted Christ. Hundreds of people, too, were healed, wonderful testimonies being given to deliverance from various kinds of diseases.

Speaking of the preaching, one who was present remarks: 'One can say that Christ has been revealed to all as never before, the preacher seeming to be freshly baptised in the Holy Spirit at every service.'

The final day of the campaign, 14 February, saw the great hall once more thronged with people. On this day over 160 souls were saved, making a total for the whole campaign of over 1,500. What an achievement! Truly the 'old, old story' is the Gospel of 'grand results'.

From Plymouth the Revivalist crossed for a short campaign in the Channel Islands where, in Guernsey, he preached to a congregation of 1,800 people in the St George's Hall, St Peter Port. Though the campaign only lasted a few days, yet God wonderfully set His seal to the ministry of His servant, and over 100 were brought to the Lord. Many others were richly blessed and drawn into closer union with Christ, whilst others again were healed.

The scene of action is now transferred from south-west to north-west, and we next find the party in Liverpool, Lancashire's great seaport, which in a short time we learn had 'been powerfully moved by the wonderful Revival Campaign in the large Boxing Stadium'.

As usual, the commencement of the campaign was small, but quickly grew from a few to hundreds, and then to thousands. Believers accustomed to the dull and stiff worship of the churches today, expressed their enthusiasm at the splendid freedom and the joyful spirit at these services.

Again the record of results was large – over 800 souls surrendering to God. Many cases of remarkable healing were also included in the results of this campaign. The *Daily Despatch* and the *Liverpool Post and Mercury* gave the following account of the last meetings:

PASTOR IN THE RING

BOXING STADIUM AS SETTING FOR REVIVAL SERVICE

Using the roped enclosure of the boxing ring as his pulpit, Pastor George Jeffreys, whose revival and healing campaign has been attracting immense crowds at Liverpool recently conducted two immense services in the Liverpool Boxing Stadium yesterday.

The evening service was attended by close on 3,000 people, and the same enthusiasm which has marked the services in the chapel in Windsor Street, where many remarkable 'cures' have been claimed was manifested last night. Over 100 men, women and children spoke of their own individual 'cures'.

Some who had suffered a wide variety of ailments were publicly tested before the congregation, who applauded each one and spasmodically burst into hymns.

TESTIMONY OF HEALING
STRANGE SCENES AT BOXING RINGSIDE

Men, women and children filed past the ringside at the Liverpool Stadium last night, to give a congregation that filled the building testimony of cures effected in them during the 'Divine Healing' campaign held in Liverpool the last fortnight by Pastor George Jeffreys. The remarkable scenes that took place at his first 'healing service' in a church in Windsor Street were described in the *Daily Post*.

WAVING HYMN-SHEETS

Last night the campaign closed to the singing of many hymns by a very large congregation, who sometimes waved their hymn papers in the air as they sang, so that the Stadium looked like a place where a distinguished visitor was being greeted with a waving of flags. At one time, a man sang a solo composed of verses like this:

Some say our doctrine's new,
And peculiar things we do,
But the ancients did them, too –

and then the people sang, fervently, a refrain, 'Praise the Lord.'

JUMPING WITH JOY

Those who later came forward to testify that they had benefited from the healing service included a man, who told the congregation that he had suffered a severe accident at a Merseyside factory, and that he had left hospital with some paralysis of the wrist, finger and foot. This paralysis, he declared, had disappeared when Pastor Jeffreys prayed over him, and he showed the congregation how supple his affected members had become. A young boy said he had a tubercular hip, and had been told by the doctors that he would have to undergo his fifth operation. 'But, thank the Lord, I won't' he called out, for he declared that his hip had benefited from the praying over him, and the people cheered his declaration. A woman who declared herself cured jumped up and down with joy as she faced the congregation from the ringside, and a girl, who had always stammered, repeated a text in a firm voice.

A girl who had suffered from weak eyes declared that she could look into the strong electric light over the boxing-ring. A man said he had been completely cured of a disease that the Pastor declined to mention by name. These testimonies were punctuated with cries of 'Alleluia' from the audience.

Some few months after this Pastor George Jeffreys paid Liverpool a further visit, this time holding his meetings under canvas. The large tent was packed with people at each service, the sides having to be lowered in order to allow the crowd outside to join in the meeting. They were excellent meetings from every point of view. But the singing was splendid! It was like a huge human organ, played by some unseen master hand. At one of these gatherings between eighty and ninety accepted the Lord as their Saviour. Who could be surprised if the huge congregation gave way to their feelings – weeping, laughing, praying, praising? Who is he that would restrain such holy fervour?

During this visit to Liverpool the Revivalist baptised over 80 believers in water. At this time many were received into membership who wished to identify themselves with the Elim Foursquare Gospel Church in Liverpool.

The parting meeting was memorable for its enthusiasm. Outside the tent, as the Pastor and his party endeavoured to make their escape to the waiting car, they were simply hemmed in by a crowd which swayed to and fro 'Like the billows of an ocean'.

Another notable campaign commenced during the month of July, down in the centre of one of the most charming holiday resorts on the south coast. Bournemouth has always retained its reputation as a prince amongst the English watering-places. Here it was that George Jeffreys' canvas tabernacle was pitched. The site selected was not the most favourable, at least from a geographical point of view. Moordown lies over two miles inland from Bournemouth, at the extreme end of one of the tram routes. Consequently, if position counted for anything, circumstances were against success. But how wonderfully it was demonstrated that when God begins to move in Holy Ghost power people will come, even though the revival rendezvous is in the most remote spot. And come they did – tram loads and bus loads of eager worshippers. Distance didn't count with them – they were drawn by the lure of an overmastering desire. God was manifesting His power in that Moordown tent, and they meant to share the glorious deluge which had come to that district.

After five weeks of continuous outpouring we learn that the tide of blessing was rising higher and higher. Testimonies from many of the surrounding districts were pouring in, telling of all kinds of diseases which had disappeared. At the end of the first month about 600 souls had been won for Christ. The congregations 'swayed like trees before the wind, but the mighty power of God', several even receiving the Baptism of the Holy Spirit in their seat, and others being healed in the same way. A minister of the Gospel who was an eye-witness, writing at the time of the awakening, says:

> We are in the midst of a mighty revival, the like of which Bournemouth has never seen before. The scenes as the great crowds disperse are wonderful, the roads being thronged with people, whilst on the ground surrounding the tent numbers of motor cars are parked during the meetings.

The *Bournemouth Echo* gave the following report after the fourth week:

MIRACLES OF HEALING

WONDERFUL TESTIMONIES AT MOORDOWN
CAMPAIGN TO CONTINUE FOR ANOTHER WEEK

People who say that the day of miracles are past should visit the tent at Moordown where Pastor George Jeffreys is holding his Healing and Revival Campaign. Though the weather was so uninviting last night, yet the large tent was comfortably full.

Among the number present were some who had been healed during the campaign. These joyfully told of their cures when the regular meeting had closed.

A lady said she had suffered with chronic asthma, and two years ago was told that she was dying. She had been cured at the mission, and had not been attacked since. 'I can sing now at the top of my voice!' she added gleefully.

'I have had rheumatism and weak eyes and couldn't see to read without glasses. But now I have left off the glasses,' said a young lady.

A gipsy girl said she had been cured of paralysis in the arms, and three young people related how they had been 'stone deaf' and were now able to hear. Then a girl came forward and emphatically declared that she had been cured of goitre, and her testimony was corroborated by her mother.

A lady aged 60, said that ever since she was 16 she had been scarcely able to see, but that now she could see quite well without the use of glasses. Head noises and indigestion were the complaints of another lady. She had suffered for years, but now she was better.

A case of prayer and faith healing was mentioned by a nurse. Prayer was offered for her at a given time one day, and at that very moment she was cured of haemorrhage. The nurse also mentioned that she had been cured of a very serious complaint. A lady testified to having been cured of arthritis which she had had all her life, and other cases related included that of a man who had pleurisy.

At the healing service Pastor Jeffreys anoints the patient with olive oil, and at the same time offers prayer for the recovery of the sufferer.

THE FOURSQUARE GOSPEL

'Something like 500 people have professed salvation since I started the meetings in this town,' declared Pastor George Jeffreys, in the course of his address at one of his recent Revival and Healing Campaign meetings, when the tent was again crowded. 'People say the Gospel has lost its power,' he continued, 'and they are introducing into the churches all sorts of things to attract people, sales of work, bazaars, concerts and tea parties. But the Gospel is still the power unto salvation, and if you preach Jesus Christ the crowds will come, and be saved,' he added.

'Many of the churches,' he remarked later on, 'have sailed away from the region of blessing and spirituality, and are manned by a frozen crew. In many places where there is modernism, higher criticism, new theology and new thought they are nothing more than floating sepulchres. Thank God,' he continued, 'the little barque I am in is allowed to sail in the region of blessing and spirituality. It is the Foursquare Gospel we are in, and it is sailing where the Sun of Righteousness sheds His beams upon her, and in His beams we find healing.' He urged the need for the 'old-time fire' again and a mighty revival which would sweep worldliness out of the churches.

Some people, he observed later, had demurred at the 'Hallelujahs' and 'Amens' which had characterised his meetings here and elsewhere. 'People say they don't believe in excitement.' 'But when God ordained me as a minister of the Gospel,' he said, 'I promised Him I would go forth to excite people to love the Master. By His Grace thousands have been swept into the Kingdom. My emotions belong to my soul, and I am sanctifying my emotions for the sake and purpose of the Gospel. How can you sit quiet,' he asked, 'when you feel the powers of another world filling you with divine life? You cannot help saying "Hallelujah!"'

The churches were asking what they should do for the young people. His reply was 'Give them the Foursquare Gospel, and you will find the young people attracted.' In his address he suggested that the signs of the times pointed to the Second Advent drawing near.

When the campaign was seven weeks' old the following telegram was received at headquarters from the minister referred to above:

Pastor George Jeffreys' Revival Campaign still continues with ever increasing momentum and far-reaching results. Over 1,500 conversions, while signs and wonders accompany the word which slays and makes alive, wounds and heals, pulls down and builds up. Tent inadequate to accommodate the great crowds. Largest hall in town taken for final rally. Pray on.

The great finale of the Campaign was simply a glorious triumph for God and the Gospel. The whole district seemed thrilled with what was taking place. The *Bournemouth Guardian* of 25 September describes the 'unusual scenes' which took place:

For some months past now one of the chief topics of conversation amongst Bournemouth religious circles has been the eventful revival and healing campaign which has been conducted at Moordown and Boscombe by Pastor George Jeffreys, who is said to be the Founder of what has come to be known as the Elim Foursquare Gospel Church, with Headquarters in London. This mission, for such it is, has been conducted in a large marquee capable of accommodating some 1,200 people, and has attracted enormous crowds representative of all social grades, who seem to have entered into the spirit of the campaign with zest. Extraordinary scenes of enthusiasm have marked all the meetings, thousands have thronged the tent, and thousands have been turned away owing to the scarcity of accommodation. Bournemouth residents, the victims of almost every conceivable ailment common to humanity, have been making the tent their regular resort. Long treks in bath chairs never before witnessed in Bournemouth have been made.

One report of these immense gatherings comes from the pen of a well-known Bournemouth authoress. It gives the impression of one who viewed the revival from an outsider's standpoint:

If I had gone to the big tent – where Pastor George Jeffreys has been holding revival and healing meetings at Moordown and Boscombe during the past seven weeks – to scoff, I should certainly have remained to pray. But I did not go to scoff; I went to see if the wonderful cures of which I had heard were really taking place, and to decide – if I could – whether they were due, as some said, to hysterical excitement, or to something much greater and more permanent in its effects.

I went, I saw, and I was conquered.

It is true the preliminary service with its emotional appeal, its ejaculated 'Alleluias' and 'Praise the Lord', left me critically cold. Yet that it caught and held the great congregations that gathered in the tent, and induced in them a spirit of worship is undeniable. And the singing, conducted with magical skill by Mr Darragh, was genuinely inspiring. That smiling young evangelist could coax a congregation of stubborn parrots to show off their vocal accomplishments! The choruses which nearly lifted the roof off the tent, were caught up and sung in perfect time and tune, after one or two rehearsals, in a way that would only come after long practice under less inspiring leadership.

A Pitiful Procession

But after this joyous – one might almost say rollicking – introduction to the healing service, a decided change was observable when Pastor Jeffreys invited the sick to come to the platform for treatment. From all parts they streamed up. The halt, maimed and blind, led by their friends, others with pale, strained faces that told their tale of suffering plainly – little children carried in their parents' arms. A hushed sympathy held everyone in thrall as that pitiful procession filed past. I felt that if any false hope were held out – any pretension to be able to help without sure ground for such a claim, it would be blasphemy, indeed. Slowly the patients were marshalled into order by kindly helpers. The strains of the hymn 'At even ere the sun was set', rose softly and reverently from a thousand throats. One's mind was irresistibly drawn back to a similar scene in Palestine two thousand years ago. There was a spirit in the air – the spirit of faith, compassion and loving service. ... The hands of the healer touched each sufferer gently with the anointing oil, a few words of earnest prayer were uttered, and faces that had been strained with pain and expectation relaxed into calm and peace.

Tears of Joy

A tiny, fair-haired girl seated on her mother's lap held my attention. One little arm was paralysed, I learned, when the mother answered the healer's quiet inquiry. He gave the treatment and passed on. But evidently the child had made an impression upon him, for he returned to her. Smilingly holding a penny above her head he told her to lift the helpless arm and take it. Waveringly, but surely, the paralysed arm was raised, the prize was grasped, and tears of joy shone in the mother's eyes.

The gift of sight to a boy, who – so I was told – was born blind, was conferred at the same meeting; and I was given the particulars of the healing of a severe and long-standing case of spinal trouble by the grateful patient himself. Cases of cancer, goitre, rheumatism, nerve trouble, curvature of the spine, hereditary deafness, asthma, and numerous others have been cured at other meetings. No wonder the great tent is packed to overflowing at every meeting, and the names of Pastor Jeffreys and his zealous colleagues figure in hundreds of grateful prayers.

A minister who for years had prayed and laboured in this district, with overflowing heart writes of those wonderful closing scenes:

The Tent Campaign closes with a great shout of praise, and as the people wend their way home, songs of praise arise from hundreds who have experienced salvation and healing.

The Great Final Rally, at the Drill Hall was filled with something like 3,000 persons, with crowds outside endeavouring to vain to gain admittance.

Once more the scene of revival is transferred from south to north. Carlisle – city of a hundred historic memories and interests – is now to experience an awakening of such magnitude that it was described as the greatest move of the Spirit Carlisle had known for 35 years. So wide was the influence of this campaign that the whole district was vitalised with the spirit of revival, people flocking in from the surrounding countryside, in some cases coming as many as thirty miles that they might not miss the showers that were falling.

Before the campaign was many weeks old, over 500 definite decisions had been registered, and the stream of converts was daily increasing. Hundreds of young people drank in the message of God and literally plunged into blessing, passing out of those meetings surcharged with the power of a 'new creation' in Christ.

Steadily the great crowds grew greater, until at last the huge Drill Hall was secured – a hall in which evangelistic services had not been held for twenty-five years – only in turn to become too small for those who thronged its entrances; almost at once packed to the doors and hundreds turned away, those without left pleading for standing room. But even this was unavailable.

Those burning addresses of the Revivalist speedily dispelled doubts and fears, and night after night, when the invitation would be given, one living stream simply poured itself towards the platform. And then, as though stricken down by some invisible hand, it was no uncommon sight to see many of them fall prostrate beneath the power of God, only to rise completely healed.

Striking healings took place. A child born with a paralysed arm was brought to the services, and was healed at once. Her mother told the congregation that the child, six years old, had never been able to move the arm. Now she could raise the arm above the shoulder and could feed herself. A sister suffering for years with rupture was instantaneously healed. Another who came in a bath chair was able to walk, after six years' suffering. One person was healed of a broken ankle, and walked up and down before the meeting without a limp and without aid. One suffering for nine years with sleeplessness was healed and is sleeping like a child. A sister suffering from bad eyesight for fifty-eight years was restored by the power of God. A young lad with broken arm in splints was healed, and the mother took off the splints. In the evening service the little fellow stood upon a chair in the middle of the hall, waving the arm above the shoulder, while the people rejoiced. A man who came to the meeting dragging his paralysed foot along the ground was prayed for, and was able to put his foot on the ground after years of suffering.

These are only a few out of the scores who have been healed, and the people all marvel. They indeed have never seen things in this fashion before. Queues form up long before the times of service.

The last five days of the Carlisle Campaign were overwhelmingly magnificent. Viewed from every standpoint, they form an astonishing commentary upon the Acts of the Apostles. Although that great Military Riding School which had now been acquired contained no heating whatever, and moreover the weather was convincingly November-like, yet the crowds continued to gather. From far and near they came, bringing their halt, maimed, and blind to the healing services, while hundreds more were drawn into the Kingdom of God, making the total number of conversions about 1,200. Said one who has since gone to be with the Lord:

> Those meetings would have melted the heart of a stoic – rows upon rows of kneeling figures, suffering from various complaints, and waiting for a touch from the Great Physician.

It was estimated that well over 3,000 listened to the Pastor's last message.

One local Anglican minister, writing of these gatherings, said:

> The Pastor's addresses were listed to with deep earnestness, he did not preach the opinions of men or even his own, but loyally held fast to the Word of the Lord. Had Mr Jeffreys been an Anglican, we should have labelled him a first-rate Gospel preacher, definitely evangelical, doctrinally, sound, and holding fast to the thirty-nine articles of our Church's belief.

His Gospel for sinners and saints alike was as clear as crystal, his heart was all afire for God, his desire was not to be known by men in the popular sense, but that men may know Jesus as their Saviour, Lord and King.

He had the joy of seeing hundreds respond to his appeal for full salvation in Christ Jesus. The sick were healed, others broken in body and mind were delivered. Carlisle will remember the Foursquare Gospel Campaign for years to come, and ever praise the Name of the Lord. Hallelujah!

Another local Christian worker adds his witness to this glorious campaign:

Five weeks ago a silent messenger in the form of a leaflet was left at every house, announcing that a Revival and Healing Campaign was to held in the Queen's Hall, Carlisle. Some glanced at it and smiled; others put it into the waste paper basket as if it did not concern them; whilst a few of the readers decided to go and see if anything would happen. The strange thing about it all was that **something did happen**.

The few attenders speedily turned into multitudes – men and women driven in their bath-chairs to the meetings, fathers bringing their crippled and paralysed sons, and mothers their sick children. When a meeting was announced for three o'clock, a queue could be seen at the doors by two o'clock.

One particular afternoon I saw a woman who I knew suffered much. I was surprised to see her, and to know how she managed to get there; but what a light came into her eyes and a note of expectancy into her voice, as she greeted me, saying: 'O Sister Lillie, I have come in to be healed.' The door then opened, and we filed in, but long before three o'clock the place was filled – what a meeting that was! The evangelist held a small packet in his hand, and it was not so much his words as the manner in which he presented that packet of requests for prayer that had come from hearts torn with suffering and affliction – it was the tremendous compassion in Pastor George Jeffreys, and his great gift of conveying that compassion to others, that caused the vast congregation to become one in a deep sympathy for the sick and afflicted. Whether he prayed or preached or anointed the sick, it was with **certainty**, because the Bible declared it. He believed that as he read those requests the sick ones could be thrilled with a new hope and be healed: and so 'something happened', and proofs abound that those who sent their requests and those who came and sought his anointing went away healed.

If the lame, the crippled, the halt and the blind were seen coming for healing to the meetings, what power drew hundreds of young men and maidens? In more than one meeting I saw more than thirty hands raised to notify that they were seeking salvation. One young lady to whom I spoke after the meeting, because I saw she had raised her hand, said: 'I have been longing for peace in my soul, and now I have got it.' Another case of a young man over six feet, strong and healthy – he too declared he had found peace and joy.

The Revivalist and his helpers have gone, but the blessing of their labours remains in Carlisle.

Some eighteen months after the campaign closed a fine large hall was purchased and added to the ever-growing number of Elim Tabernacles which are found all over the country.

Chapter 14

Miraculous Signs Follow in Scotland

Great as were the triumphs of 1925 and 1926, 1927 was destined to eclipse both years in splendid achievement and advancement. The river of revival had by this time deepened and broadened, and is seen flowing more swiftly on its course. The account of the campaigns which this year includes, reads like a modern Acts of the Apostles – every page sparkles with supernatural signs and bears the stamp of inspiration.

Early in the January of 1927 one of the more remarkable campaigns, remarkable for its prolific results, was commenced by George Jeffreys in Glasgow. By some this was regarded as a city which would not easily succumb to the Foursquare Gospel appeal; these dispassionate and self-restrained Scots were not likely to become susceptible to revival influences. Staid to a degree, it was not to be expected that they would readily respond to this unique preacher's presentation of the Gospel. Other centres might fall before the fiery eloquence of the Welsh prophet, but the Scottish citadel would not so quickly capitulate to methods so unusual and a ministry so exceptional. And yet the centre of Western Scotland's spiritual and commercial life had soon to realise that, even in this twentieth century, the same Evangel that had stirred her sons to mighty deeds for Christ in the past, possessed an undimmed and undying dynamic which was able to restore the waning spiritual glory of her religious life. 'Here was an old-fashioned, outspoken Covenanter in the land of Covenanters, a spiritual Bruce', whose voice was calling them to throw off the yoke of the oppressor. From the commencement of this campaign it was evident that George Jeffreys was a preacher who came not to trade upon the credulity of the curious, not to address himself to the connoisseurs of fantastic and fanatical religious ideas. Neither had he come as the exponent of some new creed upon which he hoped to erect the fabric of another religious sect. The constraint of his call was back to the Word. The burden of his message was the whole Gospel for the whole needs of the whole world.

The campaign had been in progress a few weeks when the following telegram was received at the London Headquarters:

> Revival fires burning in Glasgow. Crowds flocking to the services. Hundreds converted. Remarkable healing testimonies. Blind eyes opened, running wounds dried up; paralysis, rupture, tumour, growths disappear under power of God. All kinds of diseases healed daily. Hall seating two thousand taken to continue revival. Forces uniting as in Bournemouth for Foursquare Gospel. Pray on. Lord triumphs.

What a grand witness to the 'exceeding greatness' of the Divine power! Here was faith that expressed itself in stupendous facts. Here was a work that was not the creation of some human genius, but the product of the creative energy of the eternal truth.

The following report taken from the London *Daily Express* of 24 March, 1927, reveals something of the magnitude of the work accomplished and the wealth of result obtained during the Glasgow campaign:

GREAT WAVE OF EVANGELISM

'MIRACLES' AT REVIVAL MEETINGS
1,400 CONVERSIONS

Glasgow, Wednesday

A wave of evangelism is sweeping Glasgow. More than 1,400 people have been converted, hundreds have testified to faith healing, and thousands have taken part in the revival campaign which is being conducted by Pastor George Jeffreys.

The series of revival meetings which have been held by Pastor Jeffreys during the last four weeks here will conclude this weekend with a final rally which, it is expected, nearly 10,000 people will attend.

Pastor Jeffreys will hold two 'Gospel demonstrations' in the Albert Hall in London on Easter Monday.

Scenes in Glasgow and the surrounding towns during the past four weeks rival the most emotional incidents in Scottish history.

Vast crowds, moved by the passionate pleadings of Pastor Jeffreys, have risen in a body in reply to the evangelist's request to 'stand up for God'.

Scores of people, blind, paralysed, deaf, suffering from all forms of 'incurable' maladies, have been brought to the meetings to join in prayer for healing.

Crowds have been lining up at the doors to the hall each night, and hundreds have been turned away when the place was filled. Pastor Jeffreys admits that the first week of his campaign was 'uphill work'.

'The canny Scots were not too quick to believe that the age of miracles is not past,' he said. But the Lord confirmed His words with signs and wonders, and soon all reserve was broken down.

Many similar splendid testimonials from different sources reveal how profoundly the whole district was moved by this remarkable visitation of Divine power, which continued with unabated enthusiasm for upwards of eight weeks.

Perhaps the fact that St Andrew's Hall – Scotland's most historic hall – was unable to accommodate the huge crowds which sought an entrance, best serves to demonstrate the overwhelming victory gained. Glasgow was simply swept by a hurricane of heavenly blessing. It was as though a flood-tide of Pentecostal power had been let loose upon the assembled multitudes.

From one who was privileged to participate in this wonderful campaign we cull the following impressions:

From a small beginning in St Mungo Hall, the meetings grew and grew until the St Andrew's Hall – Scotland's premier hall – failed to accommodate the thousands seeking admission.

To those privileged to be present at the services it was a time of heaven upon earth – revival in flood-tide was witnessed. Impressions gathered from old saints of God who have witnessed and participated in revival meetings of by-gone days drew forth the testimony that in all their experience they have never seen anything like this. There was real revival emotion. Why deny it?

But emotion under the control of the Spirit of God. Why should not men glorify God and employ all their powers to extol His Name?

Over 1,500 souls have been saved in Glasgow and Paisley. Hundreds of bodies have been healed. God has indeed been confirming His Word with signs following. God set free those who had left the 'old paths' and had been side-tracked into roads cut by the hand of man. The Bible has now become more precious than ever to these liberated ones, and they are rejoicing once again in the 'liberty of the truth of God'.

What a sight to see these great meetings at the St Andrew's Hall during the final rally. Looking from the body of the hall, one gazes at the huge platform packed with over 600 earnest-looking men, both old and young. The subject of the address – 'The Faith once for all delivered unto the saints'. The result – thousands of believers giving heartfelt expression to their holy determination to stand for the whole counsel of God.

Another sight that lives in one's memory is the farewell meeting in Berkeley Square, outside the St Andrew's Hall. It is immediately after the final service, and the vast crowd have left the building and congregated outside. The police have hastily been summoned to control then, and they are waiting for the arrival of the Principal and his party. Five thousand people packed together to say 'good-bye' to those who had become dear to them in Christ.

The products of this revival are even greater than the most sanguine hopes raised at the commencement of the campaign. Listen to the catalogue of cures! Muscular rheumatism (after 30 years' suffering and pronounced by physicians incurable), blindness from birth, paralysis, deafness, rupture, severe internal trouble, varicose veins, etc., And all this the outcome of this magnificent mission. In addition to all this, upwards of 1,500 brought to Christ! What an argument for the Gospel's claims! What an eloquent and adequate answer to the question of agnosticism and infidelity, 'Where is God?' Let those fifteen hundred freed sin-slaves sing out their thrilling reply to the challenge of Modernism and Materialism. Is the old-time Gospel still a living power in the world? Such scenes answer, yes!

From Glasgow George Jeffreys and his party continued their triumphant tour, leaving Scotland for Leeds, one of

Yorkshire's largest and most influential cities, where a short campaign had been arranged. Already the news of what had transpired in Glasgow had preceded the party. The Leeds campaign was, comparatively speaking, even more remarkable in its outcome than the previous one had been. In the short space of two weeks, over 2,000 souls were won for Christ. The figures given in connection with this series of revival services are truly amazing, representing perhaps an almost unparalleled achievement in the history of modern evangelism. Some of the heart-moving scenes witnessed during this campaign are graphically described by one who was an eye-witness:

> The greatest feat of present-day evangelism was the overwhelming success of a fourteen days' mission conducted by George Jeffreys and party, when two thousand two hundred and ninety professed conversion, and hundreds were healed of all kinds of diseases.
>
> Why such a glorious triumph of the Gospel over sin and sickness in a few days? Not because it was an easy field of labour. It had been too often described by local Christian workers as being 'a hard place'. The lament of those most interested was, 'The time is too short to do anything', and for opposition, there was much from the class that most opposed our Lord in the days of His flesh. The why and wherefore of this phenomenal victory is that God answered prayer. The prayers of local saints that had been expressed for many a year, and the prayers of thousands of God's people throughout the land. The Revivalist preached the Word of God with real power: every address had a message for saint and sinner. Thousands praise God for his able and faithful ministry of the Foursquare Gospel.

The following press reports will suffice to show the interest the campaign created:

'BLIND MADE TO SEE'

DRAMATIC SCENES AT A MISSION
APPARENT CURES

The afternoon meeting of Pastor Jeffreys' Revival and Healing Campaign, held in Salem Hall, resulted in several apparently extraordinary cures.

During the laying on of hands a middle-aged woman who was kneeling stood up and cried: 'I can see; I can read.' then in a low impassioned voice, trembling with awe, she read aloud the words of the printed text hung above her head. Afterwards she told the Pastor that she had been almost totally blind for years, that she could not distinguish objects owing to a ball of fire in front of her eyes, but the moment his hands touched her the ball of fire was taken away.

TENSE EXCITEMENT

As the healing went on the congregation grew tense with excitement. On the platform was an aged man with a long white beard, four schoolboys, and a number of women listening with rapt attention.

Slowly the Pastor moved, anointing their foreheads with oil from a silver chalice and praying in their ears, while below, surrounding the rostrum, scores of people knelt or stood supported by crutches.

Suddenly a man gave an exultant shout and lifted both arms above his head.

The Pastor, his pale, ascetic face transfigured with joy, asked him if he could jump. In reply the man leapt into the air. It was said he had been unable to move his arms for sixteen years.

CHILD HEALED

Another 'miracle' was the healing of a little boy of about seven years of age, who suffered from infantile paralysis.

Early in the meeting, I was told, he dragged his legs down the aisle and returned walking sturdily and straight.

Hymns were sung with fervour, and the scene throughout was punctuated by deep-throated 'hallelujahs' from different parts of the hall. At the close of the meeting those who had benefited shook hands with each other and the officials in a passion of gratitude.

One unshaven old man in the clothes of a tramp walked out murmuring, 'Aye, but it's the real thing', and a fashionable dressed girl replied in a far-away voice, 'Yes, the real thing.'

(Leeds Mercury, 6 April, 1927)

FAITH HEALING SCENES IN LEEDS

A SERVICE AT SALEM
THINGS HAPPEN

Here are a few of the things that happened. There was a sudden stir on the platform and I saw the extraordinary sight of a tall, stout, elderly man, standing with his two arms stretched high above his head and then jumping into the air.

'Jump again, brother,' said the Pastor, and again and again he jumped, while we were told that for 16 years he had suffered agony from sciatica and had been suddenly relieved of all pain.

Followed a girl for eleven years deaf and now in a moment hearing all that was said to her in the lowest of voices; an elderly woman suddenly taking off her glasses and delightedly exclaiming: 'I can see better without them,' while her son tells the Pastor that she has been almost blind for more years than he can tell.

A little boy runs from the platform to the back of the church and back again. 'Are you all right, sonny?' asks the Pastor. 'Well, do it again,' and he does it again, while the congregation shout 'Hallelujah.'

'There is a brother,' the Pastor says, pointing to a lad walking strangely but briskly down the church, 'who tells me he has had stiff knees and ankles.' 'How long since you were able to kneel, eh?' 'Ten years.' 'Well, kneel now.' And he knelt.

(*Yorkshire Evening Post*, 7 April, 1927)

And so as we follow the Principal's party, a trail of triumph is traced all along the route. Victory merges into victory, each more glorious than the last. Whole districts are magnetised by the power of God. Like some huge conflagration, the revival fire swept on its course of conquest, consuming the stubble of unbelief and arousing the sleeping consciousness of the self-satisfied and self-righteous religionists whom it encountered.

Most suggestive and significant are the revival results at Leeds, as viewed some time after the actual campaign had concluded.

The revival had come, the crowds had come, the joy had come, as the salvation of the Lord and His healing power were manifested in the meetings. But the question is asked, 'Now that our beloved Principal George Jeffreys and his workers have gone, what is the outcome? What are the lasting results?' Thank God, the Christ whom Principal Jeffreys proclaimed is still with us working in our midst. Let the following facts speak for themselves:

The enrolment of a Band of Crusaders about one hundred and eighty in number – bright, happy young people, rejoicing in the God of their salvation, satisfied with their Master and eager to serve Him.

Our former hall is absolutely inadequate to accommodate the people who are seeking to hear the Foursquare Gospel. The Albert Hall has been taken for the Sunday evening meetings, and 1,000 to 1,200 people listen each Sunday night to the glorious Gospel, and at each meeting souls signify their decision to take Christ as their personal Saviour, while many sick ones seek the touch of Jesus the Healer.

On 11 May, thirty-seven candidates passed through the waters of baptism, and on 25 May, thirty-five others followed them. it was a joyful sight as, after chorus singing and prayer, the Pastor led us to the Word of God as the basis of our faith and practice. The Holy Spirit bore witness to the truth, and as a result fifteen more signified their intention to follow their Lord at the earliest opportunity.

These are some of the results of the revival campaign, whilst the following extract from the *Leeds Mercury* of 18 May, also speaks for itself:

'MIRACLE' CURES HOLD GOOD

PASTOR JEFFREYS' WORK
LEEDS PEOPLE WHO TESTIFY

'Will these miracle cures be permanent?' That was the question which many asked when Pastor George Jeffreys, the Welsh evangelist, came into the light of Leeds publicity some six weeks ago.

It can be said at once that there was no doubt about the cures at the time. Whether they were effected by religious or purely psychological means, there was ample testimony to prove that they happened.

With the object, then, of discovering whether the results claimed at the beginning of April had been sustained, a *Mercury* reporter called on several former sufferers in Leeds yesterday.

UNANIMOUS OPINION

All of them were unanimous in stating that the cures were permanent.

Perhaps the most remarkable case visited was that of a woman who had been very ill for three years with curvature of the spine, a bad leg, and internal complaints. She was wheeled about in a chair, and when she managed to walk it was with great difficulty and with the aid of crutches of a stick. She told how she heard the Pastor, and then knelt for the first time for years. 'Before he touched me I was cured. The pain had left me and it has never come back to this day. Now I walk into Leeds, do all my own cooking, washing, and cleaning, and I know that the cure is permanent.'

Another woman, whose case was quoted in the *Mercury* at the time, was blind in one eye and suffered severe pains in the head. One eye is now as clear as the other, and she can see out of both equally well. Her husband, who was badly wounded in the war, and her son, who had been undergoing injections for tuberculosis, are now in perfect condition, and there is no sign of consumption in the son.

Others also testified to the permanence of their cures.

Thus we see that the results of these two campaigns have indeed been most remarkable in every sense of the term. In the short space of three months no less than 3,750 persons had publicly accepted Christ as their personal Saviour. Whilst, in addition to all this, hundreds of healings had taken place, to which authentic testimony had been given. This gave an average of nearly 300 souls per week, and slightly over 40 for each day that the meetings were in progress. That these startling successes should create a great demand for the services of the Principal we are not surprised, as by this time his fame as a Revivalist and Teacher was well known throughout the whole country. Invitations to conduct campaigns poured in from many of the principal towns in England and Scotland. None but those who were most closely associated with Mr Jeffreys knew how greatly he longed to respond to these appeals and cover the whole country, taking the Foursquare Gospel to the perishing populations of these great industrial centres, or how deeply he was concerned at his inability to accept these urgent calls. Gladly would he have yielded to the importunate requests, but circumstances prevented him from accepting all but a few which God laid most heavily upon his heart.

Chapter 15

Pentecostal Power in the Royal Albert Hall, London – Easter, 1927

Following the Leeds campaign, the party proceeded to London for the great Foursquare Gospel Demonstration which had been arranged to be held at Easter in the world-famous Royal Albert Hall. Many eyes were turned towards the Metropolis at this time – many hearts were full of fervent prayer that God might make this mighty gathering the occasion of another even greater and more overwhelming triumph for the full Gospel in the heart of England's greatest city. Many of those who had been so gloriously saved and miraculously healed were keen to be present to join in this magnificent witness to the power of the Word of God.

What a transition from the tiny tent at Monaghan in 1915 to the princely and palatial Royal Albert Hall in 1927! Who would have dared to dream of such strides of success in twelve short years?

Easter Monday, 1927, will live long in the memory of those who were privileged to participate in the monster Foursquare Gospel Demonstration held in the Royal Albert Hall.

That these gatherings represent an unprecedented and unparalleled achievement is unquestionable. Hours before the first service was announced to commence, an eager expectant throng of people lined up at each of the many entrances waiting for admission to the great auditorium. Arena, amphitheatre, orchestra, boxes – one, two, three tiers – and balcony, all filled with an exuberant throng.

What a soul-stirring sight the choir of 1,200 Elim Crusaders presented! Stretching across the full breadth of that majestic orchestra and reaching right up to the two organ galleries, they formed an eloquent and living testimony to the power of the Gospel of Christ to sway young life, in a period when the youth of our land is given up to the pursuit of pleasure and when even the churches are rapidly becoming immersed in worldly attractions. Here were twelve hundred young lives caught in the tide of a mighty movement of God – so full of vigour and vitality. And then forth from that company of Christian Crusaders there gushed a stream of entrancing melody. One could not but be deeply impressed with the admirable and able control of that large choir by its conductor, Mr Douglas Gray. Here was no mechanical rendering of song – no perfunctory performance of music. It was the choral overflow of hearts that were simply throbbing with the very life and love of God. Surely such consecrated young life must win its way to victory in the service of the King!

Perhaps the moment for which the majority had looked and longed, came when the preacher, a figure singularly full of decision and dignity, took the platform. As he rose to his feet, a quiver of expectation and a murmur of satisfaction passed over the great audience. Every eye was riveted upon the man whose ministry is now stirring so many of the largest cities of this country. And what is the theme of the preacher who can command such a congregation? The whole of his afternoon discourse is devoted to a careful, critical and exhaustive examination of the present day claims of the Gospel of Jesus Christ to miraculous power. Step by step he conducts his hearers to the fountain of all divine revelation, the Word of God. Powerfully and persuasively he pleads for absolute faith in and obedience to the Bible. With what impassioned and earnest eloquence he holds his congregation to the subject under consideration. As the preacher proceeds, the current of thought moves on to the climax of conviction that Jesus Christ is indeed the same yesterday, today and for ever. His utterances are graced with a sublime sincerity, simplicity, and straightforwardness. There is no attempt to lose his hearers in a bewildering maze of philosophical phrases. One is struck with the balanced and forceful presentation of truth.

A shadow of sadness stole over the consciousness as George Jeffreys referred to the departed glories and desecrated ideals of the churches of today, but hope sprung to life in the soul, as he uttered that stirring and stimulating challenge to God's people to return to the old paths, and renew their devotion to the inspired truths of the grand old Book. It was wonderful to witness that crowd, as eagerly they drank in the truth. How could one listen to such preaching and remain small and narrow in vision?

That to the uninitiated spectator these meetings presented a perplexing problem can easily be understood. In vain they sought for an explanation of this extraordinary scene. Here were 10,000 people held in the vice-like grip of a profound and absorbing interest. So spontaneously responsive and receptive was that huge assembly that we are not altogether surprised to find that the press attributes to George Jeffreys the power of mesmerism. On the Tuesday morning following the Royal Albert Hall Demonstration, one of the leading London daily papers came out with the striking headline, 'Vast Audience Mesmerised'. Bless the Lord, it was the power of God which drew and dominated that mammoth crowd. It was a heavenly attraction which enthralled them, and made them willing to wait for hours to secure a seat in the great building.

One cannot recall that day, with all its wonderful events, without fervent thanksgiving to God. Ever and anon the whole place was swept by a flood of praise. Over the vast congregations hung the brooding presence of the Lord. Now a wondrous hush pervades the assemblage, and then again the place is shaken with a veritable storm of glad acclamation. Who could resist being caught in the current of that captivating enthusiasm? The atmosphere was liberating, vitalising and cheering. Again and again, as the grand organ, under the skilful touch of Mr Ronald Cooper, rolled out its glorious message of music, every heart leapt to the stirring strains, and one realised that the hand of the Lord was indeed upon the meeting in a special manner. Never has the writer witnessed a greater or more glorious exhibition of joy than on this occasion.

Again, what a magnificent moment in the meeting that was when, in response to the Revivalist's appeal, hundreds of hands were raised, and hundreds more stood to their feet to bear witness to the healing of their bodes through the ministry of this servant of God in his various campaigns in different parts of the country. Thus the preacher's claims were supported by the evidence of scores who had proved the power of the Foursquare Gospel in their lives. Here was a sermon substantiated by signs such as would gratify the heart of any preacher. People who for years had been sufferers now enjoying freedom from pain. What stories of gracious deliverance from dreadful disease these healed ones could tell.

That the remarkable results which follow the Principal's campaigns are arousing keen and widespread interest, is evident by the way in which the press have taken up the matter. These huge gatherings are the subject of comment in most of the prominent papers. Moreover, the attention of the churches is being called to the reasonableness of the claims of this twentieth-century revivalist. Through the lips of His messenger, God is undoubtedly speaking to those in as well as those outside the churches, and sooner or later organised Christianity will be compelled to admit that this is no evanescent evangelism which in a few years will pass away and be forgotten.

The occasion of this great gathering with a fitting opportunity to send a message of love and loyalty to the King and Royal Family. It was indeed a thrilling moment when the Royal reply was read to the congregation, and the whole of the vast audience rose to express their appreciation of the Royal message by singing the National Anthem.

HIS MAJESTY THE KING,
BUCKINGHAM PALACE

THOUSANDS OF LOYAL SUBJECTS WHO STAND FOR THE WHOLE BIBLE GATHERED AT ELIM FOURSQUARE GOSPEL DEMONSTRATION IN ROYAL ALBERT HALL, SEND HEARTFELT GREETINGS AND LOYAL ASSURANCES AND

UNITE IN PRAYER FOR GOD'S BLESSING ON YOUR MAJESTY
AND THE ROYAL HOUSEHOLD.

GEORGE JEFFREYS

PASTOR GEORGE JEFFREYS
ROYAL ALBERT HALL, LONDON

I AM COMMANDED TO EXPRESS THE KING'S SINCERE
THANKS FOR YOUR KIND MESSAGE OF LOYAL GREETINGS.

STAMFORDHAM

A message of loving greeting was also despatched to
Mrs Aimee Semple McPherson, whose presence with us last
year was affectionately referred to by our leader. A further
message was sent to the saints assembled at Belfast for their
annual North of Ireland Eastertide Convention.

Throughout the day the Orchestra, which numbered over
seventy players, rendered valuable service under the leadership of Douglas Gray. From a musical point of view the
Demonstration was well served. In addition to the splendid
Grand Organ, there were the two pianos, both of which
contributed considerably to the effectiveness of the service.

How glad we were to see the platform filled with such a
splendid contingent of Foursquare Gospel ministers from all
parts of the United Kingdom. Also to notice the presence of
more than one person of noble birth, who had come to show
sympathy with and interest in a movement which, although
encountering such fierce and formidable opposition, is still
forging ahead, and continually adding fresh triumphs to the
name of the Risen Lord whom it represents and for whom it
labours.

And what does this glorious gathering, with its thousands
upon thousands of warm-hearted participants portend? Does
it not tell us that we are at the dawn of a new day of
possibility for God? That heaven is about to pour out its
wealth of blessing upon the dry and thirsty land? Is it an
invitation from on high to prepare ourselves for floods of
revival – revival that shall sweep away the uncleanness of our
times, and purge the people from iniquity? God is moving in
old-time power and is asking His people to co-operate with
Him. That marvellous concourse of people which gathered

together on Easter Monday in the Royal Albert Hall is an up-to-date proof of the presence of God upon the throne. It demonstrates the sovereign power of Jehovah.

Gleaning from some of the impressions of those present at this demonstration we discover some happy and even humorous sidelights upon a day of wonderful portent and power. Says one:

> Almost at the end of the evening meeting at the Royal Albert Hall, I slipped into one of the many passages of that immense beehive and came across the sergeant of police and another. We entered into conversation, and I asked him how he liked Elim Foursquare Gospel Demonstrations. 'Well, sir,' he answered, 'I've just been talking to my pal here, and I'll say this, that of all the meetings I've been on duty at during my time in the force – **This has me beat**. The singing of all those folk, the joy on their faces, the testimonies, and the message is something new in religious meetings; what is more, he's got the voice for the Albert Hall, and can be heard all over the building. Believe me, **it's the goods!**'
>
> One final touch. Just as I was making my way to the exit, I met one of the Royal Albert Hall attendants; unbroken gross packets and boxes of cigarettes filled his arms – his daily stock unsold – and as he came along, he was singing one of our choruses that had caught on that day:
>
> > Just the same, just the same,
> > God is just the same today.
>
> I could not help but laugh at the thought that because God **was** just the same, to save and cleanse, so his stock of cigarettes was returning to the store cupboard – **just the same!**

Such widespread interest was aroused in London in these meetings that the press gave considerable attention to them. Below are two reports culled from many more which space forbids us to include in this volume:

VAST AUDIENCE MESMERISED

FERVENT SCENES AT THE ALBERT HALL
'MIRACLE' CREED OF PASTOR GEORGE JEFFREYS

Remarkable scenes took place at the Albert Hall yesterday at the annul Elim Foursquare Gospel Demonstration conducted by Pastor George Jeffreys.

The demonstration was held in two parts – the first starting at 3 o'clock in the afternoon and the second at 6 o'clock in the evening.

Hours before the doors were opened thousands of people queued up seeking admission, and spent the waiting hours singing religious songs taught to them previously by the Pastor. They stormed the great hall soon after 2 o'clock and soon every seat from the top of the Albert Hall to the bottom was occupied.

BURST INTO SONG

Several thousand Elim Crusaders from London and the provinces had formed themselves into a choir, while others organised a band. These started hymns with catchy tunes, which obviously were well-known to most of the vast audience. In a few minutes these airs were taken up by every person present with intense fervour. Indeed this fervour almost amounted to mesmerism, and independent observers must have been struck by the extraordinary hold which his young pastor exercised over his monster congregation.

There was none of that sheepish half-attention that so often characterises an audience or a church congregation.

Mr Jeffrey's flock seem to be under a spell. They would lean forward, drinking in his every word and punctuating his phrases with ecstatic 'Alleluias' or 'Thank God'.

'AMEN'

'Do you believe in miracles?' the preacher would ask. The whole congregation roared back 'Amen'.

What is Mr Jeffrey's creed? The word 'miracle' sums it up. 'I do not mind what you are,' he said, 'Catholic or Presbyterian or Nonconformist. It is all the same to me. I believe in every word of the Bible and claim that the atheist has a right to say: "I will not believe unless you can cause miracles." '

Then with a thundering voice that re-echoed through the hall he shouted: 'How many people here today have been cured?'

Immediately several hundred hands were thrown upwards, and the Revivalist and choir murmured ecstatically: 'Thank God, Amen.'

CURES CLAIMED

The evening service was a repetition of that of the afternoon. For an hour and a half the young pastor held his audience enthralled.

Again the numbers were too large for the performing of 'miracles' but prayers were said for those desiring to be cured. Many claiming to have been cured recently testified to their cure and I talked with several of them.

A man told me of his cure. 'I had an accident to my back in February 1922, and could only walk with the aid of crutches. After five years and two months of continual suffering I received the divine power. I came to the next meeting with my crutches in my hands.'

After suffering from early childhood from stammering, another was cured at the age of 40. 'I was completely cured,' he told me, 'and now I am so free that I can preach the Gospel myself.'

(Morning Post, 19 April, 1927)

10,000 people attended the service, and some of them were so overcome that they had to be provided with glasses of water. Pastor Jeffreys, who believes in miracles, spoke for nearly two hours.

When he called upon all those who had been cured of an illness by faith to signify, half the audience stood up. Hundreds of people were present, he said, who desired to be cured by being anointed with oil and by the laying-on of hands, but owing to the lateness of the hour that was not possible. But he enjoined all to pray for the suffering.

TESTIMONY

Then came the personal testimonies from people who had been healed by the power of faith.

One man, standing erect on the platform and with tears in his eyes, said that for years his legs were crossed. They dragged along as he propelled himself on his crutches. He had been completely cured at one service.

A woman from Leeds waved her left arm to the audience and said that it had been paralysed for six months. Last week she was cured.

A Grimsby woman testified that after having been bed-ridden for eleven years with spinal trouble she had been cured.

During the afternoon a telegram was sent to the King to the effect that thousands of loyal Foursquare Gospellers assembled in the Albert Hall prayed for him. A message from Lord Stamfordham conveying the King's sincere thanks was read out during the evening service.

(Daily News, 19 April, 1927)

Chapter 16

South-Coast Conquests

One might have supposed that after the incessant meetings of the past months a halt would be called in order to secure a much-needed rest, but instead of this we find that immediately following the great Easter triumph at the Royal Albert Hall, and without a single day's respite, George Jeffreys and his party commenced a fresh campaign at Southampton. Here success again speedily attended his efforts and another magnificent mission was held which yielded most gratifying and God-glorifying results.

These large seaport cities, England's doorways to the great world beyond, are usually hotbeds of sin, where a good deal of human wreckage and driftwood may be found. Moral degradation and spiritual destitution are well known in such places. Southampton was found to be no exception. Here it was at the latter end of April, 1927, that the Principal hoisted the Foursquare Gospel flag.

From the opening meeting at which several souls were saved and a number of people healed of diverse diseases, until the last gathering when well over one hundred people gave themselves to Christ and a great crowd came forward to testify of having received the healing touch of the Lord in their bodies, one could trace the rising tide of revival, with its increasing liberty and gladness. Commencing, as it did, without great promise of outpouring, the glorious ingathering of close upon a thousand souls tells a story that should make the most sceptical think seriously of the claims which these campaigns make and the source from whence they come. Southampton, like Samaria of old, had opened its heart to the Word of God, and as a result in hundreds of lives a new empire had been established – scores of ungodly lives had come under the spell of the Christ.

From the following reports and testimonies of those memorable meetings may be gathered some idea of the splendid work accomplished. Although these reports were given during the early part of the campaign, yet they reveal how, even at this early stage, the Foursquare Gospel had gripped the district. A Baptist minister from the district furnishes us with some interesting and illuminating impressions of these services. He says:

> The importance of this campaign can only be adequately understood as one looks at the mighty influence of this great city's life upon the nations of the world. The key to the very ends of the earth, the centre of that vast arterial system of ocean traffic which flings its life throb into every sea and land.
>
> 'Principal Jeffreys is here,' the notice read outside the Central Hall, and God graciously set His seal upon our brother and his noble trio from that very first night. The surroundings seemed at first like granite walls, the Principal's words like a thin ray of sunlight seeking a crevice through which to shed its light, or like the sweet melody of the Lord's song smothered by the strangeness of the land.
>
> Night after night, however, the tide rose, night after night new lights were lit, new singers sang; night after night the fire burned and leapt from soul to soul across the arena and up into the terraces, until at last the huge building was filled from end to end with a mighty full-throated crowd. God's servant, clothed with Holy Ghost power, with an unanswerable argument, descending now like hammer blows, convicting, convincing, now in soft, passionate pleading, until the iron melted and the silence was broken with loud 'Amens' and 'Hallelujahs'.
>
> Strong men were moved, young men and women by the score yielded their lives to Jesus, tears of true repentance flowed down many a sin-marked face, captives were freed, bodies healed, spiritual life revived. **Revival had started**.
>
> Yes, the walls are down. The city has yielded, and into the hum and throb of its daily life there has entered the mighty, transforming, conquering power of the Holy Ghost. Praise the name of the Lord.
>
> George Jeffreys faithfully proclaims a Foursquare Gospel, stands by the whole Word of God, uplifts Jesus and His precious blood, and it is quite clear that he is being greatly honoured of God. From

four conversions on the first night, the total rose to over 800, and definite healings took place at almost every service.

One of the many wonderful cases of miraculous healing which took place during this campaign is worthy of mention, and should serve as a stimulant to others who themselves are held in bondage to disease. The lady tells in her own words:

How overjoyed I am that you came with your little band to Southampton. Glory be to God! My cup is full and running over, for just one week ago I was an invalid, having been wheeled about in a bath-chair for between 14 and 15 years, suffering from a tubercular knee.

I was lying ill in London when your campaign started, and the doctors there gave me to understand the knee was absolutely destroyed and I should never walk again.

My mother brought me home, as soon as I was able to travel, to talk it over with my doctor in Southampton, to have my leg amputated. But, praise be to God, I never saw my doctor, but came in my bath-chair to the Central Hall, where Divine Healing was, and on that Thursday afternoon when you laid your hands upon me and prayed to God to heal me, I was healed. The power of God came upon me, and as I lay there in my chair, my knee lifted three times in the splints, and afterwards I was able to step out of my chair without aid and walk across the hall – I was healed. That night I slept without my splint for the first time for 14 years. I cannot praise the Lord enough, my heart is so full of rejoicing.

The knee which seemed destroyed and would never bend again is now bending beautifully, and the leg which was so wasted is gaining, and already there is a big improvement.

And then the modern biblical exegete would persuade us that the miraculous is impossible. In the face of such positive proofs we cannot but accept the statements of Scripture, confirmed as they are by the evidences of our eyes.

In the *Southern Daily Echo* the following reports appeared during the first part of the campaign:

HEALING MISSION

PRINCIPAL JEFFREYS AT SOUTHAMPTON
FIRST CURES IN CENTRAL HALL

A middle-aged lady with a limp was amongst those who went to the front of the Central Hall last night when, at the opening of his 'Revival and Healing Campaign' in Southampton, Principal George Jeffreys, whose meetings in the Albert Hall, London, on Monday have been given wide publicity, asked those who wished to be healed to come to him. The Pastor anointed her with oil 'in the Name of Jesus Christ', and prayed with her for a moment. He then told her to lay down the stick, with the aid of which he had walked to the platform, and walk. She walked up and down the length of the rostrum twice unaided. Then told to kneel down, she did so, whereupon the Principal informed the audience that the lady had told him that was the first time she had been able to kneel for two years.

NINE TESTIMONIES

Previous to the healing episode, Principal Jeffreys had asked all in the audience who had been touched by healing at his previous meetings to go on to the platform. Nine people responded, and the Pastor questioned each of them. A man said he came from New Milton, and after being deaf for thirty years was cured at the Principal's mission at Bournemouth last year. A little South-ampton girl of about six years was deaf, it was stated, until, taken to the Principal's meeting at Bournemouth, she suddenly told her father she could hear his watch ticking. A lady in a fur coat (the Principal said was the wife of a Harley Street specialist) told how she was wheeled in a chair by her daughter to the mission at Bournemouth and cured. The others had similar testimonies to give.

REMARKABLE STORIES OF CURES

About 100 people stood up at Principal George Jeffrey's revival and healing mission meeting at the Central Hall, Southampton, last night and testified to having experienced 'a touch of heal-ing'. Most of them were members of a party of 600 who came by special excursion train and motor coach from Bournemouth, where Principal Jeffreys conducted a mission last year.

All those who had been healed were invited on to the platform, and sufferers from deafness, blindness from birth, heart and nervous troubles, and many other ills, declared they had been cured at Principal Jeffreys' meetings.

EASTLEIGH YOUNG MAN'S DECLARATION

One young man, who said he came from Eastleigh, told the Principal he was taken to the mission on Tuesday evening stone deaf, but after prayer and being anointed by Mr Jeffreys, recovered his hearing.

A young woman stood up and testified that she had been healed of asthma at the meeting held yesterday afternoon, and a youth who had been crippled in an accident went to the afternoon meeting with the aid of a stick and said all sign and feeling of his trouble had gone. Last night he walked normally and without assistance.

All those who had testified to healing stood up in their places on the platform and sang the hymn: 'There is power, wonder-working power.'

Later on in the same year Hastings, another picturesque southern seaside resort, was visited by Principal George Jeffreys for a series of revival services. In this instance the campaign was conducted under canvas; the large tabernacle, already consecrated by many a remarkable meeting, was brought into action and once more became the scene of some soul-stirring successes. A telegram which reached the Headquarters in London whilst the Hastings campaign was in progress runs as follows:

Revival fires are spreading at Hastings. Crowds flock to the big tent daily. Souls are coming in at every meeting. Remarkable cases of healing are taking place. The largest hall in the district is now booked. Pray and believe.

We discover that the town was, at this time, in the throes of a real Pentecostal awakening.

One of the Hastings' leading Christian men writes in the most glowing terms of the campaign. He says:

At every meeting in the tent – afternoon and night – in the open air – in the Elite Theatre, immediately the Principal made the appeal for an acceptance of Jesus Christ as Saviour and Lord, hands were held up to signify their decisions – often in scores.

'Who could ever forget the solemn hush at the close of every meeting – and especially after an exposition of the Word of God upon the Second Coming of the Lord when 51 passed from death unto life – or when the miraculous Gospel was proclaimed at the Elite Theatre when some 500 could not gain admittance, and over 90 entered the Kingdom of God, born from above that night? We have been thrilled about this miraculous Gospel proclaimed by the Lord's servant. My salvation is a **miraculous** one – who wants one that isn't?

Nothing could convince those on the outside quicker than seeing the change that has come over the whole community – new-born souls in their first love (for over 800 have made confession of Jesus as Lord). Large numbers have testified that the Lord Jesus is still interested in our physical frames. Oh yes, the Risen Jesus has healed men's wounds, put smiles into withered face, and set the joy-bells ringing in hundreds of His redeemed ones. It is wonderful how quickly the Holy Ghost can teach us the Hebrew language – 'Hallelujah!' may be heard on every hand. The old Dorset woodsman who preached on Sundays was explaining to his rural congregation the meaning of Hallelujah! Said he: 'When you come across the word, it means you are to holloa louder!'

The following is a press report of the first Sunday meeting in the Elite Picture Theatre:

REVIVAL AND HEALING

OVERFLOWING CONGREGATION AT THE ST LEONARD'S ELITE
REMARKABLE SCENES

A week ago the big tent at Ore Valley Farm, Hastings, in which Principal George Jeffreys is holding his Revival and Healing Campaign, was not big enough. Yesterday evening's service was held in the Elite Picture Theatre, Warrior Square, St Leonard's, and, though this building possession three times the capacity of the tent, the attendance was so great that many people were unable to obtain entrance. Every available seat was occupied before the service was due to commence, and by the time the famous chorus: 'When Jesus came into my heart' had been struck up, the platform was crowded, and every nook which permitted standing occupied, while, in the gallery, seating accommodation was found on the stairs.

Principal Jeffreys delivered a powerful address, taking as his main theme the promise the miraculous signs should accompany the preaching of the Word of God. Atheists and agnostics, he said, had a right to demand these miraculous signs. The Church in the past had failed to take God at His word. They of the Foursquare Gospel went the whole of the way. They believed in Jesus Christ as the Saviour, the Baptiser, the Healer and the Coming King.

When Mr Jeffreys invited those who desired salvation to take God at His word, ninety-five persons professed conversion.

About a hundred people rose to their feet in evidence of having been healed by divine power.

The services are being continued at the Ore Valley tent each evening.

(Argus, 22 August, 1927)

From Hastings, Principal Jeffreys proceeded westward along the coast to Portsmouth, England's great naval base and premier naval arsenal of the Empire, thus completing a chain of Foursquare Gospel Churches along the south coast, reaching from Plymouth in Devon to Hastings in Sussex. Of these powerful services those who were eye-witnesses of what actually transpired write in words which are most expressive:

I travelled down from London to Portsmouth in company with Principal George Jeffreys in order to be present at the last services of his month's mission in that famous seaport. As we motored along, showers of rain drenched the car, but the natural showers were negligible in face of the spiritual showers which awaited us at our destination. The scenes that occurred are almost indescribable. Signs and wonders are, without a shadow of doubt, taking place in our land today. Miracles just as wonderful as when our Lord walked the earth are being seen in our midst. Neither should we be surprised – for it is the same Lord that touches and the same Lord that heals.

Critics criticise – the wildest and the unkindest things are said. But we are not angry; **we are sorry**. We are not the losers, **they are the losers**. The pulpit and the pew that stand afar off may criticise, but the needy, hungry crowds that come near – they do not. They know – they see – they feel.

The Sunday afternoon gathering in the Guildhall was packed with a mixed multitude. Many knew that God was in our midst. Others doubted, others denied. But when the testimonies commenced, all were moved to silence, then to tears, applause, laughter, hallelujahs – all combined.

Hundreds testified to healing. Two at least had been wheeled to the meetings a few days before. One for fifteen years and the other for twenty years had been carriaged about – helpless, but lo! they walked before us – healed. The useless leg of the one had faded to a skeleton. Not only was she instantly healed, but her flesh returned as fresh and full as the other. A little girlie of about three years of age had been healed of paralysis of both arms. She held them up before us. When George Jeffreys kissed her, we felt we would all like to do the same. Another had been blind in her right eye for many years. Now she sees! Growths, dislocations, deafness, rupture, even sugar diabetes, have all disappeared before the touch of the Master-Healer.

No wonder the singing was filled with joy and power. No wonder the people waved their hymn-sheets. No wonder hundreds more sought healing. But the missioner made it clear that only those who knew Christ as Saviour had a right to experience Christ as Healer. No doubt exceptional cases do take place when the unsaved are healed, but in such cases God has a special purpose – sometimes a hidden one. More than fifty saw that their first need was the salvation of the soul, and when the invitation was given, responded to the call to take Christ as Saviour.

The afternoon meeting came to an end, but the evening meeting soon commenced. This gathering was held in the Coliseum Theatre, holding about two thousand people. The place was packed – stage as well. It was the last night of a miracle-campaign. The people felt it – the missioner felt it. The message was for all – 'Earnestly contend for the Faith'. As the writer listened to the message, he marvelled that Christian people could hold aloof from such a work as this. The sermon was a mighty one from God, preached in the power of the Holy Spirit. Oh that **every Christian Editor** in the land might have been present – prejudice would surely have fled away. Some editors might have been hurt by things said, the blush would at times have risen to the cheek, their previous thoughts would have been severely challenged, but methinks at the close all would have been saying: 'Thank God. Thank God! for such a man, such a message, such a movement.' And into each respective paper would have crept a new attitude toward such a work. Not an attitude of doubt or criticism, but one of grateful support.

We are living in day of the Acts of the Holy Ghost – thank God for it! Our eyes are seeing what hundreds of thousands of the redeemed have been groaning for. We are in the midst of a **solid revival**. At this last meeting, no less than 130 people have signified their acceptance of Christ. Someone said it was like the Welsh Revival. I did not see that Revival, but I cannot doubt the similarity. And the Revival Movement is spreading and growing. This Elim Movement will grow and grow. We know not where it will end. Let God's people keep humble, let God's people keep from fleshly excitement, let God's people watch unto prayer, yea, and fasting. Let God's people seek a greater and greater outpouring of the Holy Spirit, and it will be given. This work will not cease, for it is God's work. God is in it – let His people get into it too. Let denominational labels be forgotten. Let us join together in this mighty effort. If you do not join the work, it will not stop, for it is of God, but you – you will miss the blessing. Pray for the continuation work at Portsmouth – pray for the continuation work in every part of the land. Amen!

Chapter 17

Soul-Stirring Scenes in Brighton

We who have witnessed some of George Jeffreys' greatest British triumphs find it difficult to pick out any one campaign as more remarkable than another, yet we cannot but be deeply impressed by the magnitude of the Brighton campaign. The highest expectations cherished with regard to this series of special services were more than realised. Between one and two thousand souls being literally swept into the Kingdom of God.

That Brighton was ablaze quickly became evident; this 'London-by-the-sea' soon awoke to find itself ringing with revival.

The profound impression that these gatherings made upon many of those who attended them is admirably expressed in a glowing appreciation of the campaign given by Lady Brownlow Cecil, who refers to the great revival meetings as 'truly wonderful'. She continues:

The great Revival Campaign in the Brighton Pavilion and Town Hall, Hove, has been truly wonderful. Many of us had never heard of George Jeffreys of the Foursquare Gospel, and, at these crowded meetings, growing larger each day, we have listened to the pure Gospel preached by this great teacher, God's Word explained with such wonderful simplicity and power, and the way of salvation taught, so plainly, so beautifully, so tenderly, that no heart could help being touched, no one could help longing to take Christ as their personal Saviour – a living Saviour the same yesterday, today and for ever.

The preacher explained so convincingly the Gospel of the miraculous. Jesus the Saviour, Jesus the Baptiser in the Holy Ghost, Jesus the Healer, Jesus the coming King. We know now that Divine healing for the body as well as salvation for the soul, **is true**. Many miracles have happened in Brighton and Hove, many wonderful cures have been wrought after prayer, anointing with oil, and the laying-on of hands by the Pastor.

Praise God for salvation, and praise Him for Divine healing, and for all he has done and will do for those who love and trust Him.

To those who have not been to these campaigns I would say: 'Come! See! Hear!'

An exceedingly interesting comment upon these meetings is furnished by one of the Baptist ministers of Brighton, whose attention was arrested in the first place by the remarkable happenings which characterised these meetings from the very first. He says:

My impressions of the Revival and Healing Campaign conducted by George Jeffreys in Brighton may help some if I give what has been my personal experience and some of the conclusions to which I have been forced to come. Having read a good deal from newspaper reports, and having conversed with those who have attended similar meetings in other parts, I was anxious to see for myself, and to hear what was taught.

The first meeting I went to was in the Royal Pavilion, and, frankly, I went with a prejudiced mind, but not intentionally to find fault. One became immediately conscious of an atmosphere of peace and quiet where one could commune with God and pray. And so consciously one became aware that the prejudices were all melted away, and one was in an attitude to discern whether this was of God or not. Knowing much of the joy and gladness of the Lord in one's own heart and service, one was struck with the radiant joy, and the deep love to the Lord Jesus and His Word, and also the spirit of true and loving fellowship with others who loved and served the same Lord, which Pastor Jeffreys and his co-workers manifested.

Then, the ministry of the Word appealed tremendously. It was direct, it was sound, it was fundamental. Things were in their proper order. Christ was exalted and honoured, and always pre-eminent. The new birth was insisted on as absolutely essential. The healing of the body, divine healing, was presented in such a clear way, that none but a biased mind could possibly do other than say that this is truly a blessed part of that wondrous gospel that Christ commanded to be taught to all men. Having seen many cases of wondrous healing in the past of one's ministry, one's heart rejoiced to see God's power present to heal. Everything one saw was orderly, seemly and reverent. The singing was great – an inspiration. One just had to sing – but why? Because the words sung found a responding echo in one's heart. Anyone, with any spiritual discernment, must have felt that the truth that gripped the heart, and was a blessed experience, was just finding its expression in glad song. If there was enthusiasm – and there was – it was clear it was the expression of a holy joy in the Lord.

The Foursquare Gospel taught and demonstrated in this Revival Campaign, must surely be believed by all who believe fully the Bible to be God's inspired word to man. Christ as Saviour, Christ as Healer, Christ as Baptiser – personally I think I prefer another word (filling) here, but I know what is meant and agree with what is taught, and so do not make a man an offender for a word – then Christ as Coming King.

As one listened time after time to George Jeffrey's addresses, one felt the grip of the message. It was God's word: it was manifestly in power and in demonstration of the Spirit, resulting in souls receiving Christ and being born again, and sick ones proving that touch of divine power that brought healing. And what could one say against such things? And then, my dear wife, after twenty years of continuous suffering, and having ten years ago undergone drastic operations for cancer, and several times since then having been given up as dying by specialists – but graciously preserved in answer to prayer, to their amazement – to be met in complete healing, delivered from all pain.

These are the facts, and the conclusion is this: the work is of God, and His is the honour and glory and praise. A deep joy has been revived in one's own heart and a deepened love to the Lord Jesus and to those around us who need him. And this seems to be the experience of the many one has mingled with. When Barnabas was sent to investigate the work in Antioch, we read:

*'When he came, and had seen the Grace of God, **he was glad**, and exhorted them all, that with purpose of heart they would cleave unto the Lord.'* (Acts 11:23)

I too am glad for all I have heard and seen of God's gracious work, and pray that the flood-tide of revival may increase, and prevail against all the barriers of unbelief and prejudice.

Some of the newspaper reports of the Brighton meetings are very illuminative and provide ample and authentic evidence of the greatness of the campaign. For instance, the *Sussex News* of 30 May, 1927, reports as follows:

REMARKABLE SCENES AT HOVE

Remarkably enthusiastic scenes have attended the Revival and Healing Campaign, conducted by Principal George Jeffreys at the Hove Town Hall during last week. Large crowds have flocked to both the afternoon and evening meetings, and evidence of the campaign's success is furnished by a number of written testimonies from people who claim that they have been cured by the Principal.

Among them are cases of complete deafness, lameness, stammering, and one remarkable testimony from a local minister's wife, who states she has been cured of cancer during the present campaign. Following several of the meetings, followers have congregated outside the Hove Town Hall, singing and cheering as the young Principal left.

Quite apart from his healings, Principal Jeffreys is an orator of powerful gifts. He has a vivid and striking personality, and his preaching captures the imagination. He is the Founder and Principal of the Elim Bible College, where young men are being taught for the ministry of healing and preaching, and for the past two years he has carried on his revival campaign without a single break.

REMARKABLE SCENES

Further remarkable scenes were witnessed at the Hove Town Hall yesterday, when Principal George Jeffreys began the last week of his 'Revival and Healing Campaign' there. Principal Jeffreys is the founder of the Elim Pentecostal Alliance, a movement which has attained thousands of adherents, and which held a great demonstration in the Albert hall at Easter. Yesterday afternoon's big audience joined in the popular hymns with great fervour, there was much waving of hymn-sheets, and George Jeffreys' magnetic influence gripped those who took part. When the time came for those who desired conversion, and through conversion cure, to declare themselves, hands were raised in all parts of the hall.

REASONS FOR BELIEF

Young and old, many obviously afflicted, later went up to the platform and knelt there while Principal Jeffreys anointed them. He came down to the body of the hall, where others were kneeling, and performed a similar ceremony there. Meanwhile the audience sang hymn after hymn. Principal Jeffreys, who had the assistance of several men and women in the service, gave several reasons and many scriptural quotations for his belief in faith healing. The Bible, he said, told him that Jesus Christ came into the world to destroy the works of the Devil, and sickness and disease he found came from the Devil. 'If I believe my Bible, I am bound to believe in Divine healing.' A second reason was that Divine healing was included in the Atonement. 'I believe He died for the healing of the body.' Again, Divine healing was included in the Apostolic commission – He commanded His disciples to preach and to heal. God declared Himself to be the healer of His people; healing was found among the nine miraculous gifts enumerated in the Epistle to the Corinthians and descriptions were given of how to act among the sick. Lastly, the risen Lord had promised to manifest His own Divine life in us, and there was no disease in Jesus Christ.

CURE CLAIMED

At Principal Jeffreys' request there went on to the platform a man and a woman. He said they had come from Southampton. Three weeks ago the woman was taken to one of the meetings in a bath-chair. She was unable to walk. Now she walked about the platform in a normal way. That, said Principal Jeffreys, was only one of many such cases. He has a long list of people in Brighton and Hove, and other parts of Sussex, who state they have been cured of complaints ranging from tumours to concussion of the brain.

During the earlier part of the revival the services had been held in the Royal Pavilion and the Town Hall, Hove, but these buildings became far too small for the numbers that thronged the doors for admission, and so force of circumstances demanded that some definite steps should be taken to provide for the great crowd of people who sought to hear the Principal. There was only one building in Brighton which was suitable, and that was the spacious and historic Dome, which in the past had been the scene of many memorable religious gatherings. Here day after day might be seen long queues of eager people, waiting at each of the three entrances. Tarrying until the hour should arrive which would enable them to pass into what had become a veritable Pool of Healing. What touching scenes those were! So many who for years had suffered unspeakable pain were now filled with the hope of deliverance. A preacher was in their midst who preached the same message as the Master so many centuries ago, one who was proclaiming that the Name of Jesus was as mighty in the twentieth century as in days of old, that 'this same Jesus' – the Christ of Galilee and Nazareth – was equal to every need from which humanity suffered.

The results of some of these meetings were just glorious, as many as seventy souls seeking Christ in a single service. Many remarkable cases of healing also took place from time to time during the campaign, whilst others received wonderful fulfilments of Acts 10:44–46, being baptised in the Holy Spirit in similar manner as in this instance in the house of Cornelius, whilst the Word was being preached.

We cannot close this chapter without giving in full an excellent press report from the *Sussex News* dated 6 June, 1927, which was headed 'The Age of Miracles':

THE AGE OF MIRACLES

REMARKABLE TESTIMONIES AT HOVE
REVIVAL AND HEALING CAMPAIGN

Principal George Jeffreys, whose revival and healing campaign has been drawing large gatherings in Brighton and Hove, had another large congregation at the Hove Town Hall yesterday evening, when he entered upon the final week of the campaign. The floor and balconies were crowded, every available seat being occupied, while many people had to be turned away. The sacred community singing, which is a feature of these gatherings, was taken up with much fervour, and a wonderful effect was produced by the waving of hymn sheets of various hues. When the Pastor invited those who had been healed to come upon the platform, a large proportion of the audience immediately came forward.

THE TESTIMONIES

They were further invited to give their testimonies, and one lady told how, after suffering from terrible injuries owing to an accident, she had now been able to give up her bath-chair; another had been cured of heart trouble; one of curvature of the spine; while a girl who had been blind in one eye from birth, could now see clearly with both. Others had been healed of sciatica and rheumatism; a woman who had been deaf for years was able to hear distinctly; a girl who had a lump on her side confessed that it had disappeared; the instantaneous healing of a woman who for eleven years had had to lie on her back was recorded; a poisoned finger was healed instantly by prayer; a man of 73 had lost his gout and rheumatism; while a girl who had curvature of the spine had been cured and her mother had been healed of varicose veins. One woman who had been prayed for, said Pastor Jeffreys, had been completely delivered from cancer, and another who had been unable to stand for 14 or 15 years and was wheeled to one of the meetings in a bath-chair, was able to stroll smartly across the platform.

Another interesting report appeared in the *Brighton and Hove Herald* of 18 June, 1927:

REMARKABLE ENTHUSIASM LAST NIGHT

For Principal Jeffreys' meeting in the Dome last night a queue of people waited in the Pavilion Grounds the whole afternoon and evening. In fact, the first person in the queue, a lady, arrived at 12.30, and sat patiently upon a small stool for nearly seven hours before the meeting began.

During the afternoon the queue gradually increased in number, and by tea-time there were as many as two hundred people waiting. At 7.30 when the meeting commenced, the Dome was crowded. There were remarkable scenes of enthusiasm, and at the end of the meeting the great throng of people seemed reluctant to leave. For some time they sang hymns, led by a choir on the raised platform.

What proved to be a great surprise and a splendid finish up to this truly remarkable campaign, was the acquisition of one of the oldest Nonconformist places of worship in Brighton, the Glyn Vivian Hall, situated in the heart of the town only a few minutes from the Dome – a building in which many notable preachers have ministered in former days.

This building bears the reputation of being the oldest Nonconformist place of worship in Brighton, having been erected during the reign of William the Third, in 1688. The building itself is most imposing, both from within and without. The interior arrangement is somewhat in the shape of an amphitheatre. It possesses a gallery which is supported by eight handsome circular columns. These in turn support eight Corinthian columns which carry the roof and the dome.

Amongst those preachers of eminence who have ministered within its walls are found such names as John Newton, Vaughan Price, Wade Robinson – author of the hymn, 'Loved with everlasting love' – R.J. Campbell, and J.B. Figgis. Henry Varley, the famous evangelist, preached his last sermon here, as is recorded by a marble tablet on the front of the building.

The purchase of the hall for the proclamation of the Foursquare Gospel was a venture of faith in God, and much prayer was offered that He would set His seal upon the action by giving tokens of His approval at the opening meeting. He graciously granted the request of His people, for twenty souls yielded to Christ, and two hundred and ten people – one a man over 70 years of age – rose from their seats, as an expression of their desire for baptism in the pool which is immediately in front of the rostrum.

Thus closed this remarkable campaign, a campaign so rich in fulfilment of promise, and so full of heavenly power.

Chapter 18

Three Thrilling Triumphs

With the close of the Portsmouth campaign, George Jeffreys for a season withdrew from the provinces, turning his attention to London once more. And so towards the close of 1927 we find him in the south-west of the Metropolis, Wimbledon being selected for the new campaign.

A very sympathetic nucleus of Christian people gladly welcomed the Revivalist to their midst. Soon strangers became aware of the presence of remarkable happenings at their very doors, which created the necessary incentive to attend the meetings. And so they came, curious to a degree to see this strange preacher, whose message and methods were causing such a sensation in so many places. As one writer beautifully puts it:

> Thank God they got in touch, not so much with the mission and the messenger, but with the Christ of the message.

During the first twelve days over 200 decided for Christ.

One who had been an atheist for 26 years was both healed and saved. In his case, healing came first. This is not the usual order, and not the order that George Jeffreys preaches, but God's ways are not always our ways, and God's thoughts are not always our thoughts.

But the big step forward came at the end of the second week of the campaign. Suddenly in the midst of the previous week, it was announced that the large Wimbledon Theatre had been taken for the Sunday evening services.

Blessing has attended every meeting, but the third Wednesday afternoon healing meeting was an exceptional one. I feel inclined to call it **The Bath-Chair Meeting** – yet the bath-chairs were absent! Why? Because they were no longer needed. During the testimony period, five sisters who had been brought to Principal Jeffreys' meetings in bath-chairs marched before us to the rhythm of a hymn, without the slightest sign of their past invalid condition. One was from Bournemouth, another from Southampton, and others from elsewhere, but they were all in the meeting without pre-arrangement, and it was quite spontaneously that they were asked to come to the front and witness to their healing.

One had been wheeled about for 15 years, another for five years, and the others for four years, three years, and six months, respectively. They were not ashamed to own their Lord, and their faces beamed, as with rejuvenated step they walked up and down before a wondering and worshipping people. Here is a brief summary of those who had been healed in the Wimbledon campaign:

(1) Sight restored to blind eye. First text that the new-sighted eye read, from a distance of 10 yards, was 'If thou wouldest believe, thou shouldest see the glory of God.' (2) Rheumatism over 20 years – limbs stiff and locked. Instantaneously healed. (3) Not able to kneel for six months. Knelt down in the presence of us all. (4) Eyes crossed – glasses worn for 34 years. The cross and glasses both gone. (5) Young man a week ago, unable to breathe through one nostril. Now breathing quite normally. (6) A lady over 70 years of age healed of rheumatism. (7) Asthma healed. (8) Youth healed of deafness. Time forbids the telling of all – in fact, all cannot be told, for frequently wonderful cases of healing only come to light after months of silence. Many sought healing at the close of these memorable services, but, best of all, souls professed to accept the Lord Jesus Christ.

The closing service was again held in the Wimbledon Theatre. There were about 2,600 people present, George Jeffreys spoke on the Coming of the Lord in a very clear manner. 'Are you ready for His coming? If not, get ready', was the closing appeal, and over 50 professed to get ready by yielding their lives to the Saviour. Altogether in the campaign about 500 have declared that they have accepted Christ as their own personal Saviour. When the closing benediction was pronounced, we felt inexpressibly glad and grateful for such a campaign, with such acts of the risen Lord, and such acts of the descended Spirit.

All the local newspapers reported the revival meetings. Sometimes whole columns were given to the campaign.

One of these reports is here given:

Considerable success has attended the three weeks' revival and healing campaign conducted by George Jeffreys of the Elim Four-square Gospel Movement, which he brought to a close with a meeting held in Wimbledon Theatre on Sunday night. So satisfied is he with the result of the campaign that it has been decided to start a church for Wimbledon and district in the near future. The theatre was crowded in every part, and scenes of quiet enthusiasm were witnessed until near the finish, when the great audience gave free scope to their pent-up feeling. The congregation included a number of north Wimbledon residents and titled people. The first part of the service was devoted to community hymn singing, and this was entered into with spirit by the audience. Subsequently Principal Jeffreys, who is a believer in miracles, preached on the second advent of Christ. The Bible, he said, told them the signs of the Lord's return and among these were the lust for wealth, which was to be seen on every hand; unrest in the industrial world, which was found everywhere; pleasure-seeking and wanton living, which were encountered on all hands.

When Jeffreys asked all to signify who had by faith been cured of illnesses since the campaign, at least 150 persons crowded onto the stage. Many others stood at the sides of the stalls and several scores in different parts of the building held up their hands. Then followed personal testimonies from a number who had been healed. These included five bath-chair cases, one of whom, a comparatively young woman, had not been able to walk for over fourteen years, but now walked across the stage freely. Another was a middle-aged woman who had been an invalid for twenty years, suffered from sleepy sickness three years ago, and was blind in one eye. A third was given up by the doctors; the fourth, the wife of a leading physician, and the fifth a man who suffered from a dilated stomach. Eight claimed to have been completed cured of cancers and tumours, about a score of paralysis, four of deafness, three of blindness, one of whom was a woman eighty years of age; and others claimed to have been cured of goitre, rheumatism of the spine, ulcers, consumption, meningitis, sciatica, lumbago, internal complaints and growths. Between 500 and 600 stood up in evidence of having been converted during the campaign.

(Surrey Comet, 19 November, 1927)

Leaving Wimbledon in the throes of a gracious awakening, George Jeffreys proceeded to Hammersmith, where another wonderful work for God was soon in full swing. One lady who had been mightily blessed during these campaigns, says:

Our hearts are overflowing with praise and thankfulness to our God for the wonderful things which He has done among us during the Campaign at Hammersmith.

In these western districts of London religion is not at all fashionable, but it is very respectable and **very** frigid; and many of us, struggling along in feeble isolation against its petrifying influences, have yearned and prayed for years, for a revival that would melt the icy walls of formalism and conventionalism, and kindle a fire among us which would set us aflame with ardent love to our Lord and a burning zeal for His work. And surely these revival meetings were sent to us in answer to our prayers. They have been a revelation to many of us Christians. They have taught us how to sing 'praises with gladness' – how to 'rejoice in the Lord with joy unspeakable and full of glory'. Many of us were so accustomed to lifeless ceremony that we knew nothing about the 'sacrifices of joy', and we were so swathed and bound by the etiquette of conventionalism that we had never experienced the happiness of that fellowship of believers in the Lord of which every child of Christ ought to be made a partaker. And those meetings simply swept us off our feet.

It is impossible to describe those moments when 'through the veil of the flesh' of our Great High Priest – our risen Lord – we entered into the holiest and the shekinah was manifested to us. We no longer marvelled at the miracles of healing that were taking place around us, we rather marvelled at the unbelief of a Christ-rejecting world – at the stubbornness of will and blindness of heart that could refuse the evidence of His mighty works. But the power of the Lord was mightily present in our midst to break down that unbelief and lead sinners to the Cross; and, as the numbers of souls turned to their Saviour during every meeting there, the angels must have made the courts of Heaven resound with glorious songs of rejoicing, even as we joined our Hallelujahs to theirs.

Hundreds of miraculous cures – the lame and paralysed walking – the blind seeing – the deaf hearing – deadly and torturing diseases vanishing. The following are examples:

A growth at the back of a woman's neck which prevented her moving her head, suddenly disappeared when prayed for, and she was healed.

A sister who was paralysed one side, whose brain sometimes would not function, and who suffered from loss of memory, was completely restored.

A man suffering as a result of a nervous breakdown over twenty years ago, whose limbs had been shaking ever since, came under the power of God in one meeting, was healed and became quite normal and steady.

A sister suffering from a chronic skin disease which resulted from blood poisoning eighteen months ago, was converted and miraculously healed of her trouble, no trace being left of the skin disease. Her husband was also converted as a result of this miracle.

A young man who suffered from defective eye-sight from birth owing to cataracts on both eyes, was miraculously healed and can now see quite clearly.

Another young man, quite deaf and suffering from rupture, was converted and healed in the same meeting. After giving his heart to the Lord, he was overpowered by the Spirit. While under the power he was healed of rupture and his hearing became quite normal.

Over 500 converts – not a meeting without precious souls being won for Christ and accepting Him as their Saviour. The Lord's children given a new vision, a new strength, a new love. What a proof of the 'wonder-working power of the blood of the Lamb!' What a record for four short weeks' work in a neighbourhood for the most part given over to godlessness, pleasure or ritualism!

From reports published in the *West London Observer* we cull the following:

FAITH HEALING CAMPAIGN

LARGE NUMBER OF CURES REPORTED

The phenomenal success which characterised the opening of George Jeffreys' Revival and Faith Healing Campaign at Lime Grove Baths last Sunday week has been materially substantiated by reports at the subsequent meetings, and with the conclusion of the second week of the campaign the number of conversions and cases of faith healing demonstrate that the remarkable results achieved by Principal Jeffreys in his campaigns throughout the country are being repeated in Shepherd's Bush.

A considerable time is devoted at each meeting to community singing, of which by reason of his magnetic personality, Jeffreys is a virile conductor. During the singing, numbers of men and women come forward to the edge of the platform, to signify their complete conversion. They kneel in silent prayer; the singing dies down to a whisper, and Principal Jeffreys descends from the platform, and whispers a message of spiritual comfort to each person, moving among the penitent converts with noiseless tread. These scenes are most impressive. Then the singing breaks out again with a rhythm that is seldom heard in many places of worship – although it is only led by a soloist and piano, with occasional violin obligato. Upon entering the hall while a service is in progress, one is conscious of a tense atmosphere and religious fervour – like the sanctity of a cathedral, yet more profound. Principal Jeffreys is praying. His passionate pleadings and exhortations fill the hall with a torrent of inspired eloquence, to be echoed by the audience with heartfelt 'Amens'.

Principal Jeffreys, who believes in miracles, bases his teachings upon Christ's instructions to His disciples: 'Go ye into all the world and preach the Gospel and heal the sick.' He makes no claim to supernatural gifts, but believes that the sick are healed by their own faith in answer to prayer. One healing, he declares, is worth more than a thousand sermons. He strongly repudiates all charges of insincerity, and gives a striking proof of the permanent cures effected during his campaigns.

PRINCIPAL JEFFREYS' CAMPAIGN

Principal George Jeffreys, the famous evangelist and founder of the Elim Foursquare Gospel Movement, continues to attract large audiences at Lime Grove Baths, Shepherd's Bush, where his extended revival and faith healing campaign is being conducted until next Sunday.

Following the announcement of the extension of the campaign for a further week, a huge audience of over a thousand people attended the evening meeting on Friday last. Thirteen voluntary conversions were made, following a powerful address in which Principal Jeffreys prophesied the early return of Christ in bodily form. Whatever the size of his audience, he possesses the unusual gift of being able to establish personal contact with every individual listener. By sheer personality he holds his audiences in breathless rapture as he expounds the Gospels of the New Testament, investing the old and familiar quotations with a new message of practical utility and proving that Christ is the same today as He was nearly two thousand years ago.

Scenes of great enthusiasm were witnessed at the meetings on Sunday last, and over 1,500 people were present in the evening. Forty-six conversions were reported, of which thirty were made at the evening meeting.

In spite of all the remarkable campaigns already described in these chapters, the one of which we are about to write eclipses them all by reason of its magnitude. Whilst in progress it was referred to as the 'greatest revival witnessed in the London district.' The crowds were so large and so many were turned away from the meetings, that the Headquarters of the Elim Alliance were obliged to request the members of our London Churches to refrain from attending the services. And yet the spacious North End Hall was packed, and the doors were closed long before the time for the meetings to commence. The people of all denominations in Croydon said that they had never witnessed such a movement of the Spirit of God.

For a graphic narration of the actual revival itself we cannot do better than appeal to the pen of a writer whose brilliance as a penman is well established. Let Rev. C.H. Coates tell, in his own inimitable style, the story of that glorious campaign:

We are nearing the end of the fourth week of Principal George Jeffreys' great Croydon campaign as this is being written, and still the tide of power and blessing is rising and extending, and the living waters of the old-new Gospel are feeding and healing an increasing multitude. How shall we describe the scenes?

The present writer was privileged to be present by what he cannot but regard as a remarkable providence, being a stranger both to Croydon and to the Foursquare Gospel work; and also a little prejudiced in mind, because of an adverse report, previously heard at a distance, from a too wise friend, to the effect that the result of the Revivalist's work everywhere was to crush existing churches and divide peaceful congregations to no ultimate purpose, with converts subsequently left spiritually stranded and derelict!

But after sitting through one meeting in the first week of the series, with the experience of many campaigns in memory, the conviction came home: – This is that which was spoken of by the prophets – the outpouring of the Spirit in the last days –

the ancient Gospel of the Apostles clothed still with the attesting gifts and powers of its immortal youth – armed not only with sign and gift, but with heaven-directed wisdom and discretion!

And one learned afresh that no true work of God can go uncrucified by pious slander, even in the very house and conversation of His friends!

The Holy Spirit's signs came to Croydon, a typical London business town. They are still coming as we write, for the tide of power increases. They are coming, not in ones, twos or threes, but in hundreds. Firstly, the personal individual new births in Christ Jesus, that miraculous change in the man which challenges attention and scrutiny as pointedly as ever. Secondly, the wondrous healings in all the multifarious ways by which the Holy Spirit displays His work – with some the trances induced by His power at the laying on of hands; with others nothing more than the quiet prayer of supplication and look of faith to the crucified and risen One; some healed gradually during a succession of importunate presentations before the throne, under the Pastor's hands; and yet others healed without having left their seats in the great auditorium.

These two, the spiritual conversions and the physical healings, each attest the other's origin. A typical letter of thanks from a man converted, with his family, during the present campaign ran thus: 'For ten years my home has been a hell on earth – now it is heaven.' The only possible source of this sort of heaven must needs be by **Heaven** – how then can the healings which go with it emanate from either earth or hell? And how can the doctrine taught be other than divine when beneficent physical wonders far beyond man's utmost power to perform are present to attest it? 'He hath shed forth this which ye now **see** (the healings) and **hear** (the truth)!

Are Croydon folk unusually credulous? Old inhabitants say not. They do not even seem to respond readily to that most potent of modern meseric influences – the critical agnosticism of a clever journalist, armed with a linotype powerplant. When he had done all his passes, they still poured in to the meetings, in even greater numbers. And if they are hard-headed business folk, with whom you can put nothing over which is not fact, what is the particular ingredient in the moral evidence presented by these meetings which grips them with such undeniable certitude? For the Revivalist does not work toward any mere effect – does not even trouble to ask the kneeling sufferers to say at the same meeting if they have been healed, even after trances have been experienced. He lets testimony develop spontaneously. What then can the public oral testimonies to healing mean? Is it possible to believe that these sane-looking and evidently normal people have succeeded in deceiving themselves and the vast audience into believing that they can really walk, though in fact they be still lame; to that they can read a book or recognise their friends, though still blind; or that, although they can answer questions put in a conversational tone at four yard's range, they may even yet be deaf? Or was that dear friend possibly mistaken who wept tears of joy after complete deliverance from a cancer in respect of which his physician had given him but a fortnight to live – healed during this campaign? Or was the Croydon doctor mistaken who said of another case of which he had given up hope; 'Well, I am witness to this one – the cure is perfect, I'll stand by it – it's wonderful!'?

But these masses of humanity which packed the Croydon Grand Theatre, the North End Hall, and now the still larger Baths Hall, night after night an on appointed afternoons with hundreds and sometimes thousands turned away – what is the main impression gathered from the sea of happy faces, with its foam of waving hymn-sheets, its storm of hallelujahs and its deep calm of eager waiting upon the engrafted Word? The fervent conviction, the sanity, sincerity, and happiness written everywhere on these faces are eloquent of **a delivered people**. They have no delusions, either for this life or the next. They know what they believe, and why they believe it! No one, from a higher critic in cloth and collar, to a sapient journalist, or an evil spirit, can teach them otherwise. By faith in the blood and risen life of the Son of God, they know they are delivered from the past as to sin; delivered from the power of Satan and from themselves, by the garrisoning power of Christ's indwelling Spirit; delivered from wrong knowledge and wrong courses by a cover-to-cover faith in their Bibles. Here in this rising crescendo of old-new revival power, certitude can be found, if nowhere else on the planet – for this certitude rests upon the ultimate throne of God and His revealed truth, and on the fact of His proved mercy to sinning and suffering men and women.

This closes a chapter of Elim history containing a succession of successful campaigns, the result of which, in the aggregate are simply amazing, and reveal a wealth of revival exploits scarcely excelled or exceeded at any other period in the life of the Church of God.

Chapter 19

Revival Enthusiasm
in the Alexandra Palace

The year 1928 opened auspiciously with a campaign in the North of London, in a neighbourhood, though exceedingly needy from the point of view of revival, yet one that was admittedly a hard field in which to attempt anything of this nature. A district where the Enemy was deeply entrenched and from which it would be difficult to dislodge him.

The Caledonian Road Baths Hall was engaged for the opening services of this campaign, and speedily became the rallying place of big crowds of those who had been mightily blessed through the medium of a ministry so extraordinarily owned of God. Under the transforming truths which were being given by George Jeffreys the valley of dry bones quickly became the scene of throbbing revival. The presence of a preacher whose lips are touched with living fire will soon arrest the godless and awaken concern in the hearts of those who for years have no darkened the doors of church or chapel. Let it be noised abroad that the heavens are actually being opened, and the miraculous energy of God is in evidence, and the crowd will come – first to see, and then to seek, curiosity being changed to conviction.

Within the first few weeks upwards of 400 souls surrendered to the Lord, and many wonderful cases of healing had taken place. The Baths Hall by this time had acquired a new prominence. A report of some of the earliest of these meetings appeared in the *Islington Press*.

Remarkable scenes are being witnessed at the Caledonian Road Baths each evening at the meetings of the Elim Foursquare Gospel Campaign, conducted by Principal George Jeffreys.

Thousands come to listen spellbound to the masterly oratory of this young and forceful pastor. Immaculately dressed he has an imposing appearance, and audiences are gripped with his very simplicity when delivering his addresses.

It was a wonderful calling, the calling of a Christian, he said in one address, and they were not intended to be sons only, but saints. It was a well-known fact that when a man was born anew he had a new name, and had the title of saint.

Continuing, he declared there were three great blessings in one – justification by faith, sanctification by faith, and divine healing. There was a vast difference between faith healing and divine healing. They did not believe in faith healing, but divine healing was the miraculous work of God, and they took Him at His word.

Then suddenly, he lifted the Bible above his head and cried, 'Do you believe in the Bible?' The whole congregation shouted back, 'Yes,' and there were murmured prayers by people who had come from all over London.

Then came the personal testimonies from people who had been cured of illness by the wonderful power and faith, and one nurse who had suffered terrible agony from a broken breast-bone said she had received every medical attention in vain. It was only the power of faith, she added emphatically, that had saved her.

Another woman, the wife of a well-known physician, was brought in a bath-chair at a recent campaign, but she walked joyfully up and down the hall on Tuesday.

Yet another woman, with tears in her eyes, testified to the fact that, after having had six operations for a malignant growth, she was completely cured.

There were hundreds of others – old men and women, young boys and girls, who could declare that they had been cured in the same way.

'Let those who want to be saved in both soul and body come forward,' Principal Jeffreys cried, and many ran to kneel at the front benches.

There was an expectant hush as the Principal, followed by his helpers, went to each one anointing them with oil and giving them the divine blessing. Many were so overcome that they collapsed.

The large audience filed out singing, 'I love Him better every day.'

So great had become the demand for the extension of the campaign by this time that it was decided that the meetings should be continued some time longer than originally planned. Meetings of such magnitude could have no more fitting climax and consummation than that which took place during the final three days in the Alexandra Palace. It was as though the small stream of a few weeks previous had now swollen into a mighty torrential river which threatened to burst its banks and flood the whole of the surrounding districts.

A Baptist minister, writing his impressions of the North London meetings, says:

Wake – Watch – Work

The professing Christian Church of our day and generation has been so used to a non-miraculous state that she is not only apt to overlook the fact that she started her New Testament course miraculously, and that miraculous life is the very nature of her spiritual experience, but to be so strongly prejudiced against the miraculous that miracles become ruled out as impossibilities nowadays. This great contrast between her condition now and when she started her course might well lead her to question is she is not God-forsaken. But whether that it so or not she certainly is by the vast perishing world forsaken because of her deadness and lack of spiritual power – being nigh unto trodden under-foot of men as salt having lost its savour. Nevertheless the Cross it holdeth fast – grace must triumph and God will work.

For the past three weeks and longer in North London at the Islington Public Baths and the Finsbury Park Rink Cinema and at the Alexandra Palace, Muswell Hill, God has shown that He is no respecter of places nor of times, and that all He wants in order to work is freedom, loyalty, holy lives, consecration and boldness of faith in His revealed Word and living presence and mighty spiritual energy. I write as a free, independent witness, and place on record my impression of George Jeffreys' great campaign. What we have heard with our ears, what we have seen with our eyes, what we have looked upon – that declare we. What other name but 'miracle' can describe the immediate cures of ulcers, goitres, fractures of bones, sprains, cataract and blindness, deaf- ness, paralysis etc., all of which occurred in these weeks and were publicly witnessed to by those healed? All are not cured upon whom hands are placed. That all will be cured is not claimed, but that the power of God shall be manifested to cure is expected – prayed for and justified by results – and is cause for praise and not for suspicion. That they do take place cannot be disputed, and that they are also wrought solely in the name of the Lord Jesus cannot be disputed, and by the hands of a man confessedly conscious of his own utter weakness in himself and that the channel is nothing, but that the Lord Jesus Christ Himself is everything – to whom is ascribed all the glory.

Now although marvels and wonders have been done in these meetings in the name of the Lord Jesus, the man who is used as the direct channel to convey physical blessing to many is not out for healing as such. In his own words, 'I would rather have one soul saved than 10,000 people healed.' He is first and foremost a burning evangelist of the old-fashioned Gospel of Grace and salvation by faith in the blood of Christ – the preaching of which becomes effective in the bringing to immediate decision of hundreds of souls – a special enduement of power by the Holy Spirit clothing both him and the message. In this Gospel warfare the banner which is held aloft has emblazoned on it the four-fold declaration that Christ Jesus is Saviour, Healer, Baptiser in the Holy Spirit and Coming King. Extreme utterances are avoided. Moderation and strength mark the presentation of these soul-striking truths. The Bible is believed in from cover to cover as the inspired Word of God.

The meetings have been wonderful and interest in them has rapidly spread far and wide. Increasing multitudes have gathered daily to hear the Word preached and to witness God's wonders in saving souls and healing bodies. It was computed that from four to five thousand people gathered in the Alexandra Palace to the final rally there. On the third Sunday at the Rink Cinema 220 hands were raised in acknowledgement of Christ as Saviour. And what Hallelujahs! what praises! burst forth for these fresh trophies of grace. Night by night it was just the same. Literally scores and hundreds have come out for Christ whilst the feeble embers of units have caught fire to white heat by coming together. The Lord of the harvest has answered prayer for another ingathering of souls.

Chapter 20

Notable Healing Miracles

Amongst the many remarkable cases of healing which have taken place in Principal George Jeffreys' Campaigns throughout the country can be found those of almost every class of society. Both rich and poor, the high and the humble, have been blessed through the ministry of this honoured servant of the Lord. The gospel of Divine healing has penetrated the most inaccessible circles and claimed its triumphs from the ranks of the most unlikely.

To compile a book of the testimonial of those thus healed would in itself make a most fascinating volume. But as we are only able to devote a single chapter of this work to the consideration of individual instances of healing, it becomes necessary only to make reference to few of the more outstanding cases, and that only in brief.

For twenty years Miss C. Jardine, of Southsea, suffered from shock to the whole system as a result of fright. She had undergone three serious operations, and the medical verdict was that work henceforth would be absolutely impossible. In addition to this she had contracted sleeping sickness, which rendered her unconscious for three weeks. Blind in one eye, she suddenly became the subject of a seizure which completely twisted her whole body, and left her an utter physical wreck. Whilst in this condition she was wheeled in a bath-chair into one of Principal Jeffreys' meetings, who prayed for her deliverance. We are happy to say that immediately she was dealt with her poor, pain-wracked body was freed. And as she says, 'I now go to bed to sleep, and not to lie in pain all night'. Today Miss Jardine's spine is quite straight, her sight is restored, and she is able to enjoy her food, and life is just a new glad experience to her.

During that wonderful campaign at Brighton in 1927 God, though the ministry of George Jeffreys, wrought a glorious victory in the body of the wife of one of the local Baptist ministers. Mrs Coffin had for 20 years been a great sufferer, and in 1927 it was discovered that she had been attacked by that deadly disease, cancer. At once an operation of a drastic nature was advised, and as a result her breast was removed. From the time of the operation until the time of her healing Mrs Coffin never knew a day of freedom from pain, which at times was so terrible as to indicate the end of life. Some twelve months after the operation referred to above, a specialist traced a recurrence of the trouble, and said that life could not possibly be prolonged for any length of time. In this hopeless and helpless state she attended Jeffreys' campaign in the Dome, Brighton, when she was anointed and completely healed of a threefold malady, having suffered from cancer, dropsy and heart disease.

Another remarkable instance of deliverance from a cancerous growth is that of Mrs Paul, of Croydon, who for fourteen years had been the victim of chronic indigestion and gastric ulcers, which eventually terminated in cancer. Night and day was spent in intense pain. So severe was the torture of body that often Mrs Paul was tempted to take her life. Relief was sought in drugs, and pounds were spent in this effort to drown the pain, but all attempts failed and left her a hopeless case. Hearing of Jeffreys' Revival and Healing Campaign in the North End Hall, Croydon, this poor distraught soul went and was prayed for by the Revivalist. And, to use her own words, which are most expressive, she says, 'I immediately felt the healing touch, the power of God came upon me, and I felt the cords of the cancer being dragged from me and the large lump that I had completely disappeared – not a trace remained!'

During the Bournemouth campaign in 1926 many remarkable cases of Divine healing are recorded, one of which we now give. It is that of a Hampshire Baptist minister's wife who for thirteen years had suffered from very bad eyesight. She was told by a Southampton eye specialist that from birth both her eyes were affected by cataract. In 1924 the doctor informed Mrs Dimmick that the cataracts were developing to such an extent that in two years' time she would be blind. An operation was advised, but, being anxious to prove God's healing power, she attended the campaign held at Bournemouth. So bad was the sight at this time that it was impossible to distinguish people's features. After being anointed by Principal Jeffreys three times, on the last occasion the Lord unsealed her eyes, and she 'arose a new woman'. Today the vision of this dear sister is perfectly clear – all traces of the cataracts have completely disappeared.

Perhaps one of the most wonderful cases of healing is that of Mr James Gregson of Leeds. To listen to his story is like the account which we find in Acts 3. To see this man when first of all he was brought to the revival meetings at Leeds would move the hardest heart to compassion. His pitiable physical condition was the result of an accident, which had moved every bone out of its place. An absolute cripple, whose only method of locomotion was painfully to propel himself along the ground, dragging his poor twisted legs behind him. So crippled was he that it was impossible to sit up; he could only lie in his hopeless misery.

Whilst in this condition, he read a newspaper account of a woman being healed of blindness at George Jeffreys' campaign. Hope entered his heart, and he became possessed with the conviction that if only he could get to the services he would be healed. One Saturday evening he dragged his poor, broken body to the Leeds Coliseum. That night he was gloriously saved. He says, 'God alone knows how I got there, and when I got there it was a great struggle to get in, but some people took pity on me, and then the attendants carried me in and laid me in front of the platform'. Upon being prayed for by the evangelist, he adds, 'when he laid his hands upon me I felt as if a dozen hands were placed all over by body, and I felt every bone going back into its place. I was instantly released and completely healed'. What a wonderful work of Divine power! This poor, unsightly piece of physical wreckage, all disfigured and emaciated, was able to return to his employment all sound and strong. Would that such a living demonstration of Divine and miraculous power could be dropped like a bombshell into the midst of a company of these modern mutilators of Gods' Word, who scorn the miraculous power of the Gospel.

A young lad, named Albert Peake, who for years had been deaf, came to the Hammersmith Campaign, and whilst being prayed for his ears were at once opened. In addition to the restoration of his hearing, this lad was also delivered from rupture, and at the same time gloriously saved. He also tells of the deliverance of his mother from a long-standing growth. The family numbered five – four of the family are now on the Lord's side.

A further testimony of the healing virtue of the Cross is that of a dear school teacher who was wonderfully healed whilst George Jeffreys was preaching. This took place in Hull as far back as 1922. Some years previously this sister had met with a very serious accident, in which the base of the skull was fractured and concussion of the brain resulted. A small bone was broken in the head which had punctured the drum of the left ear, rendering her stone deaf. One doctor stated that nothing less than a miracle could possibly restore the hearing. As a consequence this sister experienced severe pains in the head. It was during one of the special meetings held in Hull in 1922 that God wrought this marvellous deliverance. Without a single hand being laid upon her she was instantaneously and completely healed. She adds, 'The Lord gave me a new ear'. The Divine Life filled her whole being with an unutterable glory.

All over the country the number of these miraculous memorials to the power of God is being swollen – day by day the company increases, and new trophies of the Gospel's triumph over sickness are being witnessed. All denominations have felt the benefit of these blessed campaigns, which have yielded such splendid results: Baptists and Brethren, Congregationalist and Catholics are all represented amongst those cases of healing.

Whilst the Hastings campaign was in progress, a man – a Salvation Army bandsman – who for twelve long years had suffered intense agony both night and day, from a most malicious skin disease, and who could obtain no relief whatever from medical advice, came into one of the healing services. He asked for prayer, and immediately Principal Jeffreys anointed him whereupon the man was completely cured. Since that time he has not had a trace of the disease upon his body.

Another woman, during the Leeds campaign, was the subject of a glorious healing. For over thirty years she had been the victim of epileptic fits and kidney trouble. For many years she had undergone various forms of treatment, but all to no purpose. A visit to one of the healing meetings brought immediate, perfect and permanent healing.

Amongst the many healings which were registered in the North London Campaign was that of a man who for twelve years had suffered from rupture. This poor fellow wore a truss without which he could neither walk nor work. He came to the Alexandra Palace meetings and was completely healed. He immediately removed the truss, and after the evening meeting ran nearly the whole way home, which was some considerable distance, jubilant at the work which has been so miraculously wrought in his body.

Mrs Stephens, of Portslade, is another remarkable case. She was healed in the Dome, Brighton, during the revival services held there in 1927. For 37 years this dear woman had suffered with epileptic fits; she was also troubled with fibrous tumours. She had been in three hospitals and undergone three operations. On the last occasion she was discharged from the hospital as utterly incurable. There in the Dome Divine power was demonstrated, and in her body the Lord had revealed Himself. So much so that Mrs Stephens became a living puzzle to all who knew her. So well was her condition known to her friends that to them it came as a staggering surprise. Beyond a shadow of doubt the Supreme Power had loosed this woman from her infirmity, and she was now able to do her daily duties with ease.

Another very sad case was that of Mrs Fry, of Leeds. For years she had experienced incessant pain. For some considerable time her helplessness demanded that she should be wheeled about in a bath-chair and it was in this state that she was taken to Principal Jeffreys' meetings. She tells of that wonderful moment when healed, how her body was charged as with electricity, which brought life to her dead nerves.

And today housework, which in those old days was impossible, is a pleasure.

Mr Albert H. Stedman, of Hove, Sussex, for seven years was
a martyr to chronic sciatica and rheumatism – this rendered
it impossible for him to stoop without pain, and left him
limping along with a stick. He spent hundreds of dollars in
Canada and England seeking a cure, and found none. He
took a course of electrical treatment covering a period of 20
months, but could not get rid of his trouble. Attending
Principal Jeffreys' meetings, he was, when anointed, healed
at once, and can now walk without a stick and stoop without
pain, even touching his toes with his hands.

A case of cancer which proves so gloriously the power of
God to heal, is that of Mrs Bishop of Hastings, who at the
time of which we write was unable to raise her right arm.
Doctors diagnosed her case and stated that it was impossible
for her to live without an operation. She refused to submit
her body to the surgeon's knife, instead of which she went to
Principal George Jeffreys' Divine Healing meetings and was
completely delivered. Drugs were immediately discarded,
and sleep was secured without their aid for the first time for
four years. The pain departed and no more fainting attacks
were experienced. She can now use both her arms quite
freely.

Suffering for 30 years with a dilated stomach, during 15
years of which it was necessary to employ the use of a
stomach pump, and having been an inmate of both Brighton
and Worthing Hospitals in one of which a most serious
operation was performed, Mr G. Lelliott of Worthing, found
his way into the Dome, Brighton, whilst Principal George
Jeffreys was holding his campaign in that town. Complete
healing took place, and the old complaint from which he
had suffered so much was now a thing of the past. Well
might our brother add, 'Glory to God!'

One dear little lad of very tender years, was brought by his
mother to one of Principal Jeffreys' meetings at Forest Hill.
For nearly three years he had suffered from epileptic fits. He
had been taken to several doctors, but was pronounced
incurable, as the trouble, it was stated, was of a hereditary
nature. This dear child would have as many as four fits per

day, and the medical verdict was that as he grew older the fits would become worse, and that he might pass away in one of them. His mother, hearing of the wonders God was doing in the district, resolved to take her boy to be prayed for. He was instantaneously healed. Mrs Knowles adds: 'You ask me, "Is the day of miracles past?" My answer is, "Hallelujah! No! For my little boy is a miracle." ' For two-and-a-half years after his healing the boy had no sign of a fit. His mother describes him as 'a sturdy little boy, the picture of health'.

Miss Daisy Noakes, of Ilford, is another case of many who have been wonderfully delivered from disease. Such a confirmed cripple was this sister, that not only was she wheeled from place to place by means of a bath-chair, but in addition to this she was obliged to wear a steel jacket, also a head and chin rest were a necessary part of this poor cripple's equipment. Thus she was brought to one of Principal George Jeffreys' meetings. Humanly speaking – what hope of cure could be entertained? To expect that stricken and afflicted body to regain its freedom was out of the question. And yet she came – came believing, not in the Revivalist's power, but in the power of the Risen Lord, whose touch was able to deliver the diseased and the distressed. And faith was magnificently rewarded – the bath-chair was no longer necessary – she came forth from her jacket of steel, and rejoiced in a liberty full and complete.

A remarkable case of Divine healing is that of Mrs J.E. Gosling, of Tooting, who was suffering from a complication of diseases. At the age of 37 she had to undergo two operations for moving kidneys, and at this time Mrs Gosling was informed that her liver was enlarged and moreover that her heart was weak. Subsequent to this she developed dropsy, which in itself is a most malicious malady. Upon examination the physician pronounced her case as absolutely incurable, and acquainted her with the fact that for the rest of her life she must expect to be an invalid. From that time onward she was unable to leave the house, and life became a martyrdom. Often this dear woman was nigh unto death; on as many as 30 different occasions she was on the point of passing away. In this condition she was brought to Principal Jeffreys' meetings, was prayed for by him and thoroughly healed. The very next meeting that she attended was packed to the doors, and the only possible place to secure entrance was in the top gallery of the building, which meant a good climb, but this was accomplished with no difficulty whatever. It almost seems incredible, and yet with God all things are gloriously possible. Through faith in the Living and Eternal Healer are these wonders wrought.

Nine long, weary years of gradual death were brought to an unexpected end in the experience of Miss Edith Scarth when George Jeffreys visited Leeds in the April of 1927. A victim of tuberculosis of the spine, Miss Scarth had for eighteen months been laid flat upon her back and wheeled about in a spinal carriage – for five years she wore a spinal jacket and for three-and-a-half years of that period she was obliged to wear a spinal splint which came right up to the back of the head, and fastened around the forehead with a strap to keep the head firmly fixed in one position. Thus this sufferer came to the healing services, listened to the message of life for body as well as soul, accepted the glorious invitation to put God's promise to the proof, and was marvellously set free from the chains of sickness with which she had been so long bound. A medical examination some weeks after her healing resulted in the physician pronouncing the cure to be complete. Writing some thirteen months subsequent to the remarkable deliverance recorded above, Miss Scarth triumphantly declares the reality of the work done in her body.

Mr F.W. Hunt, of Wimbourne, for nearly two years was under the treatment of three doctors and one specialist – so crippled was he that he had to be carried up and down stairs. He was, moreover, deaf in both ears. Like so many others he found his way to the Revival Tent at Moordown, Bournemouth, where Principal Jeffreys was holding those never-to-be-forgotten meetings during the summer of 1926. Here Mr Hunt was perfectly healed – so complete was his healing that he can now hear the slightest sound.

We cannot pass the case of Miss Edith Jenkins, of Plymouth, one of the modern miracles which stagger even the sceptical and cause the materialist to muse. The subject of five operations covering a period of seventeen years, our sister was left with Bright's disease. Some four years ago Miss Jenkins was advised by a specialist that unless she consented to undergo two operations immediately she had but eight weeks to live. As a result of the first of these operations she lost both her breasts, and shortly afterward the second operation was performed, the stomach being the part of the body operated upon. Life was certainly prolonged, but years of pain followed, and the final medical verdict was to the effect that nothing more could possibly be done. As a last resort, a belt was specially made. During the Plymouth Campaign Miss Jenkins says, 'God told me to go to the platform for healing. While under the power of God I felt my right kidney, which had been forced through the intestines into the lower stomach, going back into its proper place, and my hip, which was outgrown, getting smaller. It is now quite normal and all the swelling gone. I have discarded my belt, which I had to buckle on each morning before I left my bed. Praise God, I am completely cured!'

Not only bodily ailments yield to the authority of the Name of Jesus, but also mental disorders are successfully dealt with in that all-prevailing Name. Mrs Smith, of Seven Kings, was, to use her own words, 'hopelessly insane'. A great trouble having come into her life, a serious mental breakdown followed, which eventually developed into insanity. So seriously was the brain affected, that she could not be trusted alone, and at times it became necessary that she should be tied down to her bed at night. A godly mother's prayers bore fruit in an unexpected manner. News filtered through in the distressed family circle that a 'faith-healer' had made his appearance at Barking, whose prayers brought wonderful cures to those who sought his aid. Pressure was brought to bear upon Mrs Smith to go to these meetings, but with no effect – she would not go. Later on, however, it was reported that Principal Jeffreys was conducting a campaign at the East Ham Town Hall. With great difficulty she was taken to these meetings, prayed for and immediately healed. A number of times during the days of her mental derangement had Mrs Smith attempted to end her life, but God always mercifully prevented this tragic termination to a life in which He had planned so wonderfully to reveal His glory and His power.

And so we might go on page after page and chapter after chapter, telling of these astonishing cases of Divine healing. What a trail of sickness and suffering sin has left. All around us are these dread and deadly evidences of the enemy's blighting and benumbing power. On every hand are lives all broken upon the wheel of pain. What a blessing for these poor, afflicted ones, who have for so long lain upon the rack of suffering, there is an Evangel of healing, health and hope. That the Foursquare Gospel contains that precious, priceless virtue which can remedy the ruin which sin has wrought, and restore the sick-bound bodies of those who believe its message.

To enter some of those wonderful Divine Healing services is to walk into an atmosphere that is prayer-laden and power-permeated. It is as though that arena of affliction held at its centre an invisible pool of blessing – accessible to all – into which the halt, the maimed, the blind, and the paralysed plunged – plunged from death to life, from sickness to soundness, from bondage to freedom, from blindness to vision.

Chapter 21

Unparalleled Revival Scenes at the Royal Albert Hall – Easter, 1928

For the third year in succession the annual Foursquare Gospel Eastertide Demonstration was held in the Royal Albert Hall. Each year had witnessed a decided increase in the interest displayed and the enthusiasm evinced in this great yearly Elim event.

One is simply staggered at the splendid spirit of daring displayed by the Leader of this glorious Spirit-born movement, in tackling such a colossal enterprise as that which the recent Foursquare Gospel Demonstration in the Royal Albert Hall constituted – an effort and an achievement which should and doubtless does commend the admiration of all who are able to appreciate Christian courage in the realm of Twentieth Century evangelism. The financial commitments connected with such gatherings as these would in themselves be sufficient to frighten a less lion-hearted leader than George Jeffreys, whilst the heavy burden of organisation involved might easily have dismayed less resolute hearts than those associated with him in his big forward moves. Obviously from the natural viewpoint the difficulties were legion and the risks great.

Never in the history of modern evangelism has such a scene been witnessed as that which took place on the evening of Good Friday, 1928. This stately hall, of such historic interest, commemorative of one of England's greatest princes, has been used for many and varied purposes – princes of both political and philosophical realms have graced its world-renowned platform, and the world's most famous singers and speakers have been heard within the spacious and splendid auditorium – but never had it been engaged for such a purposes as that to which it was devoted on this occasion.

We would that those who survey this Foursquare Gospel Movement with critical and censorious eyes could have been eye-witnesses of the splendid spectacle presented throughout this unique service. It would, in most cases have transformed their prejudice into praise; their fears would have melted like snow beneath the noonday sun. The sublimity and simplicity of that scene will linger long in the minds of those who were privileged to be present. It was as though in the heart of the world's great metropolis a modern John the Baptist had arisen with prophetic vision and voice to call the national consciousness back to God and His Word. Standing there, in the sparkling waters of that beautiful baptistery, amid that vast concourse of people, one was carried in thought to the banks of Jordan, and once again upon the ears of our imagination fell the stirring wilderness cry: 'Repent, for the kingdom of heaven is at hand.' As one after another of those white-robed, radiant-faced, regenerated men and women passed beneath the waters, peal after peal of praise rang through the vast gathering, as though the whole of that congregation trembled under the thrill of the Divine touch and every heart went out in glad response to the call of God.

Perhaps one of the most astonishing features of the big baptismal service was the way in which the physical power of George Jeffreys stood the severe strain of such a strenuous service. Many feared that the demand upon his strength would be too great – to immerse about 1,000 believers in one service was a task which would tax the strongest physical resources. However, in a remarkable manner God undertook and supplied sufficient strength to go right through.

Another impressive aspect of this great gathering, with its large number of candidates and its gigantic congregation, was the perfect order which prevailed throughout the whole service. How magnificently everything was managed! How splendidly the workers co-operated, succeeding in avoiding anything approaching congestion or confusion!

The resolution of that enthusiastic throng was just wonderful, providing a striking demonstration of Divine power to restrain any undesirable or unruly element that might manifest itself.

It was a moment tense with deep spiritual emotion when it was announced that some of those passing through the baptismal waters had recently been remarkably delivered from diseases of an incurable character. Several of those immersed up to the time when some weeks previously, George Jeffreys had laid his hands upon them, were confirmed cripples whilst others who had borne the stamp of death, whose days were numbered, were there full of vigour and vitality.

In an address which was clear, convincing and concise, George Jeffreys defined and declared the doctrinal basis of believers' baptism as found in the New Testament revelation, showing how this ordinance lay at the very entrance of Christian discipleship, and how essential it is to a life of obedience to the Divine Word, proving conclusively from the Scriptures that baptism by immersion is the mode of baptism authorised by apostolic example and teaching, and thus enjoined upon all true followers of Christ in this dispensation.

The Royal Albert Hall on this Easter Monday morning was the scene of a Communion Service that finds no parallel in history for numbers and holy fervour. Thousands had come to remember their Saviour's death and to commune with their risen Lord. What a company! All classes, high and low, rich and poor, learned and unlearned, were gathered together on an equal basis to commemorate the death of the one all-sufficient sacrifice. Those who had risen from couches of pain and who had lately left the sombre shadows of the sick chamber and who were now enjoying liberty of limb as well as freedom of soul were also present. There they were by the score with beaming faces, burning hearts and bubbling lips.

What a memorable message George Jeffreys gave in both the afternoon and evening service – a message calculated to clear away the mists of misunderstanding which hang so heavily over so many minds concerning this blessed

Foursquare Gospel, a message too which would speedily shatter some of the foolish and feeble arguments advanced by those who withstand the proclamation of this full-orbed Evangel. In Principal Jeffreys one is introduced to a preacher whose preaching is of the type that convinces the thinker and convicts the ungodly – a minister whose weapon is the Word, and who relies wholly upon the Spirit of God to produce the desired results. Unflinchingly and unfalteringly he proclaims the whole counsel of God, counting the consequences of secondary consideration.

God set His seal upon these services – again and again in response to the Principal's appeal souls yielded to Christ – all over the huge hall hands went up in decision, over 150 souls surrendered to the Lord on Monday alone.

As the last meeting closed amidst the rolling waves of song, one was conscious of a measure of regret that this Easter festival was over. How profound the impression created. The day of great things had come. The largest baptismal service since the Day of Pentecost had been held, one of the greatest choirs of redeemed young people that has ever sung the praises of the Lord had given forth their heartfelt message to one of the greatest congregations yet gathered to hear the Gospel preached. Though the crowds that gathered at the previous year's demonstration were great, yet this year's gatherings had surpassed the effort of twelve months earlier.

One of the best-known English evangelists writes of this day's services in the following strain:

A Never-to-be-forgotten Meeting

The scene at the evening meeting in the Royal Albert Hall beggars description, and all one can do in the space available is to give just a brief outline. Packed from floor to ceiling with nearly 12,000 people, rising tier upon tier on either side of the great organ were thousands of bright faces, happy young men and women, singing hymns and choruses until the time announced for the commencement of the meeting arrived. Then amidst a tense feeling of expectation, Principal George Jeffreys walked on to the platform, followed by a band of faithful workers.

We must pass over the singing by the choir of about 2,000 young people, but oh, what a sight! What hearty responses as the

Principal put question after question to these young people! How it must have given the lie to those who say that the Gospel is played out! Then the event of the evening – the Principal's address. We should very much like to give it verbatim, for every word sank deep down into the heart, but no doubt this address will be published. As we listened to the clear exposition of the Scriptures – the text taken from the Epistle of Jude, part of the third verse: 'Earnestly contend for the faith which was once delivered to the saints' – oh what a powerful appeal the speaker made to that great concourse of people for a return to the old paths, at one time charging home on heart and conscience the awful declension seen on every hand.

Stone by stone the man-made fortresses of false security were demolished until the Herald of the Cross stood amidst the ruins holding aloft the Bible as the only safe guide for humanity. As he drew near to the close of his wonderful address, he introduced us into the cold Roman prison cell where that mighty warrior of the Cross, the Apostle Paul, was writing to his beloved son in the faith, Timothy. Paul was exhorting Timothy to preach the Word, and as he turned to the Christian workers and ministers on the platform he made an impassioned appeal to them to preach the Word. 'Try it,' said the preacher, 'it works.' Yes, thank God, it does, and it was working. The allusion to Paul being in a cold prison, while God was there measuring his brow for a crown, was more than the writer could stand. The great tears of thankfulness ran down the cheeks of not a few in that great assemblage.

The address was over. God had spoken, and the signs began to follow; for great numbers signified the desire to accept Christ as their Saviour. There were still more signs to follow, for Principal George Jeffreys asked those present who had been brought to his meetings in bath-chairs or carriages to come up on the platform, and quite a crowd of men and women came trooping up to testify to the Divine power of Jesus Christ the Healer. What wonderful cases! And to prove this, those who had not walked for years, some who had to be held together in iron cages to support their bodies, others with one limb shorter than the other, were quite normal. They paraded and ran and jumped around the happy Principal. Then those who had been healed, but were not cripples were asked to stand, and fully 2,000 people stood up and testified to the Divine healing power in the Christ of God.

The singing of 'All Hail the Power of Jesus' Name' brought to a close one of the most remarkable and powerful meetings it has ever been the writer's lot to witness. We have only just touched the fringe in these impressions, but the writer would like to say one word in conclusion: Pray much for these dear servants of God: do not be led away by wild and untruthful statements. If possible, visit the meetings, get into touch with the leaders, and judge the movement from its centre.

The press reports of the great Baptismal Service held in the Royal Albert Hall on the Good Friday give a comprehensive commentary on this remarkable meeting. So impressive was this unique ceremony that the news was relayed throughout almost the whole world:

ECSTATIC ELIMITE CONVERTS

SINGING AUDIENCE

They had been 'saved' they had been 'born again', and Principal George Jeffreys, founder of the Elim Foursquare Gospel Alliance, baptised them by total immersion to the passionately vociferated glory of God.

A choir of 'Crusaders', as the youth of the movement is called, flanked the organ. A battery of Press cameras was focused from one end of the amphitheatre on the speaker's table, over which was suspended a microphone.

Two spot lights flamed down in a vast white 'V' from the tips of the crescent-shaped gallery.

SPIRITUAL HUNGER

Over all was an atmosphere of spiritual hunger, infinitely pathetic, a desperate craving for God to manifest Himself here – now! – that became vocal in ecstatic cries.

The service began with singing:

'Jesus, blessed Jesus,
Thou are mine, mine for evermore,'

sang the people, and the evangelist on the platform led them with swinging arms and resonantly clapping hands.

Again and again – the same verse: again and again. It was a species of trance creation. Hysteria seemed at hand. They were lashed and urged by massed melody into an unearthly joy.

Principal Jeffreys appeared and took charge. He wore a black gown. He stood there, very much in control, a tall, black-haired young man, and played on his audience as on a harp.

The procession of candidates came on the stage, passed through the tank, and wound off, wet and ecstatical.

There were some who had come curiously to the Albert Hall to look on, but no one jeered. The sincerity was too strong. One sensed it in the profundity of passion.

(*Daily Express*, 7 April)

1,000 BAPTISED IN ALBERT HALL

REMARKABLE 'FAITH CURE' SCENES
PEOPLE WAIT IN QUEUE FOR EIGHT HOURS

Principal Jeffreys stood waist-deep in the tank. The candidates walked one by one down the steps into the water, and were plunged below the surface. The women wore white dresses and the men white shirts and trousers.

All were smiling happily as they descended into the tank; some were singing, and some waved their hands to the congregation of 10,000, who shouted fervently all the time. There was no self-consciousness anywhere. That the people had been convinced by this young pastor there was no doubt.

Every member of his vast audience last night was spell-bound throughout his address, and when he had finished explaining the symbolism of baptism, no fewer than 53 people came forward demanding to be 'saved'.

'I wonder,' Mr Jeffreys said, 'that men are not being saved in thousands when they see cripples made whole, when they see vicious growths withering away, when eyes that cannot see and ears that are deaf are opened.'

His voice was carried to every part of the great hall by means of loud speakers. Specially arranged flood-lights and limelights were directed on the tank while the baptisms were taking place.

There were queues outside the Albert Hall eight hours before the meeting started, and many hundreds who had hoped to secure admission were turned away.

(*Morning Post*, 7 April)

1,000 CONVERTS PLUNGE

MASS BAPTISM SCENE IN LONDON HALL
REVIVALIST CAMPAIGN
AMAZING CURES CLAIMED

Amid fervent shouts of 'Hallelujah', 'Glory be to God', and 'Praise His Name', 1,000 converts to the Elim Foursquare Gospel Alliance were, one by one, plunged below the surface in a huge tank of water in the Albert Hall, London, on Friday night. This was the culmination of a great whirlwind revivalist campaign throughout the country by Principal George Jeffreys.

He and his colleagues claim hundreds of 'faith cures'. The first to be baptised was Miss F. Munday, of Southampton. She was stated to have been bedridden for 14 years with tuberculosis, which shortened one leg by $4\frac{1}{2}$ inches. After the 'laying-on of hands' she claimed to have been immediately cured.

As people came forward for baptism, Mr Jeffreys introduced them. A man who had been completely paralysed for many years, a woman so twisted and crippled that her head almost touched her knees, but now without trace of the complaints from which they are said to have suffered – these were merely typical of dozens baptised.

The specially constructed galvanised iron tank was covered with imitation grass and surrounded with growing roses, arum lilies, palms and other plants. It was filled with water, and by means of an inflow and an outflow represented the flowing of the River Jordan.

(*Belfast Telegraph*, 7 April)

Following the great gatherings of Easter comes the substantial triumph of Eastbourne. In the Music Pavilion, a building whose exterior is adorned with a thousand shimmering lights, George Jeffreys conducted another remarkable campaign, remarkable chiefly in result. Nearly one thousand souls witnessed to their acceptance of Christ as Saviour, whilst a great number also experienced the healing power of the Lord in their bodies. George Jeffreys preaching on this occasion was described as apostolic in character, his message being once again accompanied by signs and wonders. The last week of the campaign was indescribable. 'Cold, lukewarm, hot, red-hot religious expression had become white-hot.' At the last meeting with crowds of worshippers outside clamouring for admission, too late an hour before time, in grateful thanks and praise to God one recalled the lines:

'There's a wideness in God's mercy
Like the wideness of the sea'

as the great waves dashed and broke against the girders of the pier.

During the past few years George Jeffreys in the course of his great revival campaigns has occupied the platforms of some of England's largest and most famous halls. Almost without exception, his visit to a city means that before the campaign closes, the largest hall available must be secured in order to house the tremendous crowds that gather. During the Whitsuntide meetings in 1928 the beautiful Queen's Hall was added to the list of those historic halls where he has proclaimed the Foursquare Gospel.

The Queen's Hall has rarely, if ever, held such an enthusiastic company of Christians as that which gathered within its walls at the closing service of the great Foursquare Gospel meetings held in London during the recent Whitsuntide. One wonders where the flag of the Foursquare Gospel will be found floating next? The Queen's Hall doubtless ranks amongst the finest, foremost and more famous of London's great and historic halls, and has witnessed the performance of some of the world's greatest musical artistes. What a splendid and striking tribute to the present-day power of the Word of God, that wherever George Jeffreys goes, the crowds flock to hear his message. No matter how large the auditorium engaged, its seating capacity is almost sure to be taxed to its limit by the huge numbers that clamour for admission.

Principal George Jeffreys, with his characteristic energy and grace, gave an exposition and presentation of the Foursquare Gospel calculated to make men think, and sufficient to answer the most critical enquirer after truth. Under the compulsion of a Spirit-anointed eloquence, the hearts of many were captured.

And then to crown this glorious evening with God, nearly fifty souls surrendered to Christ, entering into union with the Living Vine, and becoming one with the Father through the Eternal Son. What a seal to a service! And thus it is that God honours the ministry of His servant in almost every meeting. Bless the Lord for such a continuous witness to the power of a Gospel that is being despised and subjected to the bitterest criticism.

Chapter 22

A Last Word

Although we have now come to the closing chapter of this book, yet the work of which we write still goes on with undiminishing power. The Foursquare Gospel frontiers are extending north, east, south and west. What the unborn future holds for this work we dare not predict. That the zenith of achievement has not yet been reached is fairly obvious. The past has been paved with surpassingly splendid proofs of Divine willingness to reward faith that is both big and bold, and counts no cost too great to win through for God. If the heavenly vision is ever kept before its Leader and his followers, then we believe that God has some blessed and more mighty ministry in store for a work which has already survived so many storms. Nothing but disobedience to that vision can ever arrest the tide of revival power which is lifting such great numbers Godward.

Even while we pen these last few lines, news is pouring in of fresh conquests of the Cross in the campaigns which are in full swing. The chariots of the Lord are still driving on from victory to victory, and on every battle front the foe is being driven from the field, whilst scores of captured prisoners are being brought into the camp of Christ; stronghold after stronghold is yielding to the conquering legions of the Lord. Districts where spiritual drought has left the land dry and dreary are being inundated with a heavenly downpour. But space forbids further record of that which is taking place. And all this glorious work going on in a period when there is a big, all-round slump in religion. When revelation is being scrapped in favour of evolution. When greyhound races, football, and cinemas draw their tens of thousands, and when many of the principal denominations are losing members so heavily.

The pages of this volume contain a record of revival which provides us with one of the most thrilling stories in the annals of Christian evangelistic enterprise, and should prove of tremendous encouragement to all believers in the Lord Jesus Christ. It is pre-eminently, as its title suggests, a record of modern miracle. It is not some far-fetched narrative too fanciful to be credited – it is a chronicle authenticated by a thousand living proofs. Some have thought that we might make Christianity more acceptable if the miraculous element was eliminated, but to this we reply, 'It is impossible to retain Christianity itself if you deny the truth of the miraculous.' The Gospels are packed with miracles, and God has been pleased to bear witness to His Word in these days with many wonderful, supernatural signs.

If it were possible to tabulate the actual results of the campaigns to which reference has been made, then the figures would astonish us. What a glorious sum total of triumph it would reveal! Thousands upon thousands of souls led into saving union with Christ! Hundreds and hundreds of pain-racked bodies delivered from disease! Multitudes more freed from formalism, purged of the poison of religion and plunged into real spiritual service for God!

Thus has God been pleased to honour the ministry of one who has always endeavoured to put first things first, making his service eloquent in mighty deeds and supernatural signs. In the pathway of obedience to God has come success in unexpected measure and manner; but mere success has been made secondary to that without which all achievement is vain. The Divine will has been the goal towards which George Jeffreys has ever sought to press. Surcharged with the power of Pentecost, his impassioned utterances have stirred thousands of souls to decision for Christ in this and other lands, whilst his Spirit-filled personality has been the consecrated channel through which God has poured Himself, and through which thousands more have been drawn to the feet of the Slain Lamb of Calvary. Beneath such burning eloquence all indifference melts like snow before a noon-day sun. Wherever he has held his campaigns, Bible study has received a wonderful impetus. Those deeply spiritual expositions of the Word of God have made his hearers hunger for more of the riches stored therein. The glory of that which has been accomplished belongs alone to Him whose power brought such wondrous miracles to pass.

It is seldom that one finds in a single ministry such a splendid combination of gifts such as those which have graced the service of this God-raised preacher and teacher. Usually when a preacher is richly endowed with unique capacity for evangelistic ministry, he does not excel as a teacher. On the other hand, when we find one who is skilled as an exponent of the Word of God, he rarely displays great power as an evangelist. But here we have a ministry in which both these gifts are beautifully interwoven and find expression in almost equal proportion. Added to this are the splendid executive and administrative qualities which have contributed so considerably towards the success with which the work as a whole has been conducted. His readiness of resource and unfailing tact have singled him out as a leader. His mastery of the great crowds which he handles so skilfully is simply splendid. As a revivalist, George Jeffreys speaks in positive terms of the power of the Word of God. He belongs to the school of Christian dogmatists who stand unflinch- ingly and uncompromisingly for the whole counsel of God, believing and proclaiming the Bible as the 'only living, life- giving, miracle-working, regenerating book in the world.' To him there is no place for a gospel of ambiguity – from his lips like a stream of lava, pours forth the old, unchanging message of Christ's power to save and heal today. To him there is no other effective and efficient remedy for the world's wounds and woes. When we look at the birth of this remarkable Foursquare Gospel work and its remarkable leader, and go carefully into its early struggles and trials, we find that at the very root of it, back of all its achievement and accomplishment, lies the mainspring of an overwhelming passion for the lost – without this it could never have reached the position of power which it now occupies and enjoys.

God has gathered around this heaven-called witness a band of earnest workers fired with the same ambition and eager to emulate the example of their leader in all his unwavering devotion and consecrated effort to extend the Kingdom of God among men and hasten the coming of the absent King. If George Jeffreys had accomplished nothing more than to bring this splendid band of Christian workers into being, then he would have left a glorious legacy of blessing to the Church of God in these days.

We who enjoy today the privileges of ministry in this blessed work certainly owe a debt to its Founder and Leader, a debt that we can only hope to discharge by giving ourselves unreservedly and wholeheartedly to the cause which lies so near and dear to his heart. We cannot but praise God for enabling His servant so manfully to shoulder the burden of a work which might easily have crushed him to the ground.

All the glorious performance recorded in these pages has not been possible without encouraging much opposition. Each new departure has been assailed by a cannonade of criticism, only in the course of time to be carefully copied by those who the most heartily hurled their condemnatory criticisms at its head. But though thus bombarded by blind and bitter antagonism, the good ship has succeeded in keeping to her God-given course, and today is making good headway for the haven of the Divine purpose.

For the past few years, George Jeffreys has been accompanied and assisted in most of his campaigns by Mr R.E. Darragh and Mr J. McWhirter, both sons of the Emerald Isle and well known to the thousands that throng the revival services. Almost like an Aaron and Hur, in the midst of fierce engagements have they held up the hands of their chief, and so assisted him to prevail when faced with fearful odds. Few have attended these remarkable revival gatherings, and have not learned to love these two valuable partners. How attractive and contagious is that sparkling spiritual sunshine, occasionally interspersed with bursts of holy humour, which radiates from Mr Darragh the song leader. Not many are able to resist of refuse his pressing and persuasive appeals to give their best in the offering of praise. Again and again have we witnessed this modern Asaph lift and lead the huge crowds to God in triumphant, jubilant song. and then how faithfully has the other member of this consecrated trio toiled, often behind the scenes, unseen and unapplauded, with no other remuneration than that which is the reward of those who diligently apply themselves to their God-given calling. And yet how much this devotion to detail in the background has contributed to the successful results realised.

Every thoughtful reader of these pages will probably have asked the question, 'How is it possible for this Revivalist to go on year after year, standing the tremendous strain of these heavy and exacting campaigns?' The way in which the strength of God's servant has been sustained is nothing short of a miracle in itself. Night after night, often for months at a stretch, with sometimes as many as twelve and fourteen meetings per week, and these gatherings at times lasting for several hours, when hundreds have to be prayed for – have these meetings continued. Nothing but a constant stream of intercessory prayer can account for this remarkable energy which is continually vouchsafed.

In the foregoing pages of this book the writer has but inadequately told the story of a work which stands today as a vital and victorious testimonial of God's glorious power. In almost every part of our land, and also in other lands, the influence of George Jeffreys' ministry has been felt; the largest buildings have been crowded with all classes of society, and marvellous results have crowned his labours everywhere, until today, in many Christian circles, he is recognised as one of the world's greatest evangelists and teachers. He as certainly succeeded in calling the attention of the Christian world to apostolic practice and experience, and proclaiming in most convincing terms the blessed fact that 'Jesus Christ is the same yesterday, today and for ever.' His is the privilege to be the exponent of a faith which has expressed itself in facts, a worker whose cardinal motive has ever been to please God.

The chronicle which these chapters contain goes to prove the contention of one great writer who affirms that 'Christianity is a living force employing an energy which performs visible miracles. It is not a theory of existence about which one may hold various opinions, but a fact in human experience which can no more be disputed that the sun can be denied as a fact in the solar system.' The same writer adds, 'Christianity in the pulpit is too often either an explanation or an apology. It should never by anything but an invitation and a challenge.' At least, we can say without fear of contradiction that this record which we have attempted to give contains both an invitation and a challenge. God grant that the Church of God may accept the challenge and rise up and claim her heritage of miraculous power.

Some say that his revival raises serious religious issues; that its teaching is distinctly provocative and creates controversy; and that its methods are of such an extraordinary character as to lead to confusion. The Foursquare Gospel certainly lays the axe of truth to the root of merely cold-blooded professionalism and rings the changes upon all conformity to the world in the Church of Christ. It undoubtedly clears the ground of much accumulated theological trash, and makes way for the fulfilment of many of the Divine promises which for centuries have been unrealised to any great extent in the life of God's people. What if its methods are startling and carry consternation into the camp of the enemy? Are we not here to awaken and arouse those that sleep? It is an Evangel which transforms the weak and wavering Christian into a lion-hearted, eagle-winged disciple of Jesus, making him invincible in the arena of spiritual conflict; he becomes a force for the foe to reckon with. And so we offer no apology for the stand we take or for the flag which we fly.

If you have enjoyed this book and would like to help us to send a copy of it and many other titles to needy pastors in the **Third World**, please write for further information or send your gift to:

Sovereign World Trust
PO Box 777, Tonbridge
Kent TN11 0ZS
United Kingdom

or to the '**Sovereign World**' distributor in your country.